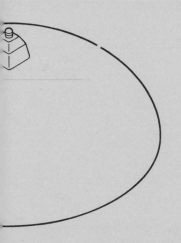

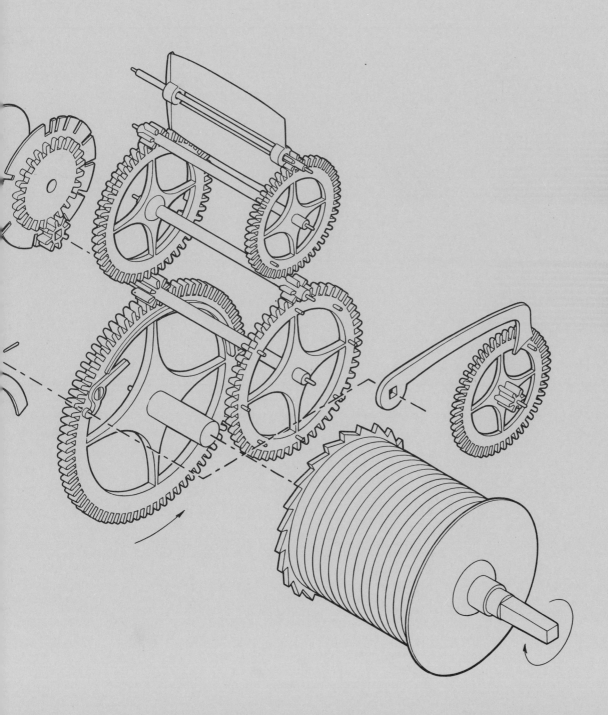

THE LONGCASE CLOCK

TOM ROBINSON

ANTIQUE COLLECTORS' CLUB

ISBN 1 85149 232 1

British Library cataloguing in publication data
A catalogue record for this book is available from the British Library

Frontispiece: Joseph Williamson solar time clock, c.1720-25, with a centre seconds dial, rare at this date, and a lunar dial.

Published for the Antique Collectors' Club
by the Antique Collectors' Club Ltd.

Printed in England on Consort Royal Satin from Donside Paper Mills, Aberdeen, by the Antique Collectors' Club Ltd., Woodbridge, Suffolk IP12 1DS

Contents

Colour Plates

Foreword

Tom Robinson brought home his first longcase clock while still a boy at school. He bought it because he was deeply interested by both its appearance and its mechanism. He belongs to that select band who collect in order to study and who constantly discover new facets of an ancient art. The result of his acute observation, spread over more than half a century, is a marvellous new book in which the plates are as good as the text. There has never been anything quite like it before. Part of what distinguishes it and makes it special is that the author seems to have thought of every question which has perplexed others and has dealt with it with the insight of the true expert. The author's practical ability has been another great asset. His experience in clockmaking and cabinetmaking has proved invaluable. Not only this, but clocks and cases are accorded equal importance by Mr. Robinson. This treatment is as useful as it is unusual, offering some historical background and furniture history alongside the development of the clocks.

The author's excellent knowledge of existing literature and his personal acquaintance with hundreds of clocks, some in the great collections but many more single milestones, has resulted in a book which no one else could possibly have written. *The Longcase Clock* will appeal to every type of reader. It has as much to offer to the man who owns (or who would like to own) one ordinary example as to the most experienced collector. In other words this is a splendid book.

Charles Allix
1981

THE ANTIQUARIAN HOROLOGICAL SOCIETY

The Society, which was formed in 1953 and now has a worldwide membership, exists to further the study of time measurement in all its forms. To achieve this, the Society holds regular lecture meetings and arranges visits to horological collections; it also produces a quarterly journal *Antiquarian Horology* and various other publications.

Details of membership may be obtained from
The Secretary
The Antiquarian Horological Society
New House
High Street
Wadhurst
Sussex
TN5 7AL

Acknowledgements

The author wishes to thank all those who have provided photographs or have permitted the photography of clocks in their possession. Most private owners have preferred the relative safety of anonymity to the dangers attendant upon publicity and their wishes have been respected.

With one exception, the drawings have been prepared specially for this work and the author wishes to thank the following for all the trouble they took to meet his rather exacting requirements: David Penney (figures 1/8; 2/12, 19; 4/23, 54; 8/41; 9/45) and Robert Gillies for the remaining drawings, with the exception of figure 3/4 which M.G. Hurst drew originally for R.A. Lee.

All illustrations are identified by chapter number/figure number and the following photographs are used by the courtesy of the owners:

Anderson & Garland 5/27
Antiquarian Horological Society 10/148
Asprey & Company 4/10, 12, 36; 5/28; 9/19, 54, 114; 11/27
Avon Antiques 10/38
David Barker 9/26
John Bly 10/106
Boardman & Oliver 6/8
Bobinet Ltd. 5/13, 14, 15, 16
British Architectural Library 2/22
British Museum (Trustees of the British Museum) 2/14, 16, 18, 20; 8/12, 13, 19, 20, 21, 22, 23, 24, 37, 38, 39, 40, 41, 42, 43, 44, 45, 46, 47; 10/61, 62, 63, 64, 65, 66, 67, 68
Aubrey Brocklehurst 5/33
Buckell & Ballard 9/89
Camerer Cuss & Co. 9/44; 10/89
Patrick Capon Colour Plate p.12
Cedar Antiques 9/100, 101, 102; G/2
Cheshire Antiques 6/9
Christie, Manson & Woods 4/34; 5/29; 7/28, 29, 36, 37, 40, 41; 8/48, 49, 50, 51; 9/26, 27, 29, 36, 106; 10/16, 95, 97; 11/53, 54, 55; 12/18; 13/22, 23, 24, 25
P.G. Dawson 5/35, 36, 37; 6/4, 7; 8/16; 9/50, 52, 52, 53, 85, 105, 115; 10/77, 105, 118
Debenham Coe & Co. 6/2; 12/13
Doveridge House 5/21
Dreweatt, Watson & Barton 11/32
Henry Duke and Son 6/3
Exeter Museums 9/98, 99, 103, 104
Fell & Davis 12/16
Fitzwilliam Museum (Syndics of Fitzwilliam Museum) 3/2; 8/27, 28, 29, 30; 11/44, 45, 46, 47, 48, 49, 51, 52; 13/7, 10
Michael Foster Colour Plate 16
Apter Fredericks 10/83, 84
Garrard & Co. 9/113
Garrod, Turner & Son 10/7
N. Goodison 10/93, 94, 95
Her Majesty the Queen 13/9, 12, 13, 14, 15, 16, 17, 18, 20, 21
F. Hudson 9/72, 73, 74, 75; G/1
P. Hunnisett 4/6

Edward James Foundation, Trustees of the, 10/79, 80, 81, 82
Kingston Clocks 4/56, 57, 58, 59
Knatchbull Collection 11/8, 9, 10, 11
Lawrence of Crewkerne 7/33; 10/40, 108
R.A. Lee 2/1, 2, 4; 3/4; 4/27, 28; 9/37; Colour Plates p.2, 3
Museum Boerhaave, Leiden 1/9
Museum of the History of Science, Oxford 2/8, 9, 10, 11, 12, 13
National Maritime Museum, London 8/3; 11/4, 5, 6, 7, 8, 9, 10, 11, 12
National Trust 10/111; Colour Plates 17, 18
Meyrick Neilson 9/1; G/4
Edward A. Nowell 9/93, 94
Partridge Fine Arts Colour Plates p.9
Philips, Son & Neale 5/6, 24; 11/40; 12/9, 10, 15; Colour Plates p.12, 13
W.A. Pinn 5/31
C.N. Ponsford 9/104
Derek Roberts 5/25, 32, 38; 9/11, 12, 34, 35, 55, 58, 59, 95, 96, 97, 107, 108, 109, 110, 111, 112; 10/1, 2, 3, 18, 69, 70, 71, 73, 119, 120, 121, 126, 127, 131, 134, 135, 145; 11/43; Colour Plates p. 6, 7
Routledge & Kegan Paul, G/6, 7, 8, 9, 10, 11, 12
Science Museum, London (Crown Copyright) 8/2; 11/59, 61
Lacy Scott and Sons 12/12
Silvester & Co. 10/72, 92, 99; 12/7, 21
Sotheby, King & Chasemore 2/23; 5/3, 5, 12, 20, 23, 26, 41, 42; 7/35; 9/22, 33, 38, 39, 41; 10/37, 96, 104, 110, 130, 141, 142; 11/36, 42; 12/8, 13, 17, 22, 23, 24, 25
Sotheby, Parke, Bernet & Co. 4/25, 26, 35, 37; 5/18, 22, 30; 8/15; 9/43, 46, 47, 48, 49, 69; 11/25, 26; 12/20; G/2; Colour Plates 3, 13
Strike One Ltd. 4/41, 42, 43; 5/1; 9/14, 30, 31, 32; 10/8, 17, 31, 32, 34, 35, 36, 74, 75, 76, 112, 113, 114, 115; Colour Plates 8, 9, 14, 19; Colour Plate p.8
Harwood Tate 10/129
Victoria and Albert Museum (Crown Copyright) 4/2, 7, 8; 9/60, 61; 10/33, 60, 78, 88, 90; 12/14
Witney Antiques 9/70, 71
Worshipful Company of Clockmakers 8/10, 11

Introduction

The longcase clock is unique among mechanical devices in that, despite the more exacting requirements of modern life, it still fulfils its purpose adequately three centuries after its invention. Its durability is also remarkable; what other machine has a working life measured in centuries of running time? These factors undoubtedly contribute to the fascination which clocks have for many of us.

Clocks are unique in requiring the skills of both the cabinet maker and the clockmaker, which has led to a curious dichotomy amongst collectors. To some a clock is a mechanical device for telling the time enclosed in a more or less decorative wooden case, whereas to others it is a piece of cabinet work which contains a time-telling mechanism. The latter point of view was normal with the early collectors and authors. Mention must however be made of the pioneer work of Alan Lloyd in studying and writing about complex clock mechanisms. My interest is primarily in the mechanism but I am also very interested in casework and furniture history generally, and in the social background to the use of clocks.

I have no conscious bias in favour of famous or humble makers, London or the provinces, north country or otherwise, and the space devoted to northern clocks in the second half of the book is purely a reflection of the horological development, caused mainly by the Industrial Revolution. Although regional variations are looked at, there is insufficient space to develop a study of regional styles. This is essentially a book about clocks rather than about makers, although some makers will be discussed as appropriate. No book can be a substitute for practical experience in handling and preferably working on clocks but suitable reading should help to develop an analytical approach.

The layout of the book is mainly chronological although some of the division into chapters is rather arbitrary. Specialist chapters have been inserted at convenient points to cover certain mechanical developments such as the search for accuracy and some decorative features such as marquetry casework. As some chapters are necessarily very long, they have been sub-divided and these headings included in the table of contents. As some clocks merit description under more than one heading, they have been described under the heading which led to their inclusion in the book. A number of typical, and convenient, clocks have been covered in detail and other related ones dealt with more briefly. An attempt has been made to show the whole range of clocks, from the simplest to the most complex and from those easily collectable to those which must remain only a dream for all except the very fortunate collector.

I have tried to state my opinions and the reasons which support them clearly without being over dogmatic, 'always' and 'never' are very dangerous words! Whenever possible I have stated the sources of information and those books most often quoted are listed on page 13 with the abbreviated form used in the text. Where I have used architectural terms such as 'plinth' they are defined in the glossary. For convenience in describing dial spandrel pieces I have used the numbers allocated by Cescinsky and Webster in *English Domestic Clocks* (e.g. C. & W. No. 3) and their illustrations of spandrels are reproduced in the glossary. I have used the Imperial system of measurement as I consider it more appropriate and if a dial is quoted as '10ins.' it implies a certain tolerance which may or may not apply to a dial '255mm square'. The dual approach '212cm high, 12ins. dial' seems nonsensical to me! However, for the benefit of those more conversant with the metric system, a conversion table follows the glossary.

Obviously a book such as this is not the work of one person working in isolation and I am indebted to many writers and to a large number of people who have helped in discussion and in various other ways. In particular I would like to thank P.G. Dawson, J. Evans, N. Goodison, J.H. Hannah, the Lord Harris, B. Hutchinson, R.J. Law, R.A. Lee and F. Smith. I am very grateful to staff at the following establishments for allowing me to examine clocks in their collections: the British Museum, the Fitzwilliam Museum, the National Maritime Museum and the Victoria and Albert Museum. I would like to express my thanks to staff at the following auction houses for their co-operation in supplying photographs and in facilitating the examination of clocks in their custody: S. Camerer Cuss and R. Garnier at Christie, Manson & Woods, K. Wills at Lawrence of Crewkerne, J. Vaughan at Sotheby, Parke, Bernet & Co. and S. Camerer Cuss at Sotheby, King & Chasemore.

Dealers in antique clocks have been co-operative in supplying photographs and I would like to thank: Asprey & Co. Ltd., Bobinet Ltd., F. Hudson, E.A. Nowell, D. Roberts and Strike One Ltd. Special thanks are due to the following for providing particularly elusive photographs: Camerer Cuss & Co. (figure 9/44), Michael Foster (Colour Plate 16) and Apter Fredericks (figures 10/83 and 84). I owe a particular debt of gratitude to the many private collectors who allowed their clocks to be dismantled and photographed but who wish to remain anonymous. If I have omitted to thank anyone who has helped me, I hope that my apologies will be accepted.

I am most grateful to Brig. R.E. Robinson and my son Richard for many useful comments on the manuscript, to my wife for countless hours of discussion as well as typing the manuscript, to my daughter Clare for typing and other help, and to John and Diana Steel and staff for their help and co-operation in seeing the book through the press.

It has been said that when one has finished writing a book one is then in a position to write it much better, which is probably true in this case. Certainly, finality is never reached as fresh evidence continues to appear and in some cases undermines existing theories. Constructive comments and additional information would be welcomed and should be addressed to me, care of the publisher. These could then be considered for inclusion in a second edition if this should be called for.

Tom Robinson
1981

Introduction to New Edition

Much has happened since the first edition appeared in 1981 and the results of some of the subsequent research and the restoration of certain important clocks have now been included, together with a few of the interesting clocks which have come to light since the book was first published.

I am very grateful to the many collectors, dealers and auctioneers who have continued to be most helpful and I would particularly like to thank Sir Geoffrey de Bellaigne, K.C.V.O., F.B.A., F.S.A. for his cooperation and assistance in connection with the royal clock by Thomas Tompion and Ben Wright of Christie's for his help with the Tompion sidereal timepiece.

Tom Robinson
1995

Abbreviated Titles used for
Books often quoted in the Text

(See Bibliography page 479 for full details)

Baillie, *Bibliography*	G.H. Baillie, *Clocks and Watches: An Historical Bibliography,* 1951.
Baillie, *Clockmakers*	G.H. Baillie, *Watchmakers and Clockmakers of the World,* 3rd edition, 1951. Now Volume I.
Britten	*Britten's Old Clocks and Watches and their Makers,* 7th edition, 1956.
Cescinsky & Webster	H. Cescinsky and M.R. Webster, *English Domestic Clocks,* 2nd edition, 1914.
Drummond Robertson	J. Drummond Robertson, *The Evolution of Clockwork,* 1931.
Lee, *Knibb*	R.A. Lee, *The Knibb Family, Clockmakers,* 1964.
Lee, *Twelve Years*	R.A. Lee, *The First Twelve Years of the English Pendulum Clock,* 1969.
Lloyd, *Outstanding Clocks*	H.A. Lloyd, *Some Outstanding Clocks over Seven Hundred Years, 1250-1950,* 1958.
Lloyd, *Dictionary*	H.A. Lloyd, *The Collector's Dictionary of Clocks,* 1964
Lloyd, *Old Clocks*	H.A. Lloyd, *Old Clocks,* 3rd edition, 1964.
Loomes, *White Dial*	B. Loomes, *The White Dial Clock,* 1974.
Loomes, *Clockmakers*	B. Loomes, *Watchmakers and Clockmakers of the World, Volume 2,* 1976.
Rees's	*Rees's Clocks, Watches and Chronometers (1819-20),* reprinted 1970.
Symonds	R.W. Symonds, *Thomas Tompion his Life & Work,* 1951.

The olivewood case shown in figure 5/2 has now been completely restored and furnished with a contemporary anonymous 10ins. dial and movement.

The hood has been re-converted to rising action and the missing front columns carefully copied from those surviving at the rear. New bun feet have been provided and all appropriate mouldings re-ebonised. Total height 6ft.3ins. with a 10ins. waist, c.1675-80.

Samuel Knibb, the maker of this fine clock, was born in 1625 and worked in Newport Pagnell until he moved to London and became a member of the Clockmaker's Company by redemption in 1663. After a relatively short career he died c.1670, his business apparently being taken over by his cousin Joseph Knibb, who had been apprenticed to him in Newport Pagnell and who moved to London about this time. Only five of Samuel's clocks are known to have survived and most of these are of considerable complexity and all are of high quality, proving him to have been a maker of great ability.

The ten inch dial has very fine matting and the spandrels are engraved with various fruit. The signature 'Samuel Knibb Londini fecit' appears in a curve just below the chapter ring. The fine original hands should be noted.

The eight day movement has a triple-divided front plate and is fully latched. The hour striking train on the left has a vertical hammer arbor and the quarter striking on two bells is on the right. The going train has bolt and shutter maintaining power to ensure that the clock does not stop during winding. Note how the movement sits on the customary wooden blocks but with the rare feature of small notches on the bottom edges of the plates engaging in iron stirrups. The normal steadying bracket is fitted at the top right of the movement. Note also the equally rare iron hooks driven into the seatboard near the front to support the catgut lines. There is a great similarity between the clocks of Samuel Knibb and those of Ahasuerus Fromanteel, proving a close association between the two makers.

The architectural case has an oak carcase veneered with kingwood, very unusual at this early period when almost all cases were veneered with ebony or ebonised. When found it was in a rough state, having lost its gilt brass mounts which have now been replaced, taking great care that they used only the original fixing holes and were correct in all respects. Note that the side windows are the same height as the dial opening.

This important clock was in the Royal Collection at Windsor Castle and is thought to have been disposed of by George IV and had been lost to view until it resurfaced recently. The probable date is c.1668-70.

Thirty-hour clock with the 10ins. dial signed 'Daniel Quare London' c.1685 and with original hands. Very substantial centre-pinion movement with five leaved pinion for fly and double-cut hoop wheel. Ebonised pine case with panelled door, original carved cresting and original tongues to rising hood. Total height including finial 6ft.10ins.

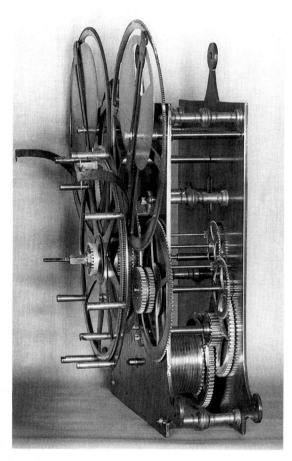

A complicated astronomical clock by Edward Cockey in a very distressed state is shown and described on pages 228, 229; it was contained in a completely unsuitable nineteenth century case.

The clock has been meticulously restored to its original design. The six wheel train has been re-modified to provide a duration of three months, using a weight of ninety pounds. The movement is shown during restoration. The dial has been completely restored including replacement spandrels to Cockey's original design. The unsuitable hands and solar disc have been replaced with those of the correct design, based on the similar clock in the National Maritime Museum.

The case of that clock is in original condition, including the japanned decoration and was the pattern for the new case. This accurately reproduces the proportions and construction of the original and the decoration employs similar motifs but is not a slavish copy. The total height is 11ft.7ins.

The whole clock is a magnificent example of detailed research and very fine craftsmanship and those interested in a more detailed account of the restoration should read *Amazing Clocks* by Derek Roberts (1987).

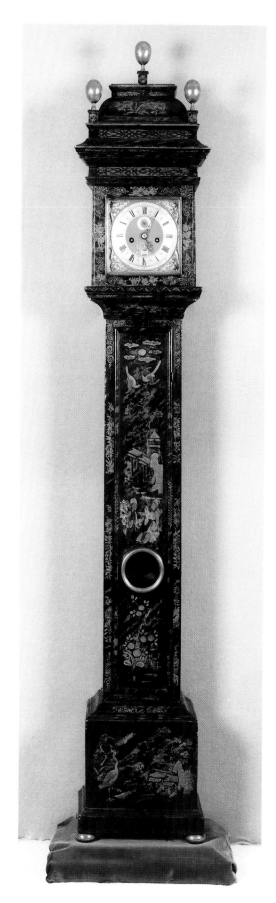

This attractive 'grandmother' clock by Manley is shown in figure 6/4 and briefly described on page 124. The present illustration shows the well balanced and nicely executed chinoiserie scenes heightened with simulated tortoiseshell on a black ground; the sides are also well decorated. The case is 5ft.9½ins. high to top of caddy and 6ft.3½ins. including finial, with a 7½ins. waist.

The clock has a 7in. square dial and an 8 day movement with hour striking controlled by an internal count wheel.

From the records of the Norwich Museums Service it is now known that the maker of this clock was Cornelius Manley, that he was established by 1710 when he advertised for lost watches and that he died in either 1721 or 1722. This additional information confirms the suggested date of c.1710-15.

This clock by W. Shephard of Millom has much in common with those by Gandy of Cockermouth and Benson of Whitehaven, see pages 304-307. It is significant that the towns of Cockermouth and Whitehaven are only twelve miles apart and Millom is a village some thirty miles to the south, all in a rather remote area in Cumberland. Both the Gandys and Benson are known to have made other complicated clocks and Benson also advertised that he made 'all sorts of Plain, Repeating, Musical and Astronomical Clocks'.[1] By way of contrast Shephard was a farmer-clockmaker who is not known to have produced any other complicated clocks. The balance of evidence therefore suggests that all three examples probably came from Benson's workshop.

The solar indications are very similar to those on the Benson with the shutters showing sunrise on left, and sunset on right and the outer pointers on the shutters showing daybreak and twilight respectively. The gilt sun is not visible in this photograph. The inner pointers show the sun's declination (left) and the signs of the zodiac in pairs (right). The top of the inner ring reads 'Sun's Amplitude Oriental. Sun's Amplitude Occidental' There is only a simple calendar, in the square opening above VI, so there is the same difficulty in setting the solar indications as with the Benson.

The movement has a dead beat escapement with centre seconds hand and hour and ting-tang quarter striking from one train.

The handsome case is almost certainly a product of one of the capable cabinetmakers working in the area. The *verre eglomisé* (painted glass) panels in the pediment, the turned wooden capitals and bases, and carved wooden mounts are typical of cases made in north-west England. The very fine quality mahogany used is also typical of this area and results from the extensive trade which ports such as Lancaster had with the West Indies and the American mainland. The lower trunk moulding and the skirting have carved members and the trunk door and plinth are inlaid with brass stringing.

The clock dates from c.1760-65.

1. J. Penfold, *The Clockmakers of Cumberland*, p.142.

This is the original case of the clock by William Lasseter which is shown and described on page 337 and is a typical Sussex case. The clock had apparently stood in the corner of a cottage room for many years and the front and one side of the case had been oak grained, probably when the room was decorated. The plinth had presumably rotted as it had been replaced by an orange box! The present paint is an accurate match for the original milk-based paint. The height is 6ft.2ins. with a twelve inch waist and a ten inch dial. The date is c.1775-80.

This is a good quality clock from south-western Scotland. It was made by John Grindall of Dumfries, probably the one who was active from c.1750. He had a son, also John, who carried on the business until the end of the century.

The dial is signed on a reserve on the engraved centre and has the earlier type of calendar shown through a square opening. The lunar dial in the arch also has the earlier arrangement where the divisions and numbers indicating the moon's age are on the disc, not on the dial arch.

The case is veneered with fine mahogany and has the typically Scottish feature of shaped sound frets, probably of satinwood, in the pediment. There are good quality brass capitals and bases, and the very rare if not unique cast brass fluted columns.

The probable date is c.1780.

Whilst it is generally known that Great Britain had a flourishing export trade in clocks in the eighteenth century, it is not common knowledge that we also exported clockmakers. This regulator is by Robert Hynam who was born in England in 1737, settled in Russia before 1776 and became court clockmaker to Catherine II. His descendants continued to hold the royal appointment until 1864.

The 11ins. painted brass dial has, unusually, a full arch and the chapter ring is reversed, to simplify the motion work. The dial was probably made in Russia as the floral decoration does not look English and no decoration would have been used on the dial of a regulator for the English market.

The high grade movement, stamped Thwaites, has six pillars and is fully latched. Thwaites were well accustomed to supplying special clocks to customers' requirements, as well as the normal range, see pages 382, 383. The train has Harrison maintaining power and stop work to the winding. The dead beat escapement has a steel escape wheel and jewelled pallets with a compensated pendulum to Ellicott's design, as shown in figures 11/5, 11/6 (page 388), which is supported on the backboard.

The mahogany case is probably English, but if so is of North Country origin as shown by the fan inlays in conjunction with the carving on the chamfered corners of the plinth and the ogee bracket feet. On the other hand it could well be Russian as the influence of English designers such as Robert Adam was strong at this period. The square pendulum window is certainly not an English feature.

The probable date is c.1790.

Handsome mahogany case with well figured veneers. It stands free in the double skirting and is 9ft.2ins. high to top of finial. It houses a year-going striking clock by Hardeman of Bridge which is described on page 459.

A Wedgwood jasper ware pendulum bob is referred to on page 47 and this is another interesting variation, a bob made of black basalt. Wedgwood developed black basalt in the second half of the eighteenth century and it was used for portrait plaques and other items where fine detail was required as it is a dense material which has a smooth matt surface after firing.

This example shows a classical scene surrounded by a laurel leaf border and was probably made in the last quarter of the eighteenth century. It has become a collector's piece and is no longer associated with a clock.

The great rarity of these bobs may be accounted for by the fact that they would be hidden away behind a solid wooden door, or were they not an official product but made by the potter in odd moments?

Chapter 1

SETTING THE STAGE

GENERAL IDEA OF CLOCK MECHANISM

A clock is essentially a machine for measuring the passage of time, so before making any serious study of the subject one must establish a clear idea of the functions necessary in such a machine; these are:

a. a **Time Standard** or oscillating system, that is something which has a natural frequency of its own so that if set in motion it will oscillate or vibrate at that frequency. As will be seen later, the pre-pendulum clock has no true oscillating system, but in later clocks the time standard normally consists of a *pendulum,* or a *balance* with its associated *balance spring* or hairspring. In a modern clock it may consist of a quartz crystal oscillator.

b. a **Driving Force** to maintain the oscillations of the Time Standard by replacing energy lost by friction. The driving force usually consists of a *weight* or a *coiled spring* acting through a train of gear wheels, or a battery for the quartz crystal oscillator.

c. a **Counting and Indicating System** to count the oscillations of the Time Standard and indicate them on a dial in hours, minutes and possibly seconds. In mechanical clocks this function is largely performed by the gear train used to transmit the driving force, but in quartz crystal clocks separate counting arrangements are necessary.

It is important to realise that the accuracy of the whole clock depends on the performance of the time standard and this in turn is affected by various factors, the most important being variation in the driving force.

CLOCKS BEFORE THE PENDULUM

Although this book is concerned only with the longcase clock, it will be useful to appreciate the position around 1650, before its introduction.

From about 1600, clockmaking in England had gradually gathered momentum and the formation of the Worshipful Company of Clockmakers in 1631[1] gave added impetus, so that by mid-century the craft was well established. Even so, the lead was still held by the European makers, particularly those of Augsburg and Nürnberg in Southern Germany.

Weight-driven clocks formed the major part of the output of English clockmakers, but spring-driven mechanisms, table clocks and watches, were also made. These were poorer timekeepers than the weight clocks because of the difficulty of making springs which would have a reasonably consistent power output.

The weight-driven clock popular in England was the *lantern clock,* a sturdily built mechanism in a brass case, which had been introduced early in the seventeenth century and which continued in production well into the eighteenth.

---

1. C. Clutton and G. Daniels, *Clocks & Watches in the collection of the Worshipful Company of Clockmakers,* 1975, p. vii.

Figure 1/1. Lantern clock c.1660, by Richard Gorslow. Brass case except for iron back plate. Note narrow chapter ring with quarter-hour divisions and half-hour markings for single hand of blued steel. Alarm setting disc with Arabic numerals. Both alarm disc and chapter ring are silvered. Dial plate with floral engraving in corners and inside chapter ring. Height 16ins., breadth across chapter ring 6¼ins.

Figure 1/2. Decorative fret above dial with maker's signature at base and first owner's initials on shield. Note form of w in Gorsselowe and also the long type of S. Hole in chapter ring at XI is for front pivot of alarm control arbor.

THE LANTERN CLOCK

Figure 1/1 shows a typical balance lantern clock of c.1660 signed 'Richard Gorsselowe, Londini'. Richard Gorslow was apprenticed in 1650 for eight years but there is apparently no subsequent record of him.

The clock is 16ins. high and 6¼ins. broad across the chapter ring, which is about the normal size, but a fair number of smaller examples and a few larger ones are also found. This example strikes the hours and has an alarm, which is typical of its period. The case is of brass with the exception of the back plate which is of iron (figure 1/7). It is supported from a hook in the wall by a stout iron loop or stirrup riveted on to the top plate and is held parallel to the wall by two square iron spikes or spurs fixed near the bases of the rear columns (figure 1/3). Later clocks were frequently supported on wooden brackets. The decorative fret above the dial is engraved with the maker's name and the initials of the first owner (figure 1/2).

The brass dial plate has floral engraving in the corners and within the chapter ring. The latter is divided into quarter hours with simple half-hour markings and, together with the central alarm setting disc, is silvered by a chemical process. The single (hour) hand is of steel blued by heat.

The going and striking trains are supported, one behind the other, by three vertical brass bars (figure 1/3), the going train always being next to the dial (on the left in figure 1/4 and on the right in figure 1/5). Friction is reduced to a minimum by following the normal practice of having brass wheels meshing with steel pinions and steel pivots running in brass

Figure 1/3. Rear view with bell, side doors and back removed. Note iron loop fixed to top plate for supporting clock on a hook in wall and iron spikes or spurs to hold it upright. Brass count wheel on rear train bar controls hour striking and square arbor to right with bent arm releases the alarm.

Colour Plate 1. Clock by William Coward, c.1680-85, in case veneered with olive crossbanding, olive oysters and small bold marquetry panels with bone or ivory leaves. Lift up hood, plinth has appropriate bun feet. 6ft. 4½ins. high and 10½ins. waist with 10ins. dial. See also figures 4/29-32.

Colour Plate 2. Clock by John Davis, Windsor, c.1685, in pine case veneered with walnut and with floral marquetry panels which include bone or ivory leaves stained green. These bone or ivory leaves, which are a feature of early marquetry, have usually faded almost to white through long exposure to light. Note hinged plinth panel with lenticle for 1¼ seconds pendulum, unusual sound frets incorporating birds (perhaps to associate with the bird in the upper marquetry panel), heavy proportions of hood and small side windows. See also figure 4/33.

Colour Plate 3. Fine quality miniature or 'grandmother' clock by Charles Goode, c.1690-95, 5ft. 9½ins. high. 7½ins. dial signed at base. Note ringed winding and seconds holes, skeleton chapter ring with minute numerals outside minute divisions and simple cherub spandrels (C. & W. No. 3), insufficient space for larger ones. Case veneered with finely figured walnut and panels of bird and flower marquetry, with floral marquetry on the moulding under the hood and on the hood door. Note identical twist columns, hood has door, sound fret.

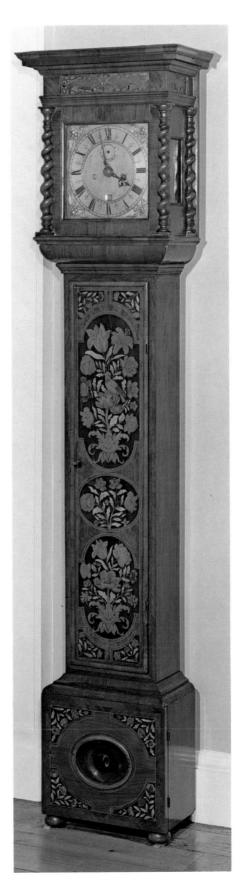

Colour Plate 1   *Colour Plate 2*   *Colour Plate 3*

pivot holes. The duration between windings is usually fifteen hours, that is the clock has to be wound night and morning. This short duration is normal for the period unless heavier weights hung on pulleys have been fitted later to make it into a thirty-hour clock. Time-keeping is controlled by a circular balance which oscillates just above the top plate (figure 1/6). It is important to note that there is no balance spring, as this was not introduced until c.1675, and never into lantern clocks. The only method of regulation is by varying the driving weight. This clock had been converted to anchor escapement and long pendulum, probably in the eighteenth century, and was restored to verge and balance some years ago. Traces of the conversion, which are visible in figure 1/6, include two screw holes for fixing the pendulum cock (top edge of plate), and the small rectangular hole used to fix the short post for the front pivot of the pallet arbor. The alarm mechanism is situated on the outside of the back plate (figure 1/7). The complete back plate had been fixed in place of the left hand door and the mechanism modified to function in that position when the clock was converted to anchor escapement.

Figure 1/8 shows details of the going train. The great wheel turns anti-clockwise, once per hour and engages with the first pinion which consequently turns clockwise. On this pinion is mounted the second wheel which in turn drives the second or escape pinion which carries the

Figure 1/4. Right hand view. Going train on left next to dial, striking on right. Note thick wheels with coarse teeth, decorative steel work. Side frets not engraved.

Figure 1/5. Left hand view. Going train on right. Note wheels mounted direct on arbors which taper towards pinion head, except for crown wheel pinion which is a replacement. Compare with figure 1/8 which shows parts of going train.

escape wheel or crown wheel and turns anti-clockwise. The crown wheel has inclined, pointed teeth which engage in turn with the two pallets or flags on the verge. One tooth of the wheel 'escapes' for each complete oscillation of the balance, that is for two swings or vibrations, one in each direction. The continuing swing of the balance after a tooth has escaped causes the escape wheel to be pushed back or to recoil and this action brings the balance to rest and then reverses its motion.

As the great wheel rotates once per hour, the number of vibrations of the balance per hour can be obtained by taking the product of the two gear ratios and multiplying by twice the number of teeth in the escape wheel:

$$\frac{56 \times 54 \times 17 \times 2}{7 \times 6} = 2{,}448 \text{ beats/hour}$$

which is approximately a one and a half second beat.

Figure 1/6. Top view showing replaced balance and balance cock. Swing of balance limited by vertical part of cock and banking pin in top plate towards right. Note supporting loop riveted into top plate.

The front end of the great wheel arbor is filed up into four pins, forming a lantern pinion which meshes with the hour wheel of forty-eight teeth to give a twelve hour rotation to the hand.

It was pointed out at the start of this chapter that the main requirement for accurate time measurement is an oscillating system having a natural frequency, something which is completely lacking in the case of a balance controlled lantern clock. The timekeeping depends on the amount of energy being imparted to the balance and on the friction at the verge pivots, so anything approaching accuracy is impossible. The only method of regulation is by adding or removing lead shot from a receptacle at the top of the driving weight. With regulation, one of these clocks will keep fair time for a period until a change of conditions causes the average rate to change by up to a quarter of an hour a day, mainly because of changes in the viscosity of the lubricant. John Smith sums it up admirably.[2]

A description of the action of the striking train will be found in Chapter 2.

2. *Horological Dialogues,* 1675, p. 43: These movements going with weights must be brought to keep true time by adding or diminishing from them: if they go too slow you must add thin shifts of lead to the weights to make it go faster, but if it go too fast then you must diminish the weight to make it go slower, so that, whensoever you find it either to gain or loose, you must thus, by adding or diminishing, rectifie its motion: note that these Ballance movements are exceedingly subject to be altered by the change of weather, and therefore are most commonly very troublesome to keep to a true time....

Figure 1/7. Rear view showing alarm mounted on iron back plate. Note double-ended alarm hammer and springy wires to prevent hammer resting on bell and marring sound of hour striking.

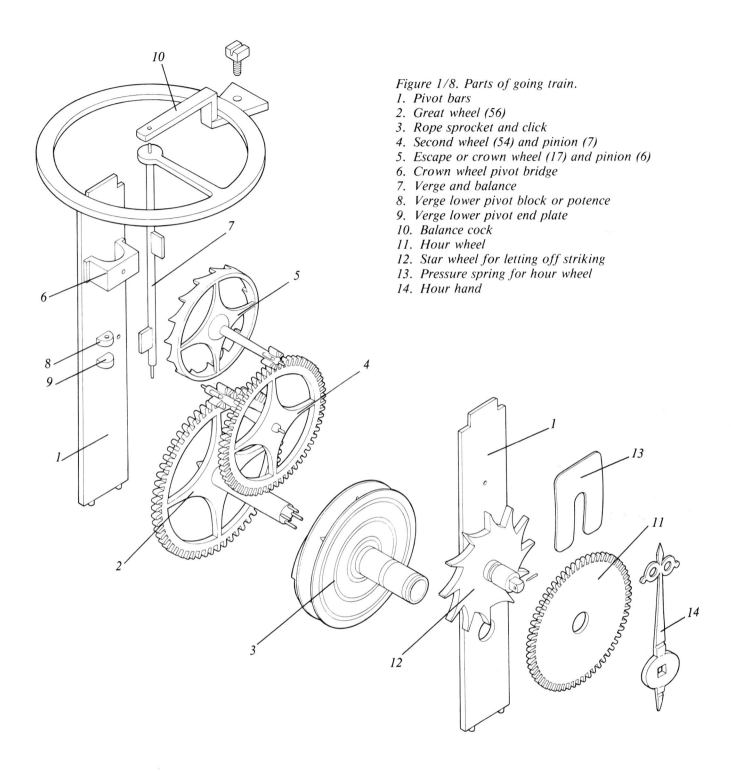

Figure 1/8. Parts of going train.
1. *Pivot bars*
2. *Great wheel (56)*
3. *Rope sprocket and click*
4. *Second wheel (54) and pinion (7)*
5. *Escape or crown wheel (17) and pinion (6)*
6. *Crown wheel pivot bridge*
7. *Verge and balance*
8. *Verge lower pivot block or potence*
9. *Verge lower pivot end plate*
10. *Balance cock*
11. *Hour wheel*
12. *Star wheel for letting off striking*
13. *Pressure spring for hour wheel*
14. *Hour hand*

THE PENDULUM INVENTION

The first public indication that pendulum controlled clocks were available in this country was provided by the following advertisement which appeared in the *Mercurius Politicus*, 27th October – 3rd November, 1658 and was repeated in the *Commonwealth Mercury*, 18th – 25th November, 1658:

There is lately a way found out for making Clocks that go exact and keep equaller time than any now made without this Regulater (examined and proved before his Highness the Lord Protector, by such Doctors whose knowledge and learning is without exception) and are not subject to alter by change of weather, as others are, and may be made to go a week, or a moneth, or a year, with once winding up, as well as those that are wound up every day, and keep time as well; and is very excellent for all House Clocks that go either with Springs or Waights; And also Steeple Clocks that are most subject to differ by change of weather. Made by *Ahasuerus Fromanteel,* who made the first that were in ENGLAND, You may have them at his house, on the Bank-side in MOSSES-ALLEY, SOUTHWARK, and at the sign of the Maremaid in LOTHBURY, near BARTHOLOMEW-LANE end LON-DON.

Ahasuerus Fromanteel had been established in London as a clockmaker since 1629; his family, of Flemish origin, had been settled in East Anglia since the sixteenth century.[3, 4]

A number of scientists, including Galileo, had been working for many years on the problem of applying the pendulum to clock mechanism,[5] but the first successful pendulum clock was designed by the eminent scientist Christiaan Huygens of Leiden in 1657. Huygens is a good example of the gentlemen-scientists who were responsible for so many of the advances in scientific knowledge during the seventeenth and eighteenth centuries. He assigned his rights in the invention to Salomon or Samuel Coster a clockmaker of The Hague, a patent being granted on 16th June, 1657 for twenty-one years. Figure 1/9 shows a clock by Coster dated 1657 and now in the National Museum for the History of Science in Leiden (Museum Boerhaave).

On 3rd September, 1657 Fromanteel's son John, who had been apprenticed in 1651, entered Coster's service until 1st May, 1658, Coster agreeing to reveal his 'secret' during this period. This 'secret' has been generally regarded as the construction of pendulum clocks but both Loomes[6] and Robertson[7] have cast doubts on this. The

Figure 1/9. Huygens' pendulum invention in a clock by Salomon Coster dated 1657. Note horizontal crown wheel driven by contrate wheel. Pendulum suspended on cord between curved 'cheeks' and operated through a crutch.

3. R. Plomp, 'The "Dutch" Extraction of the Fromanteel Family', *Antiquarian Horology,* VII (September, 1971), p. 320.

4. B. Loomes, 'The Fromanteel Story', *Antiquarian Horology,* IX (March, 1975), p. 175.

5. J. Drummond Robertson, *The Evolution of Clockwork,* 1921, pp. 75, 115.

6. Loomes, 'The Fromanteel Story'.

7. Drummond Robertson, p. 127.

former arguing, quite logically, that from the wording of the advertisement quoted above Fromanteel senior must have made pendulum clocks before John's return from Holland and that other English makers were already producing them.[8]

For the purposes of this book the last point is not very important but there is no doubt that the greatly increased accuracy available with the pendulum made it worthwhile to design new forms of clockwork and the longcase clock was born, an English invention. In support of a Continental origin for the longcase clock, Lloyd[9] cites an apparently free-standing German clock which he dates as c.1600; Edwardes[10] draws attention to German pedestal clocks, including a dated example of 1588, but rightly does not regard them as the direct ancestors of the longcase clock.

THE BACKGROUND

To understand the rapid development which followed the application of the pendulum by English clockmakers, and which led to England's supremacy in this field before the end of the seventeenth century, it is necessary to examine the social and economic background.

Until the end of the sixteenth century, the mathematical sciences had not been regarded as appropriate to a gentleman's education, but the founding of Gresham College, London in 1597 heralded a changing attitude and the sciences were studied increasingly as the seventeenth century progressed. From 1645 regular meetings were held in London, normally in the College, and Oxford instituted similar meetings within a year or two. These two societies eventually joined forces and in 1660 the *Royal Society [of London for Improving Natural Knowledge]* was born with the active support of Charles II. Horology frequently formed the subject of its discussions and demonstrations.

Another important factor was the persecution of the Protestants, or Huguenots, in France from the middle of the sixteenth century onwards, which led to many of them emigrating to England where they settled mainly in London or in East Anglia. Many of those who came here were skilled craftsmen, including clockmakers,[11] and they made a considerable contribution to horological progress, the Fromanteel family being a notable example. A particularly large influx occurred in the late seventeenth century, caused by the savage oppression which culminated in the revocation of the Edict of Nantes in 1685.

With the Restoration in 1660, Charles II and his Court brought from the Continent more luxurious ideas in furnishing than had obtained under the Puritans and in any case many of the Royalists had the need to restore and refurnish their houses after the ravages of the Civil War. There was therefore a considerable stimulus to a trade which was well equipped to meet the demand.

8. Since this was written, Dobson has suggested that the secret was Huygens' maintaining power, see R.D. Dobson, 'Huygens, the Secret in the Coster-Fromanteel "Contract", the Thirty-hour Clock', *Antiquarian Horology,* XII (Summer 1980), p. 193.

9. H. Alan Lloyd, *Old Clocks,* 3rd edition, 1964, p. 94.

10. Ernest L. Edwardes, *Weight-driven Chamber Clocks of the Middle Ages and Renaissance,* 1965, pp. 91, 104.

11. P.J. Shears, 'Huguenot Connections with the Clockmaking trade in England', *Proceedings of the Huguenot Society of London,* xx (1960), reprint.

Chapter 2

THE BEGINNING 1658-1670

THE EARLIEST LONGCASE CLOCKS

The first twelve years of so of the longcase clock, starting from Fromanteel's advertisement of 1658, are of tremendous importance, since during that time the basic designs of both mechanism and case were evolved. It is also the period which, in the author's opinion, produced the most beautiful of all longcase clocks. In spite of this they will be treated fairly briefly in this work except where the principles involved are of general importance; those wishing to consider them in more detail are referred to Lee[1] and Hurst.[2]

The transition from the typical mid-seventeenth century lantern clock as described in Chapter 1, to the earliest surviving longcase clock is very remarkable and makes one wonder whether some intermediate stage has been lost. Some early writers[3] have stated that the first longcase clocks had thirty-hour movements but there is only limited evidence to support this statement.

Figure 2/1 shows the movement of the earliest known longcase clock, c.1659-60, signed 'A. Fromanteel Londini', who made all the very early examples which have survived. It has an extremely early conversion to anchor escapement with 1¼ seconds pendulum, probably done by Fromanteel and within ten years of it being made, but this will not be described at this stage.

The trains are between brass plates joined by eight square pillars riveted into the back plate and secured to the front plates by swivelling latches (figure 2/2). The front plate is divided vertically so that each train can be dismantled or assembled independently. The gearing is of coarse pitch, as in lantern clocks of the period, and in order to obtain a duration of eight days five wheels were used in each train, a feature found only in the first few examples.

The weights are hung from pulleys on cat-gut lines which are wound on barrels connected to the great wheels through ratchets and pawls, and turned by means of a cranked key.

The going train is on the right hand side, viewed from the front, in what became its

1. R.A. Lee, *The First Twelve Years of the English Pendulum Clock,* 1969, catalogue of a loan exhibition.

2. M.G. Hurst, 'The first Twelve Years of the English Pendulum Clock', *Antiquarian Horology,* VI (June, 1969), p. 146.

3. Notably H. Cescinsky and M.R. Webster, *English Domestic Clocks,* 1914, p. 110.

Figure 2/1. Movement of the earliest known longcase clock, c.1659-60, by Ahasuerus Fromanteel. It has a very early conversion to anchor escapement with 1½ seconds pendulum and the type of micrometer regulator later used by Fromanteel. Note the very coarse pitch of the great wheels compared with the upper wheels of the striking train. The elaborate seat board is needed because of the very tall movement.

Figure 2/2. Typical latch, the shape varies with different makers. The bevelled section engages with a slot in the end of the pillar.

Figure 2/3. 8½ins. dial of Fromanteel clock. Note engraved cherub spandrels, low position of winding holes caused by five wheel trains. Note also erect Roman numerals in circles, and minutes numbered 1-15 and sub-divided into five seconds.

Figure 2/4. Case of Fromanteel clock of ebony veneer on oak with gilt brass mounts. The panelled door, stepped plinth and slightly flattened bun feet are normal, the apron piece below the hood is exceptional. Maker Joseph Clifton.

Figure 2/1

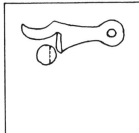

Figure 2/2

Figure 2/4

Figure 2/3

standard position and the inclusion of an intermediate wheel and pinion between the great wheel and the centre pinion causes the winding to be anti-clockwise. The centre pinion, which carries the minute hand, rotates four times per hour, an arrangement probably chosen to give relatively even gear ratios right through the train. It has the advantage of the time being indicated to five seconds by the minute hand but results in a dial which cannot be read at a glance.

The striking employs the Continental-type hammer with elongated vertical arbor mounted in its earliest position, on the front plate. The count wheel is mounted high up and is driven by a pinion on the pin wheel arbor.

The gilt dial (figure 2/3) is 8½ins. square and is secured by latches (figure 2/2). It has engraved spandrels of winged cherubs' heads, a matted centre with a reserve for the signature just above VI and a Tudor rose at the centre. The vertical Roman numerals are almost unique on early clocks and did not reappear on English dials until about the end of the eighteenth century when a few painted dials had them. The applied chapter ring is divided on the inner edge into quarter hours and on the outer edge into fifteen minutes which are numbered individually and subdivided into five seconds. To tell the time, one notes the number of quarter hours elapsed since the last hour and then reads the position of the minute hand. As shown the time is 10.53 and approximately eight seconds. The pierced and shaped blued steel hands are typical of this early period.

The case (figure 2/4) has an oak carcase veneered with ebony and is unusually small (5ft. 11ins.) but is slightly broader than usual at this time. The hood of an early case was not provided with a door but access for winding and adjusting the movement was obtained by sliding up the hood on tongues formed on the edges of the back board, the hood being retained in position by a spring-loaded iron hook. Hoods were frequently modified at a later date to slide forward and provided with hinged doors, to make them suitable for low ceilinged rooms. The presence of an apron piece below the hood sometimes indicates a conversion from a hooded wall clock, which does not apply in this instance. Bun feet were universal on early clocks but many were replaced by moulded skirtings, possibly to improve stability, and most bun feet now seen are restorations.

Figure 2/5. Early iron hinge on a case of c.1675. Note the wrought iron nails.

Figure 2/6. More decorative iron hinge on a case of c.1695.

Figure 2/7. Typical lock on an early eighteenth century case. Note the wrought iron nails.

Until at least the end of the century, all hinges and locks were of iron, fixed with wrought iron nails. Figure 2/5 shows a typical wrought iron hinge on a case of c.1675, and figure 2/6 a later, more decorative example on the japanned case shown in Colour Plate 4. Figure 2/7 shows an early eighteenth century lock, but those on seventeenth century cases are similar. It is of the type known as 'back spring', where the rear portion of the bolt is split to form a spring. Note the wrought iron nails used to fix all these examples.

The Fromanteel case (figure 2/4) has considerable historical importance, as a special recess, which was found during restoration work, contained the halfpenny token of Joseph Clifton, Bull Head Yard, Cheapside, dated 1663. Apart from establishing the provenance of this case it has made possible the identification of other cases as being from the same workshop. According to Lee,[4] the movement and case of this clock are a marriage, but surely this must be one of those arranged in heaven!

The clock dial and movement which have just been described contain a number of features which indicate their semi-experimental nature and the next example to be considered, although only some three or four years later, that is c.1663, exhibits a number of changes and more closely resembles the clocks which followed it.

Figure 2/8 shows the dial, again 8½ins. square, with the signature 'A. Fromanteel Londini' along the bottom edge of the plate, in a position which was to become the normal one until c.1690. This dial has other features which later became standard: the applied spandrel ornaments or 'spandrels' of cast, chased and gilt brass (C. & W. No. 3), and the silvered chapter ring[5] with radial Roman numerals (note the IIII)[5a] and the outer minute band containing the five minute numbering. The quarter-hour divisions and half-hour markings, although no longer really necessary, were retained until about the middle of the eighteenth century. The early chapter rings were very narrow, the record being ⅞in. on a slightly earlier clock than the present example. The shutters which close the winding holes indicate that maintaining power is provided to keep the clock going during winding. The matting on the shutters should match that on the dial centre, a point worth checking as many are modern restorations, the original maintaining power having been scrapped when antique clocks were little valued. As in figure 2/1, the dial is attached to the movement with short octagonal iron feet latched to the front plate (figure 2/9).

The movement has a divided front plate and the eight pillars are turned with fins in a design which was used until after the turn of the century. The movement rests on two tapered section blocks fixed to the seat board and is located by iron pegs through the seat board and blocks into the central bosses of the lowest two pillars. The hooked rods also fitted in this instance are a much later idea normally associated with provincial clocks.

In this clock, the first with four wheel trains, the great wheels are still of coarse pitch and are therefore over 4ins. in diameter. They have to be overlapped and are staggered (figure 2/9), the striking great wheel fitting in the space between the going barrel and its great wheel.

---

4. Lee *Twelve Years*.

5. Some early clocks had chapter rings with a silver overlay soldered on.

5a. IV is used only when a clock has Roman striking (p. 146).

Figure 2/8. 8½ins. dial of a clock signed 'A. Fromanteel Londini', c.1663. Typical early dial; note signature at base, gilt cherub spandrels, matted centre with shutters for maintaining power, five minute numbering within minute divisions.

This accounts for the small diameter, thick ratchet on the going side and necessitates an extra deep movement. The ratchet is attached to the great wheel whereas the striking has the normal layout where the ratchet forms part of the barrel. Exceptionally, the barrels are not grooved for the gut.

The going train and escapement (figure 2/9) are laid out on the same lines as in the Huygens-Coster clock shown in figure 1/9, except for the pendulum suspension. A contrate wheel mounted on the second pinion drives a vertical pinion carrying the crown wheel. The verge (figure 2/10) runs in a normal pivot hole in the front plate but the extended rear pivot is carried on the intersecting rims of two anti-friction wheels pivoted in a small sub-frame (figure 2/11). This is the only known clock with complete original suspension of this type although several others of the period retain traces of it. This suspension should be much less susceptible to wear than the knife-edge type which superseded it and which will be described

Figure 2/9. Movement of the clock shown in 2/8. Note short octagonal dial feet, turned brass pillars, very deep movement to allow for overlapping of extra big great wheels — first movement with four wheel trains. Note also verge escapement with short pendulum and very light bob, maintaining power. The plain barrels are exceptional and the fixing hooks over the bottom pillars are later. The metal projection near the top of the back board forms part of the spring catch for holding the hood in the raised position.

Figure 2/10. The same movement from above. Note the rear pivot of the verge supported by the rims of two anti-friction wheels. Note also the divided front plate and the bell stand and bell hammer mounted on the front plates.

Figure 2/11. Rear view of the movement showing the sub-frame carrying the anti-friction wheels. Note the size of the great wheels and the coarse ratchet teeth.

later in this chapter. An ordinary pivot hole at this point causes too much friction unless the pendulum bob is extremely light, which would result in poor timekeeping. The extra deep movement necessitated cutting away the back board to accommodate the suspension cage and pendulum bob (figure 2/9), and may well, as Hurst suggests,[6] have saved the clock from conversion to anchor escapement and long pendulum. The shape of the pendulum bob is of interest as Tompion used a lenticular shaped bob in a similar way on two of his surviving turret clocks. It was probably done to concentrate the mass vertically but was abandoned in favour of a space saving layout with the major plane of the bob vertical and parallel to the back plate.

Unless some form of maintaining power is fitted to a weight-driven clock, winding will cause the going train to stop or even to run back. This has several disadvantages:

   a. if the escapement jams it may cause a bent escape wheel tooth or damaged pallet.

   b. the clock may stop.

   c. the clock will lose the half minute or so occupied in winding.

   d. the oil on the pallets and escape wheel teeth will be redistributed, thus slightly affecting the rate of the clock.

6. Hurst, 'The First Twelve Years of the English Pendulum Clock'.

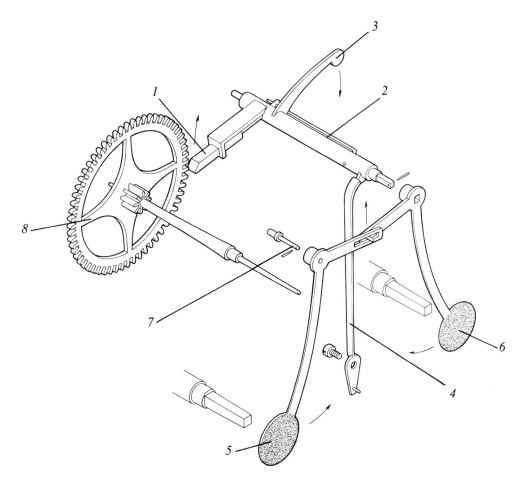

Figure 2/12. Exploded view of bolt and shutter maintaining power.

1. Chamfered bolt. 2. Bolt spring. 3. Operating lever. 4. Maintaining spring. 5. Striking shutter. 6. Going shutter. 7. Pivot stud for striking shutter. 8. Centre wheel.

As the accuracy obtainable with a verge and bob pendulum clock is of the order of a few minutes per week, points c. and d. above are of no importance, but both a. and b. are highly relevant. Where precision timekeepers are concerned, c. and d. attain considerable importance as well as a. The latter may be the sole reason for providing maintaining power on a year or other long duration clock with a delicate escapement.

The clock under consideration is fitted with what is known as bolt and shutter maintaining power and its provision became standard for the remainder of the early period. Figure 2/12 shows the operation of the mechanism and following a study of this it should be possible to find the corresponding parts in figures 2/9-11. Depression of the lever causes the chamfered end of the spring-loaded bolt to slide over the teeth of the centre wheel and at the same time the linkage on the front plate uncovers both winding holes. During winding the restoring force of the maintaining spring causes the bolt to exert pressure on a tooth of the centre wheel and the clock continues to go. After two or three minutes, rotation of the centre wheel disengages the bolt which springs clear of the wheel and the shutters close the winding holes. The shutter on the striking side serves no useful purpose but preserves the balance of the dial; occasionally it is omitted as in the Joseph Williamson clock in figure 8/31.

Figure 2/13. Ebony veneered case of Fromanteel clock shown in 2/8-11. The Doric capitals to the hood columns are very unusual for the period and the clumsy skirting has replaced bun feet. Note tall side windows.

Figure 2/14. Clock of c.1665 by A. Fromanteel with hood raised and supported on spring-loaded iron hook. Note spoon lock operated by trunk door. 8ins. dial similar to previous example but with simple calendar.

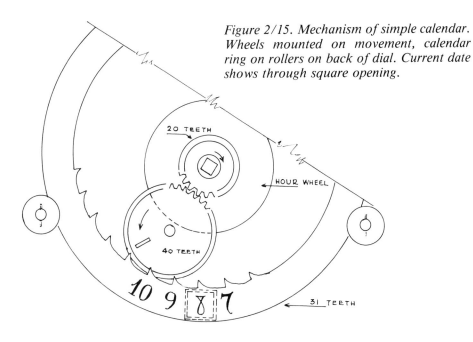

Figure 2/15. Mechanism of simple calendar. Wheels mounted on movement, calendar ring on rollers on back of dial. Current date shows through square opening.

20 TEETH

HOUR WHEEL

40 TEETH

31 TEETH

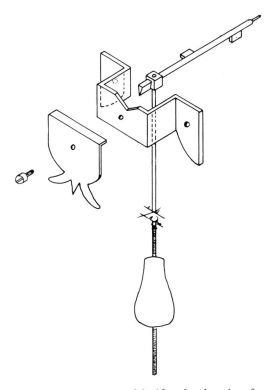

Figure 2/16. Typical movement of 2/14. Note undivided front plate, turned brass dial feet, calendar ring, angle bracket for steadying in case. Hammer mounted on back plate.

Figure 2/17. Normal knife edge bearing for verge and bob pendulum.

The striking train is laid out similarly to that of the first clock described (figure 2/1) apart from having only four wheels, which results in clockwise winding. Both bell and hammer are still mounted on the front plate but the bell stand is shorter and of the type which became standard.

The case (figure 2/13) is again of ebony veneer on oak, slightly slimmer and taller than the previous example and of a design and proportions which became normal for the period, although the Doric capitals are unusual. The moulded skirting to the plinth has replaced the bun feet originally provided.

By about 1665 the design and layout of both dial and movement had become pretty well standardised, the example in figure 2/14, again by Ahasuerus Fromanteel, being typical. One innovation is the simple calendar or day of the month indicator which was applied to most longcase clocks until well into the nineteenth century. Figure 2/15 shows the method of operation; part of the calendar ring, supported on grooved rollers on the back of the dial, is visible in figure 2/16. The dial is 8ins. square.

Figure 2/18. Going side of movement in 2/16 (compare with 2/9). Shallower movement because great wheels do not overlap (finer pitch). Note clock steadied by brass angle bracket on movement fixed to iron bracket on back board.

The front plate is no longer divided, there are five pillars and the great wheels have teeth of finer pitch so that they do not overlap. The movement is of eight day duration and bolt and shutter maintaining power is provided.

The going train is made up as follows:[7]

Great wheel	96
Centre pinion	8
Centre wheel	90
Contrate pinion	6
Contrate wheel	72
Escape pinion	6
Escape (crown) wheel	25

This gives $\dfrac{90 \times 72 \times 25 \times 2}{6 \times 6}$ = 9,000 beats/hour[8]

or 150 beats/minute and requires a pendulum with a theoretical length of 6.26ins.[9] The rear end of the verge is supported on a knife edge in a V-shaped opening in the back cock (figure 2/17), a device which was employed as long as the verge escapement continued to be used in clocks. An end plate or apron piece limits the end shake of the verge and prevents it jumping out of engagement with the crown wheel. The pendulum bob is the usual pear shape and has a wooden inset to make it grip the thread on the pendulum rod. The great wheel/centre pinion ratio of 12:1 gives two turns of the barrel per day or sixteen for the duration of eight days.

Figure 2/18 shows the movement from the going side and should be compared with figure 2/9.

The striking train has the following count:

Great wheel	80	
Pin wheel pinion	8	
Pin wheel	48	8 pins, pinion of report 8
Hoop wheel pinion	6	
Hoop wheel	48	
Warning wheel pinion	6	
Warning wheel	48	
Fly pinion	5	
Count wheel gear	78	

Figure 2/19 shows an 'exploded' view of the striking train and its associated control parts. This drawing should be studied and compared with figure 2/16 and to a lesser extent with the photographs of earlier movements so as to become familiar with the appearance and positions of the parts.

Assuming the clock to be wound and the striking at rest, the left hand projection of the detent (14), which projects through a slot in the plate, will be resting in a slot in the count wheel (11) corresponding to the last hour struck. At the same time the right hand part of the detent will be in the cut away portion of the hoop which is attached to the left hand side of its wheel (4), and the end of the hoop will be pressing against the vertical edge of the detent.

At a few minutes to the hour the lifting piece (13) is raised by a pin in the minute wheel, which rotates once per hour, and a projection on the warning arbor (12) raises the detent until it releases the hoop wheel. The train then runs and the warning wheel (5) makes about

7. The writer is indebted to the staff of the British Museum for details of this movement.

8. This type of calculation is explained on p. 21.

9. The length of a pendulum is based on the formula $t = \pi \sqrt{l/g}$ where t = time of one vibration in seconds, π = 3.1416, l = length of pendulum and g = acceleration due to gravity. For practical purposes, tables of pendulum lengths and times of vibration are given in horological reference books, e.g. D. de Carle, *Watch & Clock Encyclopedia,* 1959.

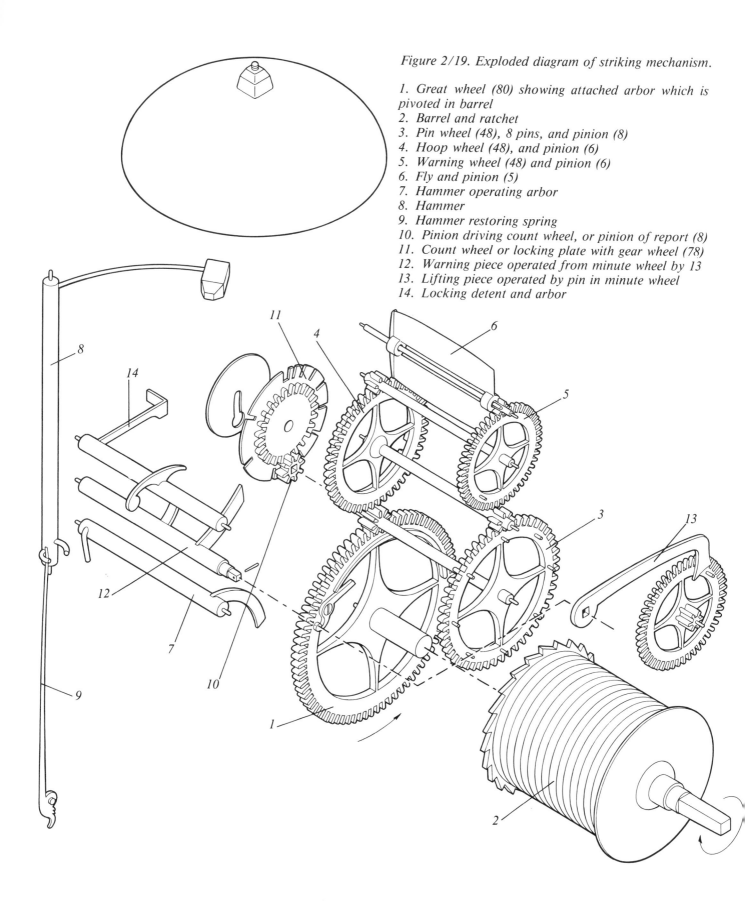

Figure 2/19. Exploded diagram of striking mechanism.

1. Great wheel (80) showing attached arbor which is pivoted in barrel
2. Barrel and ratchet
3. Pin wheel (48), 8 pins, and pinion (8)
4. Hoop wheel (48), and pinion (6)
5. Warning wheel (48) and pinion (6)
6. Fly and pinion (5)
7. Hammer operating arbor
8. Hammer
9. Hammer restoring spring
10. Pinion driving count wheel, or pinion of report (8)
11. Count wheel or locking plate with gear wheel (78)
12. Warning piece operated from minute wheel by 13
13. Lifting piece operated by pin in minute wheel
14. Locking detent and arbor

half a turn until a pin fixed in its rim hits the raised warning piece (12). This action is known as 'warning' and its object is to enable the strike to be released exactly at the hour. Further rotation of the minute wheel continues to raise the lifting piece and associated parts but has no other effect until it is released at the hour.

When the lifting piece falls, the right hand portion of the detent rests on the hoop which rotated a small amount on warning and the lowering of the warning piece releases the train. A pin in the pin wheel (3) operates and releases the hammer (7, 8) and the gap in the hoop again comes under the detent. Unless 1 o'clock is being struck, the left hand portion of the detent will then rest on the rim of the count wheel thus preventing the detent locking the train. The gear ratio (48:6) ensures that the hoop wheel rotates once for each operation of the hammer and the detent therefore checks the state of the count wheel after each stroke. When the detent finds the next slot in the count wheel it drops and again locks the hoop wheel. The count wheel is so driven by the pinion (10) squared on to the pin wheel pinion, that it makes one rotation for the hours 1 to 12, that is for seventy-eight strokes on the bell. The slots in the count wheel are progressively spaced corresponding to the hours except that those for 12 and 1 are normally run together. Apart from the gear ratios already mentioned, the warning wheel must make an exact number of turns for one rotation of the hoop wheel, eight in this example. If this were not so, the warning wheel might come to rest in such a position that its pin could jam the warning piece on operation of the lifting piece. The rate of striking is governed by the speed of the fly relative to that of the pin wheel. This example giving $\frac{48 \times 48}{6 \times 5} = 76.8$ turns of the fly per stroke on the bell. Later clocks will usually be found to have a lower ratio, so the striking tends to be faster. The ratio great wheel to pin wheel pinion and the number of pins, control the duration of the train, this clock requiring 15.6 turns of the barrel for eight days. This is a useful feature, ensuring that the going, which requires sixteen turns, should run down first. If the reverse occurs, the striking will get out of step with the hands; this can however be corrected by depressing the projecting arm on the detent arbor to release the train. It is interesting to note that replacing the great wheel of eighty teeth with one of seventy-eight would make the striking take exactly sixteen turns for eight days, an arrangement adopted on many later clocks (Chapter 3). It is worth noting that in early clocks the pitch of the wheel teeth is related to the force which they transmit, ranging from really coarse teeth on the great wheels to fine teeth, and consequently small wheels, in the upper parts of the trains. Later clocks, in general, were made with a more limited range of pitch, for economic reasons.

The case (figure 2/20) is unusual in not having attached columns to the hood and it should be noted that the frieze section just above the dial and side windows does not overhang to any extent. This indicates that columns could never have been fitted. Conversely, when the frieze projects appreciably beyond the window section of the hood, columns almost

Figure 2/20. 6ft. 4ins. case of Fromanteel clock 2/14. Oak veneered with cocus wood. Good proportions, note absence of columns, tall side windows and unusual pattern gilt brass mounts. Skirting has replaced bun feet.

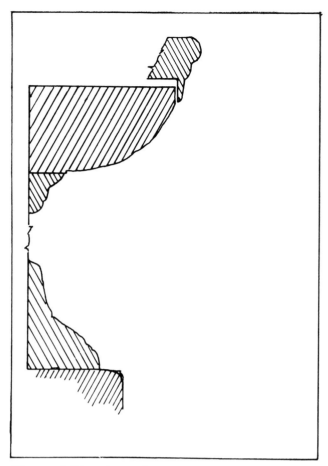

Figure 2/21. Approximate cross-section of main mouldings of 2/20 shown full size.

certainly existed originally. The gilt brass mounts are of an unusual design and the case is not thought to be by Joseph Clifton. It is 6ft. 4ins. high and is of oak veneered with cocus wood, a rich dark brown wood with a rather pronounced grain. It comes from a West Indian tree, the granadilla (*brya ebenus*) and is also known as green ebony and Jamaican or American ebony. However, in the seventeenth century Evelyn defined green ebony as a rare growth of the ash tree. Figure 2/14 shows the hood raised and supported on the spring-loaded iron hook. The pivoted spoon lock for securing the hood is shown just below the dial. Closing the trunk door pushes the lower end of the locking piece backwards and the bent over upper end enters a mortice in the bottom rail of the dial frame thus securing the hood. Almost all longcase clocks will be found to have traces of some method of securing the dial and movement against interference. The side windows should be noted — they are as tall as the dial opening and as wide as possible. From around 1670 both height and width were progressively reduced.

The mouldings at the top and bottom of the trunk are typical and their approximate section is shown full size in figure 2/21. They persisted with little alteration, apart from an increase in cross-section, until the end of the century. The convex upper moulding, in particular, being regarded as one of the signs of a seventeenth century case. The width of the trunk varies from that of the dial to about half an inch greater. One peculiar feature of this case is that the door hinges are fitted reversed, that is with their long arms on to the side of the trunk. They are of the usual wrought iron type and are apparently as originally fitted.

The plinth has lost its bun feet but the proportions are pleasing — the front approximately square, although some other examples are appreciably wider than they are high. Towards the end of this architectural period (in the 1670s) the front and sides of the plinth were frequently panelled to match the trunk, and the panels on both trunk and plinth sometimes edged with a very small moulding.

The architectural features and proportions of these early cases owe little to contemporary furniture design and this has led to the speculation that a leading architect of the period could have been responsible. Fabian, influenced to some extent by Lee, has made a good case for Christopher Wren being the designer of these masterpieces.[10] One piece of evidence used by Fabian is a Wren drawing of a weather clock, probably c.1660 (figure 2/22).

Although the majority of the clocks which have survived are by Ahasuerus Fromanteel or his son John, a few other makers are also represented, notably Edward East and the lesser-known John Hilderson whose work has a close affinity to that of East. These clocks were

10. L.L. Fabian, 'Could it have been Wren?', *Antiquarian Horology*, X (Winter, 1977), p. 550, reprint available Antiquarian Horological Society.

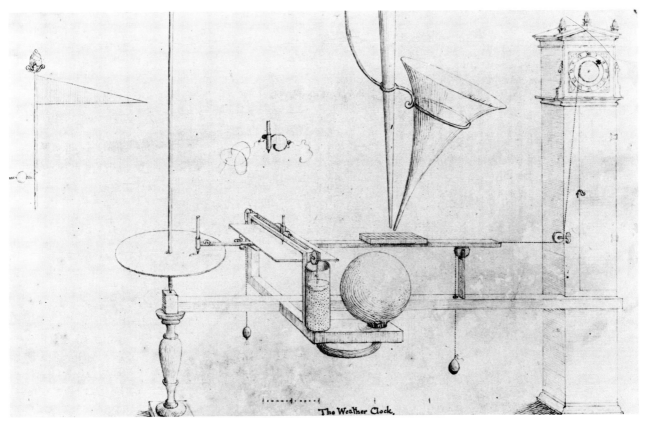

Figure 2/22. Christopher Wren drawing for a weather clock, probably c.1660, used by Fabian in support of his theory that Wren designed the first clock cases.

expensive items as may be seen from the following extracts of documents in the Scottish Record Office relating to the purchase of a clock for Holyrood House.[11]

Extract from a letter headed 'Whitehall March 17 1668'

From Lords Lauderdale and Bellenden,

"... A pendulum clock to goe a week in a plain black Case with weights to strike, will cost twenty pounds. If the case be fine and trimm'd with gilt brass, it will cost thirty. Mine is but a watch and cost sixteen, you may choise which of these three kinde you will have and it shall be made ready ..."

Discharge (authorising payment in London) 1668 May 20 to Mr. East for a pendulum clock,

Twenty pound	20-00-00
For carrying aboord the Clock to the Ship	00-02-00

Evidently a striking clock was ordered, in a plain case, probably of oak veneered with pear wood and ebonised. The term 'watch' was used to indicate a timepiece only, that is one which did not strike. In the seventeenth century, and much later, 'watch' was used to describe the going train of a clock and 'clock' was used when referring to the striking train. Late eighteenth century and even some early nineteenth century clocks will be found with W scratched on parts of the going train by the repairer, although the striking train was often identified by S.

There were apparently no cheap longcase clocks at this period corresponding to the 'country' thirty-hour clocks of the eighteenth and nineteenth centuries and the demand for

11. The writer is indebted to Margaret Swain for this information.

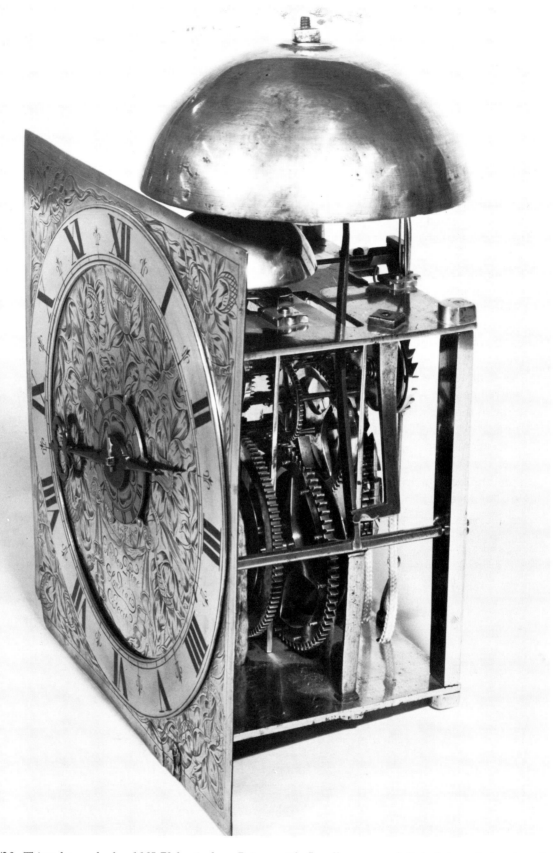

Figure 2/23. Thirty-hour clock c.1665-70 by Andrew Prime, with florally engraved dial plate and signature in drapery panel. Note alarm setting dial with unusual Roman numerals. Birdcage movement with nuts fixing top and bottom plates. Note Continental method of mounting hour hammer between corner posts and small bell for half hours.

cheaper clocks must have been met mainly by the continuing production of lantern clocks, eventually with pendulum control. Some thirty-hour clocks were made, however, and figure 2/23 shows a fine example of c.1665-70 by Andrew Prime who married Ahasuerus Fromanteel's sister.[12]

The dial centre and spandrel spaces are beautifully engraved with tulips, daffodils and other flowers, and the signature 'Andrew Prime Londini Fecit' appears in a lambrequin, or drapery panel, just above the VI. The extremely narrow chapter ring, divided only into quarter hours, should be noted. The hand is of the usual double loop pattern, but the alarm disc behind it is unusual in having Roman rather than Arabic numerals. Between approximately 1665 and 1680, engraved dial plates were used as an alternative to the more common matted centre and applied cherub spandrels. Some of them were engraved all over as this example, some had an engraved centre and cherub spandrels, and perhaps a smaller number had a matted centre with engraved spandrels.

The movement, which is of the birdcage or posted frame type, clearly shows its lantern clock ancestry, but is unusual in having nuts at the top and bottom of the corner posts. The trains are arranged as in a lantern clock with a duration of thirty hours as with later lanterns, but with separate weights; this is shown by the hammer being on the right. The verge escapement[13] is mounted on the top plate and the bob pendulum is supported on a knife edge in the usual way. The only strange feature about the hour striking is the mounting of the hammer arbor between the corner posts, which is a Continental method, instead of between extensions of the train bars. The small bell is probably arranged to provide a single blow at the half hour. The alarm train consists of a rope pulley and circular click mounted on a crown wheel with a vertical verge carrying a long horizontal hammer at its upper end. Both ends of the hammer hit the bell in turn and springy vertical wires are fitted to engage with the upper end of the hammer stem to prevent the hammer resting against the bell, thus spoiling the sound of the hour striking.

The clock has lost its case and no information about it has survived.

12. B. Loomes, *Country Clocks and their London Origins*, 1976, p. 34.

13. Since writing this I have learnt, from B. Hutchinson, that the clock originally had an anchor escapement, was converted to verge and has now been restored to anchor.

Chapter 3

THE ANCHOR ESCAPEMENT

THE NEED AND THE INVENTION

Once the verge escapement pendulum clock had become established, it was realised that its accuracy was limited by the wide arc of swing required (some 50°). This meant that the pendulum was far from isochronous,[1] any variation in arc resulting from a variation in driving force causing considerable error. The wide arc also precluded the use of a long pendulum with heavy bob which would itself have given greater accuracy. Huygens tried two methods to overcome this problem, his clock of 1657 (figure 1/9) having curved 'cheeks' to force the cord suspended pendulum to traverse a roughly cycloidal path, thus obtaining approximate isochronism. His second method, described in his *Horologium*[2] published in 1658, was to interpose reduction gearing between the verge and the crutch supplying impulse to the pendulum, thus reducing the arc of vibration but introducing frictional and other losses. A reconstruction of this design is on display at the Science Museum, London.

The only really satisfactory solution to this problem lay in the development of a simple escapement which would function satisfactorily with a relatively small pendulum arc, in other words the *anchor* escapement. The inventor of this escapement is not definitely known but there are several contenders.

John Smith writing in *Horological Disquisitions,* 1694, p. 2, said:

> From *Holland,* the fame of this Invention [the pendulum] soon past over into *England,* where several eminent and ingenious Workmen applyed themselves to rectify some defects which as yet was found therein; among which that eminent and well-known Artist Mr. *William Clement,* had at last the good Fortune to give it the finishing Stroke he being indeed the real Contriver of that curious kind of long Pendulum, which is at this Day so universally in use among us.

A clock which Clement made in 1671 for King's College, Cambridge and which is now in the Science Museum, London, has often been used to support his claim, although it is now known that the present anchor escapement dates only from a rebuilding of 1819, but there is no evidence of any other type of escapement existing previously.

William Derham writing in *The Artificial Clock-maker,* 1696, p. 96 and commenting on John Smith's statement reproduced above, said:

> But afterwards Mr *W. Clement,* a *London* Clock-maker, contrived them (as Mr *Smith* saith) to go with less weight, an heavier Ball (if you please) and to vibrate but a small compass. Which is now the universal method of the Royal Pendulums. But Dr *Hook* denies Mr *Clement* to have invented this; and says that it was his Invention, and that he caused a piece of this nature to be made, which he showed before the *R. Society,* soon after the Fire of *London.*

Robert Hooke was deeply interested in horological matters and had a great capacity for invention, being responsible for a number of important developments including the spring

---

1. Isochronism is the property of swinging through large or small arcs in equal times. It depends on the pendulum following a cycloidal rather than a circular path. For small arcs the two paths are practically coincident, hence the success of the anchor escapement which functions satisfactorily with an arc of 5°-10°. The effect of lack of isochronism is referred to as circular error.

2. A complete translation of this work appears in E.L. Edwardes' *The Story of the Pendulum Clock,* 1977.

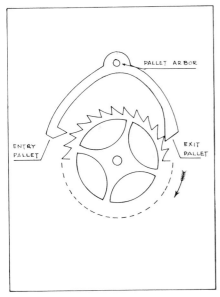

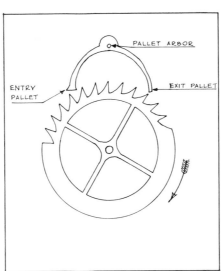

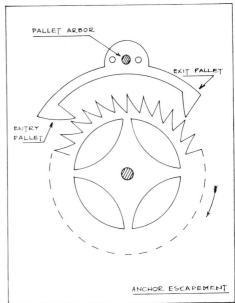

Figure 3/1   Figure 3/2   Figure 3/3

Figure 3/1. Early form of anchor escapement with pallet arbor planted well above escape wheel and with flat impulse faces. As drawn, the pendulum has swung to the left allowing a tooth to escape from the entry pallet and the wheel has been checked by another tooth meeting the exit pallet.

Figure 3/2. Experimental anchor escapement of Tompion's Astrolabe clock, c.1676, in the Fitzwilliam Museum. The escape wheel rotates anti-clockwise due to an unusual train, but is shown as from the rear to facilitate comparison with other types.

Figure 3/3. Later form of anchor escapement with pallet arbor much nearer to escape wheel and curved impulse faces.

suspension for pendulums and the wheel cutting engine, but there is no direct evidence that he invented the anchor escapement. His diary, which he started in 1672, contains many notes on his horological activities, often in association with Thomas Tompion, but is too late in date for there to be any mention of the anchor escapement.

The third contestant, who has probably the best claim to the invention, is Joseph Knibb. Dr. Beeson[3] has established that he provided an anchor escapement in a clock for Wadham College, Oxford supplied early in 1670 and also in the conversion of the clock in the church of St. Mary the Virgin, Oxford in the same year. Lee considers that "this fact, together with other aspects of his work, certainly brings Joseph forward as a possible claimant to its first production".[4] It was also in 1670 that Joseph Knibb left Oxford and set up business in London.

THE ANCHOR ESCAPEMENT

Figure 3/1 shows the principle of this escapement, which is also known as the recoil. It is much simpler than the verge as the escape wheel and pallets are all on one plane, so there is no need for a contrate wheel.

The pendulum is shown having swung to the left, and as it swings to the right pressure of the tooth of the escape wheel sliding along the right hand or exit pallet imparts energy to the pendulum. This tooth eventually escapes but the wheel is checked almost immediately by another tooth engaging the left hand or entrance pallet. With the pendulum continuing to swing to the right, the entrance pallet causes the escape wheel to recoil. On the leftward

3. C.F.C. Beeson, *Clockmaking in Oxfordshire 1400-1850*, 1962, pp. 61, 64.

4. R.A. Lee, *The Knibb Family, Clockmakers*, 1964, p. 139.

swing of the pendulum, the tooth in contact with the entrance pallet imparts impulse to the pendulum until this tooth eventually escapes and the wheel is again checked on the exit pallet. Further movement of the pendulum to the left again causes the escape wheel to recoil and the cycle of operations is then repeated.

It should be noted that the escapement is either accelerating or retarding the pendulum the whole time, as with the verge escapement. The ill effects are, however, considerably less as a much heavier pendulum with spring suspension is used. Variations in the arc of vibration have relatively little effect on timekeeping as the small total arc of vibration reduces the circular error, and the recoil action also reduces the variations in arc due to change in the driving force. The effect of an increase in driving power is to cause the clock to gain, though the magnitude depends on the degree of recoil resulting from the exact shape of the pallets. This is in contrast to the verge escapement and bob pendulum where an increase in power causes the clock to lose heavily. With a reasonably steady temperature a longcase clock with anchor escapement should keep time within a minute or so per week.

Figure 3/2 shows an early escapement of an experimental nature c.1676, by Thomas Tompion. It is in the well known Astrolabe clock at the Fitzwilliam Museum, Cambridge. For comparison with the others it has been drawn with the escape wheel rotating clockwise even though it actually goes anti-clockwise. The action is very similar to that of the one described above although the impulse angles may not be so correct. The fact that the escape wheel has the teeth facing the opposite way from the usual has little effect as all the action should be on the tips of the teeth, that is providing an excessive swing cannot cause the entry pallet to strike the backs of the teeth. Several books[5] show the anchor escapement with the wheel as in this example which may mean that a number were so made.

Early anchor escapements were made with the pallet arbor planted well above the escape wheel pinion, the distance often being about equal to the diameter of the escape wheel. Later escapements had a larger escape wheel but the pallet arbor was much closer to the escape wheel pinion, the distance being about three quarters of the escape wheel diameter or even less (figure 3/3). The pallets embraced a smaller number of teeth and the pendulum required a larger escaping arc. The pallets were also curved to reduce recoil which decreased the effect of variations in driving power but also gave rise to an increased swing and, therefore, a greater circular error. This was fine with the later broader clockcases, but when a repairer provided one of these 'standard' escapements in an early clock with a slim case there was often trouble with the pendulum striking the sides. Cases will be found with wood scooped out of the sides, or even with holes cut through them and hollowed out blocks or boxes fixed to the outside. Such cutting away normally means that the case has, or has had, a later, probably nineteenth century, movement or a replaced escapement of similar date. In a really narrow case a late, large diameter pendulum bob may be sufficient to cause trouble.

Since the anchor escapement was used in the vast majority of longcase clocks, it has been treated at length. Those interested in the practical details of the escapement should consult Rees[6] and Gazeley[7] or other practical works.

The crossbeat escapement merits a brief mention, as it apparently preceded the anchor escapement but was almost immediately superseded by it. Figure 3/4 shows the principle of this escapement and was drawn from a Joseph Knibb, Oxford, clock of 1668-69.[8] There is also a William Clement, London, clock which was scribed for a verge, drilled for a crossbeat and then provided with an anchor escapement and 1¼ seconds pendulum.[9] Careful

5. Notably *Rees's Clocks Watches and Chronometers, 1819-20,* a selection from *The Cyclopaedia; or Universal Dictionary of Arts, Sciences and Literature* by Abraham Rees, reprint (1970), pl. XXXII, fig. 3.

6. Rees, pp. 198, 214.

7. W.J. Gazeley, *Clock and Watch Escapements,* 1956, p. 21.

8. Lee, *Knibb,* p. 144.

9. Lee, *Twelve Years,* exhibit 24.

Figure 3/4

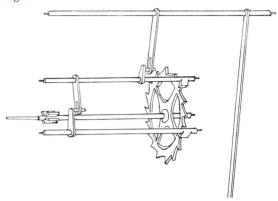

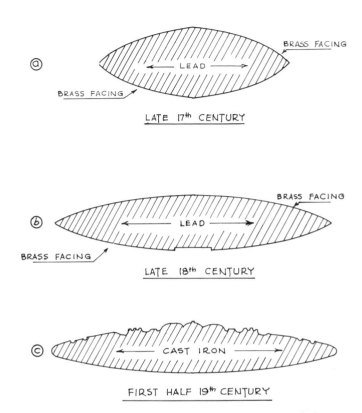

Figure 3/4. Drawing of crossbeat escapement in Jos. Knibb clock, c.1668-69. Wheel rotates clockwise and linkage between pallet arbors ensures that as one pallet allows a tooth to escape the other intersects another tooth. Some loss of impulse occurs due to friction and play in linkage.

Figure 3/5. Development of pendulum bobs, shown in cross-section.

examination of other contemporary movements would probably provide evidence of similar changes. The crossbeat seems to have been inspired by the verge escapement as the pallets bear a close resemblance to verge pallets, and are acted upon by an escape wheel with forward pointing teeth.

The pendulum normally used with the anchor escapement beats seconds, which requires a theoretical length of approximately 39ins. and an overall length of about 46ins. A number of seventeenth century clocks have 1¼ seconds pendulums with a theoretical length of approximately 61ins. and an overall length of about 68ins. As Lee[10] states: "It is a moot point as to which length was the first". Some writers have suggested that the great increase in accuracy with the seconds pendulum (with anchor escapement) led makers to experiment with the longer one in a search for even better results. It will be remembered that the earliest known longcase movement (figure 2/1) has a very early conversion to anchor escapement with 1¼ seconds pendulum. The extra long pendulum has the advantage of causing the bob to swing in the wider plinth section of the case, thus permitting a satisfactory action in a narrow case designed for a short pendulum. Pendulums beating seconds or longer periods were known in the seventeenth century as royal pendulums.

The pendulum bob normally consists of a highly domed brass front, sometimes with a similar back, filled with lead as shown in the cross-section in figure 3/5a, the approximate sizes being 3-3¼ins. diameter and ¾-1¼ins. thick. Some early bobs have two or three concentric circles turned in them and a few have engraved decoration. Later bobs are bigger, up to 5ins. across, but of flatter cross-section (figure 3/5b), the thickness remaining about the same. Quite thin cast iron bobs were introduced in the nineteenth century (figure 3/5c), some having raised decoration picked out with gold paint and others being plain with a brass facing spun over them. The writer remembers seeing a late North Staffordshire clock with a pendulum bob of Wedgwood blue and white jasper ware.

10. Lee, *Knibb,* p. 139.

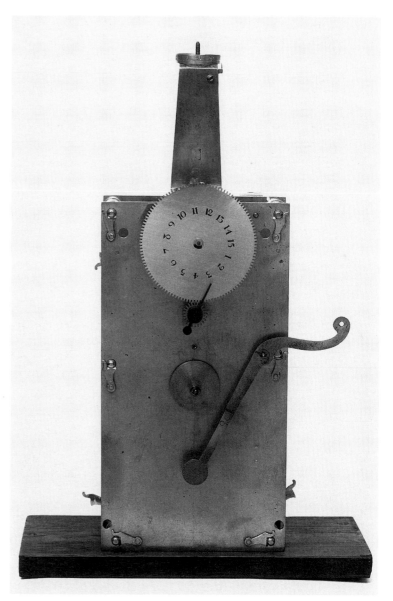

Figure 3/6. Year timepiece c.1675 attributed to Fromanteel. Five wheel train with centre pinion rotating in twelve hours. Note nineteenth century collets and non-tapering pinions, replaced pallets. Movement and dial latched. Compare pendulum suspension with that shown in figure 2/1.

Figure 3/7. Front plate of year timepiece showing restored maintaining power and drive to minute disc.

The bob usually slides on a rectangular strip or 'flat', normally of brass but occasionally of iron, mainly in provincial clocks. At the lower end is a threaded rod with a rating nut, generally square, but some better quality clocks have octagonal ones, occasionally with the facets numbered to assist in regulation; wing nuts were also used. Hexagonal nuts were not introduced until c.1850 so should not be found on clocks of earlier date. Some of the good makers used regulators which operated on the suspension spring, and these will be described later together with the clocks on which they are found.

The suspension consists of a length of very thin spring steel about ¼in. wide fitted into a small brass block at the top to support the pendulum in the back cock and a larger brass block to engage with the crutch. Thomas Tompion used a very long crutch, almost down to the seat board, with the brass block which engages with the crutch some distance below the lower end of the suspension. This design, which was also used by a few other makers, gives greater efficiency by reducing the jerk imparted to the top of the pendulum at the moment of impulse.

The rod normally consists of an iron wire ⁵⁄₆₄in.-⅛in. diameter, which is not an ideal design as some of the impulse is dissipated in flexing the rod. Quite a number of good quality

Figure 3/8. Replaced 9ins. dial of year timepiece showing unusual layout. The time shown here is 8.42 and approximately 9 seconds.

clocks have a brass pendulum rod, an unfortunate 'improvement', as the co-efficient of expansion of brass being nearly twice that of wrought iron causes an increased temperature error, a fact not appreciated even by eminent makers until well into the eighteenth century. The problem of flexing of the rod was overcome by a few makers, including Tompion, who used a brass rod of flattened oval section about ¼in. wide, or a slightly wider thin flat brass strip, which was used by Joseph Williamson. Late in the eighteenth century some provincial makers used a flat iron strip about ½in. wide, which grew to ¾in. or more in the nineteenth century.

Fromanteel's famous advertisement included a reference to clocks that '...may be made to go a week or a moneth, or a year, with once winding up' and figure 3/6 shows a year timepiece movement which came to light some years ago, having features in common with Fromanteel's work and could probably be attributed to him. It was in a very sorry state, the dial was missing and posts riveted to the front plate showed that another dial had been fitted in the nineteenth century, but this also had disappeared. The pallets and crutch, back cock, and bolt and shutter had been lost, and the pinions renewed, but the original pendulum regulator had survived and the pillars showed traces of gilding.

The train is made up as follows:

Great wheel	124	barrel diameter 2⁷⁄₁₆ins.
Second wheel pinion	16	
Second wheel	112	
Centre pinion	14	
Centre wheel	120	
Fourth wheel pinion	8	
Fourth wheel	112	
Escape pinion	7	
Escape wheel	72	

With a 1¼ seconds pendulum the escape wheel takes three minutes per rotation and the centre wheel rotates once in twelve hours. The barrel rotates once in thirty-one days, so twelve turns are required for a duration of 372 days, which means that the clock functions satisfactorily in a case of 6ft.4ins. total height. The barrel arbor is divided, the great wheel being riveted to a short arbor, the front part of which is supported in an extended bearing in the rear of the barrel as shown in figure 2/19. The six pillars and the dial feet are latched (figure 3/6).

The proportions of the escapement are interesting, the distance between the pallet arbor and escape wheel centres being approximately one and a half times the escape wheel diameter. The pallets therefore embrace almost half the wheel as in the A. Fromanteel clock in figure 2/1 and the escaping arc is consequently very small. With an adequate supplementary arc, the total swing of the pendulum is under 2ins.

The pendulum regulator (3/6) should be compared with that fitted to the Fromanteel mentioned above. It works by raising or lowering the suspension spring through the slotted block of 'chops', thus changing the effective length of the pendulum. The amount of movement can be read off the adjusting nut (which is divided 0-50) against a fixed pointer (figure 3/7).

It seems inconceivable that such a clock, designed for accurate time keeping, should indicate hours and seconds, but not minutes. Close examination of the spare holes near the top of the front plate suggested they were probably used to fix cocks, one on the inside and the other on the outside of the plate, with an arbor supported by them passing through the large clearance hole. The decision was therefore taken to provide a rotating minute disc driven from the seconds arbor in the manner used by Tompion on two short-duration observatory timers.[10a] This design uses a pinion mounted on the seconds pivot to drive the minute disc in the ratio one to five. To ensure a smooth drive, a pinion of 24 was used with a minute wheel of 120, thus giving a fifteen minute rotation see figure 3/7.

10a. See R.K. Foulkes, *Antiquarian Horology*, I (September, 1955), p.105.

Figure 3/9. 10ins. dial of anonymous eight-day clock of c.1680. Note fairly narrow chapter ring, large slender seconds ring and set back winding squares to allow for maintaining power shutters. Traces of gilding on dial plate near III and IX. Replaced hands.

Figure 3/10. Front view of the movement of the eight-day clock in 3/9. Note traces of maintaining power: hole for bolt arbor below top right hand latch, pivot stud for striking shutter just above lifting piece, screw and locating peg holes for maintaining spring to right of hour wheel. Early features include bell stand on front plate, coarse-toothed motion work for calendar, and square locating peg hole for maintaining spring. Latter is a survival of lantern clock practice. Small holes on top and bottom edges of plates were for pinning together when setting out. Note movement fixed direct to seat board by screws into bottom pillars, which became the normal method.

The dial was designed with a conventional single-hand chapter ring showing quarter hours, the minute disc was numbered 1 to 15 and the seconds ring was divided into 2½ seconds and numbered 15, 30, 45, 60, repeated three times. This layout provides a dial that is aesthetically satisfactory and is reasonably easy to read (figure 3/8). The time shown is 8.42 and approximately 9 seconds.

The clock performs very happily with a weight of 23 lbs, a tribute to the gear-cutting, no doubt helped by the clock's unconventional design which uses one less wheel and pinion than the average year clock, and by the very small pendulum arc.

The next example to be considered is a fairly typical eight-day clock of c.1680. Figure 3/9 shows the dial which is 10ins. square and is unsigned. This clock is one of a group of at least six which can be attributed to the same unknown maker because of certain peculiarities in their construction.[11] Such anonymous clocks were presumably produced by journeymen or other makers who, not being freemen of the Clockmakers' Company, were not authorised to sign their work. Unsigned clocks are becoming scarce as many of them have acquired 'important' signatures with the object of increasing their commercial value.

The chapter ring, although still fairly narrow, is broader than on the earlier dials previously

11. The writer is indebted to R.A. Lee for this information.

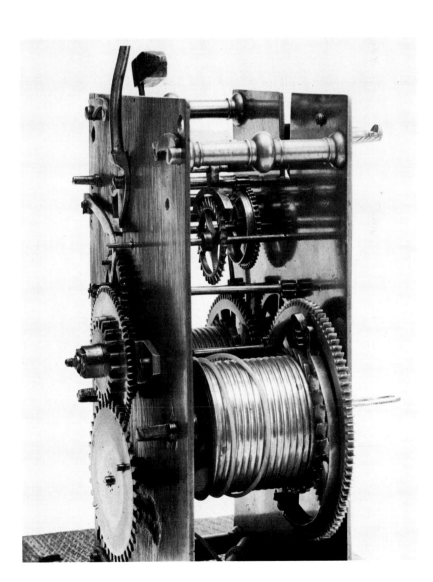

Figure 3/11. Going train of the movement in 3/10. Note small escape wheel, replaced pallets, short winding squares (short dial feet, maintaining power).

shown. The seconds ring, made possible by the long pendulum, is large and slender, and is a prominent feature of almost all early anchor escapement clocks. The hands are not original. The way the ends of the winding squares are set back from the dial indicates that bolt and shutter maintaining power was fitted originally but is now missing.

In the front view of the movement (figure 3/10) note its tall shape, also the coarse-toothed motion work to operate the calendar, and the latches securing the five pillars. The dial feet are pinned, not latched. Traces of the maintaining power include the large hole for the bolt arbor just below the top right hand latch, screw and locating peg holes for the maintaining spring to the right of the hour wheel, and pivot stud for the striking shutter near the top left corner of the plate. The movement is fixed direct to the seat board by screws into the bottom pillars, which became the normal method.

Figure 3/11 shows the going train and the escapement with its small escape wheel. The train count is as follows:

Great wheel	96 barrel diameter $1^{25}\!/_{32}$ins.
Centre pinion	8
Centre wheel	60
Third wheel pinion	8
Third wheel	56
Escape pinion	7
Escape wheel	30

This train remained in common use right through into the nineteenth century. One detail which changed was that the third wheel, which was usually mounted on a collet near the front plate on seventeenth century movements, was normally mounted on the pinion head close to the back plate on later examples. The barrel arbor is not divided, the great wheel riding loose on the arbor and being held in position by a flat collet and a pin through the arbor. The back cock (figure 3/12) made from an hour wheel bridge casting is peculiar to this maker and is one of the identifying features mentioned above.

The count wheel is now mounted direct on the barrel arbor, which is divided in the same way as that of the going barrel of the previous example. The detent is mounted outside the back plate on a squared extension of its arbor. The striking train is as follows:[12]

Great wheel	78 barrel diameter $1^{25}\!/_{32}$ins.
Pin wheel pinion	8
Pin wheel	48 8 pins
Hoop wheel pinion	6
Hoop wheel	48
Warning wheel pinion	6
Warning wheel	48
Fly pinion	6

The only differences from the train given in Chapter 2 are the great wheel of seventy-eight teeth to give exactly one rotation in twelve hours, and the fly pinion of six leaves which gives sixty-four turns of the fly per stroke on the bell. Note that the hammer is now mounted on a horizontal arbor and operated direct from the pin wheel instead of the somewhat complex arrangement used earlier and shown in Chapter 2. This method was introduced a little before 1670 and soon became standard with English makers, although some Continental makers continued to use the older method until quite late in the nineteenth century.

The screw near the top left corner of the back plate is for the attachment of an angle bracket used to steady the movement by attaching it to an iron bracket fixed to the case.

It should be noted that a 10ins. or 11ins. dial with a narrow chapter ring usually has the movement plates extending well below the great wheels. This was probably to ensure that the dial feet rivets were behind the chapter ring, ensuring that they did not mar the appearance of the dial.

12. William Dereham quotes trains identical to both these in *The Artificial Clock-maker,* 1696, p.110. He also quotes trains, some of which are not practicable, for various durations up to a year.

Figure 3/12. Rear view of same movement. Note unusual back cock made from hour wheel bridge casting and bevelled cut-away to accommodate crutch. Hole above going great wheel for pin to limit movement of maintaining bolt. Count wheel squared on to extension of barrel arbor, directly operated hammer.

Chapter 4

DEVELOPMENTS IN CLOCK DESIGN
1670 – 1700

THE EFFECTS OF THE ANCHOR ESCAPEMENT ON
CLOCK DESIGN

The immediate effect of the new escapement with long pendulum was a broadening of the trunk section of the case, made necessary to allow adequate space for the pendulum to swing. To maintain satisfactory proportions both plinth and hood had to be made wider and the overall height increased, necessitating a bigger dial.

The long pendulum had one unfortunate effect: unless the case is firmly fixed a sympathetic vibration is set up in it, thus abstracting energy from the pendulum and leading to a reduced swing or even to complete failure. According to Lee[1] this problem is most severe with a 1¼ seconds pendulum, probably because it approximately corresponds with the natural period of the case. On the other hand, with a seconds pendulum, the weights can oscillate violently when they are about 3ft. below the seat board and thus form seconds pendulums. In addition to robbing the pendulum of energy they sometimes collide with it. The problem was well known by 1675, when John Smith[2] wrote:

> In setting up long-swing pendulums ... then in the room it is designed to stand in, seek for some post if possible near the place you desire it should stand at, to which proffer the Clock and case together as it is, which done fasten the back part of the Case with a nail or screw to the post ... then when you have found it to stand in its true position, fasten it with another nail or two, that it may stand firm and not shake.

After three hundred years this advice is as sound as ever, particularly if fitted carpets are involved. It is especially important with month or longer duration movements which usually have little power to spare. This tendency of the long pendulum to rock the case is, of course, reduced as the case becomes broader, which provides another justification for this development.

The first cases for long pendulum clocks were very similar to those described in Chapter 2 apart from the small increases in width and height. They continued the architectural tradition and were mostly veneered with ebony or ebonised.

Figure 4/1 shows one of the first of these long pendulum clocks, by 'Eduardus East Londini', c.1670. The case has increased width in the trunk to allow for the swing of the seconds pendulum, but the mouldings at top and bottom of the trunk are the same cross-section as for one of the slimmer cases. Similarly the height, approximately 6ft. 5ins., has not been increased. The result is that the case is not as finely proportioned as those made a few years later when the design had been perfected.

The twist-turned, or barley sugar twist, attached columns should be noted as they were used on most, though not all, cases for the remainder of the century. They look best when made as a pair, that is with one left hand and one right hand twist, but quite a lot of cases have identical twists, as in this example and in the Charles II chairs and other furniture from

1. Lee, *Knibb*, p. 139.
2. *Horological Dialogues*, 1675, p. 34.

Figure 4/1. Clock by Edward East, c.1670, veneered with lignum vitae. Broader case to accommodate seconds pendulum but mouldings still small. Note unusual twist columns to architectural hood, very tall side windows, large octagonal lenticle to show pendulum. Skirting has replaced bun feet. Height 6ft. 5ins.

Figure 4/2. Back of English walnut chair c.1675, with carving of exceptional quality. Note winged cherub heads at the top of the cresting and the complete cherubs below it.

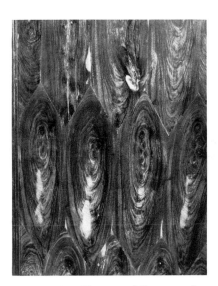

Figure 4/3. Elongated lignum vitae oyster pieces on the Edward East case, note the close rings.

Figure 4/4. Typical olive oysters on side of Thos. Johnson clock in Colour Plate 6. Note dark irregular rings. The oysters are separated from the normally cut olive veneer by a banding of, probably, sycamore.

Figure 4/5. Oyster-like knot in walnut veneer on side of Chris. Gould marquetry case in Colour Plate 5. Note the blurred rings. The panels are edged with box and ebony stringing.

Figure 4/6. Walnut oysters on a chest of drawers, c.1710. Note the blurred rings.

which the idea came. Decorative cherubs on clocks are another feature which is shared with chairs (figure 4/2) as well as architecture, and even tombstones of the period.

The window or lenticle in the trunk door is another innovation which became a very popular feature and persisted until the arched dial had become established, although some makers used it much less than others. The example in figure 4/1, being very early, is exceptional in both its size and its octagonal shape, the usual later form being round or oval. The object was to show the swinging of the pendulum bob, and if the latter does not line up reasonably well with the lenticle it suggests a marriage between case and movement. The window should be of clear glass, not the 'bull's eye' type as found in some cottage windows. This was formed in blowing window glass by hand and was discarded as unsuitable for important situations, so it would not have been used originally in clock cases. The frame to the lenticle is usually of wood polished or gilt though later ones were frequently of lacquered brass. The skirting is a replacement for bun feet.

This case shows an early use of a decorative wood, lignum vitae, in place of ebony or ebonising. The veneer is in small pieces, those on the door (figure 4/3) and plinth panel being in the form of elongated 'oysters', whilst those on the sides form a diamond design. Oyster veneers consist of slices at right angles or diagonally across a small branch or sapling and therefore show concentric growth rings and possibly some of the lighter coloured sapwood on the outside. A parquetry of oyster pieces was popular on clock cases until about 1690 and was almost always of olive wood. For other furniture, oyster pieces were cut from a variety of woods, including olive, walnut, laburnum, kingwood and lignum vitae. Like burr veneers, oyster cuts are difficult to identify and are often wrongly attributed, so figures 4/4-8 are included to show some of the commoner ones. These are shown in black and white, since the individual woods vary so much in colour that to show colour illustrations could be misleading. Early veneers, being saw-cut, were at least $1/16$ in. thick, and usually considerably thicker.

With the use of decorative woods, cross-cut pieces were applied on at least the main

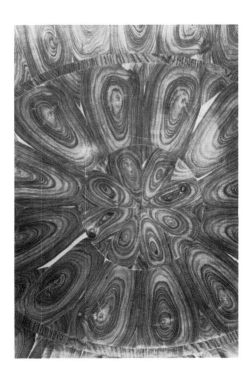

Figure 4/7. Kingwood oysters on a scriptore, c.1680. Note the very distinct even rings.

Figure 4/8. Kingwood oysters on a cabinet, c.1675. Rings less pronounced than on previous example but still quite distinct.

mouldings and the use of raised panels ceased, but panels were often outlined in cross-banding and stringing on good quality cases.

The dial (figure 4/9), like the case, shows evidence of the clock being of a somewhat experimental nature. The dial is 9½ins. square but the chapter ring is only 7½ins. diameter, the space being filled with engraving, with the cherub spandrels apparently fitted later as they cover some of the engraving. Note also the early lettering of the signature. The seconds ring is exceptional in being numbered only every fifteen seconds, instead of every five seconds as became standard until about the middle of the eighteenth century, although George Graham started numbering every ten seconds somewhat earlier.

The movement has bolt and shutter maintaining power and fine regulation is effected by means of a wing nut to raise or lower the suspension similar to that shown in figure 3/6 and described on p. 50. The pendulum bob is threaded direct on to the rod and coarse regulation is obtained by rotating the bob half a turn at a time. To ensure that the crutch and suspension are not damaged, there is a fixed wing nut just above the bob to be held during this rough adjustment. The count wheel is mounted on the extended rear portion of the barrel arbor, an early adoption of that position.

Figure 4/10 shows a clock of c.1675 also by 'Eduardus East Londini'. The beautifully proportioned case is 6ft. 10ins. high with a 10ins. waist corresponding to the 10ins. square dial. It is veneered with kingwood, which is a member of the rosewood family, and was known as Prince's wood in the seventeenth century. The decorative effect is obtained from the carefully selected matching veneers and the use of cross-cut wood on the mouldings. The twist-turned, or barley sugar twist, attached columns should be noted since they look best when made as a pair as in this case. They are of a more typical shape than those on the previous East clock (figure 4/1).

The gilt brass mounts are similar to those on earlier clocks, but metal bun feet, as in this example, are very rare and these are a restoration. With the general adoption of decorative, lighter coloured woods, metal mounts were little used except on the relatively small number of ebony or ebonised cases which continued to be made.

Figure 4/9. Experimental 9½ins. square dial of the East clock in 4/1. Note extra space outside chapter ring filled with floral engraving, early type signature, very narrow seconds ring numbered 15, 30, 45, 60, bolt and shutter maintaining power. The cherub spandrels are apparently later as they cover the engraving.

Figure 4/10. Slightly later clock by East, c.1675. Beautifully proportioned case, 6ft.10ins. high, 10ins. dial and 10ins. waist. Carefully matched kingwood veneers and cross-grained mouldings. Note twist columns more typical than previous case and made as a pair which looks better than both alike. The gilt brass mounts are exceptional on a decoratively veneered case although typical of an ebony one of the period. The metal feet are extremely unusual and these are a restoration.

Figure 4/11. Sound aperture in the hood of a country pine case of c.1780 (Wm. Lasseter, Arundel). The opening was covered with strong paper instead of the hessian used earlier.

Figure 4/12. 10ins. dial and hood of the East clock in 4/10. Beautifully proportioned dial with very slender chapter and seconds rings, the latter as large as possible and numbered 5, 10, 15, etc. Note finely detailed Corinthian capitals which came in at the end of the architectural period.

It is misleading to judge the number of black cases made from the number still extant, as like other black furniture they were quite common in the seventeenth century. Whereas much of this furniture has been lost or has been stripped and refinished, good clocks in black cases often had the latter veneered in decorative woods or the clocks were recased. This was done to make them more saleable earlier this century when antique clocks were plentiful.

When clocks were enclosed in wooden cases it was found necessary to take steps to allow the sound of the bell to be heard clearly and at a distance. A few of the early clocks had the bell and hammer above the top of the case in the Dutch manner, but usually an opening was provided and covered with coarse material to exclude dust as far as possible. Early longcases normally had a rectangular hole in the top of the hood and this idea persisted in some country thirty-hour clocks until late in the eighteenth century, see figure 4/11 which shows the hole in the hood of a clock by Wm. Lasseter, Arundel, c.1780. The absence of sound frets on many provincial clocks, particularly the humbler ones, suggests that they also may have had sound apertures in the tops of the hoods. These were probably abandoned when the dust excluding material became defective, an argument supported by the number of cases which have later, often rough, wood in this position.

Figure 4/12 shows the dial and hood of the East clock in figure 4/10. Note the large, very narrow seconds ring which is planted equidistant between the centre hole and the chapter ring. Seconds hands did not have tails until about the middle of the eighteenth century unless they were necessary for balance because of the reduced power available in a long duration movement. The Thomas Tompion year timepieces provided for Greenwich observatory in 1676[3] are notable early examples with balanced seconds hands.

3. See R.W. Symonds, *Thomas Tompion, His Life and Work,* 1951, p. 26.

Figure 4/13. 10ins. dial of a thirty-hour key wound clock by Tho. Tompion, c.1675. Note finely engraved dial centre, signature in drape or lambrequin, maintaining power shutters.

Figure 4/14. Going side of the Tompion thirty-hour clock in 4/13. Note grooved barrels for cat gut, bolt and shutter maintaining power, movement supported on tapered blocks. Indirect drive to minute hand. Latched pillars and dial feet.

The movement is of excellent quality, with five latched pillars and latched dial feet. Bolt and shutter maintaining power is provided as is normal with early anchor escapement clocks. Maintaining power is not necessary to keep the heavy pendulum swinging or to protect the escapement during winding, so its provision was gradually abandoned and by about 1690 maintaining power was restricted to clocks where accuracy was particularly important.

Figure 4/13 shows the 10ins. dial of an early Tompion clock which is contemporary with the East just described (c.1675). The dial centre is beautifully engraved and the signature 'Tho. Tompion Londini fecit' appears in a drape or lambrequin. Bolt and shutter maintaining power is provided. The hands are similar to those on the East and are typical of the period.

It has a very rare type of thirty-hour movement with the weights suspended on cat gut from key-wound barrels, see figure 4/14 which shows the going side. The movement is beautifully finished with all the pillars and dial feet latched. As usual with thirty-hour clocks each train has three wheels, and a centre arbor to carry the minute hand is provided, being operated by a small wheel which meshes with the great wheel. This form of indirect drive is referred to as 'shake minutes' from the backlash in the minute hand. The maintaining power can be seen near the top of the movement. The back plate (figure 4/15) has a number of spare holes near the top which are evidence that the movement originally had a verge escapement. The anchor escapement was quite well established when Tompion set up in business in London in 1671 so he is unlikely to have made a normal longcase clock with a verge. As

Figure 4/15. Back plate of Tompion movement. Note spare holes near top of plate, showing it originally had a verge escapement.

Hartley[4] suggests, it was most probably made as a hooded wall clock, for which purpose the plate frame, being shallower, is much more suitable than a lantern or birdcage type. Even so, the gut barrels seem a needless complication. The lantern type thirty-hour longcase clocks, made by Tompion and others, will be discussed later in this chapter.

The layout of the striking train is conventional for a thirty-hour plate framed movement except that its position on the left viewed from the front, together with clockwise winding, results in the hammer striking the inside of the bell, see figure 4/16, which also shows the angle brackets used to steady the movement in its case.

The case (figure 4/17) is some years later than the clock and very closely resembles a Tompion case. This fact, together with the quality of the early conversion to anchor, indicates that Tompion was quite possibly responsible for the change from wall clock to longcase.[5] This case has the usual oak carcase, veneered with olive oysters and with geometrical inlays of ebony with holly or box. The skirting round the plinth has replaced bun feet. The trunk door has a half round moulding, which was popular during the rest of the century and the first quarter of the eighteenth.

4. J. Hartley, 'The Thirty-hour Keywound Longcase Clock', *Antiquarian Horology*, XI (Autumn, 1978), p. 30.

5. ibid.

Figure 4/16. Striking side of Tompion movement in 4/14. Hammer strikes on inside of bell to permit clockwise winding. Note thumb screw for attaching movement steadying bracket to bracket on back board.

Figure 4/17. Tompion thirty-hour clock in slightly later case veneered with olive oysters with geometrical inlays of ebony and box or holly. Lift up hood, see 4/15 for retaining catch. Skirting has replace bun feet.

Figure 4/18

Figure 4/18. 10ins. dial of clock by Richard Lyons, c.1675-80. Note elegance resulting from absence of quarter hour divisions on chapter ring. Spandrels too small; incorrect hands; minute hand too heavy and late style, hour hand rather slight. Original bolt and shutter maintaining power.

Figure 4/19. Lyons movement with dial removed. Typical bolt and shutter mechanism with right hand shutter squared on to bolt arbor and left hand shutter pivoted on a stud.

Figure 4/20. Lyons movement. Count wheel in early high position and indirectly driven. Note cut-out for pallet withdrawal. Also recently made oil sinks and small modern screws for spandrels.

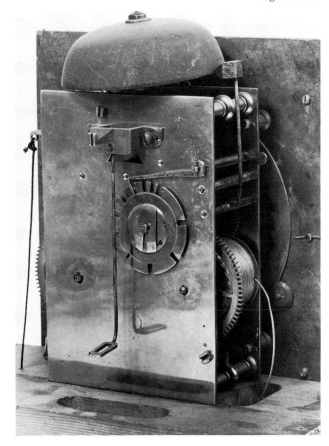

Figure 4/20

Figure 4/19

Not all makers adhered closely to the contemporary fashion and figure 4/18 shows such a dial by 'Richard Lyons Londini' on a clock of 1675-80. The absence of quarter hour divisions, which also applies to another of his clocks,[6] gives a certain elegance to the dial. The spandrels are however too small and that they are replacements is borne out by the modern fixing screws which are too small for the holes, as can be seen in figure 4/20. The hands are replacements, the minute hand being too heavy and late in style and the hour hand rather slight.

The five-pillar movement (figure 4/19) has retained its original bolt and shutter maintaining power. In the rear view (figure 4/20) note the cut-out to facilitate withdrawal of the pallets. A recent restorer has provided all the pivot holes with oil sinks, which were not invented until 1715 and took some years to come into general use. The count wheel is in the early position, being driven by a pinion on the end of the pin wheel arbor. By this time most eight-day clocks had the count wheel mounted on the rear end of the barrel arbor as shown in figure 3/12.

The use of the 1¼ seconds pendulum in a search for even greater accuracy has already been mentioned and a specimen of c.1680 by 'Robertus Seignior Londini' will be examined. The 10ins. dial (figure 4/21) shows that the clock *should* have a 1¼ seconds pendulum as the

6. See Cescinsky and Webster, p. 120.

Figure 4/21. 10ins. dial of month clock by Robert Seignior, c.1680. Note wider and lower position of winding holes for month movement, each five seconds divided into four for 1¼ seconds pendulum, half-quarter markings based on hour markings, j-type 1 used on calendar. The hands are a little too short and the hour hand is very ornate for the period.

Figure 4/22. Seignior month movement of 4/21. Latched pillars and dial feet, bolt and shutter maintaining power. Note subsidiary dial for regulation, extra long crutch, anti-clockwise winding of going train, high position of count wheel with internal detent.

seconds ring has only four divisions for every five seconds, forty-eight in all. This is achieved by fitting an escape wheel of twenty-four teeth instead of the usual thirty. Clocks with the extra long pendulum are more valuable than those with seconds pendulums and, as the conversion is quite easy to carry out, it is necessary to check that the seconds ring has the right number of divisions and is original.

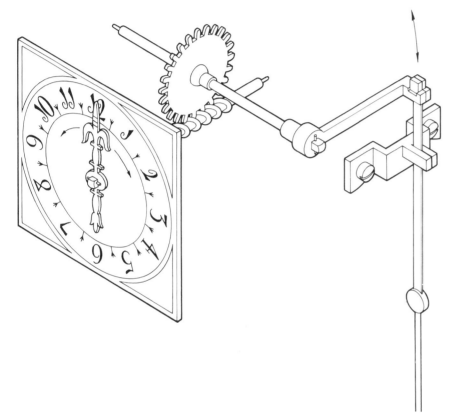

Figure 4/23. Mechanism of regulator shown in 4/22. Rotation of the hand clockwise raises the pendulum by its suspension and so shortens its effective length below the back cock. Pressure from the wheel cannot cause the endless screw to rotate and so lose the adjustment.

Figure 4/24. Burr walnut veneered case of Seignior clock. Note door in plinth to give access to 1¼ seconds pendulum for coarse regulation, unusually fine sound frets in front and sides of hood, full length side windows. Skirting has replaced bun feet. 6ft. 6ins. high.

The dial has another feature of interest, the 'half-quarter' markings at 7½, 22½, 37½ and 42½ minutes. In this example they appear to be based on the hour markings on the inner ring, but they are usually scaled down and simplified versions of half-hour marks. They were introduced around this date (c.1680) and continued in use until about 1730 or a little later, particularly in the provinces, although not all makers used them. There is very little evidence to indicate why half-quarter divisions may have been introduced; Baines[7] found a reference to clocks which chimed or struck the half-quarters in Whitehall Palace in 1685. If, as seems likely, these clocks existed, it is strange that apparently none has survived. Half-quarter repeating was developed for watches, and a few early ones, not necessarily repeaters, have their minute rings marked with half quarters. The most probable explanation however is that the hour was regarded as being divided progressively into halves, quarters, eighths, etc., in support of which Smith[8] quotes 'The Sixteenth Part of an Hour'. This successive halving also forms the basis of much of the Imperial system of weights and measures.

Certain features of the numerals used on early dials are worthy of consideration. The early j-type of 1 is frequently but not invariably used for calendars, but is rarer on seconds and even rarer on minutes. The 8 is usually flat topped as on the regulator dial in figure 4/22, but the round topped variety as on the anonymous dial of figure 3/9 is also fairly common, particularly on the relatively few dials with every minute numbered. The 7 often has a curly tail, though that in figure 4/22 is plain. The figures 3 and 5 used for minute numbering do not usually have upturned tails but this does not necessarily apply to the seconds and calendar numbers on the same dial, see figure 4/21. The hour number IIII probably derives from the old Roman notation iiii which survived in accounts into the seventeenth century. It also provides a better balance to the VIII and is always used except with a special form of striking introduced by Joseph Knibb and known as Roman striking which is described in Chapter 7 and where IV is used on the dial.

The Seignior clock has a month movement which results in the winding squares being lower down and slightly wider apart. A three-month movement usually has the winding holes very low, near the chapter ring. These are useful aids to identification. Early clocks normally have hands which exactly fit the chapter ring; surprisingly, these are a little short, while the hour hand is very ornate for the period.

For a month clock such as this an extra wheel and pinion has to be interposed between the great wheel and the centre pinion so as to give an overall ratio of 48:1. This gives a duration of thirty-two days with sixteen turns of gut on the barrel and normally uses a weight of 20-25lb. compared with the 12-14lb. of eight-day weights. The extra wheel and pinion results in anti-clockwise winding, a useful tip for quick identification (see figure 4/22). The extra duration on the striking side is sometimes obtained by providing an additional wheel and pinion between great wheel and pin wheel pinion, which again causes anti-clockwise winding. On early movements the more usual method, as here, is to increase the number of teeth in all the wheels and the number of pins in the pin wheel, and provide two notches in the hoop wheel. This retains clockwise winding, so both trains wind towards the centre. The high position of the count wheel is so that it can be driven from the pin wheel arbor.

Maintaining power is fitted and is operated by a cord which passes through a hole in the seat board. It is inconvenient to regulate a 1¼ seconds pendulum at the bob and on this clock only rough regulation is done by a nut under the bob, while the normal fine regulation is by the hand shown in figure 4/22. This raises or lowers the suspension by means of an endless screw or worm gear as shown in figure 4/23. It should be remembered that when a worm gear is used like this it cannot be driven by the wheel, so there is no risk of the device 'running back' and thus losing the adjustment.

The elegant case of the Seignior clock (figure 4/24) is 6ft. 6ins. high and is of oak veneered

7. H. Baines, 'Half-Quarter Chiming Clocks', *Horological Journal* (January, 1953), p. 41.

8. John Smith, *Horological Disquisitions,* 1694, part of heading to 'A Second Table of Equations'.

Figure 4/25. Figured walnut case with simple early cresting based on a scallop shell but lacking a gilt ball finial. Rising hood. Height without cresting 6ft. 9ins. 10½ins. dial signed at base by Joseph Knibb, bolt and shutter maintaining power. Three train movement quarter striking on three bells, c.1675-80.

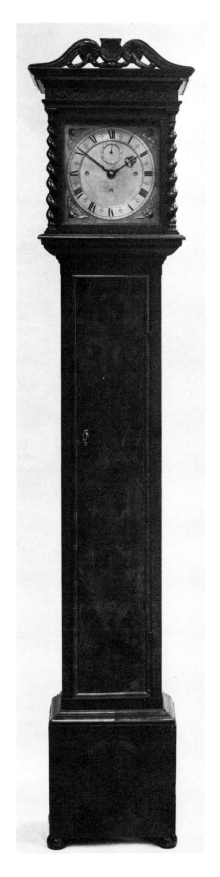

Figure 4/26. Very elegant 10½ins. dial of month clock by Peter Knibb, 1677-79. Skeleton chapter ring with every minute numbered; note the round tops on the figure 8s. Early use of cherub and foliage spandrels. Very low winding squares for a month movement. Panelled ebony veneered case 7ft. 0ins. high.

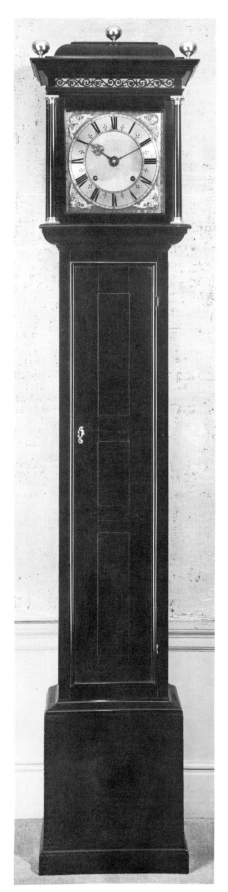

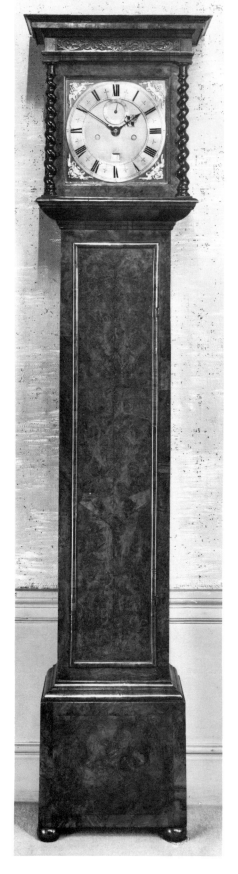

Figure 4/27. Three-month Roman striking clock by Joseph Knibb, c.1680-85. Wheat-ear border to uncluttered dial plate. Note IV on chapter ring. Ebony veneered and panelled case in early style. Skirting has replaced bun feet. Rather tall plinth. Note plain columns, simple sound fret, low caddy and gilt brass mounts. Compare with the Tompion clock in 4/28.

Figure 4/28. Eight-day clock by Tho. Tompion, no. 111, c.1685. 10ins. dial has seconds ring, calendar and shutters for maintaining power. Broader chapter ring has minute divisions set in from edge and minute numbers on outside, a Tompion innovation. Case veneered with burr walnut is only 6ft. 0ins. high. Note true pair of twisted columns and finely pierced sound fret. Equally beautiful but has a somewhat later appearance than its contemporary by Joseph Knibb in 4/27.

with burr walnut. Note the hinged door in the plinth to provide access to the pendulum. This was provided in almost all cases which were made for clocks with 1¼ seconds pendulums.

The case has the usual rising hood which is provided with sound frets on all three sides. The frets are backed with a fairly fine material such as silk and provide a pleasant decoration as well as being more efficient as dust excluders than the roof vents used previously. They were introduced at about the date of this case (c.1680) or a little earlier but the side frets were often omitted. In general the early frets were much simpler and bolder than the later ones.

Before the introduction of the frieze frets described above, some clocks had very bold frets in the side window openings with material backing and these provided an efficient alternative to the sound vent at the top of the hood. The very early Fromanteel clock shown in figure 2/3 has this feature. A number of clocks of all periods have frets in their window openings and probably many more were so equipped originally, but these have since been replaced by glass since the frets were so easily damaged. The construction of the openings is identical for both types of insert so a change leaves no traces.

One would expect clocks made up to about 1670 to have glass side windows to display the ingenious mechanisms which are at a convenient height for viewing, but this consideration does not apply to later and taller clocks when the movements were more likely to be taken for granted and are too high for easy inspection. When the windows afford a view of the ends of the seat board and the upper parts of the case sides, the result is unsatisfactory and suggests either that frets backed with material existed originally or that a marriage has been arranged. This does not occur with very early clocks with small dials which project little below their movements and where the movements are usually supported on blocks. As mentioned in Chapter 2, the windows were made the same height as the dial opening for the first fifteen years or so but after that they tended to be smaller than the dial so that by 1700 they were usually several inches less. It is worth noting that the Seignior clock just described has them the same size as the dial opening. Many later provincial cases including fine quality ones, did not have side windows, but some had tiny vestigial ones which served no useful purpose.

The cases of the Tompion (4/17) and Seignior (4/24) clocks illustrated have straight cornices to the hoods, without superstructures. Many seventeenth century cases were probably so made, in keeping with contemporary cabinets, but a number of cases were provided with carved crestings as in figure 4/25. This shows a fine figured walnut case of c.1675-80 with a simple cresting centred on a scallop shell. The small plinth above the shell shows that it should be surmounted by a ball finial. As time went on, the crestings became more elaborate and some cases had them at the sides as well. This case still has its rising hood and the height is 6ft. 9ins. without the cresting.

The 10½ins. dial is signed at the base 'Joseph Knibb Londini fecit', and the hands are typical of early Knibb work. Bolt and shutter maintaining power is provided and the movement has triple divided front plate and is latched throughout. The three train movement strikes the quarters on three bells.

All the Knibb family made clocks of great elegance and figure 4/26 shows a 10½ins. dial signed 'Peter Knibb Londini Fecit'. It is the only recorded longcase clock by this maker who became a member of the Clockmakers' Company in 1677 and moved away from London permanently in 1679. The chapter ring is cut away to leave only the minute and quarter hour rings and the numerals, this being known as a skeleton chapter ring. In addition, every minute is numbered, a rare device which must have increased the cost considerably. Note the use of round-topped 8s as already discussed (p. 68). Note the use of the larger, more elaborate cherub spandrels (C. & W. No. 5). Evidence has now come to light that this type was used earlier than had been realised.

The movement has arched top plates and is of month duration with five wheel trains. It is contained in a panelled ebony veneered case 7ft. 0ins. high.

Figure 4/29. 10ins. dial of clock by William Coward, c.1680-85. Note absence of half-hour divisions and crude engraving of minute, second and calendar numerals. Unusual but apparently original winding shutters. Fine hands. The case is shown in Colour Plate 1.

Figure 4/30. Rear of Coward dial. Note winding shutter assembly mounted on a pipe at dial centre. Slotted arm engages with pin in arm on maintaining arbor, see 4/31. A very rare type. Note six feet to chapter ring instead of four, small modern screws for spandrels.

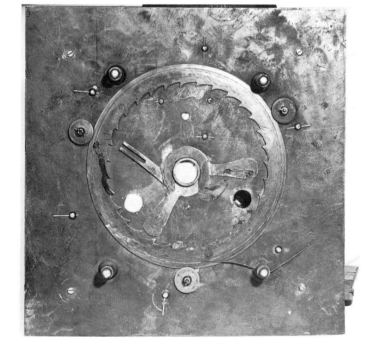

The next illustration (figure 4/27) shows a somewhat similar clock by Joseph Knibb of c.1680-85. The dial plate has a wheat-ear border and the spandrels are of the simple cherub type (C. & W. No. 3). The chapter ring is conventional except for the IV which indicates that the clock has what is known as Roman striking. This method, invented by Joseph Knibb, is particularly suitable for long duration movements as it uses less power than normal striking. It is described in Chapter 7. The position of the winding holes indicates a long running movement, in this case three months, this being obtained with high numbered five wheel trains.

The movement has arched top plates and a 1¼ seconds pendulum regulated by a wing nut at the top of the suspension.

The case is veneered with ebony and panelled in an early style. A skirting has replaced bun feet. The hood has plain columns, a typical simple fret and a low caddy top. Caddy tops were introduced c.1680 and were increasingly used as alternatives to carved crestings which they had superseded by 1700. The well proportioned case, set off by its gilt metal mounts, combines with the simple graceful dial to produce a very elegant clock.

When considering clocks by different makers it is important to remember that some makers such as Tompion were innovators and leaders of fashion, whereas others, including the Knibbs, were more conservative and tended to continue the old styles. If this is forgotten, it is easy to date some makers' work too early and others' too late.

Figure 4/28 shows an eight-day clock by Thomas Tompion, no. 111, of c.1685. The dial has one important innovation: the minute divisions are set in from the edge of the chapter ring with the numbers outside the divisions, probably for greater legibility. This idea was

Figure 4/31. Front plate of Coward movement. Six latched pillars and latched dial feet. Note arm to operate winding hole shutters, heavy steel work.

Figure 4/32. Rear view of Coward movement. Note pallet-shaped cut-out to facilitate removal of pallets and early type back cock. Iron steadying bracket at left. Early use of inside count wheel.

introduced by Tompion in the late 1670s, but most makers did not adopt it until 1690 or even later. This dial has the usual seconds ring and calendar aperture and the movement has bolt and shutter maintaining power. The spandrels are C. & W. No. 4.

The case is veneered with burr walnut and the hood has the more usual twisted columns, a true pair, and a detailed fret. The plinth has a broad crossbanding and correct bun feet. The case has no metal mounts. The height is 6ft. 0ins., and the dial 10ins. square. A beautiful clock, but its proportionately broader case with later features and its more advanced dial would at first suggest a later date than that of its contemporary by Joseph Knibb.

Figure 4/29 shows an interesting 10ins. dial signed 'Wm Coward Fecit' which lacks the fine engraving normally found on early clocks and may mean that, exceptionally, the maker did his own engraving. Note that the w in Coward is rather like n, this form quite often being found in seventeenth and eighteenth century work. Although no location is given on the dial, this is possibly the work of the William Coward of London, listed by Baillie[9] as being apprenticed in 1673 and a member of the Clockmakers' Company 1681-84, which dates are appropriate for the clock. Against this ascription, the heavy steel work and the crude engraving could result from a provincial training, rather than that of John Fromanteel to whom the London man was apprenticed.[10] Note the absence of half hour divisions and the crude engraving of the minute, second and calendar numerals. The winding hole shutters are very unusual in being engraved instead of matted to match the dial, but they appear to be original. The hands are nicely pierced and decorated.

The winding hole shutters (figure 4/30) are mounted on the dial and rotate about a short pipe fixed at the dial centre, being kept in position by a key fitted in a groove in the pipe. The maintaining arbor carries an arm with a pin near the end (figure 4/31) which engages with the slotted arm of the shutter assembly (figure 4/30). This is an extremely rare but perfectly

9. G.H. Baillie, *Watchmakers ond Clockmakers of the World,* 3rd edition, 1951, p. 68.

10. G.H. Baillie, C. Clutton and C.A. Ilbert, *Britten's Old Clocks and Watches and their Makers,* 7th edition, 1956, p. 358.

Figure 4/33. 10ins. dial of a clock by John Davis, Windsor, c.1685. Note seconds ring divided for 1¼ seconds pendulum and finely pierced and shaped hands. There are no provincial features about the dial. Case is shown in Colour Plate 2.

satisfactory arrangement. Note the unusually large number of pins holding the chapter ring and the small modern screws for the spandrels. The substantial movement (figure 4/31) has six latched pillars and the dial feet are also latched. Note the heavily forged hammer, bell stand and maintaining power lever. The back plate (figure 4/32) has a cut-out in the shape of the pallets and an early type of back cock with single screw fixing. Note the early use of an inside count wheel.

The case (Colour Plate 1) is a typical example of c.1680-85, veneered with olive crossbanding, olive oysters and small panels of bold marquetry with bone or ivory leaves. The hood lifts up and the plinth has appropriate bun feet. In all respects it appears to be a normal product of a London case maker with no provincial features. It is 6ft.4½ins. high with a 10½ins. waist.

Seventeenth century provincial clocks are rare but are usually of considerable interest. Figure 4/33 shows the 10ins. dial of a clock of c.1685 signed 'John Davis in Windsor fecit'. The dial has no provincial features and the seconds ring with each five seconds divided in four indicates that it has a 1¼ seconds pendulum. Bolt and shutter maintaining power is provided. The hands are very finely pierced and shaped. The typical eight-day movement has an angle bracket fixing it to the back board.

The case (Colour Plate 2) has a pine carcase veneered with walnut and with floral marquetry panels. The plinth has a lenticle and the front is hinged to provide access to the long pendulum. The hood retains its rising action and parts of the spoon lock and the retaining catch are visible in figure 4/33. The unusual sound frets incorporate birds. The small side windows should be noted. The case lacks the perfect proportions of a London-made example and the use of pine for the carcase is usually a sign of provincial work. The technique of marquetry cutting and the development of marquetry decoration on clock cases are discussed in Chapter 5.

Another, differing, example of about the same date (1685 or a little later) is shown in figure 4/34. The 10¼ins. dial is signed on the lower edge 'Wm. Clement Londini fecit'. There is floral engraving between the spandrels (C. & W. No. 5), and a Tudor rose at the centre. The winding holes are decorated with ornamental turning or ringing, a form of decoration which was introduced c.1685 and remained fashionable until c.1715, although not all makers used it and some provincial makers even continued to use it until at least the middle of the eighteenth century.

The rare feature is the use of only a single hand on an eight-day clock. This must have been done to meet the requirements of a customer who wanted the simple time indication of a one-hand clock with the convenience of weekly winding. It would not have been for cheapness, for which a thirty-hour clock would have been chosen.

The case, of early type, is panelled and ebonised, and is 6ft. 2½ins. high. Another similar clock by William Clement with an even simpler dial is contained in a good quality case with floral marquetry in panels, which emphasises that economy was not the reason for the single hand. Indeed, there are a few provincial eight-day one-handed clocks dating from well

Figure 4/34. Eight-day clock by Wm. Clement, c.1685. 10¼ins. single-handed dial with floral engraving between cherub and foliage spandrels (C. & W. No. 5), Tudor rose at centre and ringed winding holes. Ebonised panelled case, skirting has replaced bun feet, 6ft. 2½ins. high.

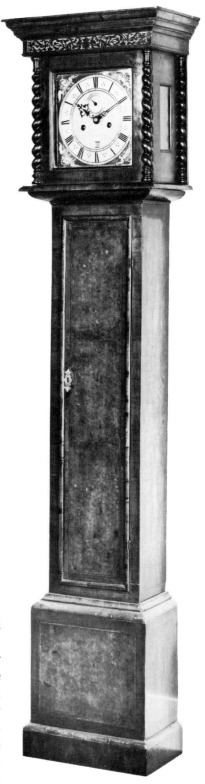

Figure 4/35. 10ins. dial of clock by Wm. Knottesford, c.1685-90. Skeleton chapter ring with one half hour mark missing. Note ringing of winding and seconds apertures, setting back of winding squares for maintaining power shutters, and incorrect minute hand. Compare effect produced with that of figure 4/26.

Figure 4/36. Eight-day clock by Charles Gretton, c.1685-90. 10ins. dial, half quarter and hour markings are crosses, remaining five minute spaces each halved by a dot. Simple cherub spandrels (C. & W. No. 4). Typical walnut veneered case, fine fret, note small side windows. Height 6ft. 6ins.

into the eighteenth century, no doubt ordered by conservatively minded customers.

Figure 4/35 shows another example of a dial with a skeleton chapter ring which should be compared with the Peter Knibb dial shown in figure 4/26. The 10ins. dial is signed 'Wm. Knottesford Londini' and is about ten years later than the Knibb, that is 1685-90. The broader, heavier chapter ring, the ringed winding holes and the seconds dial and hand, produce a rich but less elegant effect than that of the earlier dial. The minute hand is too short and not of the usual pattern; it is probably a later replacement. The setting back of the winding squares suggests that maintaining power was originally provided.

Figure 4/36 shows a typical walnut case of c.1685-90 with a fine fret and a height of 6ft. 6ins. The clock is by Charles Gretton, London, and an unusual feature of the 10ins. dial is that, in addition to half quarter markings, the remaining five minute spaces are each halved by a dot. The spandrels are C. & W. No. 4.

The panelled ebony case still continued to be made and figure 4/37 shows a fine example of c.1685-90 which retains most of the features of twenty years earlier. One later feature is the cushion moulded or pulvinated frieze below the triangular pediment of the rising hood. The decorative brass rosettes adjacent to the hinges are very rare on clock cases but common on contemporary cabinets. They may have been fitted to prevent bruising of the beading on the door against the edge of the case.

The 11ins. dial is signed at the base 'John Ebsworth Londini Fecit' and there is floral engraving between the spandrels which are the cherub and foliage type (C. & W. No. 5). A Tudor rose is engraved at the centre and the minute divisions are set in from the edge of the chapter ring with very small minute numerals on the outside. There are no half quarter markings. The wavy minute hand is unusual but probably original. The month movement is equipped with bolt and shutter maintaining power.

In contrast to the normal size longcase clocks there are a few smaller ones, under 6ft. high, which are usually called miniature or 'grandmother'.[11] They are usually of high quality and Colour Plate 3 shows a very fine example, probably c.1690-95, by Charles Goode of London. The 7½ins. dial is signed at the base, has ringed winding and seconds apertures, and engraving round the calendar opening. The skeleton chapter ring has small minute numerals outside the minute divisions. The spandrels are the simple cherub type (C. & W. No. 3), used because of the small size of the dial. The movement has ringed pillars and an outside count wheel.

The case is veneered with walnut and with panels of bird and floral marquetry. The hood has a sound fret, identical twist columns and a hinged door. The height is 5ft. 9½ins.

These miniature clocks are further discussed in Chapter 6 and their faking is considered in Chapter 12.

Seventeenth century cases which are japanned in imitation of Chinese lacquer work are not common but Colour Plate 4 shows an example of c.1690-95 which, although it is possibly of London manufacture, houses a provincial clock. The case is 6ft. 7ins. high, with a 10⅛ins. waist. The slide-up hood has been modified to slide forward but a door has not been provided. It lacks its quarter columns at the rear of the hood. There is no sound fret, but the top of the hood, which probably had a sound vent, has been replaced. A cross-section of the mouldings is shown half size in figure 4/38. The bun feet are replacements but the sockets for them existed, see figure 4/49. The carcase is of pine which often indicates a provincial origin, and the japanned decoration has had only minor restoration except on the plinth where it had deteriorated seriously. The japanning of clock cases is discussed in Chapter 6.

11. Lee, *Knibb,* p. 60, where they are discussed and examples shown.

Figure 4/37. Month clock by John Ebsworth, c.1685-90. 11ins. dial with Tudor rose at centre, floral engraving between spandrels and signature at base. Very small minute numerals outside minute divisions, no half quarter marks. Note unusual but probably correct minute hand. Bolt and shutter maintaining power. Earlier style panelled ebony veneered case except for cushion-moulded frieze below pediment of rising hood. Very rare decorative brass rosettes adjacent to trunk door hinges. Height 6ft. 9ins.

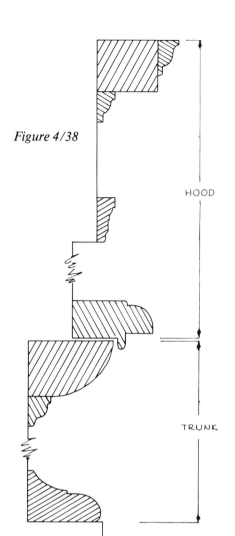

Figure 4/38

HOOD

TRUNK

Figure 4/38. Approximate cross-section of mouldings of Washington case in Colour Plate 4, shown half size.

Figure 4/39. 10ins. dial of clock by Richard Washington, Kendal, c.1690-95. Typical London dial except for extended five minute and five second divisions which are an early feature. No half quarter marks. Note finely pierced and shaped hands. Case is shown in Colour Plate 4.

Figure 4/40. Eight-day movement of Washington clock. Note wide spacing of barrel arbors caused by coarse pitch of great wheels, trace of fifth pillar below centre wheel, and substantial steel work.

Figure 4/40

The 10ins. dial (figure 4/39) signed 'Rich. Washington Kendall fecit' is very much in the London style but the extended five minute and five second divisions are a survival of an early feature. The ends of the winding squares are pleasingly file-cut and their wide spacing results from the proportions of the eight-day movement. The probable date is 1690-95; a Richard Washington was mayor of Kendal in the latter year and an apparently contemporary lantern clock by this maker has also been reported.[12]

The movement (figure 4/40) originally had the five pillars usual at this period, but the one below the centre wheel has been cut off, the hole in the front plate plugged, and all traces removed as far as possible. This may have been done because the pillar came through the front plate very close to the stud for the calendar wheel. The great wheels are of extra coarse pitch which explains the wide spacing of the winding holes in the dial. Other features, such as the substantial steel work, also support the provincial origin of the clock.

Another late seventeenth century provincial clock, but of very different appearance, is shown in figure 4/41. The case is of ebonised pine and its proportions and construction emphasise its 'country' origin. The clock has an extra long pendulum which coincides with the lenticle, thus proving that case and movement belong together. It is worth noting that quite a lot of thirty-hour clocks have trains which require pendulums longer or shorter than seconds ones. This presumably arose from convenience in wheel cutting.

The dial (figure 4/42) is well engraved and is signed 'Eduardus Clement in Exon fecit'. Edward Clement was apprenticed in London in 1662, became a member of the Clock-makers' Company in 1671 and was working in Exeter by 1684.[13] The movement (figure 4/43) is a fairly conventional thirty-hour birdcage one with brass top and bottom plates and steel corner posts. The dial is fixed by four dial feet which fit into the front corner posts.

The next clock to be described is by a well known London maker, Christopher Gould, and is in a typical case of 1690-95 with floral marquetry in panels (Colour Plate 5). This case has had some restoration which is discussed in Chapter 5, p. 117. The cresting is modern but is included to show the effect produced. The height is 6ft. 9½ins. without the cresting and the width at the waist 11¼ins. A cross-section of the mouldings is shown half size in figure 4/44. The hood slides forward and figure 4/45 shows the wrought iron bolt which engages with a staple in the bottom of the door frame and thus secures both door and hood. This was the normal method used for the first forty years or so of the forward sliding hood.

The 11ins. dial (figure 4/46) is signed 'Chr. Gould Londini Fecit' and has foliage engraved between the spandrels, a Tudor rose at the centre and curly foliage surrounding the calendar aperture. The dial and hands are typical of Gould's work. Dials and hands reached a peak of ornamentation just before 1700 and after a few years a gradual simplification began.

The movement originally had an outside count wheel as can be seen from the rear, figure 4/47. The lower pair of holes above the hammer were for the lifting piece arbor and the upper ones for the detent arbor. The square end to the striking barrel arbor resulted from cutting off the extension which carried the count wheel. The spare hole at the top left corner was for a steadying bracket. The change to rack striking was probably made in the first half of the eighteenth century, to provide for repeating the hours. Figure 4/48 shows the conversion which is not very well designed but operates satisfactorily. The original lifting piece is mounted on a stud just to the right of its original position and has a pin projecting from its rear to lift the rack hook. At the end of striking the extra fall of the latter causes an arm on its arbor to intersect a pin on the former hoop wheel, thus locking the train. Hour repeating was provided by an arm to lift the rack hook which was pivoted on a stud screwed in the hole to the right of the lifting piece and a restoring spring was fixed by the two small holes at the bottom right. The layout and action of this striking mechanism should be compared with that shown in figure 7/4 and described on p. 131.

12. The writer is indebted to Brian Loomes for this information.
13. C.N. Ponsford, *Time in Exeter,* 1978, p. 66.

Figure 4/42. Dial of Clement clock. Note competent engraving and early type of hand.

Figure 4/41. Ebonised pine case of a thirty-hour clock by Edward Clement, Exeter, c.1690-1700. Note large side windows, absence of hood columns, general primitive design. Extra long pendulum coincides with lenticle, thus proving case is original.

Figure 4/43. Typical birdcage movement of Clement clock. Now chain driven but originally was probably rope.

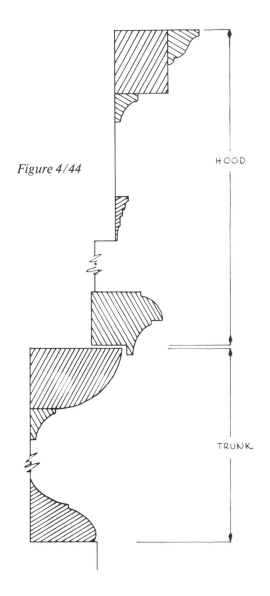

Figure 4/44

HOOD

TRUNK

Figure 4/45

Figure 4/44. Approximate cross-section of mouldings of Gould case in Colour Plate 5 shown half size.

Figure 4/45. Wrought iron bolt which secures door and hood of Gould case.

Figure 4/46. 11ins. dial of clock by Chris. Gould, c.1690-95. Note Tudor rose at centre, curly engraving round calendar aperture, ringed holes and elaborate hands, a typical Gould production. Case is shown in Colour Plate 5.

Figure 4/46

Figure 4/47. Rear view of Gould movement. Now rack striking but originally with outside count wheel. Note thick square cut pivot to striking barrel arbor where count wheel was mounted, spare holes immediately above hammer arbor for lifting piece arbor, holes above these for detent arbor. Spare hole at top left corner for steadying bracket screw.

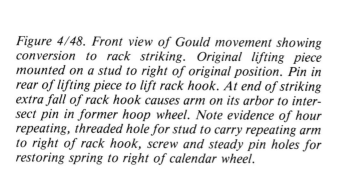

Figure 4/48. Front view of Gould movement showing conversion to rack striking. Original lifting piece mounted on a stud to right of original position. Pin in rear of lifting piece to lift rack hook. At end of striking extra fall of rack hook causes arm on its arbor to intersect pin in former hoop wheel. Note evidence of hour repeating, threaded hole for stud to carry repeating arm to right of rack hook, screw and steady pin holes for restoring spring to right of calendar wheel.

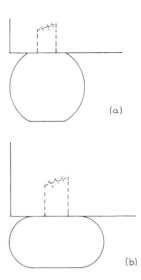

Figure 4/49. Typical construction of plinth of a case for bun feet. Replaced feet and modern strengthening at bottom of back. Case of Washington clock shown in Colour Plate 4.

Figure 4/51. Typical bun feet: (a) early, up to c.1675, (b) later. Half size.

Figure 4/50. Construction of plinth of a provincial case, c.1700-5, with old skirting. Note sockets for front feet, those for rear feet probably broken away when skirting fitted. Case of this clock shown in figure 7/23.

BUN FEET

As has already been noted, bun feet were originally provided on most if not all cases until nearly the end of the seventeenth century, but hardly any of them have survived. In this connection it is instructive to examine the illustrations in Cescinsky and Webster which show only one English example with bun feet,[14] an early Tompion which is also provided with a skirting!

There is no doubt that many bun feet must have perished through woodworm and rotting caused by damp floors, but a much higher proportion of original feet have survived on other seventeenth century furniture which was exposed to exactly the same processes of decay. The explanation must be that many clock feet were replaced by skirtings to give the greater stability resulting from the broader and deeper base in contact with the floor. This would not have been necessary if owners had heeded the clockmakers' advice and securely fixed cases to walls. Presumably in the past, as now, there was a reluctance to fasten furniture to walls if this could be avoided.

14. Cescinsky and Webster, p. 108.

Figure 4/52. 10ins. dial of lantern type thirty-hour clock by Wm. Grimes, c.1690. Note fairly broad chapter ring, cherub and foliage spandrels, bold arrow head hand.

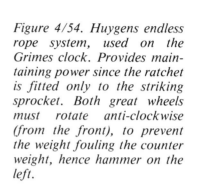

Figure 4/54. Huygens endless rope system, used on the Grimes clock. Provides maintaining power since the ratchet is fitted only to the striking sprocket. Both great wheels must rotate anti-clockwise (from the front), to prevent the weight fouling the counter weight, hence hammer on the left.

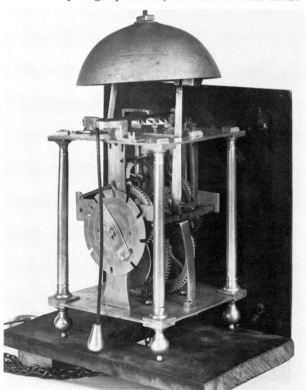

Figure 4/53. Movement of Grimes clock showing turned columns and feet. Original verge escapement. Note absence of doors, back, frets and finials. Bell supported on iron stand and hammer on left as viewed from front. Endless rope for single weight replaced by chain.

Figure 4/55. Top view of Grimes movement with bell removed. Note bell stand and absence of spare holes for fixing frets, doors or back, proving it was never a lantern clock. Similarly, absence of spare holes for fixing anchor type back cock proves it has never been converted to anchor escapement.

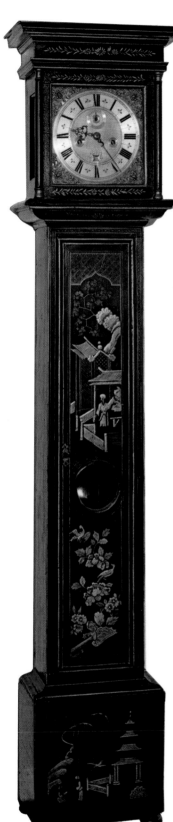

Colour Plate 4. Black japanned pine case of a clock by Richard Washington, Kendal, c.1690-95. Lift up hood modified to slide forward but not cut for a door. Rear columns missing. Decoration on plinth renewed and bun feet replaced. 6ft. 7ins. high, 10⅛ins. waist. See also figures 4/38-40.

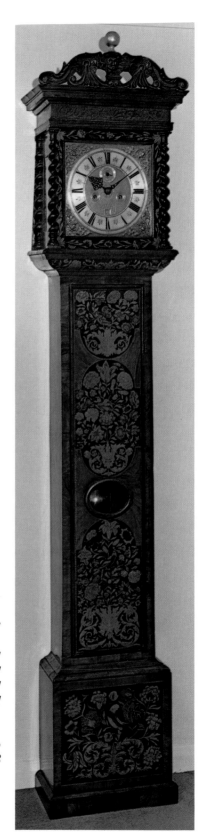

Colour Plate 5. Clock by Christopher Gould in a case veneered with walnut and floral marquetry in panels, c.1690-95. Panelled sides, see figure 4/5. Restorations to plinth and hood, and replaced cresting. Probably should have bun feet. Forward sliding hood. 6ft. 9½ins. high without the cresting, 11¼ins. waist. See also figures 4/44-48 and 5/43 and 44.

Where the original plinth has survived it will be found to have holes approximately ⅜in.-½in. diameter in the corner blocks to take the turned extensions of the feet. Figure 4/49 shows a typical construction with the side and front members of the trunk coming down into the plinth and supporting the corner blocks. The strengthening batten across the bottom of the back is modern and the feet are replacements. This is the case of the Richard Washington clock shown in Colour Plate 4. Figure 4/50 shows the plinth of a provincial case by Hawkins of Exeter of c.1700-5, which has quite an old skirting but clearly shows the sockets for the front feet. The rear sockets have disappeared, probably with the rear blocks being broken away when the feet were removed and the skirting fitted. When, as in this example, the skirting has the effect of covering the crossbanding or other decoration on the lower edge of the plinth panel (see figure 7/23), it is safe to conclude that the skirting has replaced bun feet. Conversely, if the skirting leaves the plinth panel decoration complete, it should have a skirting, or the plinth is an incorrect restoration.

Among the few clocks retaining their original bun feet Lee lists a pair supplied to St. Andrews University in 1673 and another to Ham House at about the same time.[15] These feet are slightly flattened balls and are shown half size in figure 4/51(a). The Tompion clock referred to above has feet of a more flattened bun shape, a type often used particularly for replacements, see figure 4/51(b). Dawson[16] has suggested that the feet should have a short stem as found on some bracket clocks and also on furniture of the period. Bun feet look best when their diameter is such that they are approximately in line with the sides of the plinth as shown in figure 4/51.

THIRTY-HOUR VERGE ESCAPEMENT CLOCKS

During the period under consideration a number of thirty-hour clocks were made with verge escapements, even though the simpler and cheaper anchor escapement was already well established. An early example, with plate frame, by Thomas Tompion has already been described (figures 4/13-17).

Figure 4/52 shows the 10ins. dial of a clock which is signed on the chapter ring 'Wm. Grimes Londini fecit' and which may be dated c.1690, by the position of the signature, the breadth of the chapter ring, the elaborated cherub spandrels (C. & W. No. 5) and the design of the single hand. The movement (figure 4/53) very closely resembles a typical lantern clock of the period except that it lacks frets and finials, and the bell is therefore supported on a wrought iron stand instead of by brass straps from the finials.

The trains are arranged so that both great wheels rotate anti-clockwise when seen from the front, so that both going and striking can be driven by a single weight suspended from a pulley as shown in figure 4/54. This system was invented by Huygens and was fully described in his *Horologium* published in 1658.[17] The object was to provide maintaining power for the going train since winding is effected by pulling down the right hand section of the rope on the striking side. It has, however, the minor disadvantage of making it impossible to vary the driving force on the trains individually. The Huygens system became standard on both lantern and thirty-hour longcase clocks, probably because it was cheaper and winding was simpler than with separate weights.

The Grimes clock has had the sprockets changed and a chain substituted for the rope, a common alteration as it prevented the movement being choked with rope fluff and avoided the problem of making a satisfactory splice in the rope. The reversal of the direction of rotation of the striking train, necessary to provide for the endless rope system without the weight fouling the counterweight, brings the hammer to the left hand side as viewed from

15. Lee, *Knibb,* p. 59.

16. P.G. Dawson, *The Design of English Domestic Clocks 1660-1700,* 1956, p. 8.

17. See the translation in E.L. Edwardes, *The Story of the Pendulum Clock,* 1977, p. 87.

the front. Conversely, a lantern clock or thirty-hour birdcage movement with the hammer on the right viewed from the front, had separate weights and is therefore an early example.

The top plate of the movement, with the bell removed is shown in figure 4/55 which clearly shows the layout of the verge escapement. It should be noted that there are no traces of holes which would be present if frets or doors had ever been fitted, hence the clock was made for a wooden case and was never a lantern clock.

The original case has disappeared and it is now housed in a reproduction one of ebonised pine. This type of movement requires a minimum distance of approximately 6¾ins. between the dial plate and the back board, so an exceptionally deep case is required, which makes it unlikely that it was intended for a hooded wall case.

A number of well known London makers, including Quare, Windmills and Tompion, made clocks of this type and the Clockmakers' Company collection at Guildhall contains an example by Thomas Tompion[18] which is numbered 151 and which may be dated by the breadth of the chapter ring and the spandrels to c.1690, which agrees with the number. The 10ins. dial has an engraved centre and there is an alarm as well as hour striking, but the movement is otherwise almost identical to the Grimes described above. The case is of black painted pine and has an attractive carved cresting.

A few lantern-type clocks were provided with a third train to give quarter striking and figure 4/56 shows the 9½ins. dial of a thirty-hour clock which follows this tradition. It is signed 'Joseph Knibb Londini fecit' and dates from 1670-72. The combination of a matted dial centre with florally engraved spandrels should be noted. It is somewhat unusual to find

18. See Symonds, pp. 104, 108, 276; and C. Clutton and G. Daniels, *Clocks and Watches, the Collection of the Worshipful Company of Clockmakers,* 1975, p. 78.

Figure 4/56. 9½ins. dial of a lantern type thirty-hour clock by Joseph Knibb, c.1670-72. Engraved spandrels with a matted centre. Note two hands and calendar, unusual on this type of clock.

Figure 4/57. Movement of Knibb clock, showing from right to left, going, quarter striking and hour striking trains. Note all hammer arbors pivoted on top plate and quarter count wheel mounted between great wheel and its sprocket.

Figure 4/58. Rear view of Knibb movement showing linkage between hammers and hammer tails with arbors pivoted in horizontal extensions of train bars. Unnecessary nut below pendulum bob and right hand pillar assembled upside down.

Figure 4/59. Early eighteenth century oak case containing Knibb clock. Presumably joiner-made to match panelling. Only upper panel of trunk opens as a door for winding. Height about 8ft.

two hands, and a calendar, on this type of clock. It was bought by the Duke of Lauderdale and is recorded as having been at Ham House, Richmond, from 1680 until the middle of this century.

The movement (figure 4/57) has the going train in its standard position next to the dial, with the verge escapement mounted on the top plate. The quarter striking train is in the middle and strikes on the two smaller bells. The count wheel is mounted between the great wheel and the rope sprocket, an early use of an idea which became common on eight-day clocks in the first half of the eighteenth century. All the hammer arbors are mounted on the top plate and are linked to the hammer tails, the arbors of which are pivoted in the horizontal extensions of the train bars (figure 4/58), an arrangement necessitated by the complexity of the movement. The hour striking train occupies the rear position as usual.

The right hand pillar (figure 4/58) has been assembled upside down and the octagonal nut below the pendulum bob is a later, unnecessary addition.

The case (figure 4/59), which is about 8ft. high, is of oak to match the panelling and, judging by the concave mouldings, is of early eighteenth century construction. Only the upper panel in the trunk section opens as a door for winding purposes, the lower one being fixed. The construction certainly suggests that the case was the work of a joiner, not that of a clock casemaker.

Figure 4/60. Alarm lantern timepiece by Geo. Graham in its original oak travelling case. Were the verge escapement lantern type longcase clocks similarly equipped?

It is difficult to find a satisfactory reason for the making of this group of thirty-hour verge escapement clocks. Clearly conservatism does not provide the answer, since most of them are by makers well experienced in the construction of the anchor escapement which is much simpler and cheaper to produce. Apart from the group of clocks under discussion, the verge escapement was restricted to bracket clocks — where it persisted until almost the end of the eighteenth century, to lantern clocks, particularly alarm timepieces, and to a relatively small number of hooded wall clocks. Both bracket and lantern clocks were designed to be portable and a small number of strongly built oak travelling cases have survived. Figure 4/60 shows an alarm lantern timepiece by George Graham in its original travelling case.

The verge escapement with bob pendulum has the great merit of performing quite well even when out of beat to an extent which would prevent an anchor escapement with its heavier pendulum from doing so. This undoubtedly provides the reason for the retention of the verge escapement in bracket and lantern clocks even though it resulted in some loss of accuracy. Could the same explanation apply to these verge escapement longcase clocks? It is just possible that they were intended to be portable, in which case the absence of a long pendulum with its fragile suspension would be a great help. It is perhaps significant that most of the cases which have survived are cheap ones of pine which could have been provided locally where and as required.

A passage in Smith[19] raises the possibility of another explanation:

The manner of Rightly fixing, or Setting up Pendulums *to go well.* The Difficulty of setting up *Pendulum Clocks* rightly in such places where the help of the *Clock maker* cannot be had, is the Reason that many Gentlemen who live far off from *London,* are as yet unfurnished with them; and it also too often happens, that *Clocks* who at first have been set up well as to matter of going, have by accident been misplac'd or jumbl'd awry, and so are made to stand still and become useless meerly for want of Skill in the Owner to put them again to rights; . . .

Could it be that some customers remote from London and other clockmaking centres preferred a simple clock which did not require accurate setting up?

19. Smith, *Horological Disquisitions,* p. 49.

Chapter 5

MARQUETRY CASES

INLAY AND MARQUETRY

Inlay and marquetry are two different processes used to produce a design by the use of different coloured woods. It must, however, be admitted that these distinctions are relatively modern, and it has been proved[1] that 'inlay' was the term used in the seventeenth and eighteenth centuries for both inlay and marquetry work.

True **inlay** consists of gluing suitably shaped pieces of coloured woods into prepared rebates in the ground wood. The nature of the process normally restricts the designs to geometrical patterns or simple floral effects. Examples of this type of decoration are to be found on the framing and panels of chests and other oak furniture of the seventeenth century. Inlaying is also the term used where narrow bandings or stringings of decorative woods, or coloured motifs, are set into an already veneered surface.

Inlaying into the solid carcase was used on provincial oak cases, particularly in Wales and the Border Counties, the Midlands and the North of England. In Wales and the Borders it often took the form of star inlay with chequered borders. Late in the eighteenth century mahogany crossbanding, sometimes with shell or fan inlays, was extensively used and veneered mahogany cases were often similarly inlaid.

Marquetry is a method of making a design by cutting through a number of sheets of veneer which have been temporarily fixed together, the cutting being done with a fine saw rather like a fret saw but with the work held in a vertical plane. After cutting, the pieces are separated and some of them are shaded by partially inserting them into hot sand. The design is then built up of the required coloured parts with its appropriate coloured ground. The pieces are next glued on to a paper backing and when the glue is set the panel can be handled like a sheet of veneer. It is then glued on to the carcase with the paper uppermost and the paper and surplus glue are cleaned off when the glue has set. As will be appreciated, much finer detail can be obtained this way than with inlaying. The cutting of a marquetry panel produces enough pieces for several complete designs, the number produced being equal to the number of sheets of veneer used. The colour of the ground, or of any particular detail, will be different in each design so some of them will not be suitable for use. Even so, a few examples of such pairs exist and figure 5/30 shows a pair of late marquetry cases housing clocks by the same maker. Such examples are often known as 'part' and 'counterpart'.

Marquetry was in fashionable use on the Continent before it was introduced into this country around 1665 and the type found on early clock cases shows considerable Dutch or Flemish influence. This has led a number of writers[2] into the belief that marquetry clock cases were imported from Holland, a theory rendered improbable by the English invention of the longcase clock and its adoption by the Dutch only in c.1677.[3] As already discussed in connection with clock mechanism (Chapter 1, p. 25) there was a considerable influx of foreign workmen, mainly Huguenots, in the second half of the seventeenth century and

1. Pat Kirkham, 'Inlay, marquetry and buhl workers in England c.1660-1850', *The Burlington Magazine,* CXXII (June 1980), p. 415.

2. Notably Cescinsky and Webster, p. 102.

3. According to J. Zeeman, *De Nederlandse Staande Klok,* 1977, Joseph Norris, an Englishman who settled in Amsterdam in 1677, introduced the longcase clock to Holland.

Figure 5/1. Part of a trunk door veneered with a parquetry of olive oyster pieces and inlaid with an elaborate star of ebony and box or holly. Note that the oyster pieces are cut into hexagons and that the star is inlaid as a complete unit. From the case of a clock by John Fromanteel c.1675.

Figure 5/2. Case, c.1675-80, with parquetry of olive oyster pieces and wavy edged star inlays of ebony and box or holly. All veneers and mouldings also of olive wood. Adapted many years ago to take 7ins. dial alarm timepiece. Hood altered to slide forward but not cut for a door, and has lost front columns and original top with sound vent. Tall cut-away skirting has replaced bun feet but sockets remain. Height 6ft. 6ins., 10½ins. waist for a 10ins. dial.

Figure 5/3. Case veneered with oyster pieces, probably of walnut, and with fan inlays, c.1685. Note the low caddy top with ball finials. A skirting has replaced bun feet. Height 6ft. 10ins. to top of caddy. The clock, by Joseph Windmills, has some dial features which could be post 1685: the signature on the chapter ring, elaborate spandrels (C. & W. No. 5), and ringed winding holes.

some of them undoubtedly brought the more advanced cabinetmakers' techniques with them.

PARQUETRY

Quite a long time elapsed before the fashion for decorating furniture with marquetry spread to clock cases, and the earliest examples date from c.1670 (figure 4/1), but they are very rare before 1675. At first the decoration took the form of a parquetry ground of oyster pieces inlaid with star or fan designs in contrasting woods, usually ebony with box or holly. Figure 5/1 shows part of a trunk door with this form of decoration on a ground of olive oyster pieces. It should be noted that the circular star has been inlaid complete into the ground, which consists of oyster pieces cut into hexagons. It is from the case of a clock by John Fromanteel of c.1675.

Figure 5/2 shows a case of about 1675-80 with a parquetry of olive oyster pieces inlaid with wavy edged stars of ebony and box or holly. Both the oyster pieces and the parts of the star inlays are larger than on the previous case. The inlays on the trunk door are arranged to form a pattern above the lenticle only, instead of the door being considered as a whole, which is an early sign. The hood, the sides of the case and the mouldings are all of olive wood on an oak carcase.

Probably early in the last century the case was adapted to take an eighteenth century thirty-hour alarm timepiece with a 7ins. dial instead of the original 10ins. dial and movement. The hood was altered to slide forward, but not cut for a door. The remarkably ugly cut-away skirting replaced the bun feet but the sockets remain. The hood has lost its front columns and the original top with its sound vent has been replaced with a rough piece of deal. Height as shown 6ft. 6ins. with a 10½ins. waist for a 10ins. dial.

Figure 5/3 shows another case of this type which appears to have walnut oysters and which is probably c.1685. The earliest of these cases usually had few decorative panels, those in the corners of the plinth and the lower corner ones of the door being omitted. The low caddy top with finials, as here, was introduced about 1680. Height 6ft. 10½ins. to top of caddy. The clock is by Joseph Windmills and the dial has some features suggesting a date of c.1685 or later; these are the signature being on the chapter ring and the ringed winding holes. The case of the thirty-hour Tompion clock shown in figure 4/17 has an interesting arrangement of fan motifs.

FLORAL MARQUETRY

Figure 5/4 shows an early case of c.1680 with small marquetry panels; the cushion or pulvinated moulding to the hood is also decorated with marquetry which is unusual on early cases. Cushion mouldings, which were sometime used c.1680-90, are a feature borrowed from contemporary cabinets. Notice that the panels have a walnut ground instead of the more usual ebony. The ground veneer between the panels is also walnut which gradually superseded olive wood. The later skirting has been removed but the plinth has yet to be restored and the bun feet renewed. The clock is presumably a replacement as the dial is later in style (c.1685-90) and sits too low in the case. The maker is David Roy; the hands are incorrect replacements.

Early marquetry panels are very simple but bold in design with flowers and foliage, sometimes in a vase. The cutting is cruder than in later marquetry and uses only about three different woods but the result is very effective. Bone or ivory, originally stained green to represent leaves and now usually bleached by long exposure, is a feature of early work. The vases which often appear in early floral marquetry panels may well show that the designs were derived from Dutch flower paintings.

Figure 5/4   *Figure 5/5*   *Figure 5/6*

Figure 5/4. Walnut veneered case of c.1680 with small panels of simple floral marquetry. Panels have walnut ground instead of more usual ebony. Cushion moulding in frieze of hood also decorated with marquetry which is unusual on an early case. A later skirting has been removed but the plinth has not yet been restored nor the bun feet replaced. The dial is later (c.1685-90) and sits too low in the case. It is by David Roy; the hands are incorrect replacements.

Figure 5/5. Olive wood case of c.1680-85 with olive oyster parquetry on trunk door and front of plinth, and small but numerous panels of floral marquetry. The bone or ivory leaves are particularly prominent on this example. The ebony based panels are emphasised by the banding of light coloured wood, probably sycamore or plane, which separates them from the olive oysters. The plinth is rather squat. The hood has a cushion moulding but without marquetry. The clock is later, c.1690.

Figure 5/7. Upper part of door of Johnson clock in Colour Plate 6, showing simple early type marquetry (compare with figure 5/39). Note the olive oyster pieces, the larger ones used in the side panels are shown in in figure 4/4.

Figure 5/8. Detail of hood of Johnson clock in Colour Plate 6, showing that it has lost twist columns. They would have been of ebonised beech and probably suffered from woodworm.

Figure 5/6. Case of c.1680-85 with olive oyster parquetry and marquetry panels with a walnut ground, except for one below lenticle which has an ebony ground and is probably a replacement. Note large panel full width of door, and exotic birds in larger panels. Hood has plain cushion moulding, plain columns and marquetry decorated caddy which is probably later. A skirting has replaced bun feet.

Figure 5/9. 10ins. dial signed 'Tho: Iohnson Londini Fecit.' Note wide spacing of winding squares of month movement, 3s and 5s without upturned tails, dots for half quarters. Early use of elaborate spandrels, minute hand early eighteenth century, seconds hand modern. Case is shown in Colour Plate 6.

Figure 5/10. Month movement of Johnson clock showing striking on right. Six latched pillars but dial feet pinned. Seat board with original nailing and two fixed steel pegs which fit into plain holes in bottom pillars, a very early method. Modern steadying brackets to back of case. Four wheel striking train on right, so both trains wind anticlockwise.

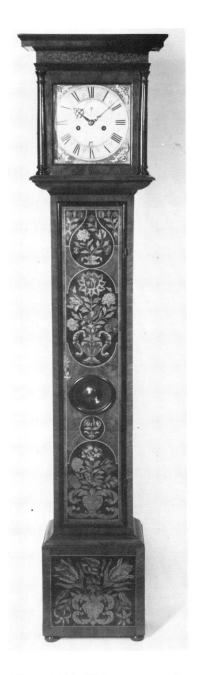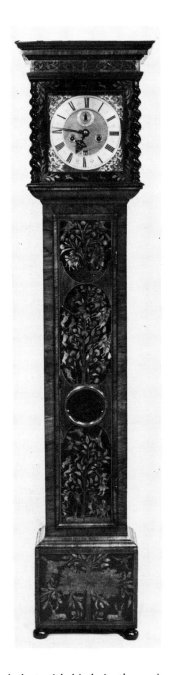

Figure 5/11. Walnut veneered case of c.1685 showing larger panels, still fairly simple but with birds in the main ones and face in urn above lenticle. Nicely proportioned case but for excessive overhang of hood cornice. Typical sound fret.

Figure 5/12. Walnut veneered case of c.1690 with what became the normal arrangement of marquetry panels on the trunk door. The marquetry is more developed with stylised acanthus leaves which became very popular, while two of the panels include birds. Plinth probably restored as marquetry does not match door panels, and the skirting has replaced bun feet without obscuring bottom of plinth. Note marquetry on hood door which became normal, unusually flat moulding under hood, repoussé brass sound fret. Height 6ft. 8ins., 10ins. dial signed on the chapter ring by Thomas Farmer. Small five minute numbers outside minute divisions. Ringed winding and seconds apertures, and foliate engraving between spandrels. Typical dial of c.1690. Much later hour hand.

Figure 5/13. Walnut veneered case of c.1690 with large panels of marquetry showing rare hunting scenes on an ebony ground. Rising hood with stags and hounds in full cry round window frame. Top panel of trunk door has birds in a tree and huntsmen and hound beneath. Remaining door panels have stag hunting in progress with men and animals in strange positions. Clock by Wm. Grimes, London.

Although it is possible to date the various developments in marquetry decoration with reasonable accuracy, it must be appreciated that the introduction of a new style did not cause the sudden demise of the previous one. Also some cases have a mixture of early and late features and must therefore be dated in accordance with the latest original features.

As time went on and marquetry cutting techniques improved the area covered by the marquetry increased. This sometimes resulted from an increase in the number of panels, but more usually from an increase in their size. Figure 5/5 shows a case of c.1680-85 with two extra panels in the upper part of the door. The marquetry panels have the usual ebony ground and are given emphasis by the bandings of a light coloured wood, probably sycamore or plane. The same banding around the door and plinth panels contrasts with the ebonised beading and bun feet. Olive oysters are used for the background. The height is not known but the plinth is rather low for its width. The dial is later, c.1690.

Another case (figure 5/6) of about the same date (c.1680-85) has full-width panel above the lenticle, while the panel below is odd in having an ebony ground and being in a somewhat earlier style than the others. It is probably a replacement. Colourful birds, which became very popular in floral marquetry appear in three of the panels. The hood has plain columns and a marquetry decorated caddy which is later. A skirting has replaced bun feet.

It is not very often that one can be absolutely certain that an early clock and its case have always been together, but provenance and physical evidence both support this view for the example shown in Colour Plate 6 which dates from c.1685. The case has never been restored, and has had only first aid repairs by the local joiner or cabinetmaker.

The usual oak carcase is veneered with olive, with olive oysters on the door and in the panels on the trunk sides. The panels are outlined with a light coloured wood such as sycamore and a number of the mouldings and the door beading are ebonised to match the ebony ground used in the marquetry panels. Note single large panel on plinth and two large ones on door, but the marquetry is the simple early type (figure 5/7). A close up view of the large oyster veneers used in the side panels is shown in figure 4/4.

Colour Plate 6 also shows a very high softwood skirting which has been painted black and has replaced the bun feet but the plinth has not been cut and the sockets for the feet remain intact. There is an unusual simple gilt wooden fret incorporating two birds. Although it is not obvious on casual inspection, the hood has lost its original twist columns, evidence of which can be seen in figure 5/8. They would have been made of ebonised beech and probably became badly infested with woodworm. The hood has been modified to slide forward but has not been cut for a door.

Figure 5/9 shows the 10ins. dial signed at the base 'Tho: Iohnson [Johnson] Londini Fecit.' Note that the figures 3 and 5 are the very early type without upturned tails, and dots are used for half quarters. The use of the larger, foliated, cherub spandrels (C. & W. No. 5) is unusual on such an early dial. The seconds hand is a much later replacement and the minute hand is early eighteenth century.

The month movement (figure 5/10) has the striking train on the right and as this is the four wheel type, both trains wind anti-clockwise. There are six latched pillars but the dial feet are pinned. The striking parts are very delicately made. The seat board, of oak which matches the carcase, is fixed with wrought iron nails and has apparently always been so attached. Instead of screws there are two steel pegs fixed in the seat board which fit plain holes in the bottom pillars of the movement. This is a very unusual method of locating a movement at this date but it is found on very early clocks. The normal angle brackets for steadying the top of the movement are modern replacements.

The last example discussed showed the introduction of one large marquetry panel for the plinth, with a tendency to use larger panels on the door also. Figure 5/11 shows this development with fairly simple panels, although each of the main ones includes an exotic bird, and the urn above the lenticle incorporates a face. A very pleasing case of c.1685, except that the

Figure 5/14. Lower panel of trunk door showing hunt defying gravity. Note varying sizes of animals and men, also relaxed stag in foreground.

Figure 5/15. Part of lower panel showing archer shooting at birds. Note naïve drawing of designs.

Figure 5/16. Plinth panel. Note oak tree with acanthus-like leaves and birds fitted into top corners.

cornice at the top of the hood has an excessive overhang. As stated earlier, sound frets were introduced c.1680 and will be found, as here, on practically all cases after about 1685.

A large number of cases were made with four panels arranged as in figure 5/12 which shows an example signed 'Thomas Farmer Londini Fecit' of c.1690, the year he became a member of the Clockmakers' Company. The door panels incorporate birds perching rather precariously on pinks or carnations, and stylised acanthus leaves which became a prominent feature of later floral marquetry. The plinth panel is unusual in having two floral groups but lacks acanthus leaves, so is probably restored. Marquetry has spread to the hood window frame and there is a repoussé brass fret. It is very probable that brass frets were much more common originally but that many have perished, being made of thin metal, and have been replaced by wood. There is an unusually flat moulding under the hood. The skirting is a later addition and the height is 6ft. 8ins.

The 10ins. dial has cherub and foliage spandrels (C. & W. No. 5) with foliate engraving between them. The chapter ring has the minute divisions set in with very small five minute numbers outside and the signature is on the chapter ring between VII and V. The winding holes and seconds hand opening are ringed, a development of c.1690, and the whole dial is typical of that date. The hour hand is a much later replacement.

Figure 5/13 shows a clock signed on the chapter ring 'Wm. Grimes Londini fecit' and housed in a case with most unusual marquetry panels which portray hunting scenes. The hood window frame has stags and hounds in full cry. The top panel of the trunk door has birds perching in a rather strange tree with huntsmen and hound beneath. The remaining door panels have huntsmen, hounds and stags in various positions defying gravity and the lowest panel is shown in figure 5/14. A bowman is shooting at the birds flying above the tree. Note the varying scale used for the various figures and animals, also the stag at rest apparently oblivious of the hunt. Part of the same panel is shown in detail in figure 5/15. The plinth panel (figure 5/16) shows a peaceful scene with stags resting under a fruiting oak tree and birds acting as spandrels for the top corners of the panel.

The naïveté of the designs for the panels suggests that they were composed by taking elements from a design book such as was used for embroidery in the seventeenth century. Altogether a most interesting case which has had very little restoration. The whole clock is c.1690 and the dial and hands are typical of that date.

The four panel style of case gradually developed so that the panels became more closely filled with decoration and also tended to join up with one another and the lenticle frame. Marquetry also appeared on the convex moulding under the hood. At about this time the marquetry became more finely cut. Figure 5/17 shows a case of c.1690, or a little later, with these characteristics but with pairs of curly tailed dolphins instead of the usual acanthus foliage in the three main panels. The canted corners to the plinth are an incorrect restoration.

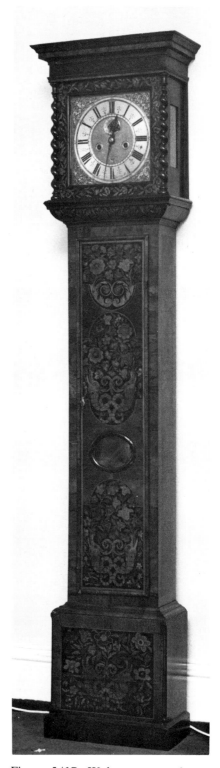

Figure 5/17. Walnut veneered case of c.1695 or slightly later with larger, more detailed panels and marquetry on moulding under hood. Pairs of curly tailed dolphins instead of usual acanthus foliage. Incorrect canted corners to plinth.

The next example (figure 5/18), a month clock by 'Nathaneal Barrow London' of c.1700, shows some early features. The panels have well spaced floral designs with rather unusual acanthus foliage and the lower door panel is quite small. The panels as well as the door and the plinth are edged with a leaf design. The case is veneered with walnut, except on the door between the panels, which has olive oysters. This case may always have had a skirting but the present double one with feet is later. Although the height is 7ft. 1in., the hood was originally made to slide up.

The 12ins. dial has a broad chapter ring which is exceptional in not having quarter hour divisions although it has half quarter marks on the outer edge. In contrast, the slim seconds ring is of an early type and the engraved Tudor rose at the centre is also often an early feature. The heavily ringed winding holes are typical of 1690-1700 and their low position is determined by the month movement. This position probably accounts for the exceptionally high calendar aperture. The whole dial is something of a puzzle, but should be compared with the Richard Lyons dial in figure 4/18.

A logical development of the increasing size of the marquetry panels was to design one large panel for the door as shown in figure 5/19. This is an early example, probably c.1685-90, and the design shows signs of being built up of three elements, rather than being one continuously flowing design as in the later ones. Notice the absence of marquetry on the moulding under the hood. The case lacks sound fret and bun feet. It is not known whether the dial is original to the case but it appears to be c.1685, as it has the early type minute numbering, plain winding holes and simple spandrels (C. & W. No. 4).

Figure 5/20 shows a later case, c.1695, where the door panel design is more integrated. It has marquetry on the moulding under the hood and the trunk sides are panelled with oyster pieces. The small mouldings, bun feet and columns are ebonised, with the capitals and bases gilt. The hood lifts up in spite of a height of 7ft. 3ins.

The 11ins. dial is signed at the base 'Chr. Gould Londini fecit', with foliate engraving between the spandrels (C. & W. No. 5) and a Tudor rose at the centre. Altogether a typical clock by this well-known maker.

From this time onwards a few of the most expensive cases were made with marquetry decoration on the sides of the case as well as on the front.

A later case with more closely packed marquetry and a fully integrated design on the door panel is shown in figure 5/21. Marquetry has now spread to the large caddy top, the finial plinths and each end of the fret opening. A probably broken fret has been filled in. The hood slides forward and has an opening door with lock. The side finials are missing. The plinth skirting is probably original. The dial has a broad chapter ring with quite large minute numbers, but all the hands are much later. The probable date is 1700-5.

The final stage of floral marquetry is shown in figure 5/22 where the decoration has spread to every available surface. This is one of the few marquetry cases designed for an arched dial and the wide, shallow arch shows it to be one of the first, probably c.1710. The point is stressed because cases will be found which have been 'modernised' in past centuries to take an arched dial. Similarly, at all periods square dials have had arches added to make them fit cases with arched hood doors. The straight columns and plinth skirting are typical of the period but gilt brass frets, as here, are exceptional so late. The marquetry has an ebony ground and the columns, sides of the case and so on are of walnut. The height is 7ft. 11ins. The 12ins. dial is signed on a convex boss in the arch 'John Wise London', and the rest of the arch has engraved scrolls. The dial plate is in one piece, proof that it has not been altered to fit the case. The calendar opening is circular not square, a change introduced about 1700. The spandrels are cherubs with foliage (C. & W. No. 5). It has a month movement.

Figure 5/18. A month clock by Nathaniel Barrow signed on chapter ring of 12ins. dial. Walnut and olive oyster veneered case with well-spaced marquetry which has unusual acanthus foliage and leaf borders. Small lower door panel for period. Case may always have had a skirting but double one with feet is later. Height 7ft. 1in., but hood originally made to slide up. Note broad chapter ring without quarter hour divisions but with half quarter marks on outer edge. Slim, early type seconds ring, Tudor rose at centre. Low winding squares for month movement and very high calendar aperture.

Figure 5/19. Case of c.1685-90 with early example of one large marquetry panel for door. This appears to have been built up from three elements rather than one flowing design. No marquetry on moulding under hood. Lacks sound fret and bun feet. Typical c.1685 dial.

Figure 5/20. Case of c.1695 with more integrated design on door. Marquetry on moulding under hood, panelled trunk sides with oyster veneers. Small mouldings, bun feet and columns ebonised, capitals and bases gilt. Plinth may be restored as marquetry does not match that in door panel. Rising hood in spite of height of 7ft. 3ins. 11ins. dial signed at base by Christopher Gould. Typical clock by this well-known maker.

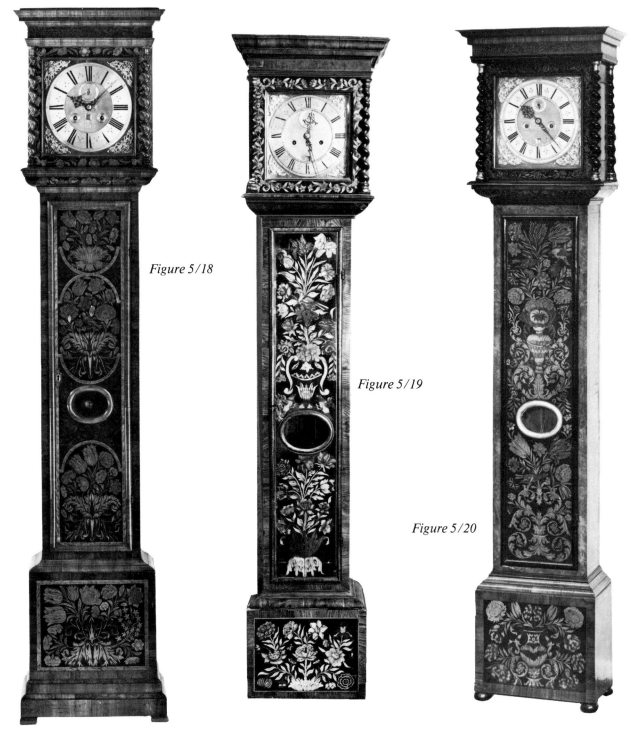

Figure 5/18

Figure 5/19

Figure 5/20

Figure 5/21. Case of c.1700-5 with closely packed marquetry and fully integrated design on door panel. Marquetry has spread to large caddy top, finial plinths and each end of fret opening. A probably broken fret has been filled in. Forward sliding hood with lockable door. Skirting probably original. Side finials missing. Much later hands.

Another change introduced about the end of the century was the use of formal borders which did not necessarily match the other marquetry on the case. Figure 5/23 shows a clock of c.1700 signed 'Richard Colston London', which is a late example of floral marquetry in panels, where the acanthus leaf decoration has become quite open and scroll-like. The border surrounding the trunk door is of dark wood on a light ground and is a type known as 'seaweed', described below. The dial is signed on the chapter ring with 'Richard Colston' between VII and V and 'London' between 35 and 25, the latter made possible by the larger minute numbers. The movement has an inside rack for the striking.

ARABESQUE MARQUETRY

As already discussed, the naturalistic marquetry owed much to influence from the Low Countries, but in France more formal designs became popular largely due to the work of Jean Berain (the elder), 1637-1711. He was appointed designer to Louis XIV in 1674 and published many drawings which incorporated grotesque and other figures, draperies, arabesques and trailing foliage. He greatly influenced André-Charles Boulle (1642-1732), whose furniture had marquetry designs carried out in brass, pewter, tortoiseshell and other exotic materials, and whose name is often applied to this type of work.

The designs of Berain resulted in the appearance in this country towards 1700 of more formal marquetry designs and a style usually known as 'arabesque' was developed. This is characterised by strap-work, usually human or other figures, and formalised foliage, with the whole design made symmetrical.

All-over marquetry was popular when the arabesque style was introduced so it normally takes this form, but figure 5/24 shows an example which is based on the earlier panel arrangement. The clock is by Matthew Bunce London and dates from c.1695-1700. Note the symmetrical designs and the figures in the main panels of the trunk door.

Usually the decoration consists of light colours on a dark ground, but when the reverse obtains the effect can be very striking as in figure 5/25, where presumably the counterpart has been used. The panels consists of formalised floral designs, with those on the door each including a human figure and the plinth having a human face. The rest of the case is veneered in walnut with gilt wood capitals and bases to the plain columns. There are no signs of restoration.

The dial is signed on the chapter ring 'John Wise London' and has a mixture of early and later features. The chapter ring has the minute divisions at the outer edge, the crown and cherub spandrels (C. & W. No. 8) have foliate engravings between them and there is a Tudor rose at the centre. Other clocks by John Wise have a similar mixture of dial features and he continued to use the outside count wheel after 1700. In this example, which is c.1700, his casemaker also appears to have been somewhat conservative.

Colour Plate 6. Case of c.1685 veneered with olive, with olive oysters on door and trunk side panels. Note single large panel of floral marquetry on plinth and two full width panels on door. Ebonised mouldings and bandings of light coloured wood such as sycamore round panels. Hood has unusual gilt wood sound fret incorporating two birds, but has lost its columns (see figure 5/8). It has been modified to slide forward but not cut for a door. The high skirting has replaced bun feet but the sockets for these remain intact. The month clock by Thos. Johnson has a 10ins. dial. See also figures 5/7-10.

Colour Plate 7. Very rare case with seaweed marquetry of pewter and burr elm, an English version of French marquetry, often called boulle work. Note formal borders to plinth and trunk door; also coarse, probably later work on frieze. Height 6ft. 8ins. with an 11½ins. waist and probable date c.1700. 11ins. dial signed by Jacob Wallis, London. See also figure 5/38.

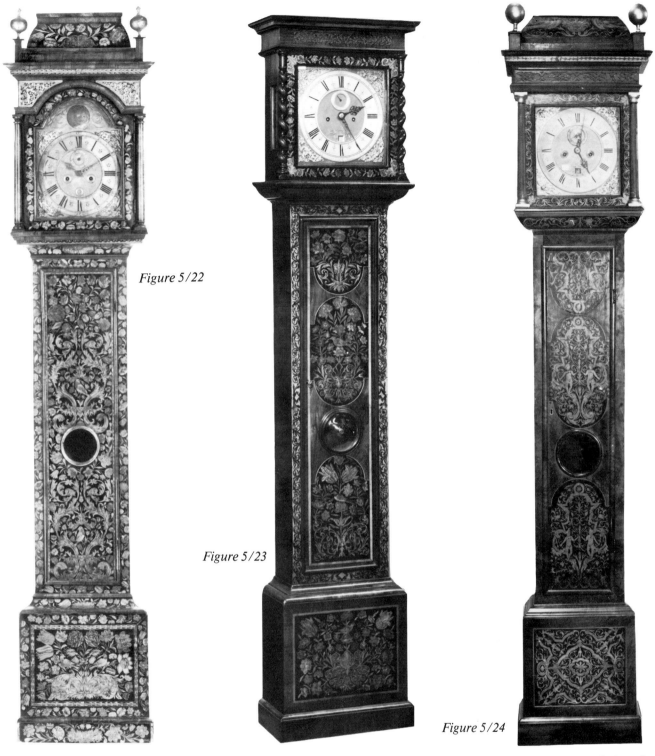

Figure 5/22

Figure 5/23

Figure 5/24

Figure 5/22. Final stage of floral marquetry, covering every available surface. One of few marquetry cases designed for an arched dial, c.1710. Note wide, shallow arch, typical of the earliest. Plain columns, caddy top and skirting typical of the period. Very late use of gilt brass frets. Marquetry has ebony ground. Columns, mouldings, sides of case are walnut. Height 7ft. 11ins. 12ins. dial plate in one piece, signed on boss in arch by John Wise. Rest of arch has engraved scrolls. Circular calendar opening.

Figure 5/23. Case of c.1700 with floral marquetry in panels but with formal border of seaweed type surrounding trunk door. Note how the acanthus leaf decoration has become open and scroll-like. Dial signed on chapter ring by Richard Colston, wheat-ear border to dial plate. Inside rack striking.

Figure 5/24. Arabesque marquetry case, c.1695-1700, decoration in panels, unusual with this type. Note symmetrical designs, strapwork, and figures in main panels on trunk door. Clock is by Matthew Bunce.

A more conventional arabesque case of similar date, c.1700, is shown in figure 5/26. It is of high quality and the door panel is without a vertical joint being made in two sections which come together each side of the lenticle. Although the whole design is symmetrical, the birds in each of the five pairs are not identical, nor are the tiny grotesque figures halfway between the lenticle and the top of the door. The twisted cord border to the door, which is a Dutch feature, strikes a slightly jarring note. It is a month clock and the dial is signed on the chapter ring 'Geo. Etherington London.'

Figure 5/27 shows a very exotic example by a provincial maker which incorporates two grotesque mermen as well as birds and foliage. It employs a greater variety of woods than many cases of this period. The case is 7ft. 4ins. high but the plinth skirting and the lower trunk moulding are incorrect replacements. The twist columns and the convex moulding under the hood are a late use of these features.

The dial is signed 'Wm. Ball of Bister fecit' (i.e. Bicester) on the chapter ring which is broad but has the early type of minute markings. The seconds ring is very small and is planted exceptionally low. The spandrels are of the crown and cherub pattern (C. & W. No. 8) which was introduced c.1700, but the probable date for the clock is c.1710-15.

The next illustration (figure 5/28) shows a high quality case of typical London design where the fine marquetry has spread over every possible surface, including the hood columns. As we come to later cases, the number of 'creatures' inhabiting the marquetry decreases and this example has just two pairs of rather inconspicuous birds. The hood has fine sound frets including the one in the large caddy top. The height is 7ft. 11ins.

The 12ins. dial (figure 5/29) is signed on the chapter ring 'W. Stokes Fecit' with no indication of place of business. The dial is quite standard apart from the enormous minute numbers which rival the hour numerals. Such minute figures are found on very late eighteenth century provincial clocks but that cannot be the explanation here as the clock has all the other characteristics of early eighteenth century work. Perhaps it was a special commission for an owner who had difficulty in reading a two hand clock or who wished to stress the importance of the minutes. A somewhat later clock with similar minute numbers, by a Somerset maker, is shown in Colour Plate 8, so possibly W. Stokes was also a west country maker. The ringing of the hands aperture at the centre of the dial to match the other holes is an unusual feature. The clock has a three month striking movement. The maker has not been traced, but he could well be provincial as the use of 'fecit' was rather old fashioned by this time. The probable date is c.1715.

When describing the technique of marquetry cutting it was noted that the production of a panel resulted in sufficient pieces to make several more panels of the same design but with differing colour schemes. Figure 5/30 shows a pair of such cases with fine arabesque decoration, elaborate sound frets and carved gilt wood flambeau finials. The cases are 8ft. 2ins. and 8ft. 3ins. high.

The clocks are both signed 'Nicholas Lambert LONDON' on the chapter rings and the 12ins. dials have engraved borders and turbaned head spandrels (C. & W. No. 19) which were introduced by Tompion about 1700. Strike/silent levers in slots marked S N are fitted just above the chapter rings at XII. The eight-day movements have rack striking for hours and half hours. Unfortunately this is another apparently unrecorded maker, but the clocks are c.1715 and their maker is discussed later in connection with figures 9/98 and 99.

Figure 5/25

Figure 5/27

Figure 5/26

Figure 5/25. Case of c.1700 veneered with walnut and with counterpart panels of arabesque marquetry, that is with dark decoration on a light ground. Note human figures in all trunk door panels and human face in centre of plinth. Gilt wood capitals and bases to plain columns. No signs of restoration. Dial signed on chapter ring by John Wise, with minute divisions at outer edge. Crown and cherub spandrels (C. & W. No. 8) with foliate engraving between, Tudor rose at centre.

Figure 5/26. Conventional all-over arabesque marquetry case of c.1700. No vertical joint to door panel but horizontal joint at lenticle. Whole design is symmetrical but birds in each of five pairs are not identical, nor are tiny grotesque figures in centre of upper part of door. Bold twisted cord border to door, a Dutch feature, striking a somewhat jarring note. Month clock signed on chapter ring by George Etherington.

Figure 5/27. Exotic provincial arabesque marquetry case, probably c.1710-15. Design includes grotesque mermen as well as birds and foliage, all in a greater variety of woods than is usual at the period. Twist columns and convex moulding under hood are a late use of these features, but lower trunk moulding and skirting are incorrect replacements. Height 7ft. 4ins. Chapter ring has minute divisions on outer edge and signature of Wm. Ball of Bicester. Very small and low positioned seconds ring. Crown and cherub spandrels with scrolled engraving between.

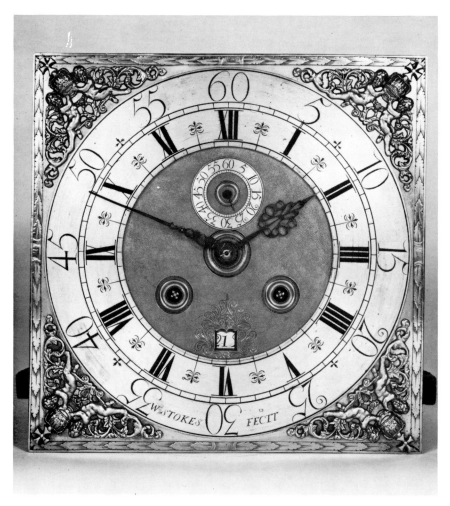

Figure 5/28. Fine, later London style arabesque marquetry case with only two pairs of small birds. Note marquetry has spread everywhere. Fine sound frets. Height 7ft. 11ins. Probably c.1715.

Figure 5/29. 12ins. dial of 5/28. Normal apart from enormous minute numerals (compare Colour Plate 8, Clark, Frome). W. Stokes is apparently not recorded but probably provincial. Ringing of hands aperture to match other holes is unusual.

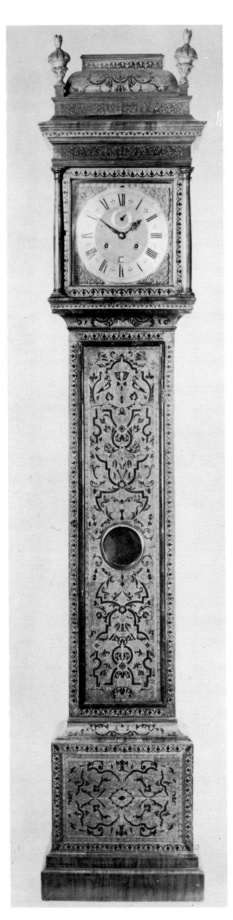

Figure 5/30. Rare pair of fine arabesque marquetry clocks of c.1715 which are 'part' and 'counterpart'. Note fine sound frets and gilt wood flambeau finials. Cases 8ft. 2ins. and 8ft. 3ins. high. 12ins. dials signed on chapter rings by Nicholas Lambert, London, and with engraved borders. Turbaned head spandrels (C. & W. No. 19). Strike/silent levers above XII. Eight-day movements have rack striking for hours and half hours.

Figure 5/33

Figure 5/32

Figure 5/31

Figure 5/31. Case of about 1700 with seaweed marquetry in panels. Note only two woods in design, very mellow colouring, no 'creatures' of any kind. Incorrect skirting probably replaces bun feet. Bold sound fret probably also a replacement. Rather heavy cornice to hood. Dial signed on chapter ring by Joseph Saer.

Figure 5/32. Case, probably c.1715, with fine seaweed marquetry panels, note concave moulding under hood and very fine sound fret. Skirting fits correctly and is probably original. Chapter ring, signed by John Everell, London, has fairly large minute numbers. Crown and cherub spandrels.

Figure 5/33. Case of c.1700-10 in all-over marquetry with some strapwork amongst the seaweed, but no 'creatures'. Ogee feet and double moulding replace a simple skirting. All case mounts are of brass. Dial with engraved border and signed on chapter ring by Peter Trumball, London, apparently an unrecorded maker. Cherub and crown spandrels.

Figure 5/34. Detail of a trunk door with seaweed marquetry showing traces of arabesque. Note the vertical joint.

SEAWEED MARQUETRY

Within a few years of the introduction of arabesque marquetry a further variation was developed. This is known as seaweed marquetry and retains the fine scrolling foliage of the arabesque type but without the 'creatures' and the strapwork. It may also have been influenced by the formalised acanthus foliage of later floral marquetry.

An early example of seaweed marquetry is shown in figure 5/31, where the decoration is in panels and has mellowed so that there are no strong contrasts. The skirting is an incorrect replacement which covers the border round the plinth panel and probably replaces bun feet. The sound fret has a very bold design for the period which suggests that it too is probably a replacement. The dial is signed on the chapter ring 'Joseph Saer in Perpoole Lane London' and has cherub spandrels (C. & W. No. 5). The chapter ring has very small minute numbers outside the minute divisions. Joseph Saer is recorded by both Britten (1686-1700) and Loomes (1687-97) and this clock is c.1700.

A slightly later example, but still with the marquetry in panels, is shown in figure 5/32. This has the eighteenth century feature of a concave moulding under the hood. The skirting fits correctly, leaving the border round the plinth panel exposed. There is a very fine sound fret. The dial is signed on the chapter ring 'John Everel London' and has an engraved border and crown and cherub spandrels (C. & W. No. 8). The chapter ring is quite broad and has fairly large minute numbers. The probable date is c.1715.

Some cases have marquetry incorporating characteristics from both the seaweed and the arabesque types and an example is shown in figure 5/33. The decoration is in the more usual all-over style and includes some strapwork amongst the seaweed, but it has no 'creatures', human or otherwise. The ogee feet and double moulding replace a simple skirting. All the case mounts, including the trunk door hinges, are of brass. The dial is signed on the chapter ring 'Pet. Trumball London', an apparently unrecorded maker. The dial plate has an engraved border, there is no engraving round the calendar aperture, and the spandrels are cherub and crown type (C. & W. No. 8). The date is c.1700-10.

Figure 5/34 shows in more detail part of the door of a case with the type of seaweed marquetry just described. Note the vertical joint, proving that the two halves of the pattern were cut at the same time.

A very fine arabesque marquetry case housing a grande sonnerie clock by Quare is illustrated in Colour Plate 10 and figure 7/26, and figures 5/35-37 show details of the intricate marquetry on this case which exhibits quite a lot of seaweed influence.

In spite of the fact that French marquetry work of the period normally incorporates metal inlays, hardly any examples of this type are found in English cases, but Colour Plate 7 shows a most attractive specimen veneered with burr elm and pewter marquetry. It is tempting to think that it might have been made by a Huguenot settled in this country, but it is more likely to have resulted from the direct request of a customer who wanted a case decorated in the French manner. Although the decoration is completely symmetrical, it does not incorporate any form of animal life. The formal borders to the trunk door and plinth panels are a late feature and the rather coarse design on the frieze appears to be by a different hand. The sides of the case are panelled with crossbanding and the forward sliding hood has a door. The height is 6ft. 8ins. with an 11½ins. waist and the probable date is c.1700.

The 11ins. dial of this clock (figure 5/38) has a ringed calendar opening to match the other apertures and the seconds ring has the early style five seconds divisions. It is signed on the chapter ring 'Jacob Wallis London', an apparently unrecorded maker. The movement has an inside count wheel.

RESTORATION

Although the general subject of restoration is dealt with in a later chapter, it is appropriate to discuss a few points at this stage.

Any form of veneering, particularly marquetry, is affected by changing atmospheric conditions which cause slight lifting of the veneers in places and a tendency for the glue to exude and stand slightly proud of the joints in the marquetry. Unless serious lifting of the veneers occurs, which is particularly likely at the cross battens on trunk doors, it is far better to leave these irregularities of both glue and marquetry than to sandpaper them down and repolish. Such a refinished surface often has a new look which contrasts with the rest of the case. It is of course a useful method of blending in the new work on a case which has had major restoration.

Figure 5/35. Trunk door of fine seaweed and arabesque marquetry case shown in Colour Plate 10. Very finely cut marquetry with small grotesque heads. c.1715-18.

Figure 5/36 (above). Very fine sound frets in hood of the same case.

Figure 5/37 (right). Frets in side of hood and marquetry on column of same case.

Figure 5/38. 11ins. dial signed on chapter ring by Jacob Wallis, London, an apparently unrecorded maker. Fine quality hands. Movement has an inside count wheel. The very rare case with seaweed marquetry of pewter and burr elm is shown in Colour Plate 7.

Figure 5/39. Case of c.1690 with floral marquetry in panels. Plinth replaced with great care, walnut veneer matches that on trunk, boxwood stringing used round panel and to form panels on plinth sides to match trunk. Ebonised bun feet to match black mouldings and columns prove this is a recent restoration. Effect completely ruined by marquetry panel different in design and treatment from rest of case. Clock by John Austin, Watford, is c.1710 with quite large minute numerals and turbaned head spandrels (C. & W. No. 19).

Figure 5/40. Case of c.1700 with interesting marquetry design on door, showing Berain influence in grotesque figures supporting urn. Plinth restored with completely unsuitable panel of St. George and Dragon which looks like japanning. Small piece of original border at top of plinth. Skirting too deep and probably replaces bun feet. Whole of hood apparently replaced, probably at same time as plinth.

Figure 5/41. Case of c.1690 where plinth had been cut down and a very rough attempt has been made at completing the marquetry panel. The clock is by Thomas Budgen, Croydon, and dates from c.1735-40. The dial has four seasons spandrels, which could be replacements.

Figure 5/42. Floral marquetry case of c.1710 with lower trunk moulding and whole of plinth wrongly restored. Trunk section also shortened below door and marquetry border missing below door and a short distance up each side. Plinth skirting much too high. Plinth veneered with nineteenth century mass produced border. Sound fret in caddy replaced with same type of border. Nineteenth century dial and movement by Lund & Blockley in late eighteenth century style.

Figure 5/43. Lower door panel of Gould marquetry case shown in Colour Plate 5. Note fine cutting, particularly in carnations. This should be compared with figure 5/44.

Figure 5/44. Replaced plinth of Gould case shown in Colour Plate 5. Compare with 5/43 and note coarser marquetry work, completely different treatment of acanthus foliage and different type of walnut used for crossbanding. Bun feet would have been better than a skirting.

The plinth is the part of the case which normally requires most restoration, so some restored examples will be discussed and their shortcomings pointed out.

Figure 5/39 shows a completely replaced plinth which has been done with considerable care and attention to detail. The walnut crossbanding matches that on the trunk, boxwood stringing is used to match that round the door panels and to panel the sides of the plinth. The ebonised bun feet match the black mouldings and columns, and prove that this is a fairly recent restoration, otherwise a skirting would have been provided. The whole effect is ruined however by the marquetry panel which is completely different in design and treatment from that on the rest of the case, and suggests Victorian needlework! The clock, signed 'Jno. Austin Watford', is c.1710 (the spandrels are C. & W. No. 19), whereas the case is c.1690.

Figure 5/40 shows a much less skilful restoration. A sample of the original marquetry border has been fitted at the top of the new plinth, there is no border below the panel and the subject of the panel is quite out of keeping, resembling japanned decoration — which it probably is. The door panel is very interesting, showing the influence of Berain in the grotesque figures supporting the urn. The skirting is too deep and replaces bun feet. The hood appears to be a complete replacement, probably contemporary with the plinth.

In the case shown in figure 5/41 the top half of the plinth survived and an attempt was made to complete the design in the panel without much success. This case, of c.1690, houses a clock signed 'Tho. Budgen Croydon', of c.1735-40. The dial has four seasons spandrels (not in C. & W.), but these may be replacements.

Quite a lot of cases were restored by men who were unable to make or obtain marquetry panels, a good example being shown in figure 5/42. The trunk section has been shortened so that the door almost touches the lower moulding and the marquetry border is missing below the door and a short distance up each side. The lower trunk moulding and the whole of the plinth are replacements, the top half of the plinth being edged with a mass produced border as found on some American clock cases, the lower portion of the caddy having the sound fret replaced by a length of the same border. The present dial is signed on the chapter ring 'Lund & Blockley 42 Pall Mall London' and is a reproduction of a late eighteenth century one. The movement has a dead beat escapement. In all probability, the case was restored when the new dial and movement were supplied about a hundred years ago.

Figures 5/43 and 44 show details of the case of the Gould clock shown in Colour Plate 5 and are worthy of careful study. The plinth was rebuilt some years ago, utilising a comparatively modern marquetry panel which happened to be available. Although this is similar in style to the old work, it is much less finely cut and the acanthus leaves in particular are treated quite differently. The cabinet work and matching-in are both competently executed, but the walnut veneer used for the cross-banding does not match that on the trunk door frame. It would have been better to have provided bun feet instead of a skirting.

Figure 5/45 shows a close up of a case where the original plinth has survived. The marquetry on both door and plinth appears to be by the same hand and the crossbanding on both door frame and plinth matches.

It must be remembered that a specialist case restorer will design and cut a marquetry panel which will harmonise perfectly with the rest of the case and will select his walnut veneer and other materials with equal care. The final result may well be practically undetectable and well worth the not inconsiderable cost.

Figure 5/45. A case where the original plinth has survived. Note the similarity of treatment of the carnations in both panels and the matching walnut crossbanding on plinth and trunk.

Chapter 6

LACQUERED OR JAPANNED CASES

There was some interest in Oriental arts and crafts from the late sixteenth century and this was fostered by the formation of the East India company in 1599 and its Dutch equivalent in 1602. Probably because of vague geographical notions, 'Indian' was often the term used to describe any far eastern work, but 'China' and 'Japan' were also used. Although there are records, and some examples, of English furniture with lacquer-type decoration from the first half of the seventeenth century, it did not become popular until after the restoration of Charles II in 1660. Interest was stimulated by the return of the Court from the Low Countries where lacquer and japanned work was already popular, and by items such as Oriental lacquer cabinets brought from Portugal by Charles' queen, Catherine of Braganza.

Although the two terms lacquer and japanning are often used indiscriminately, it is as well to know what they mean.

True **lacquer** is the finish obtained by applying many coats of the sap of the lac tree (*Rhus vernicifera*) with polishing between coats. The final product has a deep gloss and is hard and durable. It is then decorated with raised gilt decoration. The basic material is not available in Europe.

Japanning consists of the application of two or more coats of a varnish consisting of gum-lac, seed-lac or shellac dissolved in spirits of wine. Before varnishing the wood is prepared by coating it with whiting and size. It is then well rubbed down. The gloss obtained depends on the care expended in polishing but the finish is not as durable as true lacquer and, if exposed to damp, it may flake off. Japanning was available in various colours, including red, blue, green, yellow and tortoiseshell, but black was the most common. Decoration in the form of Oriental or pseudo-Oriental scenes was applied to this ground in various shades of gold with the main features built up of a whiting paste to highlight them. This raised work was usually confined to the trunk door and in some cases the plinth also. Gold leaf was often used for the most important decoration, but much of it consisted of powdered brass, bronze or tin used very much like modern gold or silver paints.

Japanning became so popular with both professionals and amateurs (especially ladies) that a number of textbooks were produced, of which the best known is *A Treatise of Japaning and Varnishing* by John Stalker and George Parker (1688, reprinted 1971). This makes fascinating reading and has twenty-four plates of designs which show Dutch influence and which provided inspiration for many pieces of furniture.

Lacquered screens were imported and cut up to make other pieces of furniture, the lacquer being supplemented as necessary by English japanned decoration, but clock cases were not made by this method. In addition, some furniture was sent to China for lacquering, a service offered by the Dutch East India Co., but probably not used very much because of the long delay and the expense involved. Even so, a number of writers have stated that clock cases were shipped to the Far East for lacquering but it is difficult to find any evidence for this.

The quality of English japanning varies enormously, the best having quite a deep gloss and carefully executed raised work, whilst the cheapest consists of flat decoration applied to a coat of paint and varnish. Unlike a polished wood finish, japanning deteriorates with time

Figure 6/1   Figure 6/2   Figure 6/3

Figure 6/1. Black japanned case decorated in shades of gilt with chinoiseries and some European touches resembling some of the designs in Stalker and Parker's Treatise. *6ft. 9ins. high, c.1690. 10ins. dial, thirty-hour lantern type striking and alarm movement by Tho. Tompion.*

Figure 6/2. Unrestored japanned case of c.1705. Note how raised work on trunk door has survived better than decoration on rest of case. Interesting carved and gilt wood brackets under hood. Elegant caddy top marred by incorrect finials and rough filling in of sound fret. Brass hinges, lenticle frame and capitals. Clock by Francis Gregg, signed on chapter ring. Crown and cherub spandrels and ringed winding and other apertures.

Figure 6/3. Black japanned case in good condition but decoration on plinth and skirting apparently renewed. No brass mounts other than escutcheon. Clock by Fran. Hussey, c.1705-10.

and is also very susceptible to damage by atmospheric changes and rough treatment, so most unrestored cases present a somewhat shabby appearance. Many of those offered for sale have therefore been restored to some extent, varying from a light touching up to complete stripping and re-japanning. As with the original, the quality of this work varies, with some examples being difficult to detect whilst others are terribly garish.

Probably the earliest japanned clock case to survive is that of a Joseph Knibb bracket clock of c.1672-74,[1] but there are a number of seventeenth century longcases even though the main flowering of English japanning was in the next century and they were made until the 1770s, at least in the provinces. London made cases generally had an oak carcase, possibly with pine mouldings, and with the trunk door veneered with pear or other fine grained wood to provide a smooth surface. Provincial cases usually had a pine carcase, a characteristic which also applies to marquetry or other veneered cases.

THE SEVENTEENTH CENTURY

Figure 6/1 shows a case of c.1690 with a black ground, decorated in shades of gilt with chinoiseries which have odd European touches somewhat in the manner of Stalker and Parker's *Treatise* and with some restoration. The case is 6ft. 9ins. high with a 10ins. dial opening and houses a thirty-hour striking and alarm clock signed in a drapery cartouche 'Tho. Tompion Londini Fecit.' This has a lantern type movement with verge escapement of the type discussed in Chapter 4, pages 86-90, where a similar Tompion clock in the Clockmakers' Company collection is described.

Another seventeenth century case, with simple decoration, is illustrated in Colour Plate 4, and houses a clock by Richard Washington of Kendal.

THE EIGHTEENTH CENTURY

Mention has already been made of how japanned work deteriorates and figure 6/2 shows an unrestored example of c.1705 signed 'Fran: Gregg London'. Raised work was usually confined to the trunk, as here, and generally survives better than the flat decoration on the rest of the case. The carved and gilt wood brackets under the hood are an interesting feature and the graceful caddy top has fortunately survived. A broken sound fret above the cornice has been roughly filled in. The hood column capitals and bases and the lenticle frame are brass, but the extra large finials must have come from some other piece of furniture.

The dial has crown and cherub spandrels (C. & W. No. 8) and the winding and seconds holes and circular calendar aperture are ringed. The latter is surrounded by engraved birds and scrolls.

1. Lee, *Knibb*, p. 77.

Figure 6/4. Japanned case of 'grand-mother' proportions, 5ft. 10ins. to top of caddy and 7½ins. waist. Its size can be judged by comparison with the chair. Note absence of hood columns and elaborate caddy which may be a later addition, sound frets being c.1750. Note also flattened bun feet with skirting, quite possibly correct. Clock by Manley, Norwich, 7ins. dial with cherub spandrels. Probably c.1710-15.

Colour Plate 8. Fine decorated black japanned case. Mellow appearance but probably some restoration. Note well integrated scene on trunk door. Approximately 8ft. high without finials. Dial signed on chapter ring, between 35 and 25, 'James Clark' with 'Frome Fecit'. below the name. This layout is made possible by very large minute numbers rivalling in size those for the hours. In the arch is an early type moon dial with a hand indicating its age and the phases shown through a circular opening. The spandrels have a female head amongst scrollwork (C. & W. No. 21), a common type for the period. Winding holes, seconds and date apertures are ringed. Probably c.1730.

Colour Plate 9. Red japanned case with graceful broken arch pediment and detached columns. Gilt wood bases, capitals and finials. Note how outer finials line up with hood columns. 7ft. 7½ins. high. 12ins. dial signed on boss in arch 'James Goodyer, Guilford'. Note unusual four seasons spandrels (not in C. & W.). These are comparatively rare on English clocks but quite common on Dutch ones. c.1750 or slightly earlier.

Figure 6/5. Well proportioned case with rare tortoiseshell coloured ground and good quality decoration, note St. George and Dragon on trunk door. All brass mounts. 8ft. 8ins. high without finials. 14ins. dial signed on plaque in arch, 'Edmund Bullock Ellesmere 301.' Late example of floral engraving between spandrels and wheat-ear border to arch. Provincial variety of crown and cherub spandrels. Complete simple calendar, day of month below XII, day of week in aperture by IX and month with its number of days in aperture near III. Top left subsidiary dial for strike/silent, top right for pendulum regulation. c.1734. Illustrated in Cescinsky and Webster, English Domestic Clocks, p. 191.

Figure 6/6. Red japanned case in un-restored state. Note unusual feature of raised decoration on hood door and on frame round trunk door, well integrated design. Probably c.1740. Broad masking frame round dial, together with the fact that the dial has later features than the case, suggest present dial and movement have replaced original larger dial. Dial signed on boss in arch 'Charles Manson London.' Note absence of half and quarter hour markings, large seconds ring, and absence of ringing round apertures. A later, plainer style of dial, c.1750 or later.

Figure 6/5

Figure 6/6

Figure 6/7. Fine quality unrestored case with very complex scenes on plinth and trunk door. Reserves on mouldings and hood door beautifully painted with birds, animals and flowers. Note detached columns and graceful caddy, figure of Atlas probably Dutch. Approximate height 9ft. Dial signed on a plaque 'John Laight Birmingham', with later type moon disc in arch. Dial and case c.1750.

Figure 6/8. Case with decoration applied direct to ground without any raised work, a cheaper method. Note truncated pagoda top popular from c.1760, which is probably the date of the case. Wheat-ear border to dial plate and name boss, quarter and half-hour markings on chapter ring and style of hands suggest c.1740. Maker, Simon of Romford, was lagging well behind London fashion, or this is a marriage.

Figure 6/7

Figure 6/8

Figure 6/3 shows a case of c.1705-10 where the decoration has a black ground and is in very good condition, probably the result of careful restoration. The decoration of the plinth is rather different in character and suggests that it has been completely renewed. The lenticle frame is not normally decorated as in this case and the capitals and bases to the hood columns are of gilt wood. The dial is similar to the Gregg example described above but has an engraved border. It is by Fran. Hussey, London.

Miniature longcase or 'grandmother' clocks are exceedingly rare and have in consequence been much sought after. Whilst there is no exact definition of what constitutes a 'grandmother', a height of less than 6ft. usually qualifies.[2] The interesting example in figure 6/4, with the height to the top of its caddy being 5ft.10ins., should certainly be included. Its size can also be judged from that of the chair alongside. With a 7ins. dial it has a 7½ins. waist. The elaborate caddy top incorporates some upward facing mouldings which would not be required on a case of normal height with the caddy well above eye level. The sound frets in both cornice and caddy are later in design than the rest of the case and the caddy may be a later addition to give the case a more imposing appearance. The hood door was apparently not made with columns as the decoration extends to the outer edges. The plinth has the unusual but possibly correct combination of a skirting with flattened bun feet. The japanned decoration has the appearance of age but unfortunately the writer has not had an opportunity of examining it.[2a]

The 7ins. dial is inscribed on the chapter ring 'Manley in Norwich', presumably Cornelius Manley who is recorded by Loomes as 1702-14. The dial plate has an engraved border and matted centre with floral engraving round the square calendar opening. Simple cherub spandrels (C. & W. No. 3) are fitted as on bracket clock dials or other small dials at this period. There is a seconds dial and, judging by the position of the lenticle, a seconds pendulum. The probable date is c.1710-15. Because of their scarcity these miniature clocks have been faked in some numbers and this aspect is discussed in Chapter 12.

Figure 6/5 shows a fine example of japanning with the rare tortoiseshell coloured ground. The scenes are well drawn and animated, with St. George and the Dragon in the middle of the trunk door. The well proportioned case has a height of 8ft. 8ins. without finials and all the mounts are of brass.

The 14ins. dial is signed on a plaque in the arch 'Edmund Bullock Ellesmere 301', the arch has a wheat-ear border and there is a late example of floral engraving between the spandrels. The latter are a provincial variation of the cherub and crown pattern (C. & W. No. 8) but the standard dolphin design (C. & W. No. 38) is used in the arch. There is a complete simple calendar, the day of the month is shown on the dial in the normal seconds position, the day of the week appears in the opening near IX and the month with its number of days in the opening near III. The top left subsidiary dial is for strike/silent and the top right one is for pendulum regulation and is marked 5, 10 . . . . 30. The purpose of the opening above VI is not known to the author. This clock was illustrated by Cescinsky and Webster[3] but the name plaque was then covered by a disc painted with an eighteenth century ship and the number was quoted as 303. Proof that it was the clock illustrated here is provided by the nineteenth century minute hand shown in both photographs. The probable date is c.1734 as Bullock died in that year.[4]

Another fine provincial example is shown in Colour Plate 8. The excellent even state of preservation of the decoration suggests it has been restored but the overall effect is mellow and very pleasing. The problem of designing one continuous scene for the trunk door has been neatly solved. It is about 8ft. high excluding finials.

The dial is signed on the chapter ring, between 35 and 25, 'James Clark' with 'Frome

2. Lee, *Knibb,* p.60.
2a. See page 8.
3. Cescinsky and Webster, p.191.
4. D.J. Elliott, *Shropshire Clock and Watchmakers,* 1979, p.39.

Fecit' below the name. Somewhat difficult to date but probably c.1730.

Figure 6/6 shows a very similar case to that in Colour Plate 8, but with a red ground and definitely in unrestored condition. It has the unusual feature of raised decoration on the frame round the trunk door and on the hood door. The broad masking frame round the dial suggests that the present dial has replaced a larger original one. The case is probably c.1740.

The dial is signed on a boss in the arch 'Charles Manson London', an apparently unrecorded maker. It is a later and plainer dial than the dial seen in Colour Plate 8, although the spandrels are the same type, but the chapter ring has no half or quarter hour markings and the seconds ring is large and slim, a reversion to a very early style. Also, none of the apertures is ringed. The dial must be about 1750 or later.

A fine quality unrestored case is shown in figure 6/7. The main scenes are very complex with a fine ship at the base of the door which however seems to have little relation to the rest of the scene. Some of the reserves on the mouldings and the hood door are beautifully painted with birds and animals as well as flowers. The hood columns are not attached to the door. The height is approximately 9ft. without the figure of Atlas — which would be more at home on a Dutch clock.

The dial is signed on a plaque 'John Laight Birmingham' and has the later type of moon disc in the arch. Baillie records Laight as 1730 but the whole clock is approximately 1750.

Colour Plate 9 shows an interesting case with red japanning and a graceful and unusual broken arch pediment with gilt wood finials and detached columns. This is of a more convenient size, 7ft. 7½ins. high.

The 12ins. dial is signed on the boss in the arch 'James Goodyer Guilford.' The date of the clock is again c.1750 or perhaps a little earlier.

An interesting case of rather later date, c.1760-70, is shown in figure 6/8. This has a truncated version of the pagoda top which was often used in the second half of the century. The pediment is later in style than some other features of the case, such as the half round beading on the trunk door. The decoration appears to be painted direct on the flat surface without any raised work.

The dial has a wheat-ear border round the dial plate and the name boss in the arch. The chapter ring with half hour marks and quarter hour divisions, and the hands, suggest a date c.1740. The dial is signed 'Simon Romford' and is either an example of provincial work lagging considerably behind the London fashion or the clock has been married to the case in comparatively recent times.

Another good quality Birmingham clock is shown in figure 6/9, although the case has been somewhat restored, the plinth panel and some of the mouldings appearing rather out of character with the fine work

Figure 6/9. Good quality case with fine decoration on trunk door but plinth and mouldings restored. Note unusual break arch panelling of door and sides of trunk. Giltwood flambeau finials resting too low on their plinths. Dial boldly signed on curved strip round arch, Edward Gratrex Birmingham, otherwise similar to Birmingham example in 6/7. Note that bold type of signature with large minute numbers is usual on Midlands and north country clocks of the second half of the eighteenth century.

Figure 6/10. Example of good quality decoration showing how discontinuities in design can be avoided by setting scenes on islands as in Chinese work.

on the door. The panels formed by the applied beadings on the sides of the trunk are a very unusual feature. The gilt wood flambeau finials have lost their lowest sections and rest squatly on their plinths.

The dial is boldly signed 'EDWARD GRATREX BIRMINGHAM' on a silvered strip round the arch and this, with the equally large numbers on the moon disc and for the minutes, is quite usual on Midlands and north country clocks of the second half of the eighteenth century. The date is about 1760.

Mention has already been made of the difficulty of designing a continuous scene the shape of a trunk door, and figure 6/10 shows how this discontinuity can be overcome by setting the scene on a series of islands as is often found in Chinese work. An example of good quality decoration.

Information has recently come to light concerning a London casemaker active in the first half of the eighteenth century who specialised in japanned cases and supplied a large number of both London and provincial clockmakers. Whilst it is far too early to publish any useful results, there is a clear indication that such a casemaker dominated the market.

Chapter 7

TELLING THE TIME AT NIGHT

To appreciate the importance of striking work, particularly the complex and ingenious devices sometimes encountered, it is necessary to consider the conditions prevailing at the time it was made. In the seventeenth century clocks were still relatively scarce, so one had to serve for a number of rooms or even a whole house. Except in the entertaining rooms of the wealthiest homes the level of artificial lighting was very low[1] and 'striking a light' with flint and steel presented some difficulty. Added to this, skilled oculists did not yet exist, so there must have been a lot of people who had difficulty in seeing the time particularly in dim light. All these factors enhanced the importance of an aural indication of the time.

THE COUNT WHEEL

By far the commonest arrangement provides simple hour striking using count wheel control as described in Chapter 2. This method survived with only minor modifications in the vast majority of thirty-hour clocks until production ceased in the nineteenth century. It was also used in most month or longer duration clocks, possibly because it required slightly less power to operate it than rack striking which is described later.

From c.1670 the count wheel, although still mounted outside the back plate on eight-day clocks, was on an extension of the great wheel arbor, which required the arbor to be divided with the rear portion fixed to the great wheel and running in an extended bearing in the barrel. This was apparently normal practice on many early movements including those with indirectly driven count wheels (see figure 2/19), so re-positioning the count wheel did not necessarily require major changes. The new position had the advantages of saving a wheel and pinion in the drive to the count wheel and giving a more even motion to the latter. Figure 3/12 shows this type of count wheel on an anonymous clock of c.1680. This clock has an undivided barrel arbor on the going side but many had divided arbors to both barrels and it should be noted that the year timepiece of c.1675 shown in figure 3/6 has this type.

Shortly before the lower position was adopted for the count wheel, the detent was in most cases brought outside the back plate on an extended arbor instead of operating through a slot in the plate.

From about 1690 many eight-day movements had the count wheel between the plates and attached to the great wheel, which removed the need for a divided barrel arbor. This development is found on a few special clocks from c.1675, but some London makers continued to use the external count wheel until at least the turn of the century. The first type of internal count wheel was mounted between the great wheel and the back plate with the detent at first still mounted externally and operating through a slot in the plate, the reverse of the layout employed in the first eight-day clocks. The example of c.1705 by Henry Perry (figure 9/8) is of this type. However most internal count wheels consist of a slender ring attached to the front of the great wheel and with an internal detent. The count wheel on thirty-hour or month and longer duration clocks was mounted externally whether indirectly or directly driven. Figure 7/1 shows the indirectly driven count wheel on a late seventeenth

---

1. This is discussed at some length by Peter Thornton in *Seventeenth Century Interior Decoration in England, France and Holland,* 1978, p. 268.

Figure 7/1. Indirectly driven count wheel on a late seventeenth century month movement with four wheel striking train. Note the flat tension spring to take up the play in the wheel teeth.

Figure 7/2. The earliest form of rack striking known as the inside rack, where most of the mechanism is between the plates, with only the snail and rack tail mounted on the front plate. Note locking of pin in pallet wheel on projection on rack. The earliest examples had a rigid rack tail which jammed against the long step of the snail if the striking failed.

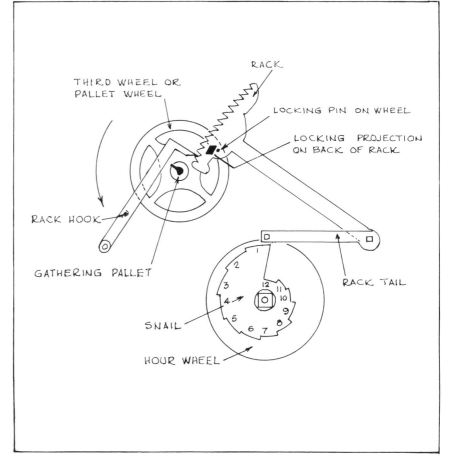

128

century month movement with four wheel striking train.

In eight-day clocks the count wheel was gradually supplanted by rack and snail striking which had been invented in 1676, but its use was exceptional until around 1700 and it did not become standard even on London-made clocks until about the end of the first quarter of the eighteenth century. Provincial makers often continued to use the count wheel until about the middle of the century.

Whilst it must be admitted that a badly worn or bodged count wheel striking system can prove very troublesome, one which is in good condition is perfectly reliable providing the hands are not moved without allowing the clock to strike. It also permits of the striking being silenced by simply wedging the fly or omitting to wind the striking train, neither of which is satisfactory with the average rack striking clock which is not fitted with a strike/silent device. To enable the striking to be corrected if it became out of step with the hands, two devices were used: the hour wheel pipe was attached to its wheel by means of a friction disc so that the hour hand could be turned to agree with the last hour struck, and the arbor carrying the locking detent had a projecting lever which could be depressed to release the striking (figure 9/8). Sometimes the lever had a cord attached so that it could be operated without disturbing the hood.

THE RACK AND SNAIL

Rack striking was invented by the Rev. Edward Barlow (born Booth) in 1676, initially so that repeating could be incorporated in spring clocks. In fact a few early repeating clocks have count wheel striking with rack and snail repetition of hours and quarters, the repeating mechanism being completely separate from the striking train.

The essential feature of rack striking is that the number struck depends entirely on the position of a stepped cam or 'snail' mounted on the hour wheel, hence the striking cannot get out of step with the hands even if it is allowed to run down, and it can be repeated as often as desired.

Figure 7/2 shows the earliest type known as the inside rack, where most of the mechanism is between the plates. The rack, which is mounted on an arbor between the plates, is held in the position shown by the rack hook which is also pivoted between the plates. A locking projection on the rack locks the train by means of a pin in the third wheel or pallet wheel (this corresponds to the hoop wheel in a count wheel movement).

When warning occurs the warning wheel is intercepted in the usual way and the rack hook is raised so allowing the the rack to fall. The rack tail is squared on to an extension of the rack arbor and carries a stud which comes to rest on the appropriate step of the snail. The snail has twelve even steps and the rack tail and the rack arm are so proportioned that when the rack tail drops on to a particular step the corresponding number of teeth pass the rack hook.

When the striking is released at the hour the rack hook restores, the pallet wheel rotates once for each blow struck and the gathering pallet lifts or gathers up one rack tooth. This continues until the rack is returned to the position shown, when it is locked as before.

Some makers used a steel pin driven into the wheel collet instead of filing the gathering pallet out of the pinion arbor and normal wheel teeth were sometimes used on the rack in place of the usual ratchet teeth.

On the earliest examples the rack tail was rigid so if the striking failed for any reason the stud in the rack tail jammed against the edge of the snail between 12 and 1 o'clock, thus stopping the clock. This difficulty was overcome by modifying the rack tail so that it could ride up on to the snail, which will be described in connection with the next development.

Figure 7/3 shows an inside rack striking movement by Henry Stocker, London, c.1700. This is a month movement and has the striking train on the right, whereas figure 7/2 is

(a)   *(b)*

Figure 7/3. Inside rack on month movement by Stocker. Four wheel striking train on right. In view (a) note spring stud on rack tail and raising of rack hook by warning piece, also latched pillars. View (b) shows large pallet wheel with two locking pins and two gathering pallets as it makes half a turn for each blow on bell.

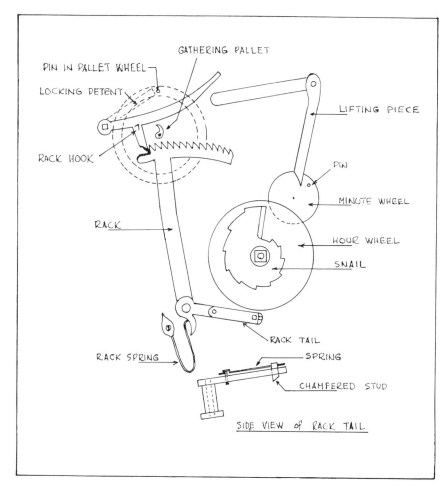

Figure 7/4. Early type of outside rack striking, where everything has been brought out on to the front plate except the locking which is still by a pin in the rim of the pallet wheel. At the end of striking the rack hook drops lower for the locking detent to intersect this pin. Note the sprung stud on the rack tail to enable it to ride up the chamfered edge of the snail if the striking fails.

130

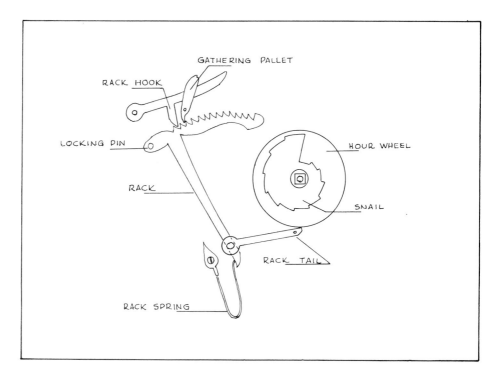

Figure 7/5. Final form of rack striking where locking is effected by a tail on the gathering pallet striking a pin or block in the rack. The gathering pallet tail may be arranged either in front of or behind the rack but the actual pallet should be as shown. Note the cheaper and less satisfactory springy rack tail which superseded the sprung stud on a rigid tail.

drawn with it in the usual position on the left. The Stocker movement has the rack behind the pallet wheel and as it has a four wheel striking train the pallet wheel has two locking pins and two gathering pallets. Note how the rack hook is raised by the warning piece. The rack tail has a spring stud to enable it to ride up on to the snail if the striking fails. The device is shown in detail in the drawing of the outside rack in figure 7/4.

The internal rack is comparatively rare in longcase clocks because not many makers had adopted rack striking before the external version came in shortly after 1700 and few inside racks were made after c.1730.

The early type of outside rack is shown in figure 7/4 where everything except the locking of the train has been brought out on to the front plate. The rack and rack tail are riveted to a pipe which rides on a stud in the front plate and as the rack is more or less vertical a spring is provided to bring the rack tail into contact with the snail. The rack tail has a chamfered stud mounted on a spring and working in a slot in the end of the rack tail (see drawing). The long step of the snail is also chamfered so that in the event of failure to strike the rack tail rides on to the snail and the clock keeps going. This imposes some strain on the mechanism so the clock should not be run without striking unless it has a strike/silent device or steps are taken to prevent the rack falling on to the snail.

The gathering pallet is mounted on a squared extension of the front pivot of the pallet wheel pinion. The rack hook is similarly mounted on an arbor which carries a locking detent between the plates. At the end of striking the rack hook drops much lower than when it is engaging in the rack teeth and this brings the locking detent into the path of a pin in the rim of the pallet wheel. Gordon[2] mentions another type where the final movement of the rack was used to move a locking piece pivoted between the plates. This is sometimes found on provincial movements and an example is shown in figure 10/21.

2. G.F.C. Gordon, *Clockmaking, Past and Present*, 1925, p. 70.

The highly satisfactory rigid rack tail with its flexibly mounted stud was replaced from about 1720 by a springy rack tail, a cheaper but much less reliable device.

Around 1740 another change was introduced in the locking arrangements which gave the striking its final form (figure 7/5). The gathering pallet is provided with a tail which locks on a pin or other projection on the rack, so the rack hook is simply mounted on a stud in the front plate. This modification was adopted only slowly and some clocks were made with internal locking until practically the end of the eighteenth century. The gathering pallet tail may be arranged either behind or in front of the rack, the former position imposing less strain on its fixing on the extended pivot.

When considering the various developments in striking systems or in other mechanical devices it is important to remember the very considerable time lag which occurred before they were universally accepted. Arising from this, when arriving at a date for a clock one must take note of the *latest original features,* not the earliest. It is quite useless to formulate rules that provincial or country makers were so many years behind their London contemporaries, the time lag varying from virtually nothing to fifty years or more, since it depends on so many factors.

HALF HOUR STRIKING

A few clocks were made to strike one at the half hour.

With a count wheel this was effected by having double width slots and arranging the gear ratios so that the count wheel made one rotation for 90 (i.e. 78 + 12) blows on the bell. Two diametrically opposite lifting pins were provided on the minute wheel.

With rack striking the lifting pin for the half hour was placed nearer the minute wheel centre than that for the hour and the first tooth of the rack made shorter. When the clock warned for the half hour the rack therefore fell one tooth only, independent of the position of the snail. The same result was sometimes obtained without shortening the first tooth of the rack, in which case the rack was merely over-gathered and fell back at the half hour.

Using the same bell for hours and half hours was liable to cause confusion, particularly at 12.30, 1 o'clock and 1.30, so some seventeenth century clocks were provided with a second, smaller bell of higher pitch for the half hours. The hammer arbor was then pumped over to bring the hammer opposite the second bell, by means of a lever operated by an edge cam on the minute wheel.

A more comprehensive form of half hour striking was occasionally provided in the last quarter of the seventeenth century, when the previous hour was repeated on a smaller bell. With a count wheel this necessitated two equally spaced slots for each hour and the gear ratios such that one revolution of the count wheel was made for 156 (i.e. 2 × 78) strokes. With rack striking, the snail had to be correctly positioned and two similar lifting pins provided, as were also required for the count wheel system. The other requirements were a pump action on the hammer arbor as described above and modifications to the striking train to give it twice the duration of a normal striking train. This form of striking is often somewhat misleadingly called 'Dutch' striking. The system used in Dutch clocks sometimes repeats the previous hour at the half hour as described above but in other examples the next hour is struck at the half hour.

QUARTER STRIKING AND CHIMING

Quarter striking was introduced to give a more frequent audible indication of the time. The correct terms are 'quarter striking' when not more than three bells are used and 'quarter chiming' when four or more bells are employed. In general, small numbers of bells were used in early clocks and larger numbers in later ones. Clocks with quarter striking or chiming usually have a third train for this purpose but in all periods a few were made where both hours and quarters were sounded by the same train.

Thirty-hour clocks were not often provided with quarter striking or chiming, but

Figure 7/6. Unusual three train quarter striking thirty-hour movement. Probably c.1740, but maker not known as dial has been changed at least twice — note holes in front plate and bridge over motion work to accommodate shortened dial foot.

Figure 7/7. Front view of same movement showing four-armed snail in front of cannon pinion, to let off quarters and snail behind pinion (just visible on right) to let off hours. Hour striking train on right as usual, going in middle and quarter striking on left. Note crude stand for quarter bells, possibly a replacement.

Figure 7/8. Rear view of same movement showing hour and quarter count wheels. Note nicely finned pillars and decorative turning sprockets, count wheels and motion work (see 7/7).

figure 7/6 shows an example where quarter striking on three bells is provided by means of a third train with count wheel control. Unfortunately the maker is not known as the dial has been changed at least twice — note the holes in the front plate. The date is probably c.1740. The hour striking train is in its normal position on the right, the going train is in the middle with the usual indirect drive to the hands and the quarter striking is on the left.

Figure 7/7 shows the arrangements for letting off the striking trains. The cannon pinion has a snail behind the pinion to let off the hours. This is just visible pointing to the right. In front of the pinion is a four armed snail which operates the quarter lifting piece. Figure 7/8 shows the back plate with the count wheels. The quarter count wheel is squared on to its great wheel arbor, so the great wheel has ten pins (1 + 2 + 3 + 4 quarters) and makes one rotation per hour. The three quarter hammers are lifted in sequence by the pins in the great wheel (figure 7/6).

At the hour it is essential to ensure that the four quarters have been struck before the hour train is released. One method would be to delay the release of the hour lifting piece sufficiently to allow plenty of time for the quarter striking, but to be reliable this introduces an unacceptably long interval between the end of the fourth quarter and the first blow on the hour. The usual method, as in this case, is for the arbor carrying the quarter detent to have an extension piece which intercepts the warning wheel of the hour striking train. The hour striking is then released when the quarter detent drops into a count wheel notch.

The dial of a conventional eight-day three train chiming clock is shown in figure 7/9. It is signed on an arched plaque 'Samuel Thorne London' and the probable date is c.1740. Figure 7/10 shows the rack and snail control used for both hours and quarters. It is the later type where a tail on the gathering pallet locks on a projection on the rack. The hour striking is on the left and the quarter chiming on the right. The lifting piece, which is just above the hour wheel, is mounted on an arbor and when the hand is moved to 'silent' it allows this arbor to move forward under pressure from a spring on the back plate. This takes the lifting piece out of the path of the four pins on the cannon pinion.

Raising the lifting piece and its attached warning piece intercepts the pin in the quarter warning wheel and, by raising the rack hook, allows the quarter rack tail to drop on to its snail on the minute wheel. As soon as the quarter rack is released a pin in the front of it releases the hour warning piece which is pivoted just below the quarter bells. A spring under the hour warning piece raises it into the path of the pin in the hour warning wheel. It remains in the warning position until the quarter rack is gathered up. This movement of the hour warning piece has no effect except at the hour.

When the quarter rack tail falls on to the lowest step of the snail in warning for the hour, the left hand end of the quarter rack strikes the tail of the hour rack hook and raises the latter so releasing the hour rack. The hour warning piece has already intercepted the hour warning wheel so the hour striking train remains held on warning until the final movement of the quarter rack at the end of chiming moves the hour warning piece clear of the warning wheel.

The hour striking is therefore always released just at the end of chiming the four quarters. To ensure reliable action at the hour the quarter rack must have a strong spring to ensure that it will always lift the hour rack hook. This means that the quarter rack assembly must be strongly made or the rack tail will go out of adjustment as a result of its heavy blows on the snail. This is the usual arrangement, but some movements are made with the hour rack hook lifted by a separate pin in the motion work just after the quarter train has warned, as is arranged in the thirty-hour movement in figure 7/7. This system is more reliable and is much quieter in warning.

Repeating of hours and quarters is provided by the spring loaded lever at the top left. When the cord is pulled, pins in this lever lift the quarter warning piece and the hour rack hook. Release of the lever allows quarter chiming followed by striking as at the hour. For

Figure 7/9. Dial of an eight-day three train chiming clock signed 'Samuel Thorne London', probably c.1740.

Figure 7/10. Movement of Thorne clock. Conventional layout of chiming and striking mechanism. The lifting piece is mounted on an arbor which is pumped forward for silencing so that the lifting piece clears the pins on the cannon pinion.

Repeating lever

Hour rack hook

Hour gathering pallet

Hour rack

Lifting piece

Hour snail

Hour warning piece

Quarter rack hook

Quarter warning piece

Quarter rack

Quarter snail

more reliable repetition of the last hour the snail would have been mounted on a star wheel and flirted over to its next position just before warning for the hour.

Although quarter striking or chiming normally requires three trains it is possible to design a clock to operate with two, but usually by omitting the four quarters at the hour. Such a movement is often described as a 3 × 2 chime and the dial of one is shown in figure 7/11. This is signed 'Jos: Cobham LONDON' who is not recorded in the usual lists but the probable date for the clock is c.1725.

The 12ins. dial has a well engraved laurel leaf border. Engraved borders were used approximately 1680-1730 on London clocks and are usually a sign of quality although their absence does not prove the contrary. A pleasing alternative took the form of flowers or foliage between the spandrels and was used approximately 1685-1710, but it was not suitable for use with the later types of spandrel such as those on this dial (C. & W. No. 21). Note the tiny arrows used as hour, half hour and five minute marks. From about 1715 the signature was usually in the arch or, when the arch was occupied by some other device, on a reserve[3] or on an applied plaque in the dial centre as here. Latinised signatures are rare after about 1700, except on provincial clocks.

3. A reserve is a plain area surrounded by matting or decorative engraving.

Figure 7/11. 12ins. dial of a two train quarter chime clock, c.1725, by Jos. Cobham, London. Earliest type of lunar and tidal dial in arch. Dark blue painted disc with gilt stars has circular hole to show phases by exposing varying amounts of bright metal ground and dark blue paint. Hand rotates with the disc and shows age of moon by Arabic numerals and high tide at London Bridge by Roman numerals. A good quality dial.

Figure 7/12. Front plate of Cobham movement. Striking and chiming train on right so that hammers will strike towards centre of movement with clockwise winding. Two racks on common arbor, with rigid rack tails and sprung studs, very unusual in having two sets of teeth, lower for gathering pallet and upper for rack hook. Train is locked when rack hook drops into very deep last teeth of both racks. Lifting piece squared on to an arbor with internal warning piece. At the quarters lifting pins do not raise rack hook sufficiently to release hour rack as well as quarter rack. At the hour both racks are released but high step on quarter snail prevents quarter rack dropping. Repeating cord releases both racks, strikes hour first then quarters.

Figure 7/13. Right hand view of movement. Pin barrel normally held in rearward position by shaped piece on hour rack holding long stud on L-shaped lever (see 7/12). Other end of lever presses on arbor of pin barrel. In this position radial pins in barrel operate chime hammers. Release of hour rack releases L-shaped lever and spring on back plate pushes pin barrel forward so chiming pins miss hammers but axial pins operate hammer for hour bell.

Figure 7/14. Left hand view showing drive to 59 tooth moon wheel. Note early use of small bevel wheels behind twenty-four hour wheel which operates calendar. Upper end of vertical arbor carries pin which advances moon wheel one tooth for each half turn. Spring pawl holds wheel in position.

Figure 7/15. Pendulum of Cobham clock. Note faceted rating nut and pulleys made to dismantle for cleaning.

Figure 7/16. Case of Cobham clock, approximately 8ft. high. Oak carcase, some pine mouldings and pear or similar veneer on trunk door. Japanning with dark green ground, with restoration. Should have gilt wood finials, probably flambeaux.

Figure 7/17. Approximate cross-section of mouldings on Cobham case shown half size.

HOOD

TRUNK

A very few lunar dials were made in the seventeenth century but they did not become popular until the arch dial provided a suitable setting and this is the earliest type usually found. Although an average lunar cycle is 29.53 days this is normally approximated to 29½ days to allow the use of a 59 toothed wheel stepped on twice a day. In figure 7/11 the disc, which is painted dark blue with gilt stars, has a circular hole which exposes a varying amount of bright metal ground and dark blue paint to to show the phases. The hand rotates with the disc and indicates the age of the moon by the outer Arabic numerals and the time of high tide by the Roman numerals. The fact that the high tide at the new and full moons is at 3 o'clock shows that it is intended for London Bridge. Some universal tidal dials were made by engraving the hour numerals on a separate ring which could be rotated to bring the appropriate time for a port opposite new and full moon. Some of these moon dials are made with a circular hole in the dial plate and a rotating disc behind it but the principle is the same. Information about the state of the moon was useful when planning land journeys and the tides affected use of the river as a highway as well as a port.

Figure 7/12 shows the dial removed. The going train is conventional except that it is planted on the left so that the chime hammers will strike towards the centre of the movement. The two racks are pivoted on a common arbor, the quarter rack being next to the front plate and its tail engaging with a snail on the minute wheel. Both racks have rigid tails with sprung studs and are extremely unusual in having two sets of teeth. The upper teeth are only for the rack hook and the lower ones are for the common gathering pallet. The lifting piece is operated by pins in the cannon pinion, the three for the quarters being nearer the centre than the pin for the hour. Both lifting piece and rack hook are squared on to arbors and these carry the warning and locking pieces respectively. As shown in figure 7/12 both racks have been released but when the train is at rest both have been gathered up and the shaped steel piece attached on the right of the hour rack will have pushed the long stud projecting from the L-shaped lever (see figure 7/13). This lever is mounted on a vertical arbor and when operated the lower end of the lever pumps over the pin barrel against the pressure of a flat spring on the back plate.

When the lifting piece rises for warning at a quarter, the rack hook is raised sufficiently to release the quarter rack but not the hour rack because the quarter rack teeth are lower than those of the hour rack. As the hour rack has not been released, the pin barrel remains held in its rearward position so that its pins will engage with the chime hammers. When the lifting piece falls the appropriate number of quarters are sounded on the eight bells as the quarter rack is gathered up by the rear portion of the gathering pallet and the deep drop of the rack hook then locks the train.

When warning for the hour, the rack hook is raised sufficiently to release both racks but the quarter rack cannot fall because the quarter snail has a high step for the hour. Movement of the hour rack releases the pin barrel which moves forward. In that position the chiming pins miss their hammers but the longitudinal pins at the front end of the barrel engage with the hammer for the hour bell (figure 7/13). When striking occurs, the hour rack is gathered up in the usual way, the pin barrel is again pumped over to its chime position and the rack hook holds both racks.

Repeating is provided and pulling the cord on the left releases both racks as shown in figure 7/12 and the pin barrel moves forward ready for hour striking. As the hour is struck the gathering pallet gathers both racks but the quarter rack falls back each time because its teeth are lower than those of the hour rack. At the end of the hour striking the pin barrel is again pumped over to the chime position and during chiming the quarter rack is gathered up and now held by the rack hook which has dropped about halfway down the deep cut-away on the hour rack. At the end of chiming the final drop of the rack hook holds the train.

The drive to the moon wheel is shown in figure 7/14. Mounted on the back of the wheel

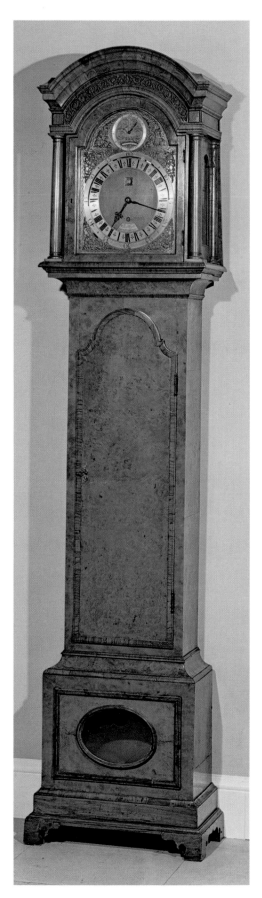

Colour Plate 10. Superb case of grande sonnerie month clock by Daniel Quare, no. 145, c.1716-18. Height approximately 8ft. 10ins. excluding finials. Oak carcase veneered with walnut and arabesque marquetry of holly or similar wood in a walnut ground. The marquetry is even applied to all main mouldings and columns. The small mouldings are of cross-cut walnut and the sides are panelled with herring-bone banding. The finials, capitals and bases, and trunk door hinges are of gilt brass. Detailed views of decoration in figures 5/35-37 and 7/26. See also figures 7/24 and 25.

Colour Plate 11. Month equation timepiece by Wm. Wright in a case veneered with burr yew which has mellowed to a lovely lightish brown resembling walnut. 8ft. 3ins. high, c.1730. Oval lenticle in plinth in fixed panel as regulation is by dial and hand in arch. A fine case but the bracket feet are an addition. See also Frontispiece and figures 8/25 and 26.

which operates the calendar is a small bevel gear wheel and this engages with a similar one on the almost vertical arbor with a pin through the top. Like the calendar wheel, the vertical arbor rotates once a day and during each half turn the projecting pin at its top advances the moon wheel one tooth. There is a spring pawl to hold the wheel in position.

The pendulum has the refinement of an octagonal rating nut with the facets numbered to facilitate regulation (figure 7/15). The weights are approximately 12lb. for the going and 18lb. for the chiming and striking.

The case (figure 7/16) is a mixture of pine and oak, the oak trunk door being veneered with pear or some other fine grained wood to make a better surface for the japanning, which has a dark green ground. Unlike polished wood, japanning deteriorates with age, so like most of those in good condition this case has had extensive restoration. The height is approximately 8ft. and it should have finials, probably carved and gilt wood flambeaux. The approximate cross-section of the mouldings is shown half size in figure 7/17.

GRANDE SONNERIE STRIKING AND CHIMING

The systems of striking or chiming so far described do not give full information other than at the hour and in the case of 'Dutch' striking at the half hour.

A system giving full information every quarter of an hour was in use by 1675 and was

Figure 7/18. 11ins. dial of grande sonnerie striking clock by Ambrose Hawkins, Exeter, who died 1705. Good quality dial but engraver had some difficulty in setting out signature. Note early use of crown and cherub spandrels by a provincial maker.

Figure 7/19

Figure 7/20

Figure 7/21

Figure 7/19. Front plate of Hawkins movement. Note late use of divided front plate, with ten pillars and braces to ensure alignment. Count wheel quarter striking on right, rack hour striking on left. Hour rack is outside back plate. Note unusual hexagonal socket for hour hand.

Figure 7/20. Back plate showing quarter count wheel with pins to warn and let off the hour strike. Hour rack with very deep last tooth for internal locking. Several striking parts replaced. Note shaped aperture for easy withdrawal of pallets and engraved decoration matching that round calendar aperture (see 7/18).

Figure 7/21. Quarter striking train of Hawkins movement. Both striking barrels are plain because of anti-clockwise winding. Note lifting pins in count wheel, also decorative steel work and substantial pillars.

Figure 7/22. Hour striking train. Note coarse teeth on great wheel of five wheel train, also coarse ratchet teeth. Rack spring is on inside of back plate.

Figure 7/22

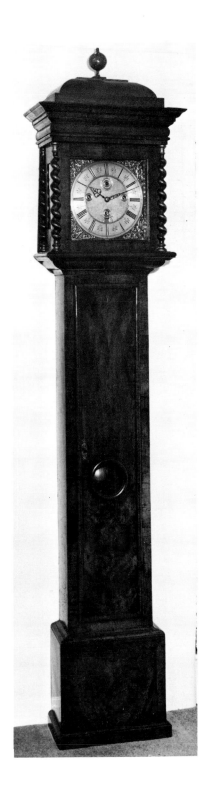

Figure 7/23. Case of Hawkins clock of pine veneered with walnut, height 7ft. 2ins., excluding finial. Note cushion moulding to hood, caddy is a restoration. Skirting has replaced bun feet (see 4/50). Heavy proportions of hood confirm provincial origin.

described by Smith under the heading *Repeating Clock:*[4]

> They not only strike the hour and quarter, but also, immediately after the striking of each quarter, it repeats or strikes over again, on a different bell, the last hour that was strucken, by which you are given to understand, that it is 1, 2, or 3 quarters past that hour which was repeated; this Clock is of excellent use for the night.

This is now described as *grande sonnerie* striking, the term repeating clock being reserved for one which strikes hours or hours and quarters on demand, usually by pulling a cord.

Grand sonnerie striking is rare, particularly in longcase clocks. The mechanism is complicated and therefore must have been expensive to produce, and the invention of quarter repeating action in 1676, usually restricted to bracket clocks, provided a simpler and more acceptable solution to telling the time at night.

Few examples were the work of provincial makers but figure 7/18 shows the 11ins. dial of one signed 'Amb: Hawkins de EXON fecit' which should be dated 1700-5 as he died in the latter year. The engraving is of good quality, note the wheat-ear border and small minute numerals with simple half-quarter markings. The crown and cherub pattern spandrels (C. & W. No.8) came into use c.1700, so this maker was not behind the times!

The movement is shown in figure 7/19. Note the divided front plate with a separate section for each train and braces to preserve alignment between the sections. Divided front plates are not often found as late as this, probably because of the extra work involved — this movement has ten pillars! Note also the unusual hexagonal socket for the hour hand.

The hour striking is by rack, and despite the four strikings of each hour the snail is attached to the hour wheel so the positioning of the latter is critical. On a later movement the snail would have been mounted on a star wheel and stepped on quickly just before the hour to prevent the risk of wrong numbers. The rack tail is squared on to an arbor and the rack is on the back plate (figure 7/20), with the rack spring between the plates. Locking is effected by the downward movement of the rack hook after the last stroke. The quarter striking is controlled by a count wheel, and pins projecting from the face of the latter depress a warning lever squared on to an arbor carrying a lever to raise the rack hook and a warning piece to intercept the warning wheel. The warning lever is released by the count wheel just as the latter comes to rest. The quarter striking is let off by four pins in the minute wheel (figure 7/19).

4. Smith, *Dialogues*, p. 50.

In the back view (figure 7/20) note the cut-away section to enable the pallets to be withdrawn without the complicated manoeuvre so often required. The engraving round the square aperture for the pallet arbor, matching that round the calendar aperture, is a rare feature. The next view (figure 7/21) shows the pins in the count wheel and some of the decorative steel work. Because of the hammer position, the quarter striking train winds anti-clockwise and has a plain barrel. The hour striking needs a five wheel train (figure 7/22) because eight days of grande sonnerie is equal to thirty-two days of normal hour striking, so winding is again anti-clockwise. If, at the design stage, the two striking trains had been transposed, their direction of running would have been reversed and all trains would have wound clockwise. Then all the barrels could have been grooved — evidently the barrel grooving engine used here could not cut a reversed groove. As has been indicated, the movement contains many interesting features as is often the case with the better quality provincial work.

The case (figure 7/23) is of walnut veneered on pine and is of provincial origin, indicated by the pine carcase and slightly clumsy proportions of the hood. The caddy top is a restoration and the skirting round the plinth covering the lower crossbanding indicates that it should have bun feet. This is confirmed by figure 4/50 which shows the sockets for the front feet, the rear sockets presumably having been broken away. Note the cushion moulding on the hood. The height is 7ft. 2ins. excluding the finial.

Figure 7/24. 12ins. dial of grande sonnerie striking and chiming clock by Dan. Quare, no. 145, c.1716-18. Typical Quare calendar in arch. The right hand subsidiary dial, marked 'Hours & Quarters/Silent' is to silence the striking and chiming at the quarters and the left hand one, marked 'Strike hours alone/ Silent' is for silencing the hour striking also. Note the widely spaced winding squares for the month movement. Case is shown in Colour Plate 10.

Figure 7/25. Quare movement showing chiming train. Note anti-clockwise winding of five wheel trains.

From an example by a relatively unknown maker we now pass to one by a Royal maker, Daniel Quare. Figure 7/24 shows the 12ins. dial with a reserve[5] inscribed '145 Dañ: Quare London.' The clock presumably dates from just before 1718 when Quare's ex-apprentice Stephen Horseman joined him in partnership. The dial and hands are typical of the period 1715-25 and the calendar in the arch is very much a Quare feature. The right hand subsidiary dial marked 'Hours & Quarters/Silent' is to silence the striking and chiming at the quarters. The left hand dial marked 'Strike hours alone/Silent' is for shutting off the hour striking also. So that silencing can be effected without upsetting the sequence, rack and snail are used to control both hours and quarters. This also provides quarter repeating facilities when required.

The movement (figure 7/25) is of month duration, an outstanding achievement for grande sonnerie as the hour striking is required to strike 18,736 blows per winding. The chiming on six bells consists of straight runs up and down the scale, the more tuneful 'change ringing' type of chime is not normally used until much later in the century. The movement is of high quality with all trains winding anti-clockwise.

The case (see Colour Plate 10) is superbly proportioned and is approximately 8ft. 10ins. excluding the central finial. The oak carcase is veneered with walnut and arabesque marquetry of holly or other light coloured wood in a walnut ground, which is even applied to all the main mouldings and the columns.[6] The next view (figure 7/26) shows more clearly the marquetry, the mouldings and the panelling of the sides. It also shows the exceptionally fine frets in frieze, caddy and side windows. Mention was made earlier that the clock was equipped for repeating and the small hole with brass bushing, on the left near the top of the trunk, was provided for the repeating cord.

5. Although this looks like an applied plaque, it can be seen from figure 7/25 that it is in fact flush with the dial plate.
6. Detailed views of the marquetry are shown in figures 5/35-37.

Figure 7/26. Hood of Quare clock showing fine marquetry and very detailed frets. Note panelling of sides with herring-bone-banding. Small bushed hole on left near top of trunk provided for repeating cord.

ROMAN STRIKING

Joseph Knibb invented a system of striking on two bells which has become known as Roman striking because the small higher pitched bell represents the Is and the large lower pitched bell represents the Vs in the Roman notation. Thus one, two and three are represented by those numbers of blows on the small bell, four by one on the small bell followed by one on the large bell, and five by one blow on the large bell. The complete notation is shown in figure 7/27 which represents the rim of the pin wheel with pins projecting on the appropriate sides to operate the hammers of the small or the large bell.

Because the striking is rather confusing it did not become popular and its use was almost entirely restricted to Knibb. Its great advantage is the saving in the power required as it takes only thirty strokes for twelve hours compared with seventy-eight for normal striking. It was used for month and three month clocks of which Knibb made quite a number. A three month Roman strike uses only a sixth more power than a month ordinary strike, which is important as it is much more difficult to make a clock strike satisfactorily for longer than a month than to arrange for a longer going period. For this reason three month striking clocks are rare and six or twelve month examples almost non-existent.

Figure 7/28 shows the month movement of a clock of c.1685 by Joseph Knibb. The distinctive spacing of the count wheel notches is clearly shown and its crossing out is a typical Knibb feature. The large pin wheel has the pins to lift the hammer for the small bell on the right and those for the hammer of the large bell on the left. The pendulum suspension has the wing or butterfly nut adjustment which Knibb normally used with a 1¼ seconds pendulum. Making the pendulum detachable as shown has the great advantage of not exposing the suspension to the risk of damage during transport.

The case (figure 7/29) is a typical Knibb example of the period with beautifully matched walnut veneers, a typical simple fret and a low caddy top which should probably have three flattened ball finials of gilt metal. It is 6ft. 7ins. high. Note the IV on the chapter ring which always indicates that the clock has Roman striking.

STRIKING DIRECT FROM THE MOTION WORK

A few longcase clocks, mostly of long duration and without striking trains, struck one at each hour, a method usually described as a 'passing strike.' This is of limited use but does draw attention to the passage of time and was popular on Victorian skeleton clocks. A pin, or preferably a smooth snail, mounted on the minute wheel is arranged to lift gradually a hammer which is released at the hour. In the case of a year clock the lifting action must be very smooth and spread over as much of the hour as possible or the clock will stop.

The principle just described is used to provide quarter striking on the thirty-hour clock shown in figure 7/30. The 9½ins. dial is signed on the chapter ring 'Jos[e] Kirk of Harstoft.' Loomes[7] quotes an I. Kirk, Harstoft, date unknown, who is probably the same man as the initials J and I were interchangeable. Loomes also records Joseph Kirk, Skegby, c.1730, who again is probably the same maker, for Hardstoft and Skegby are villages a few miles apart in the Mansfield district of Nottinghamshire. This clock is probably appreciably earlier than the 1730 quoted above.

The movement has an internal rack with its tail projecting through the cut-away section of the front plate and going behind the huge snail, with the tip just visible behind the minute hand. The spring loaded lifting piece has a tail to the right which suggests that hour repeating was originally provided, probably using the spare holes just below the snail. In fact, repeating almost certainly provides the reason for rack striking on a thirty-hour clock.

Quarter striking uses three bells, the largest being at the front and the hammer tails are arranged to lie side by side. There are three graduated lifting pins in the minute wheel. The

7. B. Loomes, *Watchmakers and Clockmakers of the World*, Vol. 2, 1976, p. 135.

SMALL BELL   LARGE BELL

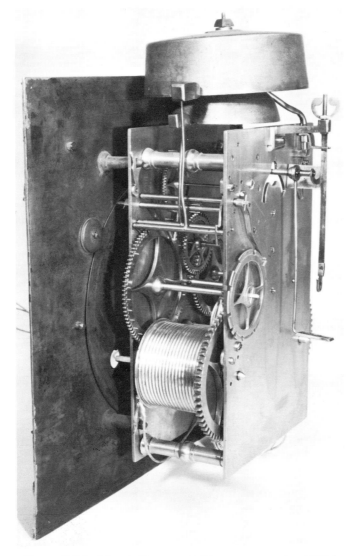

Figure 7/27. Layout of pins in pin wheel for Roman striking; compare with 7/28. Note that twelve hours requires only thirty blows against seventy-eight for normal striking.

Figure 7/28. Month Roman striking movement c.1685 by Joseph Knibb. Note distinctive count wheel with typical Knibb crossing out, also large pin wheel with pins on right for hammer of small bell and on left for hammer of large bell. Good quality movement with latched pillars and dial fret, and typical Knibb wing nut adjustment on suspension.

Figure 7/29. Beautifully proportioned case of Knibb clock. Well matched veneers, true pair of twist columns, typical Knibb feet. Low caddy probably had flattened ball finials of gilt metal. Height 6ft. 7ins. Note simple, elegant dial with IV on chapter ring which always indicates Roman striking.

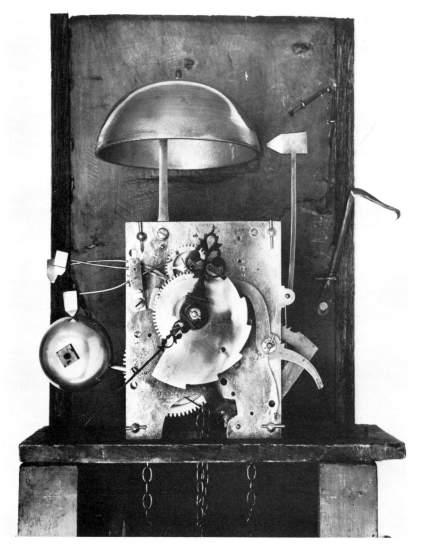

Figure 7/30. Thirty-hour movement with quarter striking direct from the motion work, by Joseph Kirk, Hardstoft, early eighteenth century. Internal rack with its tail behind the huge snail and the tip just visible behind the minute hand. Would have had hour repeating, note tail to spring loaded lifting piece and spare holes just below snail. Quarter striking on three bells with hammer tails side by side and three graduated pins in minute wheel. Shortest pin for first quarter lifts only rear hammer for smallest bell. Middle size pin for half past lifts hammers for smallest and middle bells. Longest pin at third quarter lifts all three hammers. Stud in snail operates calendar once a day via a star wheel. Note iron hook to support rising hood.

Figure 7/31. Ebonised pine case of Kirk clock, height 6ft. 8ins. Many seventeenth century features, but puzzling broken pediment if original. Pleasing dial and hands.

Figure 7/32. Roughly made thirty-hour two hand movement with rack striking to provide repeating. Spring loaded lever on right raises lifting piece when pulled down. Movement has reversed trains, going on right with centre pinion. Note bodged rack and rack hook. Spring stud on rack tail may indicate an early eighteenth century date.

Figure 7/33. Key wound thirty-hour striking and alarm clock by Thomas Johnson, c.1680. 10ins. dial with fine quality engraving, note usual Arabic numerals on alarm setting disc. Movement with latched plates, anchor escapement and usual pull up winding for alarm.

shortest pin, for the first quarter, lifts only the rear hammer, so one blow is sounded on the smallest bell. At half past, the medium length pin lifts the two hammers nearest the rear, so the smallest and middle bell are each struck once. At the third quarter all three hammers are lifted so each bell is struck once. The hammer tails are graduated in length so that they are released in sequence starting from the rear. A stud in the snail operates the calendar once a day via a star wheel with pins on alternate teeth.

The ebonised case is substantially built of pine and has a rising hood with large side windows. Note the spring loaded catch on the right hand side to hold the hood. The spoon lock for securing the hood when the trunk door is closed is just visible at the bottom left of the photograph. The case (figure 7/31) has many seventeenth century features, but the broken pediment, if original, is something of a puzzle. The height is 6ft. 8ins. Due to the delay in adopting new styles and technical innovations country clocks are notoriously difficult to date but this one is probably c.1710-20.

REPEATING

As stated earlier, repeating was applied to bracket clocks from 1676 and eventually superseded other methods of telling the time in the dark, such as grande sonnerie striking. Quarter repeating, that is indicating the last hour and the number of quarters which have since elapsed, is normal on bracket clocks but is very rare on longcase clocks. A year timepiece with this facility is described in Chapter 12.

Hour repeating was provided on many clocks, which of course needed to have rack striking. Occasionally an early clock was converted from count wheel to rack to provide repeating, an example being the Gould shown in figures 4/44-48. Quite a number of thirty-hour clocks exist with rack striking which was provided so that they could repeat and a rough example is shown in figure 7/32. On the right is a spring loaded lever to which a cord was attached. When operated this raised the lifting piece and when released the clock struck the last hour providing the same step of the snail was still opposite the rack tail. This is obviously a rough-and-ready method depending on how accurately the steps of the snail are cut to length and how carefully the motion work is assembled. To overcome the uncertainty of whether the last or the next hour would be repeated, a few makers mounted the snail on a star wheel which was stepped on smartly just before the clock warned for the hour. A good quality thirty-hour clock with this refinement is shown in figure 10/21. The repeating lever has a restoring spring to ensure that it does not remain operated and thus cause a failure of striking.

Eight-day clocks had similar repeating arrangements but many of the levers and their springs have been removed by repairers from both eight-day and thirty-hour clocks. A cord attached to the lever was led out of the case, sometimes in the waist, but sometimes it was led round a pulley and then out through the top of the hood and through the ceiling to an upstairs room, see figure 9/82. A rocking lever was also arranged to respond to an upward pull.

Quarter striking or chiming clocks were also arranged to repeat hours and quarters by letting off their rack controlled hour and quarter trains. The clocks by Thorne (figure 7/10), Cobham (figures 7/12 and 13) and Quare (figure 7/26) are provided with this facility.

ALARM WORK

Many early lantern clocks were provided with alarm as well as striking, but when the longcase clock was introduced it did not usually incorporate an alarm, or alarum to use an old name. In general the facility was provided by small lantern timepieces, some of which had oak travelling cases as in the Graham clock in figure 4/60. Another solution was the hooded wall timepiece alarm developed from the lantern clock. However a few longcase clocks were

Figure 7/34. Anonymous thirty-hour alarm time-piece with 7ins. dial, probably c.1710-20. Rope sprocket on crown wheel, verge with cranked top and double ended hammer inside bell. Alarm normally locked by pin in crown wheel and short arm on alarm control arbor. At appropriate time pin in disc carried round by hour wheel raises long arm of alarm control arbor thus releasing alarm. Note cast openings in dial plate and plate frame, both mainly but not exclusively north country features.

Figure 7/35. Spring night clock with striking and alarm, by John Hilderson, c.1665. Probably the earliest type with dial and hands for day time as well as a perforated disc carried by the hour wheel and lit from behind for night time. Time is read off against key-hole shaped aperture at top. Wrongly assembled as hands and disc do not agree.

made with alarms and one of c.1665-70 by Andrew Prime is illustrated in figure 2/23.

Figure 7/33 shows an example of c.1680 signed 'Thomas Johnson Londini Fecit.' Although a thirty-hour movement it is key wound like the Tompion movement in figure 4/13, but the usual pull up winding is employed for the alarm. The 10ins. dial has fine quality tulip engraving and the movement has latched plates and an anchor escapement.

The clock has lost its original case which raises the possibility of it having been a wall clock originally, but if the anchor escapement and long pendulum are original this is unlikely as seventeenth century makers provided such clocks with verge escapements and short pendulums.

Provincial makers made more longcase alarm clocks than the London makers but even so they are rare from any period.

The usual alarm mechanism consists of a rope or chain pulley acting direct on a crown wheel with vertical verge, the latter having a bent over top with a double ended hammer which operates inside the bell. This is the same arrangement as that shown on the lantern clock in figure 1/7, and it is interesting to note that it continued in use with little change well into the nineteenth century. Figure 7/34 shows the alarm mechanism on an anonymous hooded wall timepiece with 7ins. dial and c.1710-20.

The alarm control arbor is pivoted between the dial and the extension piece screwed to the back plate. A pin in the rim of the alarm crown wheel is intercepted by the short arm on the alarm arbor to hold the mechanism when wound. At the appropriate time a pin in a disc, associated with the alarm setting disc and carried round by the hour wheel, raises the long arm on the alarm control arbor and thus releases the alarm.

NIGHT CLOCKS

All the methods so far considered in this chapter announced the time by audible signals, but one solution which gave a visual indication in the dark merits a description. A quotation from the diary of Samuel Pepys is worth repeating:

> 24th. June 1664 .... After dinner to Whitehall and there met with Mr. Pierce and he showed me the Queen's bed-chamber .... with a clock by her bed-side wherein a lamp burns that tells her the time of the night at any time.[8]

Night clocks were in use in Italy by about 1660[9] and were probably also being made in England soon after the application of the pendulum. English night clocks are very rare as quite soon after their introduction, the invention of repeating clocks in 1676 provided a better solution without the smell and risk of fire associated with oil lamps. Also, it is probable that night clocks suffered a high rate of wastage once they were superseded, those without normal dials and hands, especially, being much less convenient for ordinary use.

Figure 7/35 shows a spring night clock of what was probably the earliest type, the back plate being signed 'John Hilderson Londini Fecit.' It dates from about 1665 and has a normal chapter ring and hands as well as a perforated disc for night use, emphasising its dual function. The night facility is provided by a large brass disc with cut out numerals and quarter hour divisions which is mounted on the hour wheel. Part of the disc shows through a curved slot in the dial plate and the time is read off against a key-hole shaped perforation near the top of the plate. When photographed, the clock had been wrongly assembled, the times shown by the disc and the hands should, obviously, agree. The case has a glazed back so that a lamp placed behind the clock would light up the appropriate pierced numerals. In addition to hour striking, the clock is also provided with an alarm.

No longcase clock of this type has been recorded but there is or was a similar spring clock

8. This quotation has been used as evidence of night clocks in England at that date, notably by Lee in *Knibb*, p. 150.

9. Guiseppe Campani, 'Discourse of Guiseppe Campani, on his silent clocks'. See G.H. Baillie, *Clocks and Watches, an Historical Bibliography,* 1951, p. 59.

Figure 7/36. Dial 10¾ins. by 11½ins., of longcase night timepiece by Edward East, c.1670. Piercings for sixty minutes, half quarters and Roman numerals for quarter hours. Pierced Arabic numeral for hour appears on left and takes one hour to traverse slot, small arrow-head piercing points to minutes. Lamp supported on back board of case shines light through openings (7/37). Squared arbor at centre for setting to time.

Figure 7/37. Movement of East night clock. Eight latched pillars, latches for dial feet and dirt excluding plates also. Eight-day movement, disc assembly carrying numerals rotates in two hours.

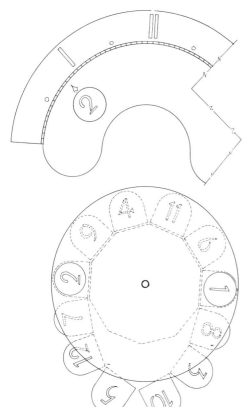

Figure 7/38. Principle of disc assembly. Ten sided wheel carrying chain of twelve hour plaques is sandwiched between two discs with round apertures diametrically opposite one another. Hour plaques assembled as shown so that when one hour number disappears on the right the next number appears on the left.

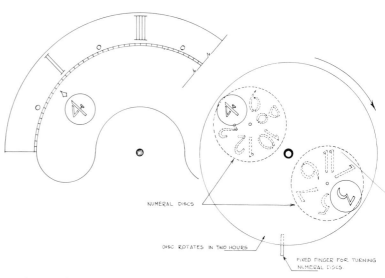

NUMERAL DISCS

DISC ROTATES IN TWO HOURS

FIXED FINGER FOR TURNING NUMERAL DISCS.

Figure 7/39. Alternative system used in some spring clocks, much simpler but gives smaller numerals for a given size of dial.

Figure 7/40. Case of East clock veneered with olive oysters and marquetry on an ebony ground. Lift up hood has sound fret but no smoke vent. Double skirting in place of bun feet and other restorations. Height 6ft. 10ins. and 10½ins. waist. Case c.1680 and not original to clock but has been with it since early this century.

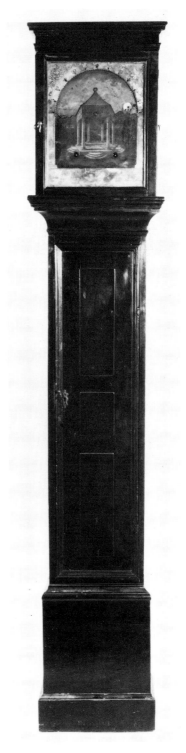

Figure 7/41. The only other known long-case night clock, with doubtful signature of Joseph Knibb. Similar display to East clock but size of numerals suggests it uses mechanism of 7/39. Dial plate pierced with five minute numerals and with painting in centre. Latched movement with outside count wheel striking. Ebonised case, rising hood, height 6ft. 5ins.

by Edward East.[10] It is not at present known what connections there were between the two makers but Hilderson's work normally closely resembles that of East and the clock described above is no exception.

The night clock just described gives only an approximate reading of the time, like a one hand clock, but an improved design was introduced into this country from Italy, probably c.1670. The dial of a longcase example of about that date signed 'Eduardus East Londini' is shown in figure 7/36. It measures 10¾ins. wide by 11½ins. high and is beautifully engraved. The outer edge of the semi-circular opening has sixty slits for the minutes and piercings for the quarters and half quarters. A pierced Arabic numeral for the hour appears on the left and takes one hour to traverse the slot, a small arrow-head piercing pointing to the minutes. As the hour numeral disappears on the right the next one appears on the left. The squared arbor near the bottom of the dial is for winding the movement and the upper one (at the centre of the semi-circle) is for setting to time.

Figure 7/37 shows the eight pillar latched movement with sloping cover plates to protect it from dust as well as from smuts or oil drips from the lamp. The latter was supported on a metal bracket on the back board so that its light was approximately level with the dial piercings. The numerals are carried round on a ten-sided wheel as shown in figure 7/38. The wheel carrying the numerals is sandwiched between two discs each provided with two diametrically opposite circular holes, with the discs positioned so that the holes coincide. The assembly rotates once in two hours and the numerals are pierced in twelve plaques which are linked together as shown. In the diagram 1 is just disappearing on the right as 2 emerges on the left. The numerals are arranged so that each successive hour is five places behind the previous one. This ingenious design is necessary so that the numerals appear in turn at the appropriate apertures. The drawing of this mechanism and the accompanying description in *Cescinsky and Webster* (pp. 128-9) are both rather misleading.

East used this mechanism in at least one spring driven clock, but some other makers including Joseph Knibb used two rotating discs, one behind each aperture in the large disc (figure 7/39). The latter idea was also used in the late seventeenth century 'wandering hour' watches.

The present case (figure 7/40) is of oak veneered with olive oysters and with panels of marquetry on an ebony ground. The lift up hood has no smoke vent in the top, and the presence of a sound fret indicates that the case was intended for a striking clock. The double skirting is a replacement for bun feet and there are other restorations. The case stands 6ft. 10ins. high and has a 10½ins. waist. Its probable date is c.1680 and it has certainly been associated with the clock since early this century.

The only other longcase night clock known to have survived is shown in figure 7/41. The dial employs a similar display of wandering hour figures but the dial plate is pierced with five minute numbers and there is a moralising verse and the apparently spurious inscription 'Joseph Knibb Londini Fecit' at the base. The dial centre has a painting somewhat similar to those found on Knibb spring night clocks. The latched movement has hour striking with an outside count wheel and a bell between the plates.

The case is ebonised, has a rising hood and a lamp shelf on the back board. The height is 6ft. 5ins.

10. H. Cescinsky, *The Old English Master Clockmakers and their Clocks*, 1938, p. 124.

Chapter 8

THE QUEST FOR ACCURACY

The anchor escapement with seconds or longer pendulum gave sufficiently accurate results for all normal domestic purposes, although it must not be forgotten that there was no quick and easy way of verifying the time such as exists today in the form of radio and telephone time signals. The main demand for more accurate timekeepers came from astronomers who needed to be able to record precisely the apparent motions of the heavenly bodies as a step towards solving the urgent problem of finding the longitude at sea. There was also a number of amateur astronomers with their private observatories who would be equally interested in accurate time measurement.

In this chapter a survey will be made of the main improvements in longcase clock design until the middle of the eighteenth century.

MAINTAINING POWER

The need for maintaining power[1] is discussed in Chapter 2, p. 32, and the third reason for its provision applies in the context of this chapter, that is to avoid the clock losing time during winding.

Bolt and shutter maintaining power, fully described in Chapter 2, is the type usually found throughout the period. Huygens endless cord maintaining power was very little used in English precision clocks.

John Harrison, who made the first successful marine timekeepers[2] invented a fully automatic device by 1735[3] which was not popular during the period under review but later became the standard method for precision clocks, watches and chronometers. The principle is shown in figure 8/1 and the device is often known as the going ratchet or occasionally as the perpetual ratchet. The pawl for the barrel ratchet is mounted on a larger or going ratchet with fine teeth facing in the opposite direction from those of the barrel ratchet. During normal running, power is transmitted from the going ratchet to the great wheel through the springs which are therefore compressed. The teeth of the going ratchet pass freely under the large pawl which is on an arbor pivoted between the plates. When the clock is wound this pawl prevents clockwise rotation of its ratchet and the energy stored in the compressed springs causes the great wheel to continue to drive the clock. Maintaining power is normally available considerably longer than is required for winding. The going ratchet has fine teeth to ensure minimum loss of energy when winding commences. The maintaining springs must be strong enough to drive the clock but not so strong that the weight is unable to compress them. Before winding it is a good idea to exert slight reverse pressure on the key to ensure that the springs are fully compressed. Figure 8/2 shows a nineteenth century example from a clock by Walsh of Newbury.

---

1. Some earlier writers (e.g. in *Rees's Clocks and Watches and Chronometers,* 1819-20, reprint 1970) used this term for the normal driving power and called the bolt and shutter mechanism a forcing spring.

2. See H. Quill, *John Harrison, the man who found Longitude,* 1966, and W.S. Laycock, *The Lost Science of John 'Longitude' Harrison,* 1976.

3. It was first used in his first sea clock (H.1) of that date.

MORE ACCURATE ESCAPEMENTS

The most important improvement in clock mechanism during the period was undoubtedly the introduction of more accurate escapements. In particular, the dead beat escapement gives remarkably consistent results and remained the standard escapement for precision clocks until Riefler's almost free pendulum of 1893 superseded it for observatory use.

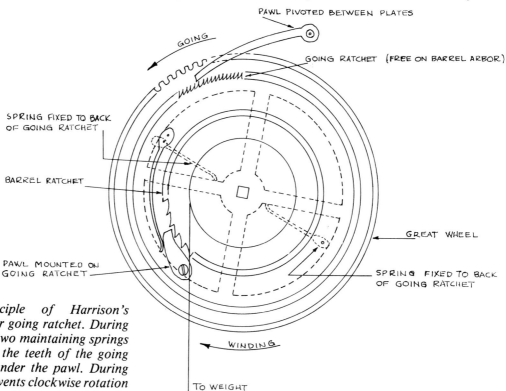

Figure 8/1. Principle of Harrison's maintaining power or going ratchet. During normal running the two maintaining springs are compressed and the teeth of the going ratchet pass freely under the pawl. During winding the pawl prevents clockwise rotation of the going ratchet and the springs drive the clock.

Figure 8/2. Harrison's maintaining power on a clock by Walsh of Newbury, 1836.

The dead beat escapement

George Graham is usually credited with the invention of the dead beat escapement, c.1720, but Howse[4] has proved that in 1675-78 different forms of dead beat escapement were being tested on the two Tompion year timepieces at the new Greenwich observatory and elsewhere. The source of this information is a long series of letters from John Flamsteed, first Astronomer Royal, to Richard Towneley an important scientist living in Lancashire who had evidently designed such an escapement. Figure 8/3 shows three-quarter size a tracing taken by Flamsteed in 1675 of the escapement of a Tompion clock owned by Sir Jonas Moore (Flamsteed's patron). Howse commissioned a working model from the drawing, which indeed bears a close resemblance to a type of dead beat escapement, with teeth on the side of the wheel, which is found on a number of late eighteenth century turret clocks, probably because it is less liable to damage than the conventional form.

4. D. Howse, 'The Tompion clocks at Greenwich and the Dead-beat Escapement', *Antiquarian Horology*, VII (December 1970, March 1971), pp. 18, 114.

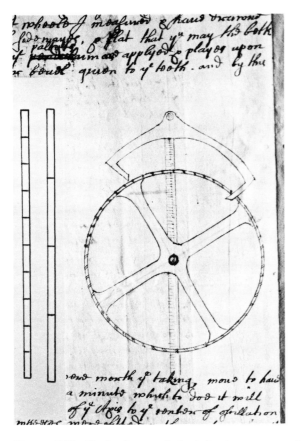

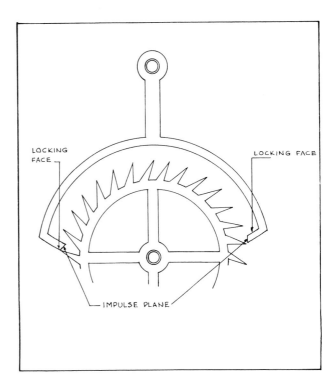

Figure 8/3. Early form of deat beat escapement shown in a tracing of the escapement of a Tompion clock owned by Sir Jonas Moore. It was taken by Flamsteed in 1675.

Figure 8/4. Dead beat escapement as invented by Graham. In this early version the pallets embrace the maximum of fourteen teeth, while later examples embrace as few as ten or even eight, depending on the quality of the movement.

As both the Tompion year clocks were eventually made into domestic clocks with one second pendulums replacing the original two second ones, they have necessarily lost their early escapements. However the absence of any known surviving dead beat escapements earlier than Graham's of c.1720[5] suggests that they may not have been very successful and justifies Howse's conclusion that Graham should be credited with the first successful dead beat escapement. It is of interest that he apparently never published any claim to its invention.

The principle of Graham's escapement is shown in figure 8/4. Essentially each pallet consists of a short impulse plane having an angle similar to that of a recoil pallet and a long locking face which is part of a circle concentric with the pallet arbor. As shown in the drawing the pendulum has swung to the right and the point of an escape wheel tooth is resting on the locking face of the entry pallet (on left). When the pendulum commences to swing to the left, the tooth will slide down the impulse plane thus imparting energy to the pendulum and will then escape. A tooth will then drop on to the locking face of the exit pallet (on right), and during the supplementary arc the tooth will slide along the locking face with the wheel remaining stationary. When the pendulum again swings to the right, the tooth will slide down the impulse face of the exit pallet and will then escape and another tooth will drop on to the locking face of the entry pallet. In the escapement shown in figure 8/4 the pallets embrace the maximum of fourteen teeth, which was the early arrangement,[6]

5. See A.J. Turner 'The Introduction of the Dead-beat Escapement: a new document', *Antiquarian Horology*, VIII (December 1972), p.71. Since this was written an early Tompion dead beat escapement has been found in Holland.

6. See 'Observations on the New Scaping for Clocks and Watches', *The Gentleman's Magazine* (September 1754), reprinted *Antiquarian Horology*, VII (September 1972), p. 720. This shows the pallets embracing twelve teeth.

but later examples were made to embrace only ten or even eight teeth. Pallets spanning the smaller number give the best results in a high grade movement but those embracing more teeth work better in a lower quality movement such as a domestic clock.

The escapement requires a heavy pendulum for satisfactory operation so the latter is often hung from a stout bracket on the back board of the case. In high grade clocks the pallets are usually jewelled with agate, sapphire, or other hard stone. To protect the pallets and the escape wheel, maintaining power is necessary, as the momentum of the heavy pendulum can cause serious damage. Surprisingly, a number of house clocks with dead beat escapements but without maintaining power have survived quite well.

The excellent performance of Graham's escapement arises mainly from the absence of recoil which leaves the pendulum almost free from interference from the escapement except during impulsing. The lack of recoil has the effect that any increase in power reaching the escapement causes an increase in the arc of vibration, which results in the clock losing. This is the opposite effect from that obtained with an anchor escapement where the increased recoil limits the increase in supplementary arc and accelerates the pendulum. With the dead beat escapement, the effect of circular error arising from variations in driving power can be made very small by designing the escapement to operate satisfactorily with a total arc of 3° whereas the recoil type needs 5° to 10°.

The opposite reactions of the recoil and dead beat escapements to variations in driving power led to the development of the half dead beat escapement.[7] This has impulse planes as in the dead beat type but the locking faces are made to give a small amount of recoil. It gives excellent results in bracket clocks but was little used (if at all) in longcases, where variations in the driving force should be much smaller.

7. See W.H. Gazeley, *Clock and Watch Escapements,* 1956, p. 90; also *Rees's Clocks Watches and Chronometers,* 1819-20, reprint 1970, pp. 201, 215, where it is attributed to F. Berthoud.

Figure 8/5. Movement by Daniel Delander showing duplex escapement. Small escape wheel between plates for impulsing, large escape wheel outside back plate for locking. Note bolt and shutter maintaining power and long Tompion style crutch.

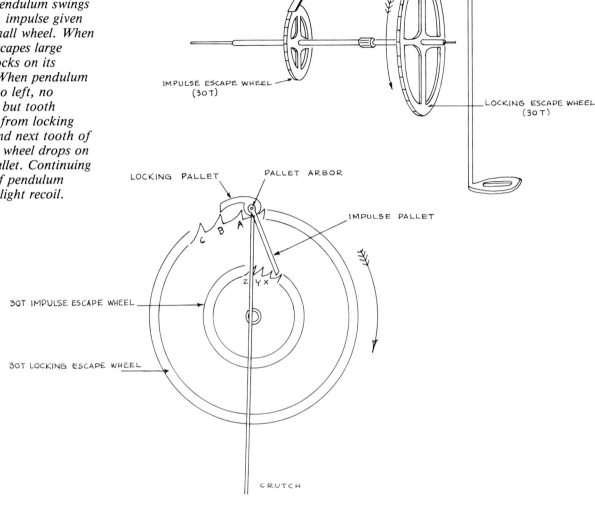

Figure 8/6. Principle of duplex escapement. When pendulum swings to right, impulse given from small wheel. When tooth escapes large wheel locks on its pallet. When pendulum swings to left, no impulse but tooth escapes from locking pallet and next tooth of impulse wheel drops on to its pallet. Continuing swing of pendulum causes slight recoil.

The duplex escapement

Daniel Delander, a noted clockmaker who had been a journeyman with Thomas Tompion, made a number of clocks with an ingenious escapement with two wheels which bears some resemblance to the early form of the well known duplex escapement used in watches. Delander's escapement pre-dates that used in watches and he deserves credit for its design although he apparently never published any report of his work.

Figure 8/5 is a side view of a movement by Delander incorporating his escapement. Note the bolt and shutter maintaining power necessary to protect the escapement and the extra long crutch probably resulting from Delander's association with Tompion. There are two escape wheels each of thirty teeth on the same arbor, a normal sized one between the plates for impulsing and a very large one outside the back plate for locking. The movement has been pulled forward for photographing.

The upper part of figure 8/6 shows the layout and the lower part explains the action of the escapement. The front faces of the teeth of both escape wheels are radial and the pallet arbor is planted at the circumference of the locking wheel with a section cut away to allow the teeth to pass. As shown in the lower part of figure 8/6, tooth B has just escaped from the locking pallet and tooth X has come into contact with the impulse pallet. With the pendulum

Figure 8/7. 12ins. dial of duplex escapement clock by Daniel Delander, No. 6, c.1715. Note seconds ring numbered 6, 12, 18, etc. to agree with two second steps of hand, but still divided into sixty. Late use of divisions extended through two figure numbers on seconds and chapter rings.

now swinging to the right, tooth X gives impulse until it finally escapes and then tooth C drops on to the locking pallet. The supplementary swing causes no recoil due to the positioning of the pallet arbor. When the pendulum swings to the left, tooth C escapes and tooth Y drops on to the impulse pallet. Further movement of the pendulum to the left causes recoil as tooth Y slides up the pallet.

To summarise, as the pendulum swings to the right the escape wheels move forward one tooth, that is two seconds on the dial, and then remains stationary. When the pendulum swings to the left, nothing happens until near the end of the swing when a small forward movement is followed by a slight recoil.

The pendulum has an unusually heavy bob and is provided with a graduated rating nut and a steel rod.

The escapement has a number of features which should ensure accurate timekeeping. The pendulum is more independent of the escapement, receiving impulse only on alternate swings and the large locking wheel exerts only a light pressure on its pallet, thus reducing frictional drag. Also the limited recoil should help to even out variations in the driving force. Against this, the escapement requires a large arc of vibration, some 10°, which involves the risk of serious circular error. Unfortunately the author has not had sufficient experience of this escapement to be able to assess its performance accurately.

Figure 8/7 shows the 12ins. dial of this clock, with plaque engraved 'Dan. Delander London No. 6.' The seconds ring is divided into sixty as usual but is numbered 6, 12, 18, etc., to accord with the two second steps of the hand. The extension of the divisions through the two figure numbers of both seconds and chapter rings is a very late use of a feature which was popular until about 1690.

The case (figure 8/8) is approximately 8ft. high to the top of the central gilt wooden finial and is of oak veneered with burr walnut. The raised panel in the plinth became popular later but is unusual at this date, that is c.1715.

Figure 8/8. Delander case of 8/7 veneered with burr walnut, height approximately 8ft. overall. Note early use of raised panel on plinth.

Delander made a number of these clocks with his duplex movement and they are numbered serially on the oval name plate. A fine example of c.1725, no. 17, is shown in figure 9/37. In contrast to these special clocks, Delander normally did not number his productions which had more conventional escapements.

The grasshopper escapement

As explained above, Graham obtained his excellent results by eliminating recoil and the circular error arising from a large arc of vibration. The Harrison brothers, John and James, were not inhibited by any formal horological training and by 1726 they had produced an unconventional escapement, later known as the grasshopper which, in spite of a large escaping arc (some 10°) and a fairly large recoil, produced outstandingly good results.[8]

Figure 8/9 shows the principles of this escapement. The pallet arbor carries a frame which supports a pair of pallet arms on a common pivot. These pallet arms are weighted so that they come to rest clear of the escape wheel teeth. A pair of controllers are mounted on the same pivot and these are made just heavy enough to overcome the weights on the pallet arms. The travel of the controllers is limited by stop pins in the pallet frame, so a free pallet takes up a position determined by its controller stop pin.

As shown in the drawing, the pendulum is at the right hand limit of its swing and the exit pallet is engaged on a tooth of the escape wheel. As the pendulum swings to the left the escape wheel exerts a pull on the pallet and rotation of the pallet frame lowers the entry pallet into the path of a tooth on the escape wheel. When the pallet has engaged a tooth, further movement of the pendulum and pallet frame, by reducing the angle between the

8. For an excellent description and assessment of this escapement see H. Quill, 'The Grasshopper Escapement', *Antiquarian Horology,* VII (September, 1971), pp. 288-296.

Figure 8/9. Principle of the Harrison grasshopper escapement. With the pendulum moving to the left the right hand pallet intercepts a tooth, and continuing movement of the pendulum causes recoil of the escape wheel and the left hand pallet then springs clear of the wheel. The reverse swing of the pendulum produces a similar sequence of operations. There is no drop of the teeth on to the pallets nor any sliding action so no oil is necessary.

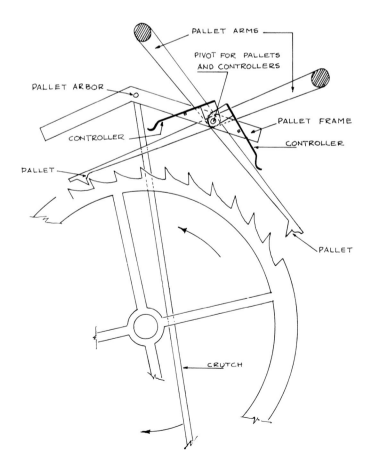

Figure 8/10. James Harrison movement of 1728 with grasshopper escapement. Brass escape wheel but all other wheels of oak and pinions with brass-pivoted lignum vitae rollers. Arbors have brass pivots in lignum vitae bushes, so no oil required. Essential maintaining power operates on pins in third wheel (top left). Harrison gridiron pendulum.

frame and the entry pallet, causes the latter to make the escape wheel recoil. As soon as this happens the exit pallet loses contact with the escape wheel and the pallet quickly lifts clear of the wheel due to its counterweight. It then drops to its final position as determined by the controller. The reverse swing of the pendulum produces a similar sequence of operations which does not need further description.

This escapement is remarkable in several ways: the pallets engage the escape wheel without any drop, so it is therefore silent in operation and wear is greatly reduced; there is no sliding action between pallets and wheel teeth, so oil is not required. The Harrisons used lignum vitae pallets on oak arms with a gold pivot pin, all without lubrication. For satisfactory operation a total pendulum arc of about 12° is necessary and cycloidal cheeks, as invented by Huygens, were used to minimise circular error, together with other devices to reduce friction and eliminate the need for oil in any part of the clock.

In spite of their theoretical shortcomings, the Harrison longcase clocks performed extremely well and a variation of not more than one second a month with a total error of less than thirty seconds in fourteen years was obtained. However, the escapement is difficult to make and to adjust, and is liable to destroy itself if power be temporarily removed from the escape wheel as this causes disengagement of both pallets. Turning back the hands against a stiff clutch or failure of the maintaining power can provoke this catastrophe.

The grasshopper escapement never became popular but Benjamin Vulliamy took it up and developed several variations, examples of which survive, including a fine regulator made for George III's private observatory, now in the British Museum.

Figure 8/10 shows the wooden movement of an eight-day striking clock by James Harrison.[9] The brass escape wheel and the grasshopper pallets are visible towards the top of the photograph and the bent wire attached to the pallet arbor is the crutch. The other wheels each consist of an oak disc with a

9. A detailed description of Harrison's clock movements and his working methods is given in W. Andrews, 'John Harrison, a Study of his Early Work', *Horological Dialogues*, I (1979), p. 11. *Horological Dialogues* is published by the American Section of the Antiquarian Horological Society.

Figure 8/11. James Harrison clock, signed on dial arch and signed and dated 1728 on calendar wheel. Silvered chapter ring and steel hands, ebonised and gilt wooden dial. Case 7ft. 4ins. high, ebonised and with restored gilt decoration. Note blocks over cut-outs in sides of trunk to allow for large pendulum arc, suggesting case may have been intended for an anchor escapement. Door has equation table in John Harrison's writing.

groove in its rim in which are glued pieces of oak with the grain radial and each shaped into three or four teeth. The lantern pinions have loose lignum vitae rollers on brass pivots and the arbors have brass pivots running in lignum vitae bushes. Due to the greasy nature of the lignum vitae and the properties of the escapement no lubrication is required. A Harrison type of bolt and shutter maintaining power is used, the suspension has adjustable brass cheeks and the pendulum is to Harrison's gridiron design. The striking is controlled by a count wheel formed on the great wheel.

The dial (figure 8/11) is of ebonised wood with gilt decoration and is signed in the arch 'Barrow James Harrison.' There is a conventional silvered chapter ring with steel hands and the seconds and the date are shown through apertures. The calendar wheel bears the additional signature 'James Harrison 3rd 1728 Barrow.'

The case is obviously the work of a joiner, not of a casemaker, and has a rather short trunk and tall plinth. The trunk door is unusually shaped for a period when a square or break arch top would be normal. The sides of the trunk have been cut away to accommodate the wide swing of the pendulum, a modification which suggests that the Harrisons may have originally intended the case for a movement with an anchor escapement which they used on earlier clocks. Like the dial, the case is ebonised with gilt decoration and has been restored, some of the decoration having a strangely Edwardian appearance. The height is 7ft. 4ins. The glazed panel on the trunk door contains an equation table in John Harrison's handwriting which has been corrected for the adoption of the Gregorian calendar.

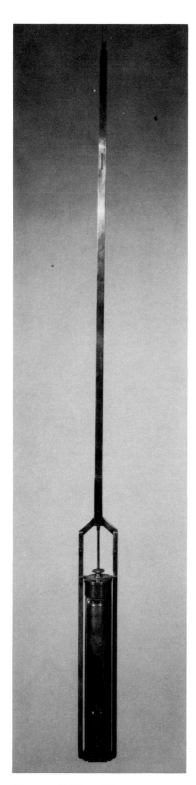

Figure 8/12. Mercury compensated pendulum from a Graham regulator. This example has a brass rod, but no rating nut as there is a micrometer adjustment to the suspension.

TEMPERATURE COMPENSATION

As other sources of error were reduced it became evident that changes of temperature affected timekeeping and as early as 1705 a writer to the French Royal Academy[10] reported his conclusions that the main cause of variations in timekeeping was the expansion and contraction of the pendulum rod by changes of temperature.

Detection of the effect of changes in the length of the pendulum rod must have been made more difficult by the temporary changes in viscosity of the lubricant with temperature variation as well as its fairly rapid deterioration with time.

The mercury pendulum

In 1726 Graham wrote to the Royal Society[11] to report his experiments on temperature compensation. He said that about 1715 he had investigated the differences in expansion of various metals but had found these differences insufficient for his purpose (as will be seen below, a satisfactory design was in fact being developed at about this time). Graham then accidentally discovered the large coefficient of expansion of mercury and designed a very successful pendulum. This remained standard for precision clocks until the invention in 1896 of an alloy, invar, with a practically zero coefficient of expansion.

Figure 8/12 shows the pendulum from a Graham regulator. The flat brass rod is formed into a stirrup at the lower end to support the bottom of a glass tube containing mercury. The height of the latter is so adjusted that the downward expansion of the brass rod is counteracted by the upward expansion of the mercury, so that the centre of oscillation remains at the same distance from the point of suspension. One great advantage of this design is that the quantity of mercury can readily be adjusted until the compensation is correct. As will be appreciated, a higher column of mercury will be required with a brass rod than with a steel one. In this example regulation is by a micrometer adjustment to the suspension, there being no adjustment at the bottom of the pendulum.

One minor source of error is that the rod responds more rapidly to a temperature change than the mercury and to reduce this some later regulators have a cast iron container instead of the glass one because iron is a better conductor of heat. Probably for the same reason Graham also experimented with a varnished brass tube. Another idea sometimes adopted was to divide the mercury between two narrow jars, one each side of the pendulum rod, which again reduces the response time.

The gridiron pendulum

John Harrison, working with his younger brother James, produced in 1726 two regulator clocks of outstanding accuracy. These had, in addition to his grasshopper escapement, what he called the gridiron pendulum. This resulted from considerable research into the rates of expansion of different metals from which he chose iron and brass which expand in the ratio 3:5 approximately.

10. Phillippe de la Hire, 'On the Irregularity of Pendulum Clocks', *Histoire et Mémoires de l'Académie Royale des Sciences,* 1705. See G.H. Baillie, *Clocks and Watches — an Historical Bibliography,* 1951, p. 133.

11. George Graham, 'A contrivance to avoid irregularities in a clock's motion', *Philosophical Transactions of the Royal Society,* 1726. See Baillie, *Bibliography,* p. 169.

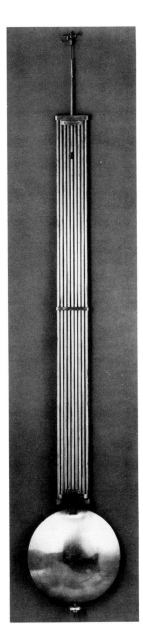

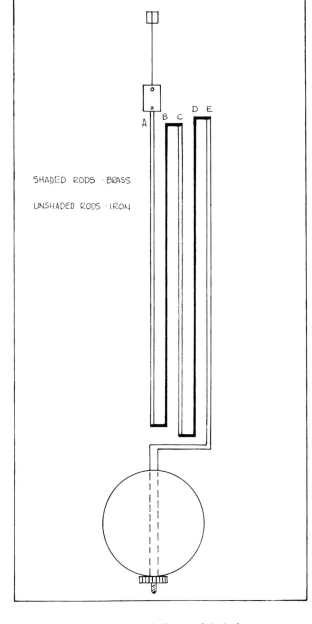

Figure 8/13. Gridiron compensation pendulum as invented by the Harrisons but from a Mudge regulator. Five rods of iron and four of brass.

SHADED RODS · BRASS

UNSHADED RODS · IRON

Figure 8/14. Principle of the gridiron pendulum. Upward expansion of brass rods B and D, plus rise in centre of gravity of bob, equals downward expansion of iron rods A, C and E plus suspension and flat through bob. Rods B, C, D and E have to be duplicated on left to balance whole assembly.

Figure 8/13 shows a gridiron pendulum made by Thomas Mudge and figure 8/14 shows the principle on which it works. The iron rod A, carrying the suspension, has its lower end joined to a brass rod B, the upper end of which is joined to another iron rod C. The lower end of C is joined to a second brass rod D, the top of which is joined to the iron rod E which carries the pendulum bob. Therefore the iron rods are in tension and expand downwards and the brass rods are in compression and expand upwards. In working out the relative lengths of the rods it is necessary to include the top portion of rod A including the suspension and the lower part of rod E including the flat through the pendulum bob, with the iron rods. Similarly, half the upward expansion of the pendulum bob[12] must be included with the brass rods. With these corrections applied, the ratio *total length of iron rods:total length of brass rods* must be the same as *coefficient of expansion of brass:coefficient of expansion of iron.* In other words, for correct compensation, *length of iron × its coefficient of expansion = length of brass × its coefficient of expansion.*

12. The centre of gravity will rise half the increase in the diameter of the bob.

In practice it is necessary to duplicate the rods shown on the other side of the rod A to balance the whole assembly, and to keep the rods parallel with one another by means of the horizontal bars shown in figure 8/13. These bars serve to unite the rods where required and have clearance holes for the other rods. For example, the top bar is fixed to the two outer rods at each side and slides freely on the central one. The central bar is fixed only to the outer rods and is provided to prevent buckling of the brass rods. If the compensation is incorrect it can be altered only by changing the effective length of the rods by moving one of the bars and if necessary fitting longer rods. Simplified versions of the pendulum were also made, having five or seven rods instead of nine. Some of the later examples used zinc instead of brass, as the greater coefficient of expansion of zinc permitted the use of fewer rods. Pendulums of this type are shown in figures 11/30 and 34.

The gridiron pendulum has been very widely used and there are examples by many well known makers such as John Shelton[13] and the Vulliamy family. It is of course, cheaper to produce than the mercury pendulum.

To appreciate the pioneer work of both Graham and Harrison it must be remembered that little was known about the expansion of metals before their researches led to the invention of almost perfect compensation devices. As already mentioned in Chapter 3 on page 50, brass pendulum rods were often provided on good quality clocks, and somewhat surprisingly several by George Graham are so equipped. A brass pendulum rod, of course, seriously increases the temperature error.

The wooden pendulum rod

It is not clear when wooden rods were first used, but they are capable of good results if well seasoned, straight grained wood is employed and it is sealed to prevent it being affected by moisture. According to Baillie,[14] Pierre Le Roy writing in 1751 reported that "several makers had used pendulum rods of ebony, walnut or boxwood, and that Graham, though inventor of the mercury compensation, always used wooden rods for his regulators". The last statement is most surprising and rather misleading, as few such Graham pendulums have been recorded.

A report to the Royal Society in 1771[15] quoted the performance of a clock by John Holmes with a deal pendulum rod. Over a period of a year the daily rate varied from a maximum gain of 2.4 seconds to a maximum loss of 1.9 seconds. The rate at the end of the year was within half a second of what it had been at the beginning.

THE EQUATION OF TIME

More accurate timekeeping served to highlight the fact that the solar day, that is the period between two successive crossings of the meridian by the sun, is by no means of constant length, although the maximum daily deviation from the mean day is only about half a minute. This variation is caused by the elliptical path of the earth round the sun together with the varying inclination of the earth's axis with respect to the sun. The result is that the sun varies between maxima of over fourteen minutes slow on February 11th and over sixteen minutes fast on November 3rd (modern calendar). The relationship between solar and mean time is known as the equation of time.

More accurate results can be obtained by measuring the earth's rotation against a distant fixed star. This gives what is known as a sidereal day which has a duration of 23 hours 56 minutes 4.1 seconds. The sidereal day is shorter than the mean solar day because the earth

13. William Stukeley's diary, 12 November 1740, refers to "Mr. Shelton's new pendulums for clocks ... after Mr. Harrison's method ..."

14. Baillie, *Bibliography,* p. 222.

15. F. Wollaston, 'An account of the going of an astronomical clock', *Philosophical Transactions of the Royal Society,* 1771. See Baillie, *Bibliography,* p. 286.

TABULA

Æquationum Dierum Naturalium

Temporis Intervalla

Inter Horas ab *Horologiis Ofcillatoriis* æquabiliter moventibus, & à *Sciotericis Solaribus* accuratis indicatas, ad Diem quemlibet fingulum Anni 1690. St. Novi, ex hibens: Futuris etiam Annis hujus fæculi, abfque fenfibili differentiâ inferviens.

Dies	Januar Mi.	Sec.	Februa Mi.	Sec.	Mart. Mi.	Sec.	April Mi.	Se.	Maii Mi.	Se.	Junii Mi.	Se.	Julii Mi.	Se.	Aug. Mi.	Se.	Sept. Mi.	Se.	Octob Mi.	Sec.	Novem Mi.	Sec.	Decemb Mi.	Sec.
1	4	42	14	20	12	37	3	44	3	20	2	50	3	04	5	35	0	31	10	30	16	01	10	02
2	5	09	14	27	12	25	3	26	3	28	2	41	3	16	5	31	0	50	10	48	16	00	9	38
3	5	36	14	32	12	12	3	08	3	35	2	31	3	27	5	27	1	09	11	06	15	59	9	14
4	6	04	14	37	11	57	2	49	3	42	2	21	3	38	5	22	1	29	11	24	15	57	8	49
5	6	30	14	41	11	43	2	31	3	47	2	11	3	48	5	16	1	49	11	41	15	55	8	23
6	6	57	14	44	11	28	2	13	3	52	2	01	3	59	5	10	2	07	11	58	15	52	7	57
7	7	23	14	47	11	13	1	55	3	56	1	51	4	09	5	03	2	27	12	14	15	48	7	31
8	7	48	14	48	10	58	1	38	4	00	1	40	4	18	4	56	2	47	12	29	15	43	7	05
9	8	12	14	49	10	42	1	21	4	03	1	28	4	27	4	48	3	08	12	45	15	37	6	38
10	8	35	14	49	10	25	1	05	4	06	1	17	4	35	4	39	3	28	13	00	15	31	6	10
11	8	59	14	48	10	08	0	49	4	09	1	05	4	43	4	30	3	48	13	14	15	23	5	42
12	9	21	14	47	9	51	0	32	4	11	0	53	4	51	4	20	4	09	13	28	15	15	5	13
13	9	43	14	45	9	34	0	16	4	12	0	40	4	58	4	10	4	29	13	42	15	05	4	45
14	10	05	14	42	9	17	0	*01	4	13	0	28	5	04	4	00	4	50	13	56	14	55	4	16
15	10	26	14	38	8	59	0	14	4	12	0	16	5	11	3	49	5	10	14	08	14	44	3	47
16	10	45	14	33	8	42	0	29	4	11	0	03	5	17	3	37	5	31	14	20	14	32	3	17
17	11	04	14	28	8	24	0	44	4	10	0	10	5	23	3	24	5	51	14	31	14	20	2	47
18	11	23	14	23	8	05	0	58	4	08	0	23	5	28	3	11	6	12	14	41	14	06	2	17
19	11	40	14	14	7	47	1	12	4	06	0	36	5	32	2	58	6	33	14	51	13	52	1	47
20	11	57	14	09	7	29	1	26	4	04	0	49	5	35	2	44	6	53	15	01	13	38	1	18
21	12	14	14	01	7	10	1	38	4	01	0	*01	5	38	2	30	7	14	15	11	13	21	0	48
22	12	30	13	52	6	52	1	51	3	57	0	14	5	41	2	16	7	34	15	20	13	04	0	18
23	12	44	13	43	6	33	2	03	3	52	1	27	5	43	2	02	7	54	15	26	12	47	0	*12
24	12	58	13	34	6	15	2	14	3	47	1	40	5	45	1	46	8	14	15	32	12	28	0	42
25	13	12	13	24	5	56	2	24	3	41	1	53	5	46	1	30	8	33	15	38	12	09	1	12
26	13	24	13	13	5	37	2	35	3	35	2	05	5	46	1	13	8	53	15	44	11	50	1	42
27	13	35	13	02	5	18	2	46	3	29	2	17	5	45	0	56	9	13	15	49	11	30	2	11
28	13	46	12	50	5	00	2	56	3	23	2	29	5	44	0	39	9	32	15	52	11	09	2	40
29	13	56			4	41	3	04	3	15	2	41	5	42	0	21	9	52	15	55	10	47	3	09
30	14	05			4	22	3	12	3	07	2	53	5	40	0	03	10	11	15	57	10	25	3	38
31	14	13			4	03			2	58			5	38	0	*14			15	59			4	07

Vertical italic annotations printed within the columns read: **Horolog. Ofcill. velocius. Scioterico.** (January, February, March, May), **Horolog. Ofcill. tardius.** (April, May, June, August, September, October, December), **Horolog. Ofcill. velocius.** (July, October, November).

O Bfervato accuratè tempore apparente, Scioterici ope vel alterius alicujus inftrumenti Mathematici, capiatur è Tabulâ præcedente temporis Æquatio diei competens, & difponantur indiculi Horologii tardiùs aut velociùs tempore apparente (juxta Æquationis in Tabula Titulum) quantum præcisè ea eft: Tunc fi motu æquabili moveatur Horologium, differentiæ temporum ab eo, & à Scioterico commonftratorum, Temporis Æquationibus, *obfervationum diebus*, in Tabula adfcriptis, femper deinceps æquales erunt.

LONDINI:
Sumptibus *Thomæ Tompion*, Automatopœi, ad Infigne *Horologii* & *trium Coronarum* in Vico vulgò dicto Fleetftreet, 1690.

Figure 8/15. Equation table in Latin published by Tompion in 1690. Corrected for the Gregorian calendar thus indicating it must have been for export to Europe, proving that Tompion had a good export trade by that date.

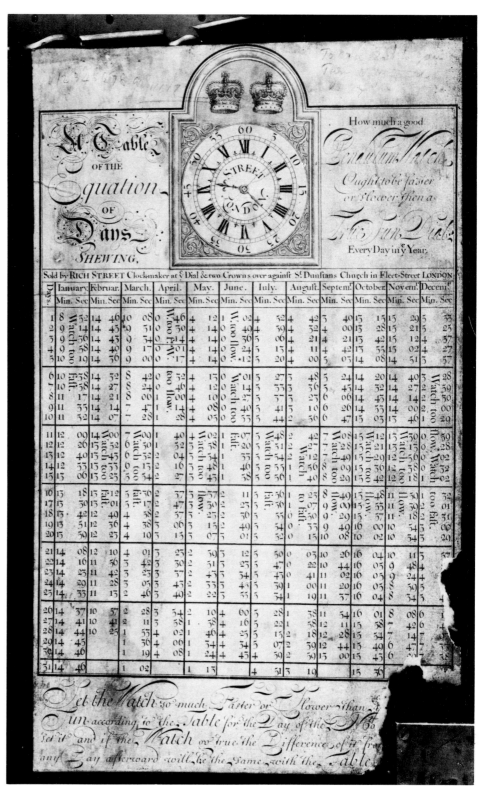

Figure 8/16. Equation table in English, published by Richard Street but identical to one by Tompion also in English.

actually rotates 366 times in a year, but the annual path of the earth round the sun causes the earth to rotate only 365 times a year with respect to the sun.

Astronomers use sidereal time, and a clock can easily be converted from mean solar time to sidereal time by a slight shortening of the pendulum. A few very complicated clocks have been constructed to indicate both sidereal and mean solar time simultaneously and an example will be described later.

Sidereal time was obviously unsuitable for general use,[16] so clocks had to be checked, as they had been for centuries, against the sun, and a correction applied for the equation of time. Which meant that the appropriate variation for the date in question needed to be readily available. This information was supplied in a variety of ways, which will be considered in turn, starting with the simplest devices.

Equation tables and annual equation dials

By the late seventeenth century equation tables were being published and Smith[17] lists several. It is worth noting that as late as the middle of the nineteenth century some almanacs were still including the equation of time. Nowadays it is included in the *Astronomical Ephemeris* published by H.M. Stationery Office.

A number of clockmakers published equation tables which quite often also included instructions for setting up and adjusting a clock. These tables were often stuck in a convenient position on the inside of the trunk door, and figure 8/15 shows such a table by Thomas Tompion published in 1690. Many were in English but this example is in Latin, which was the international language of science. Note *Horol. Oscill. tardius* (clock slow) and *Horol. Oscill. velocius* (clock fast). It is correct for the Gregorian calendar which was adopted by the Roman Catholic states of Italy, Portugal, Spain and France in 1682 and parts of Germany in 1683. The adjustment required was ten days, as in this example, up to 1700 and eleven days afterwards. The printing of this table is proof that Tompion had a considerable export trade by 1690. This is supported by the number of his clocks which have come to light on the Continent during this century.

A somewhat later example by Richard Street, entitled *A Table of the Equation of Days shewing How much a good Pendulum Watch Ought to be faster or slower than a True Sun Dial Every Day in ye Year,* is shown in figure 8/16. It is interesting to note that this table is identical to one by Tompion in its title and instructions as well as in the equation table. It will be noted that this table is still in position on a clock door. Any such tables or maker's instructions for setting up and regulating should be carefully preserved, a suitable method being by fixing a sheet of perspex over them. If it is intended to use an equation table or an equation clock, for example to check a sundial, it must first be ascertained whether the table or clock dates from before or after the adoption of the Gregorian calendar in England in 1752 when eleven days were omitted. Failure to do so can result in an appreciable error.

As a development of this idea, the equation table was incorporated in the clock dial, often in a simplified form. Figure 8/17 shows the 13ins. arched dial of a month clock by Daniel Delander, c.1725. Behind the arch is a disc continuously driven from the going train and arranged to rotate once per year. A sector of this disc appears behind the four concentric openings which indicate the month with its number of days, the date every seven days, the equation of time to the nearest minute every seven days, and Sun Faster or Sun Slower. Below this is engraved *Tabula Æquationis.* When photographed on November 13th the clock indicated that the sun was fifteen minutes (approximately) ahead of mean time.

16. Even so, Smith, *Disquisitions,* p. 90, includes such a method submitted by Samuel Watson.

17. Smith, *Disquisitions,* p. 16: "As first, by Mr. *Hugens,* Printed *Novem. 29.* Of the *Philosophical Transactions:* Secondly, by Mr. *Flamsteed,* commonly made use of by Mr. *Tompion,* Printed also in *Parker's Almanack.* Thirdly by Mr. *Molyneux* in his *Sciothericum Telescopium* ... Fourthly, by the learned Dr. *William Salmon,* in his *Almanack* for this *Year* 1694. And fifthly, by Mr. *Samuel Watson,* the curious contriver of that rare *Celestial Orbitery,* now in the present Queen *Mary's* posession."

The day of the month is read on the usual indicator above the VI and this needs correcting for months of less than thirty-one days as indicated in the arch. The subsidiary dial on the left is for pendulum regulation and that on the right for strike/silent.

The elegant case (figure 8/18) is veneered with burr walnut and the break arch hood is of a type which was used from time to time from c.1720 until quite late in the century. The fine sound frets in the front and sides of the hood should be noted. The height is approximately 8ft. 4ins. to the top of the hood.

The clock by Joseph Finney shown in figure 10/41, has the equation

Figure 8/17. 13ins. arched dial of a month clock by Daniel Delander, c.1725. Annual calendar in arch showing: month with its number of days; date every seven days; equation of time to nearest minute every seven days; Sun Faster or Sun Slower. Below this is engraved 'Tabula Aequationis.' Usual simple calendar below dial centre. Left hand sub-sidiary dial for pendulum regulation, right hand for strike/silent. Note non-standard cast ornaments in arch.

Figure 8/18. Elegant burr walnut case of Delander clock in 8/17, height approximately 8ft. 4ins. to top of break arch hood.

of time given in tabular form in the arch, a very simple way of giving the required information.

An alternative idea was to mark the equation of time on the sundial, and many fine horizontal sundials by eighteenth century instrument makers will be found to have this information engraved outside the hour and minute markings.

True equation dials

The next stage was to provide a direct reading of the equation of time for the day, usually by means of a separate dial and hand. As will be seen, this requires special mechanism involving difficult design problems. The term equation clock is reserved for examples which incorporate this special mechanism.

The dials of an important year equation timepiece are shown in figure 8/19. It is by Daniel Quare, c.1710 and is thought to have been made for Hampton Court Palace, a view which is supported by the royal arms on the upper part of the dial. The latter is 14ins. by 17ins. and has specially designed foliate spandrels. The upper left dial indicates the day of the week and the upper right one provides an up and down adjustment for pendulum regulation.

The equation mechanism is quite separate from the rest of the clock, a point which will be returned to when Joseph Williamson's work is discussed later in this chapter. The equation work is connected to the clock by a long vertical arbor and its dial (figure 8/20) appears behind a glazed opening in the trunk door. The fine engraving on the lower half of the silvered ring explains how to read the dials: "The long Hand is 365 days in going Round and points the Days of the Months. The Hand with the Figure of the Sun shews how many

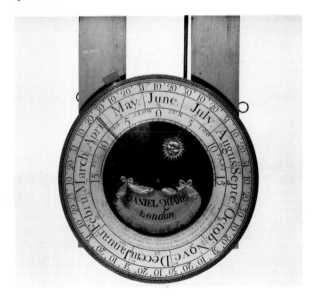

Figure 8/19. Dial of year equation timepiece by Daniel Quare, c.1710. Dial plate 14ins. by 17ins. Note special foliate spandrels and royal arms in upper part. Left hand subsidiary dial for day of week, right hand for pendulum regulation. Equation mechanism separate and driven by a vertical arbor.

Figure 8/20. Equation dial of Quare clock. Long hand points to annual calendar, essential for setting the mechanism, hand with gilt sun points to equation of time.

Figure 8/21

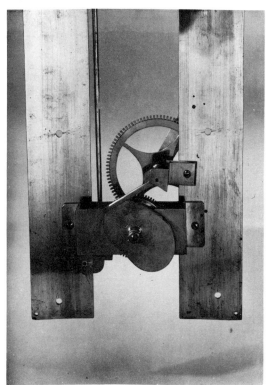

Figure 8/22

Figure 8/23

Figure 8/21. Front view of equation mechanism, driven by vertical rod on right. Endless screw or worm on rod drives wheel between plates. This rotates once per year and is mounted on its arbor with a clutch to permit hand setting. Front end of arbor carries calendar hand, rear carries equation cam or kidney.

Figure 8/22. Rear view of equation mechanism showing cam and pivoted arm which rides on it. Large wheel at front of mechanism is fixed to same arbor as arm and drives loose pinion on centre arbor (8/21). This pinion carries the equation hand.

Figure 8/23. Massive year movement of Quare clock. Note small sub-frame carrying lightly made upper part of train to reduce inertia. Up and down mechanism consisting of snail moved by regulating hand through gearing. Pivoted arm carrying pendulum suspension rides on edge of snail.

minutes (computed from the Cypher under ♋)[18] a true Sun Dial is Faster or Slower than this Clock, the Sun dayly varying from equal Time''. It must be appreciated that an annual calendar is essential on an equation clock to enable the owner to set the mechanism correctly.

The lower end of the vertical arbor has an endless screw or worm gear which meshes with the wheel between the plates (figure 8/21). The gear ratios are such that this wheel rotates once a year. It is connected to its arbor through a friction clutch to permit hand setting. The front end of the arbor carries the calendar hand and the rear end carries the equation cam or kidney as it is often called from its shape (figure 8/22). An arbor pivoted above the cam carries an arm which follows the contour of the cam and therefore imparts a backward and forward rotary motion to the arbor. This motion is magnified by the wheel on the front end of the arbor meshing with the pinion which rides freely on the central arbor and carries the equation hand (figure 8/21).

The movement (figure 8/23) is massively constructed with the upper part of the train delicately made and supported in a small sub-frame to reduce inertia as much as possible. Note the substantial steel cable for supporting the very heavy weight[18a]. The pendulum suspension is hung on a pivoted arm, the free end of which is supported by a snail. Regulation is effected by turning the latter through a reduction gear from the regulating hand.

The case (figure 8/24) is veneered with burr walnut and is 9ft. 10ins. high overall. The feet are of brass and repoussé brass mounts cover the skirting to the plinth. These mounts and the spandrel-like mounts on the trunk door are an exceptional feature but somewhat similar mounts appear on other 'royal' clocks, by Tompion.

Because of the mathematical and other skills required in the design and construction of equation clocks most of them are by eminent makers, but figure 8/25 and Frontispiece show an example c.1730 of unusual design and excellent quality by an almost unknown maker, William Wright of Southwark.

The dial is 13ins. wide, is well engraved and has the rare floral spandrels with cornucopia in the arch (neither in C. & W.). There appears to be no special reason for the twenty-four hour chapter ring. The dial in the arch is for pendulum regulation and the curved slot within it displays the annual calendar necessary for setting the equation mechanism. The usual simple day of the month indicator is provided in the upper centre of the dial. The equation of time is shown by the small gilt sun which traverses the slot in the chapter ring between 44 and 15 minutes. The greatest difference occurs early in November when the sun is approximately 16¼ minutes ahead of mean time, so readings to the left of 60 have to be subtracted from solar time to give mean time and those to the right added.

The timepiece movement is of month duration and the bolt and shutter is operated by a lever in a slot just outside the chapter ring at

18. The zodiacal sign for Cancer, the Crab.

18a. Very thick catgut would have been used originally.

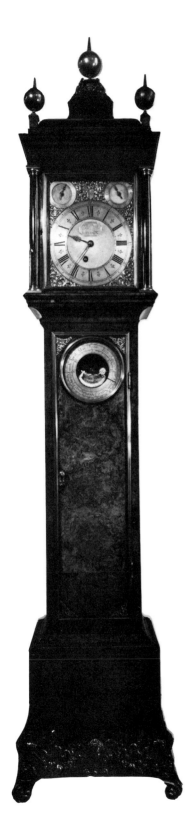

Figure 8/24. Magnificent burr walnut case of Quare clock, 9ft. 10ins. high overall. Gilt brass mounts including feet, repoussé work on skirting and small spandrels on trunk door.

37½ minutes. Figure 8/26 shows the movement with elegantly shaped plates and brackets which support the rise and fall mechanism. Both dial and movement are latched. The drive to the equation cam and annual calendar is taken off the forty-eight hour wheel for the common calendar which is mounted on a pinion between the plates towards the bottom of the movement. There are two wheels and two pinions between the plates followed by a similar number mounted on the front plate. The equation cam can be seen immediately behind the 'spider' carrying the annual calendar ring. The pendulum beats 1⅓ seconds and has a substantial brass rod with an enormous bob.

The case (Colour Plate 11) is of oak veneered with burr yew. The bracket feet are not original. The large oval lenticle in the plinth is mounted in a fixed panel as access to the pendulum is not required for regulation which is carried out from the dial. The total height is 8ft. 3ins. but the whole clock is beautifully proportioned.

Figure 8/25. 13ins. dial of month equation timepiece by William Wright, c.1730. Well engraved dial with rare corner and arch spandrels. Equation of time indicated by gilt sun which moves in slot between 44 and 15 minutes. Readings to left of 60 have to be subtracted from solar time to give mean time and those to right added. Annual calendar in slot in arch and simple calendar above centre. Up and down regulation dial in arch and bolt and shutter operated by lever at 37½ minutes. No special reason known for twenty-four hour chapter ring. The case is shown in Colour Plate 11. See also Frontispiece.

Figure 8/26. Elegant movement of Wright clock, seven pillars and dial feet latched. Drive for equation cam and calendar is by a pinion on arbor of forty-eight hour wheel for common calendar. This pinion drives a four wheel train, with first two wheels between plates and remainder on front plate. Equation cam is just behind annual calendar. Rack and pinion up and down regulation to 1⅓ seconds pendulum with stout brass rod and huge bob.

Figure 8/27. Dial of direct reading year equation time-piece by Tompion, c.1700 ('The Drayton Tompion'). Dial 10¾ins. square within engraved lines which is all that shows with hood door closed (figure 8/30). Essential annual calendar showing months with days numbered every six and sun's position in ecliptic in opening above square. Upward extension of dial plate supports and protects calendar and equation mechanism. Days of week with their deities in opening below centre. Typical Tompion spandrels with fine engraving between. Minute hand rotates in two hours to allow more efficient gear ratios. Twenty-four hour dial follows naturally from this. Outside normal minute ring marked 'EQUAL TIME' is a movable minute ring marked 'APPARET TIME.' Counterbalanced minute hand indicates mean time on inner ring and solar time on outer ring. Design of hands confused by heavy shadows. Inverted movement with bolt and shutter operated by lever on right hand edge.

Figure 8/28. Tompion dial with centre and chapter ring removed. Apparent time ring is mounted on three-armed wheel with wheel at centre which meshes with rack on bell crank which follows shape of equation cam. Note vertical arbor taking drive from endless screw on motion work to calendar and cam. Pendulum suspension visible just below centre.

Direct reading equation clocks

All the methods so far described are indirect, that is the user reads off the equation of time and then has to carry out a simple calculation to convert from solar time to mean time or vice versa. Other developments which will now be described give a direct reading of solar time without any mental effort being required by the user.

Thomas Tompion made at least three direct reading equation clocks[19] and the dial of the second of these, chronologically, is shown in figure 8/27. It is now in the Fitzwilliam Museum but it was made for Drayton House, Northamptonshire, c.1700 and remained there until 1928.

19. Symonds, *Tompion*, p. 129.

Figure 8/29. Tompion movement showing massive construction of early part of train. Note calendar disc next to dial plate, then equation cam and wheel driven by endless screw on vertical arbor.

Figure 8/30. Burr walnut case of Tompion clock, 8ft.8ins. overall. Note early use of gilt metal mounts including mounts on trunk door as on Quare case, 8/24. Despite height, hood lifts up but has a door. The annual calendar is visible when the hood door is open but the zodiac dial is visible only when the hood is raised. Pendulum swings in front of weight and is isolated from it by a silvered plate carrying a degree scale.

The dial is signed, like his first equation clock, 'THO. TOMPION. LONDON. INVENT'; the section within the engraved lines, which is all that shows with the hood door closed, is 10¾ins. square. The essential annual calendar appears in an opening just above this square and the upper slot shows the sun's position in the ecliptic, that is its apparent annual path through the heavens. This is divided into twelve equal arcs of 30° each with its appropriate constellation of the zodiac. The upward extension of the dial plate is necessary to support and protect the calendar and equation mechanism. Immediately below the centre of the dial is a day of the week indicator showing the appropriate deity for the day. The spandrels (C. & W. No. 7) are of a type which Tompion and a few other makers adopted as successors to the larger cherubs at about this date. It has a year timepiece movement and the minute hand rotates once in two hours as this permits more efficient gear ratios to be used. The twenty-four hour dial follows naturally from this. Outside the normal minute ring marked 'EQUAL TIME' is a movable minute ring marked 'APPARĒT TIME', so that the minute hand indicates mean time on the fixed ring and its gilt tip shows solar time on the outer ring. The hand is counterbalanced to reduce the load on the movement. The winding hole at the upper 12 o'clock position shows that the movement is inverted and the bolt and shutter mechanism, necessary to protect the delicate escapement, is operated by a lever at the right hand edge of the dial plate.

Figure 8/28 shows the mounting of the apparent time ring and how it is moved backwards and forwards by means of a rack under the control of the equation cam mounted behind the annual calendar. The drive to the calendar and equation cam is taken off the motion work by an endless screw or worm driving a small wheel on a long vertical arbor with another endless screw at its upper end. This meshes with a wheel on the arbor carrying the calendar and equation cam. The movement (figure 8/29) consists of a small back plate carrying the strongly built early part of the train with a large front plate on which are mounted the rest of the train and all the calendar and equation work. The annual calendar disc is next to the dial and just to the right is the equation cam. The pendulum (figure 8/30) swings in front of the weight from which it is isolated by a silvered metal plate carrying a degree scale. This is for accurately levelling the clock and recording the amplitude of swing by means of two sliding indices. There is an enormous oval section weight of some 80lb.

The case (figure 8/30) is veneered with burr walnut and is 8ft.8ins. high including the gilt metal figure of a warrior, and it is stated to be the earliest extant Tompion clock with gilt metal mounts. Figure mounts are rare on English clocks but common on Dutch ones; perhaps it is worth noting that the original owner of this clock was described as a 'Dutch gamester...'[20] and that other figures are found on clocks made for 'Dutch' William III. Another point of interest is that in spite of the gilt mounts this case still has iron hinges, exceptionally three, to the trunk door.

The hood slides up, but has a later door. When the latter is closed, the annual calendar is covered, which emphasises that it is provided for setting the equation mechanism rather than for normal use. Opening the hood door exposes the calendar but not the slot for the zodiac, which is visible only when the hood is raised. This is in contrast to the other Tompion year equation clocks which are of similar design but which each have an upward extension of the central part of the hood door so that all the indications can be read with it closed. With more ordinary clocks such an apparent misfit usually means that case and movement have been 'married', but the special features which do correspond rule out this possibility. Like other special productions by Tompion, neither case nor movement is numbered. The case is discussed in more detail in pages 445 to 454.

20. Symonds, *Tompion,* p. 269.

Joseph Williamson had a different approach to the problem, he designed and made a number of clocks which kept and indicated solar time, not mean time. This solution had the advantage that such a clock would automatically agree with the sundial so no corrections would be necessary. It would have been perfectly satisfactory at that time, providing all the clocks in a community were regulated in the same way,[21] as local time depending on the longitude was used until 1848.

The dial of one of these clocks, made shortly before Williamson died in 1725, is shown in figure 8/31. On a recessed plaque is inscribed 'Horae indicantur. Apparentes involutis Æquationibus Ioseph Williamson Londini', which has been translated as: The apparent hours are indicated by complicated equations.[22] The dial plate is 12ins. across and bolt and

21. There is some evidence for this: see J. Wenzel, 'Equation Clocks', *Antiquarian Horology*, XIII (September 1981), p.24.
22. H. Von Bertele, 'Equation Clock Inventions of Joseph Williamson', *Antiquarian Horology*, I (December 1955), p.123.

Figure 8/31. 12ins. dial of solar time clock by Joseph Williamson, c.1720-25. Note late use of Latin inscription. Maintaining power with shutter on going side only. Broad chapter ring with large minute numerals and no half quarter markings. Essential annual calendar in arch with signs of zodiac. Hand same design as on Quare clock in 8/20.

Figure 8/32. Williamson movement showing drive to equation work. Twenty-four hour wheel as for a common calendar, mounted on a pinion which drives contrate wheel on long vertical arbor. Endless screw at upper end drives wheel on arbor carrying cam and calendar hand. Note clutch on wheel for adjusting calendar.

Figure 8/33. Rear view of Williamson movement. Note almost circular cam with bell crank riding on its periphery. Lower arm of crank has stud which carries pendulum suspension. Hence length of pendulum varied as in normal rise and fall mechanism.

Figure 8/34. Front of movement showing maintaining power in unusual position because of drive to equation mechanism. Normal rack striking with inside locking, probably had hour repeating. Note spare holes to right of lifting piece.

shutter maintaining power is provided but without a matching shutter on the striking side, the winding square projecting into the hole in the dial plate. Note the broad chapter ring with large minute numbers but without half quarter markings. The half hour markings are of a type found on some late Tompion and on Graham clocks. The annual calendar in the arch has on its inner edge the twelve constellations of the zodiac with their appropriate signs. The hand is the same pattern as that on the Quare equation clock shown in figure 8/20.

The side view of the eight-day movement (figure 8/32) shows the drive to the equation cam and calendar. A twenty-four hour wheel as used to operate an ordinary day of the month calendar is mounted on a pinion which is between the plates. This drives a contrate wheel on a vertical arbor with an endless screw or worm gear at its upper end and the endless screw drives a wheel on the arbor for the cam and the calendar hand. A large friction clutch operates on the side of the last wheel (see figure 8/33) to provide a definite drive with ease of hand setting. The cam, at the right hand end of the same arbor in figure 8/33, is much less elongated than those used on conventional equation clocks and a bell crank pivoted on a

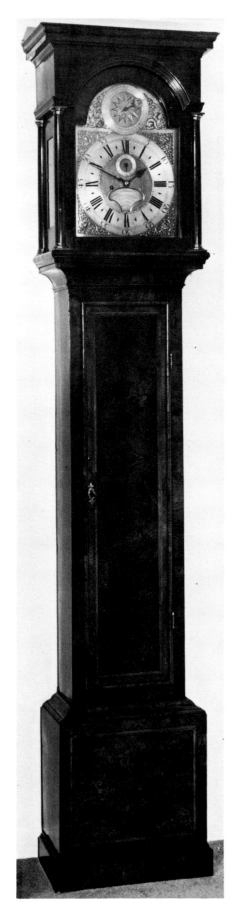

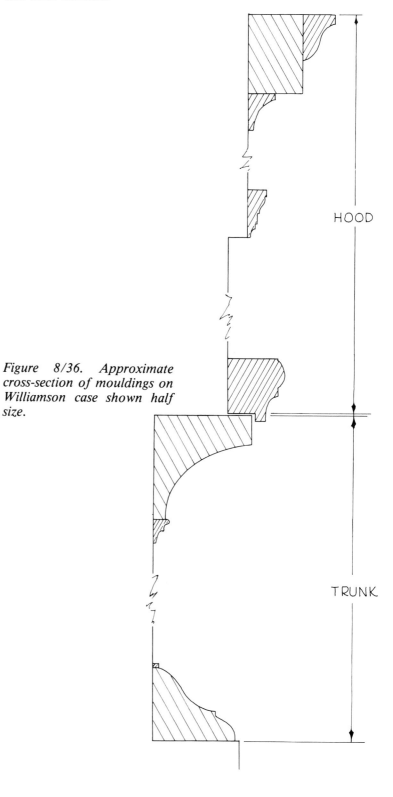

Figure 8/35. Walnut veneered, herring-bone banded case of Williamson clock, 7ft. 7ins. high. Caddy and sound frets missing. Original brass hinges and other mounts.

HOOD

Figure 8/36. Approximate cross-section of mouldings on Williamson case shown half size.

TRUNK

stud follows the shape of the cam. The lower arm of the crank has a small post which supports the pendulum suspension. The effective length of the pendulum is therefore varied as the suspension is raised or lowered through the chops attached to the back cock. The whole device is very soundly but economically designed. Figure 8/34 shows the front of the movement with the maintaining arbor unusually placed because of the space occupied between the plates by the drive to the equation mechanism. The maintaining power is a restoration. Normal rack striking is provided and spare holes on the right of the front plate suggest that it originally had hour repeating.

A flat brass pendulum rod is fitted, which is unfortunate for the increased temperature error it causes, but brass rods were common on good quality clocks at this period.

The well proportioned case (figure 8/35) is veneered with walnut and is 7ft. 7ins. high without its caddy, which was presumably removed so that the clock would fit a room with a lower ceiling. Broken frets above the hood door have been covered over with plain wood. The columns have brass capitals and bases and the trunk door has original brass strap hinges. An approximate cross-section of the mouldings is shown half size in figure 8/36.

Joseph Williamson undoubtedly played an important part in the development of equation clocks and the following letter which he wrote to *Philosophical Transactions* (of the Royal Society) in 1719 is worth reproducing in full:[23]

> Having been informed of a *French* Book[24] lately published, wherein the Author speaks of making Clocks to agree with the Sun's Apparent Motion: and supposeth that it was a thing never thought of by any before himself: I was therefore willing by the advice of some of my Friends, to write this short Account of what I have performed in this matter myself.
>
> And in the first place I must take notice of the Copy of a letter in this Book, wrote by one P. Kresa, a Jesuit, to me *Mr Williamson,* Clockmaker to his Imperial Majesty: of a clock found in the late King *Charles the Second of Spain*'s Cabinet, about the year 1699 or 1700 which sheweth both equal and apparent Time according to the Tables of Equation, and which went 400 days without winding up. This I am well satisfied is a clock of my own making: for about six years before that time, I made one for Mr Daniel Quare, for whom I then wrought mostly, which agrees with the Description that gives of it, and went for 400 days. This clock Mr. Daniel Quare sold, soon after it was made to go to the said King *Charles the Second of Spain*: and it was made so that if the *Pendulum* was adjusted to the sun's mean Motion, the Hands would show equal Time on two fixed Circles, on one the Hour, and the other the Minute... Soon after this clock was sent to *Spain*, I made others for *Mr Quare* which showed Apparent Time by lengthening and shortening the *Pendulum,* in lifting it up and letting it down again, by a Rowler in the form of an *ellipsis,* through a slit in a piece of Brass, which the Spring at the Top of the Pendulum went through... For one of those, and not the first, made with the rising and setting of the Sun, Mr Quare sold to the late King *William* and it was set up at *Hampton Court* in his lifetime, where it hath been ever since... So that I think that I may justly claim the greatest right to this contrivance of making clocks to go with Apparent Time; and I have never heard of any such clock sold in *England* but was of my own making, though I have made them so long.

If Williamson was claiming the invention only of those clocks which *kept* apparent or solar time he would appear to be justified, but if he meant all equation clocks this is

---

23. H.A. Lloyd, *The Collector's Dictionary of Clocks*, 1964, p. 200.
24. H. Sully, *Regle artificielle du Tems*, 1717.

probably incorrect. Lloyd[25] states that Christiaan Huygens invented the equation cam in 1695 just before he died and suggests that Tompion made the first in England, c.1695.[26] He also suggests that Tompion, and Quare with Williamson, independently developed the equation mechanism.

As can be seen from the example described above, Tompion made his equation work an integral part of the clock movement and signed the earlier examples 'Tho. Tompion, London. Invent.', whereas Quare had a separate unit which was presumably made for him by Williamson. In clocks signed by Williamson the equation work is integrated into the movement and at least one of his earlier solar time clocks is signed 'Joseph Williamson Londini. Inv. & Fecit.', thus supporting his claim.

Williamson also made a remarkable clock with two dials, one each side of the movement.[27] The movement keeps mean time, which is shown on one dial. The other dial indicates solar time which is obtained by applying the correction from an equation cam through a differential gear, the first known use of such a device in horology.

Precautions with equation clocks

As the equation cam must have a certain position relative to the calendar hand or the calendar dial if the latter rotates, it is not advisable to dismantle this mechanism without marking the parts to ensure accurate positioning on reassembly. The correct setting up of the calendar can be verified by checking the equation of time displayed against an equation table for various months of the year, if necessary making an allowance for the calendar adjustment of 1752.

The Williamson type of solar time clock is not so easy to check but it is just possible to see the bell crank rise and fall as the cam is rotated by the calendar hand. The bell crank should fall for January-February and rise to its highest level around October-November. As both hand and cam are squared on to the arbor, incorrect assembly will produce an obvious error of at least 90° or three months.

PRECISION CLOCKS

After considering the various developments required to provide precision timekeeping it is advisable to examine two clocks which include them all. Figure 8/37 shows the 12ins. dial of a month equation timepiece signed on a plaque at the base of the arch 'Geo. Graham, London', of c.1740. It incorporates Graham's inventions, the dead beat escapement and the mercury pendulum, and has bolt and shutter maintaining power operated by a lever in a slot near 3 o'clock. The position of the seconds dial indicates that the escapement is inverted at the bottom of the movement. Solar time is indicated directly by a gilt minute hand with an effigy of the sun. The right hand winding square is provided for setting the calendar and hence the equation work.

The calendar disc provides a number of indications which will be described, starting from the outside. The first two rings give the date and the month, and the next two the equation of time and 'Sun too Fast' or 'Sun too Slow'. The equation is given in minutes but at its maximum values the number of seconds is also shown, for example 49 S at 11 February indicates that the value then is 14 minutes 49 seconds slow and similarly on 2 November it is 16 minutes 13 seconds fast. The next three rings give information relative to the sun. The first one gives its declination, that is its position north or south of the equator in degrees of latitude, with the maximum declination of 23° 30′ at the summer and winter solstices (June 21st and December 22nd). The equinoxes (March 21st and September 21st), when the sun is

25. Lloyd, *Dictionary*, p. 77.
26. Ibid., pp. 148, 174.
27. See H.A. Lloyd, *Some Outstanding Clocks over Seven Hundred Years*, 1958, p. 82.

Figure 8/37. 12ins. dial of month equation timepiece by Graham, c.1740. Arabesque design silver spandrels probably later. Chapter ring made more elegant by omission of quarter hour divisions and half hour marks. Large slender seconds ring with balanced hand. Simple calendar just below centre. Annual calendar dial in arch shows: day of month and month; equation of time and Sun too Fast/Sun too Slow; sun's declination north or south of the equator; sun's position in the ecliptic; times of sunrise. Blued steel hands indicate mean time, gilt hand with sun shows solar time. Inverted movement with dead beat escapement and maintaining power operated by lever at III. Left hand winding square for winding train, right hand for setting calendar.

Figure 8/38. Back of Graham dial. Note substantial dial feet screwed to plate and sub-plate to carry mechanism for common calendar. Sliding shutters for maintaining power.

Figure 8/39. Graham movement. On right note bell crank on maintaining arbor. Pin in upper arm engages in slot in shutter mechanism (8/38) and pin in other arm projects through slot in dial. Annual calendar is driven by pinion on arbor with square for setting.

Figure 8/40. Drive to annual calendar. Wheel mounted on hour wheel drives larger wheel carried by bridge on front plate. Pinion of this wheel drives wheel (visible to right of plates) which is mounted with a clutch on arbor carrying pinion to drive calendar. Epicyclic gear assembly to drive solar hand is held by a cock towards bottom left. High grade movement, note beautifully shaped plates, latched pillars, end plates to reduce pivot friction.

over the equator, are marked '$\AE$'. The next markings show the position of the sun in the ecliptic, that is its apparent annual path through the heavens. This is divided into twelve equal arcs of 30°, each marked with its appropriate zodiacal sign. Finally the innermost ring gives the time of sunrise with the hours divided into five minutes, with the earliest and latest times being indicated directly, for example 13 M at the winter solstice shows that the sun then rises at 8.13.

This calendar disc poses an interesting problem as it conforms to the Gregorian calendar adopted in this country in September 1752, whereas Graham died in November 1751. The change involved the omission of eleven days so existing equation clocks and equation tables needed substantial amendment. The most likely explanation is that the present calendar disc was made either by Graham in 1751 when legislation was introduced for the change in the calendar, or by his successors (Barkley and Colley) in, or shortly after 1752. In support of this theory, the engraving appears to be by the same hand as that on the rest of the dial. In addition, H.M. Smith states that the calendar dial has been renewed,[28] but the evidence for this is not stated. Another possibility is that it was intended for export as most of Europe had adopted the Gregorian calendar by 1700.

The spandrels are of silver, of a highly individual arabesque design, quite different from the turbaned head type used on other Graham equation clocks and are presumably later replacements.

The chapter ring (figure 8/37) has been made more elegant by the omission of half hour ornaments and quarter hour divisions, only the hour and half hour divisions being retained. These also were omitted on Graham's last productions. The hands are original, with balanced seconds hand to prevent interference with the action of the escapement. Larger seconds rings as on the early pendulum clocks, but with balanced hands, gradually spread to ordinary domestic clocks.

Figure 8/38 shows the mechanism mounted on the back of the dial. Note the substantial dial feet screwed in position. The maintaining power shutters are arranged to slide horizontally. A small sub-plate, screwed and pinned to the dial plate, accommodates the pivot holes for the large grooved wheels which carry the simple calendar ring. This has external teeth and is operated by a stud in the twenty-four hour wheel which is also mounted on the sub-plate. This wheel is operated by the small wheel on the hour wheel.

The drive to the annual calendar disc is shown in figure 8/39. The disc has 365 teeth and is driven by a thirty tooth pinion mounted on an arbor which is squared to take a key for correcting the calendar. Figure 8/40 shows most of the drive to the calendar. The hour wheel carries a wheel of thirty-two teeth which meshes with one of ninety-six teeth which is pivoted in a bridge on the front plate. The arbor of this wheel has a six-leaved pinion which drives a 120 tooth wheel between the plates and visible on the right. This wheel is mounted with a clutch on the arbor of the thirty tooth pinion which drives the calendar disc. By calculation, this pinion turns once in thirty days, so the calendar disc is advanced one tooth per day. The equation cam is mounted on the rear end of the arbor of the calendar disc.

In figure 8/40 note the beautifully shaped and latched plates; the dial feet also are latched. The small bell crank on the right is mounted on the maintaining power arbor. The pin in its upper arm engages in a slot in the shutter mechanism on the back of the dial (figure 8/38) and the pin in the other arm projects through the slot in the dial plate near III.

Figure 8/41 shows the layout of both the normal motion work and the epicyclic gearing used to operate the solar hand. The ordinary motion work consists of the cannon pinion (1), the minute wheel (2) which carries the minute pinion (3), and the hour wheel (4) on which is mounted the wheel (5) to operate the twenty-four hour wheel for the simple calendar.

28. H.M. Smith, 'The Solar System as an Astronomical Clock', *Horological Journal,* March, 1953, p. 178.

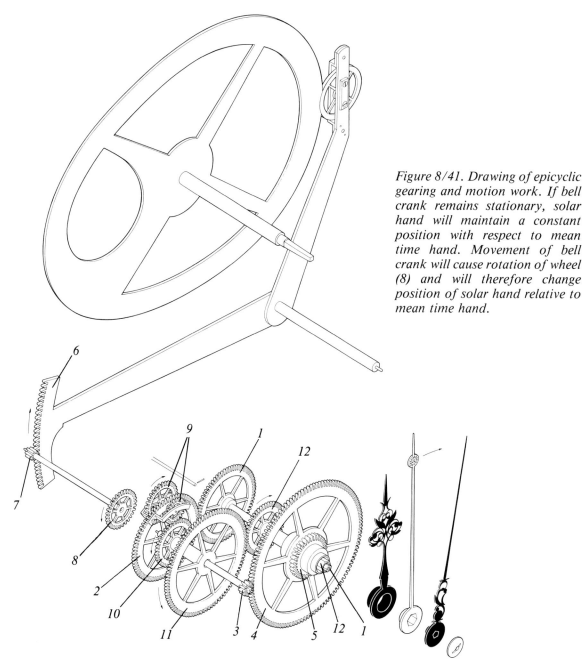

Figure 8/41. Drawing of epicyclic gearing and motion work. If bell crank remains stationary, solar hand will maintain a constant position with respect to mean time hand. Movement of bell crank will cause rotation of wheel (8) and will therefore change position of solar hand relative to mean time hand.

The lower end of the bell crank terminates in a rack (6) which meshes with a pinion (7). The pinion arbor extends through the plates with a wheel (8) on its front end and has a concentric hole to take the rear pivot of the minute wheel arbor. Pivoted in two bridges on the rim of the minute wheel (2) is an arbor carrying a pair of wheels (9), the rear one engages with (8) whilst the front wheel meshes with a wheel (10) which rides free on the minute wheel arbor. Rotation of the minute wheel will therefore cause the pair of wheels (9) to rotate on their arbor and turn wheel (10). Wheel (10) has fixed to it a larger wheel (11) which drives the cannon pinion (12) for the solar minute hand. The gear ratios 8:9, 9:10, 11:12, are so chosen that if wheel (8) remains stationary, cannon pinion (12) makes exactly one rotation per hour. In other words, the solar minute hand will maintain a constant position with regard to the mean time minute hand. Rotation of the equation cam will cause angular movement of the bell crank and consequent movement of wheel (8). Wheel (12) will therefore be advanced or retarded with respect to wheel (1) to show the change in the equation of time.

This complicated mechanism provides a most elegant solution to the problem of showing mean and solar time simultaneously. It is also the simplest from the clock user's point of view.

Figure 8/42. Rear view showing equation cam and bell crank with anti-friction wheel running on periphery. Note careful lightening of parts. Lower end of crank has rack which engages with pinion connected to epicyclic gearing. Note fixing brackets, four to seat board, one to back board.

Figure 8/43. Right side of movement. Arbor at top on which are squared calendar wheel and equation cam. Note extreme thinness of latter.

Figure 8/44. Left side of movement. Micrometer adjustment to pendulum suspension. Pendulum hooks on to a pin in the suspension. Long crutch hanging below seat board. There is a screwed beat adjustment.

Figure 8/43 *Figure 8/44*

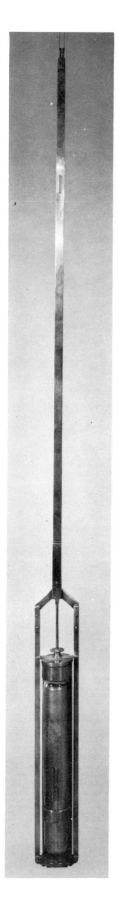

Figure 8/42 shows the back of the movement. It is fixed to the seat board by four angle brackets. Several refinements have been introduced; note the end plates to the pivot holes which reduce friction by ensuring that the shoulders of the pivots do not touch the plates, the rounded ends of the pivots, offering much less friction. Note also the delicate wheel which rides on the edge of the equation cam, which is carefully balanced and very lightly made (see figure 8/43). A screwed beat adjustment is provided on the pallets and there is a micrometer adjustment above the back cock. The slot though which the suspension spring passes is fitted with two small angle strips to ensure a perfect fit (see figure 8/42). Small threaded holes in the vertical edges of the plates and in the flattened bosses of two upper pillars indicate that dust excluding plates were fitted at some time. Figure 8/44 shows the left hand side of the movement.

The mercury compensation pendulum is shown in figure 8/45. It has a brass rod with a hook at the top which fits a pin in the suspension (figure 8/44). The position of the slot for the crutch pin shows that a long Tompion type crutch is used. The pendulum is not provided with a rating nut.

The case (figure 8/46), which is 7ft. 8ins. high is of figured mahogany veneer on a mahogany carcase and the hood is of an unusual but elegant design.

It was definitely made with a solid trunk door but this was subsequently cut for glazing, probably early in the nineteenth century when it had become fashionable to provide regulators with glass doors to show their compensated pendulums. The glass panel was later replaced by a wooden one, probably in a search for

Figure 8/45. Mercury pendulum of Graham clock. Brass rod with no provision for adjustment.

Figure 8/46. Case of Graham equation timepiece, mahogany veneer on mahogany carcase, c.1740, 7ft. 8ins. high. Unusual but elegant hood. Trunk door panel cut out and glazed, probably early nineteenth century. Note brass strengthening strip at top corner and see 8/47. Compare case design with 8/51.

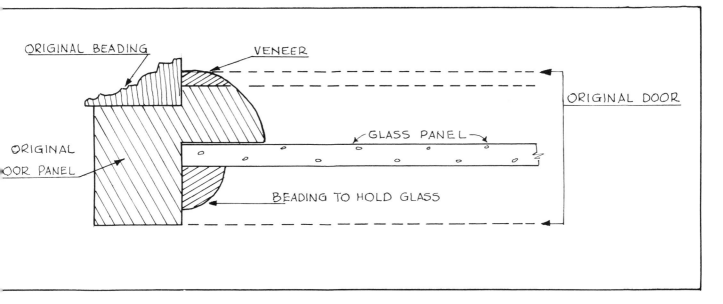

Figure 8/47. Cross-section through modified door of Graham case.

originality, for Lloyd[29] wrote: "a later owner has removed the glass door panel and substituted a mahogany panel". When acquired by C.A. Ilbert c.1951 it had again been fitted with a glass panel. Figure 8/47 shows the construction of the door, but the following is additional evidence for the alterations:

a. the long arms of the strap hinges have been cut off somewhat roughly.

b. brass strengthening strips have been fitted across the top and bottom of the door (see figure 8/46). As there were no battens the end grain would have been very weak.

c. an old key hole has been blocked in the rounded section in front of the glass.

The modification of the door has been discussed at some length because if it were originally glazed it would have set a precedent which was not followed until about the beginning of the nineteenth century.

The dial of an earlier (c.1735) but similar equation timepiece is shown in figure 8/48. The signature 'Geo: Graham London' is engraved on the dial plate just above XII instead of being on an applied plaque. The turbaned head spandrels (C. & W. No. 19) are typical. The annual calendar disc, unlike the previous example, does not show the equation of time. The changes necessary to accommodate the Gregorian calendar were made by providing a new centre to the disc so that the solar indications could be engraved in the correct positions. The outer portion of the disc with its finely cut teeth was too valuable to scrap. A slight change in colour is visible in the photograph and the flat ring used to unite the two parts can be seen in figure 8/50. The hands are of a different pattern from those on other Graham equation clocks and look rather heavy so may not be original. The equation hand is incorrectly positioned as the equation of time never exceeds approximately sixteen minutes.

Figure 8/49 shows the front of the movement and should be compared with figure 8/40. The main difference is in the drive to the calendar disc which is taken from the first pinion of the going train instead of from the motion work. This results in an anti-clockwise rotation of the arbor carrying the last wheel between the plates and which is squared for setting the calendar with a key. The direction of rotation is reversed by a pair of small wheels on the

---

29. H.A. Lloyd, *Old Clocks,* 3rd edition, 1964, p. 115, but this entry may have survived without correction from the 1st edition, 1951. See also Lloyd, 'George Graham, Horologist and Astronomer', *Horological Journal,* November 1951, p. 712, which shows the case with a wooden door panel.

Figure 8/48. Dial of a similar but earlier equation timepiece by Graham, c.1735. Compare with 8/37. Typical turbaned head spandrels, signature on dial plate, not on a plaque. Annual calendar disc does not show equation of time. Disc modified for Gregorian calendar by replacing inner part, note slight change in colour, see also 8/50. Hands probably replaced. Solar hand incorrectly positioned as equation of time never more than approximately sixteen minutes.

front plate and the pinion on the arbor of the second one meshes with the calendar wheel. There are also minor differences in the mounting of the epicyclic gears.

Figure 8/50 is a back view of the movement and should be compared with figure 8/42. Note the absence of the end plates to the pivots and the less careful lightening of the bell crank assembly. There is no micrometer adjustment for the pendulum nor is there a beat setting adjustment. The pendulum is a gridiron type instead of a mercury compensated one. To sum up, although it is a very fine mechanism, this earlier clock lacks some of the refinements which Graham incorporated in the first clock described (figures 8/37-45).

The case (figure 8/51) is very similar in design to the one illustrated in figure 8/46 but has

Figure 8/49. Movement with dial removed, compare with 8/40. Drive to calendar disc taken from first pinion of train instead of from motion work. This gives anti-clockwise rotation of squared arbor of last wheel between plates, hence pair of small wheels to reverse rotation.

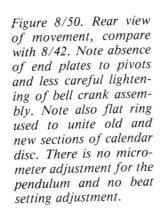

Figure 8/50. Rear view of movement, compare with 8/42. Note absence of end plates to pivots and less careful lightening of bell crank assembly. Note also flat ring used to unite old and new sections of calendar disc. There is no micrometer adjustment for the pendulum and no beat setting adjustment.

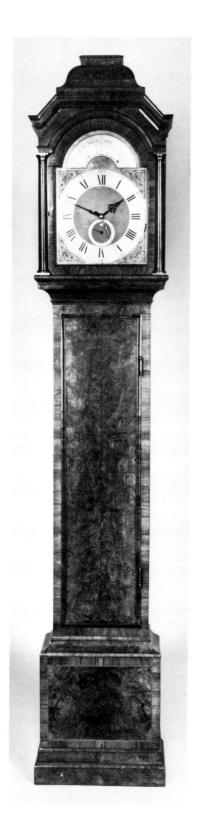

not been modified. It is veneered with burr walnut and has the earlier feature of a simpler moulding on the trunk door.

A third somewhat similar equation clock by Graham is illustrated by Cescinsky.[30] The dial resembles the previous ones in layout, has turbaned head spandrels, but the chapter ring is rather broader and has no markings on the inner edge. The annual calendar disc lacks the equation of time but has additional rings for sunrise and sunset times in hours and minutes. The disc has not been modified for the Gregorian calendar. The movement is apparently eight day and it may lack maintaining power. The clock is probably c.1745 and is in an elegant break arch walnut case with detached reeded columns which bears no resemblance to the two other cases.

30. H. Cescinsky, *The Old English Master Clockmakers and their Clocks,* 1938, p. 84.

Figure 8/51. Walnut veneered case of Graham timepiece, c.1735. In original state, compare with 8/46.

Chapter 9

THE AGE OF ELEGANCE
1700 – 1750

By 1700 the longcase clock had become very well established and fine, beautifully made clocks were being supplied in quite large numbers. Although technical advances continued in the first half of the eighteenth century, many of these did not affect the ordinary domestic clock which responded mainly to stylistic changes. As clocks had become accepted as useful furnishing items rather than still being regarded as scientific wonders, fewer were now made with a duration greater than eight days and the thirty-hour clock became popular for the cheaper market. With the very much wider range of quality being made it is important to recognise these variations. Where convenient, a group of clocks by one maker has been discussed to show that country makers were not necessarily restricted to the simple thirty-hour clocks which formed their staple product. It must not be forgotten that, in spite of the ingenious and complicated mechanisms described in Chapters 6 and 7, the vast majority of longcase clocks were simple, straightforward devices with only hour striking. Even so, amongst the exceptions are some of the most complicated clocks ever made.

THE SQUARE DIAL

Although Tompion had used arched or other shaped extensions on some of his dials in the first decade of the eighteenth century, square dials were normal on the more straightforward examples until c.1715 and their use was never entirely abandoned. George Graham, for example, normally used the square dial unless an arch were required for accommodating a complicated calendar dial or other device.

Figure 9/1 shows a month clock, the 11ins. dial of which is signed at the base 'Tho. Tompion Londini Fecit'. The spandrels are of the turbaned head type (C. & W. No. 19) and bolt and shutter maintaining power is provided. Both movement and case are numbered '365' and it probably dates from just before the start of Tompion's partnership with Edward Banger in 1701.

The case is of finely figured walnut with herring-bone banding and crossbanding, and is 7ft. 10ins. high including the finial. The trunk door has brass hinges which could be original as they were introduced at about

Figure 9/1. Tompion no. 365, c.1700. 11ins. dial, turbaned head spandrels and maintaining power to month movement. Both movement and case are numbered. Case veneered with finely figured walnut with herring-bone banding and crossbanding. Forward sliding hood with hinged door and lock, graceful caddy top and fine frets. Concave moulding under hood introduced about this date. Plinth with probably original skirting which does not obscure crossbanding. Gilt brass mounts, note especially capitals and bases, and trunk door hinges, introduced about this time.

Figure 9/2. Brass hinges. Near right, strap type introduced c.1700 for finest cases and used until mid-century and often afterwards. Note nail, not screw, holes in strap hinge. Decorative butt hinges then used on trunk doors and also used on some hood doors. Example shown far right is probably for latter.

this time on the finest clocks although iron ones continued to be used for some years. Figure 9/2 shows a typical early brass strap hinge, but many are less graceful in design than this pattern. Strap hinges were always used until at least the middle of the eighteenth century, when decorative butt hinges were introduced, though strap hinges continued to be used on many high grade cases. A rather small butt hinge is also shown in figure 9/2. Hinges on trunk doors are usually larger than this one which may have come from the hood door of a good quality case for which such hinges were also used.

The concave or cavetto moulding under the hood is an important change which was introduced about 1700, although the convex moulding continued to be used for some years, particularly on provincial cases. The moulding at the base of the trunk is similar to that used in the seventeenth century. This type continued in use for some time but from c.1710 it was often replaced by a concave section similar to the upper one. The change from convex to concave mouldings reflects a similar change which occurred on cabinets and other furniture. Most mouldings of decorative wood were still made cross-grained.

The hood slides forward and its lockable door is hinged by means of pins in the ends of the right-hand column which pivot in the frame of the hood. The columns are usually attached to the door until about 1750, but from c.1730 a few good quality cases have the door fitting between separate posts. Note the return to brass capitals and bases, but the capitals are Doric until much later in the century when Corinthian ones had a limited revival. Note also the elegant caddy top incorporating an additional fret and the gilt metal ball finials on plinths. When correctly fitted, as in this example, the side finials and their plinths will be found to line up with the hood columns. Many later, mainly provincial, cases have the finials not in line with the columns, making them look like the afterthoughts they probably were.

Bun feet were out of fashion by this time although still being used in the provinces. The skirting is probably original and it should be noted that it does not mask any of the cross-banding on the plinth.

Figure 9/3 shows the 11ins. dial of a month clock, c.1700-10, signed 'Hen Harper London.' It is unusual in showing the day of the week with its planetary sign as well as the date. Calendar information other than the date is very rare on square dial clocks but became more common, though still unusual, on arch dial clocks where the extra space available probably encouraged such devices.

Figure 9/4 is a detail view of the calendar apertures and figure 9/5 shows the complete day of the week disc with its unusual spellings. The mounting of the calendar ring and disc is shown in figure 9/6. The edge of the disc is thinned off to prevent it coming into contact with the date ring. Disc and ring are operated by different pins in the normal twenty-four hour calendar wheel.

The hands are typical early eighteenth century design and are well finished. The month movement is unusual in having outside rack striking instead of the usual count wheel.

Figure 9/7 shows the 11ins. dial of a typical London clock of c.1705. The signature 'Henry Perry Soho' is in its usual position on the chapter ring between VII and V. The minute numerals are slightly larger than were used earlier. The crown and cherub spandrels

Figure 9/3. 11ins. dial of month clock by Harper, c.1700-10, with rare feature of day of week as well as date. Typical well finished hands. Movement is unusual in having outside rack striking.

Figure 9/4. Calendar apertures of Harper dial. Planetary sign is given above day of week. Note spelling of 'Munday'.

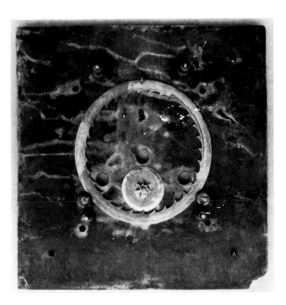

Figure 9/5. Complete day of week disc.

Figure 9/6. Mounting of calendar ring and disc on back of dial plate. Outer edge of disc thinned off to clear date ring. Disc and ring are operated by different pins in normal twenty-four hour wheel.

Figure 9/7. 11ins. dial of typical London clock of c.1705 by Perry. Crown and cherub spandrels (C. & W. No. 8) which were introduced c.1700. Beautifully finished original hands, including baluster shaped seconds hand. See Colour Plate 12.

Figure 9/8. Eight-day movement. First type of inside count wheel with outside detent. Raised bushes for barrel arbors are a repair.

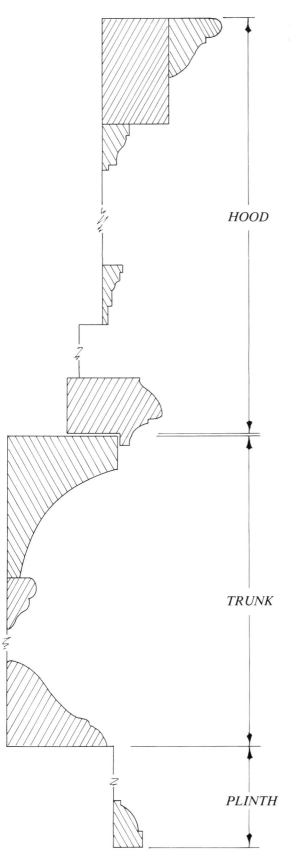

HOOD

TRUNK

PLINTH

Figure 9/9. Cross-section just under two-thirds actual size of mouldings on Perry case.

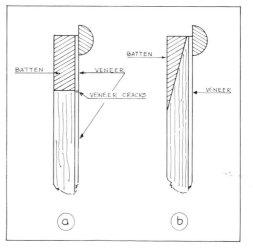

Figure 9/10. Construction of trunk doors: (a) normal design giving rise to cracking of veneer due to shrinkage; (b) method used on Perry case to overcome difficulty.

(C. & W. No. 8) were introduced around 1700 and came into general use. The original hands are beautifully finished, the seconds hand having a slight baluster shaping.

The eight-day movement, which has an inside count wheel with outside detent, is shown in figure 9/8. It has no special features, the raised bushes for the barrel arbors being a repair of some years' standing. The original brass cased weights have domed caps as well as domed bases, a type which was apparently introduced about this time but did not immediately displace the flat topped variety.

Colour Plate 12 shows the case, which stands 7ft. 0ins. high and is of oak veneered with burr walnut which has faded to a honey colour. It has lost its caddy top but is otherwise in original condition and the graceful fret (figure 9/7) still retains its original green silk backing. Notice that the fret is in one piece, quite a lot were (and still are) made of two pieces joined at the centre. These were cut at the same time to ensure symmetry and save work.

The whole case is gracefully proportioned, the waist measuring 11⅞ins. The trunk door has herring-bone banding immediately inside the half round beading, and

Figure 9/11. Year timepiece by Edmund Wright, c.1700-10. Single handed to permit a simpler and more efficient train. Apart from usual quarter hour divisions, outer edge is divided into minutes and numbered every ten. Lunar dials are very rare at this period but this type became common on north country clocks later. Bolt and shutter maintaining power is provided.

Figure 9/12. Case of Wright clock. Substantial carcase veneered with arabesque marquetry incorporating birds. Lower, walnut, skirting probably added later to protect marquetry one. Brass capitals and bases to hood but iron trunk door hinges.

the lenticle surround is of walnut. The sides of the trunk and the front of the plinth are panelled with broad crossbanding, a sign of quality. The mouldings are cross-grained and a cross-section of all the mouldings appears in figure 9/9.

The trunk doors of veneered cases usually have battens glued across at top and bottom to prevent warping, as shown in figure 9/10a. Subsequent shrinkage causes movement of these glued joints and results in cracking of the veneer. This is particularly serious when the veneer is of marquetry or burr wood and is almost the hallmark of an early case. The problem has been solved very simply in the Perry case. The battens are fitted on a long bevel as shown in figure 9/10b, which is a complete cure as the joint between door and batten is kept away from the veneer.

Brass capitals and bases for the hood columns became usual in the eighteenth century, as on the Tompion case described above (figure 9/1), but the Perry has walnut ones (figure 9/7). Note that they are squared like the metal ones, whereas most of those of c.1680-1700 have no squared section. The hood door is secured by a wrought iron bolt operated from inside the trunk and the only brass mount is the keyhole escutcheon.

Figure 9/11 shows the dial of an interesting year timepiece signed on the chapter ring by an almost unknown maker 'Edm: Wright Londini fecit' and contemporary with the Perry, c.1700-10. It is single handed to reduce friction by allowing for a simpler and more efficient train. In this respect it should be compared with the early movement described on page 50 and illustrated in figures 3/6-8. The chapter ring has the usual quarter hour divisions on the inner edge and divisions for every minute near the outer edge with further divisions for the five minutes and numbers 10 to 60 for the minutes in each hour. Some north country thirty-hour clocks used a somewhat similar idea with a single hand pointing to quarter hour and five minute divisions on the outer edge of the chapter ring and one is shown in figure 9/67. The moon phase and age indicator is very unusual at this period although this type became popular on north country clocks later. The disc carrying the moon face and numerals has two ratchet shaped teeth per day and is stepped on one tooth every twelve hours by a pin or other projection on the hour wheel. Bolt and shutter maintaining power is provided to protect the delicate escapement.

The case (figure 9/12) is similar to the Perry case but is more stoutly built to cater for the heavy driving weight and ensure stability to avoid the case swaying with the pendulum. It is veneered with arabesque marquetry incorporating birds but no other figures. The hood columns have brass capitals and bases but the trunk door still has iron hinges. The lower, walnut, skirting was probably added later to protect the marquetry one.

Figure 9/13 shows another similar clock of c.1710 with the 11ins. dial signed on the chapter ring 'J. Windmills Londini fecit.' The calendar aperture is circular and ringed to match the winding holes, a change which was introduced about this time although the square opening continued to be used. The movement has latched plates.

The case is 6ft. 10½ins. high and is veneered with burr walnut. It has the unusual feature of brackets under the hood, carved with acanthus scrolling. Some cases have similar decoration at the lower rear corners of the trunk also. The moulding at the bottom of the waist is the concave type which became very popular in the eighteenth century. There are no brass mounts.

The use of subsidiary dials was rare with the square dial but figure 9/14 shows an example with one in each corner. The 12ins. dial plate is signed in a curved reserve just below the centre 'Langley Bradley London' and foliage is engraved round the calendar aperture and the signature. The four subsidiary dial rings have Tudor roses engraved within them and are surrounded with fragments of, probably cherub, spandrels (C. & W. No. 5). The eight-day movement has count wheel hour striking and quarter chiming on eight bells, also controlled by count wheel.

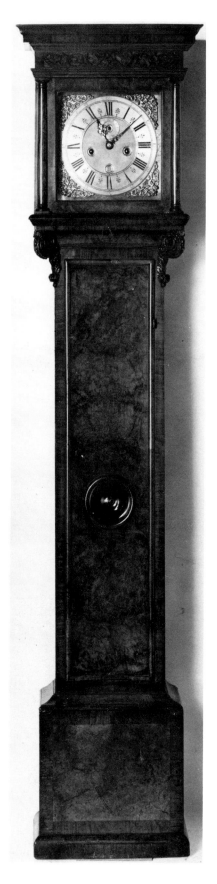

Figure 9/13. Clock by Windmills, c.1710. Note change to circular calendar opening, ringed to match winding holes, introduced about this time. Case veneered with burr walnut with unusual feature of brackets under hood, carved with acanthus scrolling. Note lower trunk moulding concave to match upper one. There are no brass mounts. Height 6ft. 10½ins.

Figure 9/14. Chime clock by Langley Bradley, c.1710. 12ins. dial signed just below centre, with rare feature of four subsidiary dials. Upper dials indicate last hour and quarter struck and lower ones are for correcting the striking and chiming, probably a unique feature. Case is veneered with mellowed seaweed marquetry and has brass mounts except for iron trunk door hinges. Height to top of caddy 7ft. 9ins.

The upper left hand dial is marked 1-12 and its hand points to the last hour struck. The upper right hand dial is marked 1-4 and its hand similarly indicates the last quarter chimed. The hands for these two dials are driven from their respective count wheels so the spacing on their dials corresponds to the slots in the count wheels. The lower left hand dial is marked 'Turne to the Right to Sett of [i.e. off] the Clock', and momentary movement of its hand releases the striking as necessary if it is out of step with the hands. The lower right hand dial is marked 'Turne to the Left to Sett of the Chimes', and its hand is used to correct the chimes. These elaborate arrangements for correcting the striking and chiming are very rare, if not unique, on an English clock, but dials like the two upper ones are quite usual on sixteenth and seventeenth century Continental table clocks.

The case is veneered with seaweed marquetry which has faded to a lovely mellow colour and there are brass capitals and bases to the hood columns but iron hinges to the trunk door. The height to the top of the caddy is 7ft. 9ins. and the date is c.1710.

Figure 9/15. 8ins. country dial, unsigned but dated 1712. Very crude engraving, so probably done by clockmaker. Replaced spandrels.

Figure 9/16. Dial with chapter ring removed. Note practice engraving including '1712' and 'Joh...'

Figure 9/17. Birdcage movement of anonymous clock. Soundly made but with iron frame for economy. Thin dial plate also for economy.

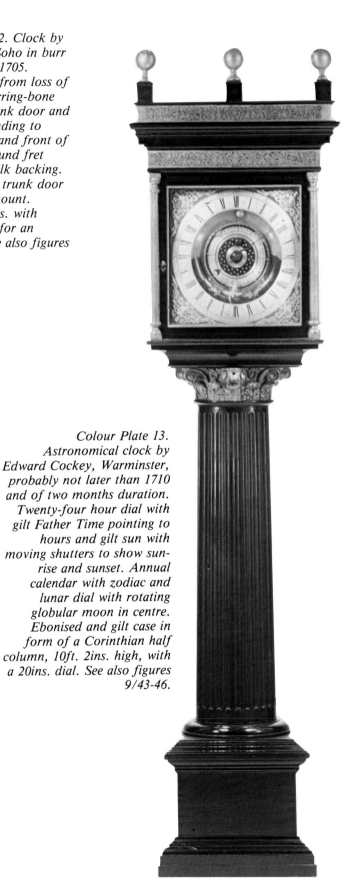

Colour Plate 12. Clock by Henry Perry, Soho in burr walnut case, c.1705. Original apart from loss of caddy top. Herring-bone banding on trunk door and broad crossbanding to sides of trunk and front of plinth. Fine sound fret with original silk backing. Escutcheon on trunk door is only brass mount. Height 7ft. 0ins. with 11⅞ins. waist for an 11ins. dial. See also figures 9/7-10.

Colour Plate 13. Astronomical clock by Edward Cockey, Warminster, probably not later than 1710 and of two months duration. Twenty-four hour dial with gilt Father Time pointing to hours and gilt sun with moving shutters to show sunrise and sunset. Annual calendar with zodiac and lunar dial with rotating globular moon in centre. Ebonised and gilt case in form of a Corinthian half column, 10ft. 2ins. high, with a 20ins. dial. See also figures 9/43-46.

Country clocks are notoriously difficult to date accurately but the crudely engraved dial in figure 9/15 is an exception. It is 8ins. square, is not signed and, by its poor quality, the engraving was done by the clockmaker. The spandrels are replacements. Figure 9/16 shows how the maker practised on the dial plate, from which it is reasonable to deduce that the clock was made in 1712 and that the maker's christian name was John!

The thirty-hour birdcage movement (figure 9/17) has iron plates and pillars and the dial is attached to it by means of lugs which are pinned to the top and bottom plates. The iron frame and a very thin dial plate were made for economy of brass, but the movement is nicely made with file-cut decoration on the hammer springs. Proof of the soundness of the move-

Figure 9/18. More elegant brass framed birdcage movement with turned columns showing its lantern ancestry. Note bad work, vice marks on pillars, soft solder repair to dial plate. Hammer spring reversed to use unworn surface.

Figure 9/19. Fine clock by Boyce, Puddletown, probably c.1710-20. 11ins. dial has cherub and foliage spandrels and is very much 'London' style. Case veneered with walnut and floral marquetry in panels, note how acanthus foliage has developed into a seaweed design. Formal borders to trunk and plinth indicate a late date. Skirting is rather too narrow.

Figure 9/20. Good quality dial of thirty-hour clock by Kefford, Royston, probably c.1710-20. Early type chapter ring with crown and cherub spandrels. Hour hand original, minute hand probably later.

ment is given by the fact that it goes very happily with a weight of 3lb. on the usual double line, although this is not sufficient to operate the striking. It is worth noting that birdcage movements were made with heavy flies like those in lantern clocks, whereas thirty-hour plate frame movements had light flies as in eight-day clocks.

The case has been lost. It would have been made by the local carpenter or joiner of any readily available wood such as oak, elm or pine. The small size dial (8ins.) necessitated a trunk width greater than that of the dial to allow an adequate clearance for the pendulum. The result was a crude 'straight up and down' case where the three sections – hood, trunk and plinth – were ill defined. These unattractive cases must once have been quite common but are now extremely rare and have been almost completely neglected by horological authors.[1]

The movement shown in figure 9/18 clearly shows its lantern ancestry in the nicely turned brass corner pillars. Unfortunately the maker is not known but some west country makers used decorated pillars; for example Peter Bower of Redlinch, Somerset used square brass ones with decorative capitals and bases. Note the bad work – vice marks on the pillars through not using fibre jaws or other protection, and the soft soldered repair to the dial plate where brass strips and rivets would have been better. The hammer spring has been reversed to present an unworn surface to the hammer.

The next clock to be considered (figure 9/19) is also provincial but has nothing else in common with the previous examples. The 11ins. dial is signed on the chapter ring 'Laurence Boyce Piddle Towne' (now Puddletown, Dorset). Baillie records only that Boyce made a clock for Bere Regis church in 1719, but he was apparently born c.1677 and died in 1738.[2] The dial is very much in the London style of 1695-1700, having cherub and foliage spandrels (C. & W. No. 5) with floral engraving between them and the five minute and five second divisions extended between the numerals. The only provincial feature is rather complicated engraving round the calendar aperture, consisting of three coronets and scroll work. The hour hand is also typical of 1695-1700 but the minute hand suggests a date of 1710-20.

The case is a fine example of walnut and floral marquetry, in panels, but the acanthus foliage has developed into a seaweed design. The formal borders surrounding the trunk door and plinth panel indicate a late date, as does the concave moulding under the hood. The skirting is very narrow and is probably a replacement. A difficult clock to date and one wonders how much of it was made in the Dorset village. Its probable date is 1710-20.

Figure 9/20 shows the dial of a thirty-hour clock signed on the chapter ring 'Tho. Kifford Royston', almost certainly the Thomas Kefford recorded as 'early eighteenth century'. The dial is of good quality and in the London style, but the chapter ring has the minute numbers within the divisions in the seventeenth century manner. The cherub and crown spandrels (C. & W. No. 8) did not come into use until about 1700. The hour hand fits the dial in style and in size but the minute hand appears later and is too short; it may well be a replacement. In summing up, this is probably a clock of 1710-20 but could be slightly later. The case has not been shown as it is c.1750 or even later, so is unlikely to be the original one.

THE ARCHED DIAL

This should properly be called the 'break arch' dial, to distinguish it from the full arch, that is one which is the full width of the dial (figure 9/21e). This latter type is rare and is normally found mainly on a small number of nineteenth century clocks, although Hindley of York used it in the mid-eighteenth century, see figure 9/116.

Tompion used small semi-circular arches on the dials of his equation clocks[2a] and a few other makers also used this type to accommodate a strike/silent or other device as in figure 9/21a. The early arches, provided purely as decorative features, were usually much wider

1. Brian Loomes is an exception, see his *Country Clocks and their London Origins*, 1976, p. 124.
2. See T. Tribe and P. Whatmoor, *Dorset Clocks and Clockmakers*, 1981, p. 69.
2a. As in his Bath Pump Room Equation Clock of 1709.

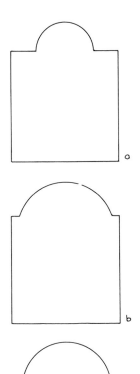

Figure 9/21. Development of the arched dial:

(a) Small semi-circular type introduced by Tompion c.1709 on equation clocks.

(b) Wide, shallow break arch introduced c.1710 for decorative purposes.

(c) Full size semi-circular break arch introduced c.1715.

(d) Serpentine or ogee arch introduced by Delander c.1725 and used later by a number of makers.

(e) Full arch, introduced by Hindley c.1750 but used very little until the nineteenth century.

Figure 9/22. Month clock by Gretton having 12ins. dial with typical shallow arch used for signature surrounded by scrolling foliage, c.1710. Spandrels are cherub head with flowers. Case veneered with arabesque marquetry including mouldings and columns. Break arch hood following line of dial but note square topped trunk door. Plinth seriously cut down and present height 7ft. 1½ins. All brass mounts but elongated bases to columns are exceptional.

Figure 9/23. 12ins. dial of month clock by Windmills, c.1710. Low arch with fine gilt cartouche for signature and scrolling foliage. Rare floral spandrels. Fine, typical hands and strike/silent at VI.

Figure 9/24. Case of Windmills clock, veneered with burr walnut and with very rare Corinthian pilasters with gilt capitals and bases, a furniture feature. Height 7ft. 4ins. with a 12½ins. waist for a 12ins. dial.

and shallower, being, like the later ones, 2-2½ins. smaller than the dial width but considerably less than half a circle, as in figure 9/21b.

Figure 9/22 shows a typical early arched dial of c.1710, signed 'Chā Gretton London' in the arch amidst scrolling foliage. The dial has an engraved border and is 12ins. across, the usual size except for clocks of monumental size and later examples. The spandrels are a version of the cherub head with flowers (C. & W. No. 7), which was popular with Tompion. The movement is of month duration and has the usual outside count wheel striking.

The case has arabesque marquetry on an oak carcase, the marquetry even being applied to the trunk mouldings and hood columns. The break arch hood, following the line of the dial, was introduced at this time and was used to some extent for the rest of the century. It was probably derived from the dome-topped bureau cabinets of the Queen Anne period. Many of these break arch hoods are surmounted by a superstructure or caddy. The trunk door remains square topped until c.1720 when a break arch top was introduced to match the arched dial. The plinth has been seriously cut down and the present height is 7ft. 1½ins. The case has the usual brass hinges and other mounts, but the elongated bases to the hood columns are very unusual.

Figure 9/23 shows another 12ins. dial with low arch, very similar to the Gretton and contemporary with it (c.1710). The arch is again filled with scrolling foliage but the signature 'Joseph Windmills London' is on a fine gilt brass cartouche and the spandrels are a rare floral type not in C. & W. The month movement has rack striking, probably provided so that it could be silenced when required, note the lever just below VI.

The case (figure 9/24) is veneered with burr walnut and is of fine quality. The Corinthian pilasters with their fire gilt brass capitals and bases are extremely rare on clock cases but are found on some fine bureau cabinets and other furniture of the period. The case is 7ft. 4ins. high and has a 12½ins. waist.

Another example of a dial before the arch had become standardised is shown in figure 9/25. It is signed on the chapter ring 'Rich: Penny London' and probably dates from c.1715. The arch is a full semi-circle but unusually large being barely an inch smaller than the square part of the dial. The engraving resembles that used on the back plates of bracket clocks of the period and, as the reserve fits the spandrel which occupies it, one has to assume that was the original idea. The striking is controlled by an inside count wheel.

Figure 9/25. Dial of clock by Penny probably c.1715. Arch is semi-circular but unusually large and with a crown and cross sceptres spandrel surrounded by scrolled engraving which fits accurately round it.

Figure 9/26 shows a semi-circular arch smaller than the later ones and provided to accommodate a dial and hand for pendulum regulation. The clock is signed 'Geo. Graham London' and was made within a very few years of Graham succeeding Tompion when the latter died in 1713. Later Graham simplified his chapter rings by marking only the half hours on the inner edge and using a diamond half hour mark like the half quarter marking on this dial. He also abandoned engraving between the spandrels. Note the large slender seconds ring which Graham reintroduced. The turban head spandrels (C. & W. No. 19) were first used by Tompion about the beginning of the century. The movement has bolt and shutter maintaining power operated by a lever in an unusual cutaway between IX and X.

The case (figure 9/27) is veneered with ebony or possibly ebonised pearwood, and resembles some of the cases housing clocks by Richard Street in having elaborate break arch panels. In particular it calls to mind the huge clock which Sir Isaac Newton had made by Street and which he presented to the Observatory at Trinity College, Cambridge in 1708.[3] As Lloyd comments, there appears to have been some connection between Street and Tompion although none has yet been discovered. Apart from similarities in their movements they probably used the same casemaker. Graham undoubtedly carried on for a time as his master had done.

The next illustration (figure 9/28) shows the standard type of arch, that is normal size and

3. See H.A. Lloyd, *Old Clocks,* 3rd edition, 1964, pp. 107, 113, pl. 25, 39.

Figure 9/26. Dial of clock by Graham, c.1715, with a fairly small semi-circular arch used for pendulum regulation. Note bolt and shutter operated by lever near IX and reintroduction of larger, slender seconds ring.

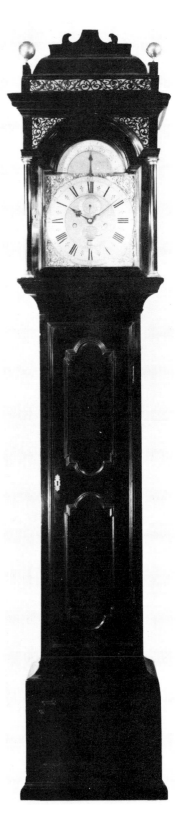

Figure 9/27. Case of Graham clock, veneered with ebony or ebonised pearwood. Elaborate break arch panels to trunk door and shaped panel to plinth. Elegant caddy top and fine sound frets.

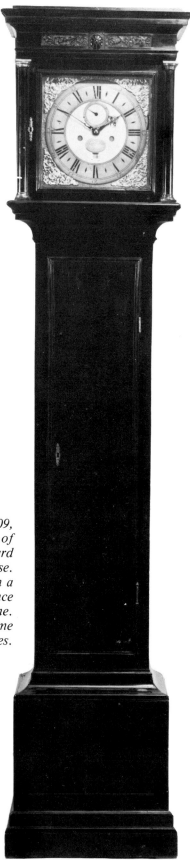

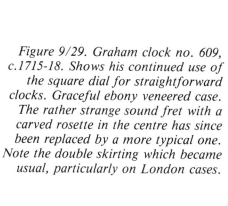

Figure 9/28. Month clock by Quare, no. 109, c.1715. Normal sized semi-circular arch used for typical Quare feature, a simple calendar. Beautifully proportioned case veneered with burr walnut and with graceful caddy bearing gilt wooden finials. Compare with slightly later Quare no. 145 in figures 7/24 and 26 and Colour Plate 10.

Figure 9/29. Graham clock no. 609, c.1715-18. Shows his continued use of the square dial for straightforward clocks. Graceful ebony veneered case. The rather strange sound fret with a carved rosette in the centre has since been replaced by a more typical one. Note the double skirting which became usual, particularly on London cases.

Figure 9/30. Dial of an unusual clock by Jordan, c.1720-25. Note wheat-ear border to dial plate but no ringing of winding holes. Unusual calendar in arch.

Figure 9/31. Arch of Jordan dial with large calendar which is reset at end of month by pulling a cord. Apertures show month and its number of days. Scrolled engraving used to fill spaces in arch.

Figure 9/32. Graceful black japanned case of Jordan clock with original decoration. Overall height 7ft. 11½ins.

Figure 9/32

approximately semi-circular. The dial is signed on a reserve below the centre 'Dan. Quare London 109' and the whole clock dates from c.1715. The arch is used for a typical Quare feature, a simple calendar but this example has every day numbered. The spandrels are of the cherub and crown design (C. & W. No. 8) and the arch has the dolphin pattern (C. & W. No. 38) which was very popular as long as applied spandrels were used. As can be deduced from the low position of the winding squares, it has a month movement.

The case is veneered with burr walnut and is beautifully proportioned with a very graceful caddy surmounted by three gilt wooden finials. It is worthwhile to compare the whole clock with the slightly later Quare No. 145 described in Chapter 7, p. 145, figures 7/24, 26 and Colour Plate 10.

PERSISTENCE OF THE SQUARE DIAL AS AN ALTERNATIVE

The arched dial has now become established as a normal feature so clocks will be shown chronologically independent of whether the dial be arched or square.

The next example (figure 9/29) has an 11ins. square dial signed on a plaque and at the base of the dial plate 'Geo. Graham London', and numbered twice on the movement '609', which dates it c.1715-18. It demonstrates Graham's continued use of the square dial for a straight-forward clock without elaborate calendar or equation work. The gilt dial plate has a finely matted centre and the spandrels are of the turbaned head pattern (C. & W. No. 19). The eight-day movement has latched plates, rack striking and a dead beat escapement, with bolt and shutter maintaining power operated by a lever in a slot in the dial near III.

The ebony veneered case is simple but beautifully proportioned and is 7ft. 0ins. high. The rather strange fret with a carved rosette in the centre has now been replaced by a more typical one. Note the double skirting which became a normal feature, particularly with London cases.

Figure 9/30 shows the dial of an unusual clock signed 'John:Jordan:London', of c.1720-25, which demonstrates once again that interesting mechanisms are to be found amongst the output of 'unknown' makers. Although the dial plate still has a wheat-ear border, the matted centre is like the two previous examples, free from ringed apertures. The spandrels are the female head amidst scrolling foliage, often known as mask and scroll (C. & W. No. 21), a type which came in about 1720 and had a long run of popularity. The arch (figure 9/31) has a large calendar with every day numbered and the hand is reset at the end of the month by pulling a cord, a very rare feature. To assist in resetting the calendar, apertures show the month and the number of days in the month. The scrolled engraving was often used to fill spaces for which suitably shaped spandrel castings were not available.

The graceful case (figure 9/32) retains most of its original japanned decoration with a black ground. The caddy top should be noted as many of these have been removed to suit low ceilings. It is almost certain that all eighteenth century square headed clocks, other than cottage examples, had caddy tops originally. The overall height is 7ft. 11½ins.

Another clock of similar date (c.1720-25) is shown in figure 9/33. The 12ins. arched dial is signed on a silvered plaque below the centre 'Edward Bodenham London'. The dial plate has a wheat-ear border, elaborate engraving in the arch and, unusual with a London clock, large engraved birds on the matted centre. The spandrels are the crown and crossed sceptre type (C. & W. No. 10). The sector shaped opening in the arch shows a day of the week indi-cator with the appropriate deity for each day being displayed. It has a month movement.

The case is veneered with burr walnut with herring-bone banding used on the trunk door and to form panels on the plinth and the sides of the case. The hood columns have turned walnut capitals and bases and the unusual arched side windows should be noted. Height 7ft. 9ins. A good quality case.

The arch dial provided clockmakers with plenty of scope for variety in decorative treat-ment, and figure 9/34 shows an interesting variation by 'William Sellers Longacer London' of c.1725. The arch is almost filled by a casting which incorporates a crown and two pairs of cherubs, and surrounds the name plaque. The spaces left in the arch are filled with scrolled engraving. The crown and crossed sceptre spandrels (C. & W. No. 10) were obviously chosen to harmonise with the arch decoration. The fact that the spandrels and the arch casting slightly overlap the engraving here and there does not mean that they have been changed. The broad chapter ring with large minute numbers should be noted. The eight-day movement has quarter chiming on eight bells.

The case (figure 9/35) has matched walnut veneers with herring-bone crossbandings and the break arch hood is matched by the trunk door, an early use of this design. The skirting would not have been cut away originally. The height is 6ft. 11ins.

Mirror doors, which were often used on early eighteenth century bureau cabinets, were also used occasionally on clock cases. Apart from their decorative value they also reflected what light was available, a useful feature with the bureaux which were provided with candle slides. The mirrors were often known as Vauxhall mirror plates after the glass works established at Vauxhall by the Duke of Buckingham c.1670.

Figure 9/36 shows a case with the somewhat unusual combination of a mirror door and japanned decoration. The sharpness of the bevelling suggests that the mirror plate has been renewed, as early mirrors have a not very obvious rounded bevel resulting from hand work. The black japanned work also appears to have been restored. The height is 8ft. 0ins. excluding the figure of Atlas which is probably of Dutch origin.

The dial is signed on a plaque below the centre 'Claudius du Chesne Londini' and the dial plate has a wheat-ear border. There is a strike/silent hand in the arch flanked by figures of cupids mounted on eagles instead of the more usual dolphins. The spandrels are the pattern with a head amidst scrolling foliage (C. & W. No. 21). The whole clock is c.1725.

Two clocks by Delander have already been illustrated and described but no excuse is needed for including the beautiful specimen in figure 9/37. The dial has the flattened or ogee arch pioneered by this maker and used by some others later in the century. The signature 'Dan Delander London No. 17' is on a silvered plaque in the arch and is surrounded by scrolled engraving. The spandrels are an unusual pattern with a head

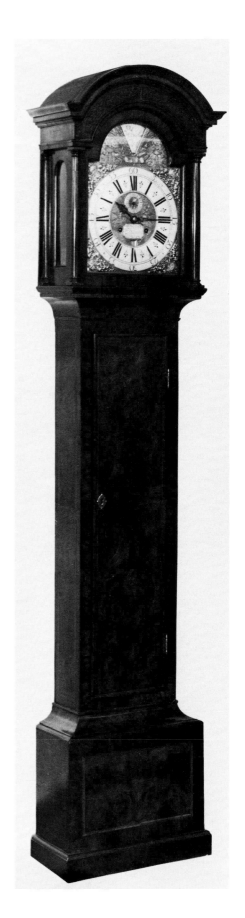

Figure 9/33. Month clock by Bodenham, c.1720-25. 12ins. dial, signed on silvered plaque below centre and with day of week and appropriate deity in aperture in arch. Elaborate engraving in arch and birds engraved on matted centre. Good quality case veneered with burr walnut and with herring-bone banding on trunk door and to form panels on plinth and case sides. Note unusual arched windows in hood. Height 7ft. 9ins.

Figure 9/34. Dial of clock by Sellers, c.1725. Arch is almost filled by a casting incorporating a crown and two pairs of cherubs with a silvered plaque in the centre. Crown and cherub spandrels chosen to match arch decoration. Note broad chapter ring with large minute numerals. Eight-day quarter chiming movement.

Figure 9/35. Case of Sellers clock with matching walnut veneers and herring-bone banding. Note early use of break arch trunk door. The skirting would not have been cut away originally. Height 6ft. 11ins.

Figure 9/36. Clock by du Chesne in black japanned case, c.1725, with unusual mirror door. Sharp bevel to mirror plate suggests it has been renewed and some of japanned work has been restored. Height 8ft. 0ins. excluding figure of Atlas which is probably Dutch. Dial has strike/silent in arch flanked by unusual cupids mounted on eagles.

Figure 9/37. Delander no. 17 with ogee arched dial introduced by him. Name on silvered plaque in arch surrounded by scrolled engraving. Unusual head and foliage spandrels. Duplex escapement and bolt and shutter maintaining power. Elegant burr walnut case with very early use of canted corners. Note also octagonal plinth panel, trunk door shaped to match dial and well designed caddy. c.1725.

  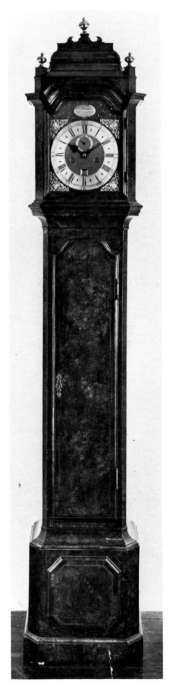

amongst scrolling foliage, not shown in C. & W. The seconds ring is numbered 6, 12, 18 . . . . . to agree with the two seconds steps of the hand. Bolt and shutter maintaining power is provided and is operated by a lever at III. The movement has Delander's duplex escapement as illustrated and described in figure 8/6. The pendulum has a rectangular steel rod and a very heavy bob.

The elegant case is veneered with burr walnut and shows a very early use of canted corners. Other features of interest are the raised octagonal panel on the plinth and the top of the trunk door shaped to match the dial. The whole is completed by the well designed caddy. The date is c.1725.

FOUR CLOCKS BY A PROVINCIAL MAKER

Four clocks by an almost unrecorded maker,[4] Thomas Baker of Portsmouth will now be considered. It is fortuitous that these examples happen to be available, but they exhibit some interesting as well as puzzling characteristics.

Figure 9/38 shows a very attractive clock with 12ins. dial, signed on a reserve below the centre 'Thos Baker Portsmouth'. There is a wheat-ear border to the dial plate and scrolled decoration in the rather small, shallow arch and it has crown and cherub spandrels (C. & W. No. 8). The left hand subsidiary dial is for pendulum regulation, the central one is a simple calendar and the right hand dial is for strike/silent. The five pillar movement has heavy steelwork and, of course, rack striking to permit silencing.

The slim case is veneered with walnut with herring-bone banding and crossbanding. There is a form of convex moulding under the hood, a survival fairly often found on early eighteenth century provincial cases. The hood columns have gilt wood capitals and bases. All the Baker cases have iron trunk door hinges. The very small moulding at the top of the plinth suggests that it has been restored. The height is 7ft. 0ins. and the date probably c.1715-20.

The dial of the next example (figure 9/39) again has a wheat-ear border and crown and cherub spandrels. It is given a very provincial appearance by the engraving which almost covers the matting and by the unusual engraving of the chapter ring. This is in contrast to the other dials which have no provincial features. It is difficult to date this clock, but it is probably c.1720-30 and may be by another maker of the same name.

The pleasantly proportioned case (figure 9/40) is, like the other two, veneered with walnut and has herring-bone banding and cross-banding. The twisted columns are an extraordinary feature and are

4. *Baillie's* only date is 'ante 1753'.

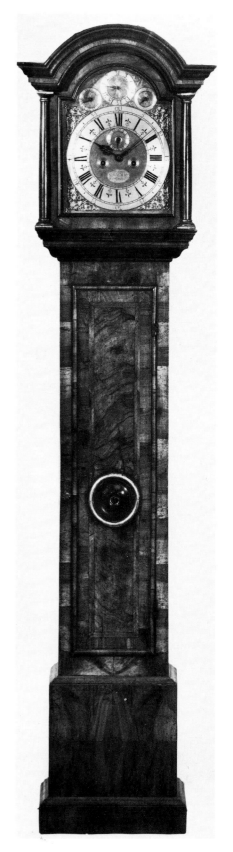

Figure 9/38. Clock by Thomas Baker, Portsmouth, c.1715-20, in attractive walnut veneered case with herring-bone banding and crossbanding. Note survival of convex moulding under hood. Gilt wood capitals and bases and no brass mounts. Very small moulding at top of plinth suggests a restoration. Height 7ft. 0ins. 12ins. dial has shallow arch with subsidiary dials for pendulum regulation, calendar and strike/silent.

Figure 9/39. Dial of another clock by Baker. Note provincial feature of extensive engraving on matted centre, also unusual chapter ring. Different from other Thomas Baker dials illustrated and could be by another maker of same name. Probably c.1720-30.

Figure 9/40. Case of clock shown in 9/39. Veneered in walnut with herring-bone banding and crossbanding. The twisted columns are strange and could be a recent 'improvement'. Arched side windows to hood, a provincial feature when combined with a square dial.

Figure 9/41. A third Baker clock. The conventional 12ins. dial has crown and sceptre spandrels. Replaced hands. Attractive walnut veneered case similar to the others but with an arch and double beading to trunk door, both provincial features. Gilt wood capitals and bases. Cut-away skirting probably a replacement. Height 6ft. 11ins.

probably a recent 'improvement'. The hood has arched side windows, something which a London casemaker would not have done on a square dial case. The clock may have been recased, but if so it was put in another provincial one.

The third example (figure (9/41) has a conventional 12ins. dial but with crown and sceptre spandrels (C. & W. No. 10) which may make it slightly later than the other two. The hands are very late eighteenth century style and look like modern stampings. The striking is controlled by an inside count wheel.

Again, an attractive case, but with the provincial feature of an arched trunk door in conjunction with a square dial. The double beading round the trunk door is a furniture feature of this date not often found on clock cases. The capitals and bases to the columns are again of gilt wood. The cut-away skirting is probably a later replacement. The height is 6ft. 11ins.

The last of the group (figure 9/42) is a thirty-hour clock with an attractive dial. The engraving of the signature, the foliage between the spandrels, and the half-quarter marks very closely resemble that on the previous example, but the spandrels are of a pattern not often found on provincial clocks (C. & W. No. 7). The circular date aperture is usually later than the square ones. The hour hand is apparently original but the minute hand is too long and is probably a replacement. Nothing is known about the case.

These four clocks have been discussed together to illustrate the interest as well as the difficulties which may be found with provincial clocks.

COMPLICATED CLOCKS

Over the years a number of clockmakers, famous or little known, produced some very complex masterpieces which appeal strongly to the lover of ingenious mechanisms as they undoubtedly also did when they were first made, and this is a convenient point at which to discuss some examples.

Edward Cockey of Warminster made at least six complicated astronomical clocks and yet surprisingly little is known about him. According to Bellchambers[5] the Edward Cockey who was born in

5. J.K. Bellchambers, *Somerset Clockmakers*, 1968, p. 43.

Figure 9/42. Thirty-hour clock by Baker. Dial has features in common with those in figures 9/38 and 41 but cherub and flower spandrels are a type seldom found on provincial clocks. Circular date aperture is usually later than square type. Hour hand apparently original but minute hand too long so probably a replacement.

1701 and died in 1786 was the second of that name but there seems little definite information about the earlier man. The astronomical clocks are so individual in design that they are difficult to date, but stylistic changes in the dials suggest that they were made over a fairly long period.

Figure 9/43 shows the 20ins. dial of one of the early productions, signed on the chapter ring 'Warminster' with below it 'Edward Cockey'. The twenty-four hour chapter ring has simple half hour markings as used on seventeenth century London dials and is divided into twice sixty minutes. The very large spandrels are of a special design which Cockey used on nearly all his astronomical clocks. They incorporate a crowned female figure, could it be intended to represent Queen Anne? There is a long balanced minute hand and the hours are indicated by the scythe of a figure of Father Time. There is a gilt sun which is carried round on an assembly which also carries the figure of Father Time. The sun shows its passage through the heavens and indicates the hours during the day. The times of sunrise and sunset are shown by means of rising and falling shutters.

Within the ring carrying the gilt sun is an annual calendar dial which is also marked with

Colour Plate 14. Clock by William Morgan, Southwark, with urn spandrels and strike/silent in arch, c.1765. Dark green japanned case with well raised gilt decoration. Note early type of pagoda top. Height 7ft. 9ins.

Colour Plate 15. Complicated clock by Gandy, Cockermouth, 1757. Annual calendar on chapter ring, twenty-four hour dial in arch with gilt sun and moving shutters for sunrise and sunset. Lunar and tidal dial at centre of arch. Case of red or Virginia walnut with plinth and trunk door veneered and crossbanded. Ogee feet, canted corners to plinth, reeded quarter columns to trunk and detached plain columns to hood. Height 7ft. 2¼ins. with a 14ins. dial. See also figures 10/31 and 32.

the signs of the zodiac, each divided into 30 degrees. A decorative gilt pointer, almost behind the minute hand in the photograph, indicates the date, and another gilt pointer, to the left of Father Time, indicates the position of the sun in the zodiac. Both these pointers are carried round on the ring which rotates in twenty four hours. The calendar ring has 365 teeth and is mounted friction tight on the twenty-four hour assembly. The latter also carries a six leaved pinion meshing with the calendar ring and provided with a six pointed star wheel which is advanced one tooth as it passes a fixed stud on the dial plate. The calendar is therefore stepped on one tooth every twenty-four hours.

Inside the calendar ring is a rotating disc which has a scale 1 to 29½ anti-clockwise round its periphery for showing the age of the moon. This is read off against the extended foot of Father Time. Within this scale is a star spangled sky with a rotating globular moon, half dark blue and half silvered, to show the phases. In a lunation of 29½ days the lunar dial has to make one turn anti-clockwise with respect to Father Time. As Father Time will have made 29½ turns clockwise in a lunation, the moon dial must make 28½ turns clockwise. It therefore makes one clockwise turn in approximately 24 hours 50½ minutes.

The dial also shows the relative positions of the sun and moon as viewed from the earth. At new moon, it is between the earth and the sun, and at full moon it is on the side of the earth remote from the sun.

Figure 9/43. 20ins. dial of astronomical clock by Edward Cockey, Warminster, rather difficult to date but probably not later than 1710. Twenty-four hour chapter ring, note early style half hour markings. Very large special design spandrels may represent Queen Anne. Long, balanced minute hand, and scythe of Father Time to point to hours. Father Time is mounted on a rotating ring which also carries a gilt sun and there are rising and falling shutters to indicate sunrise and sunset. Within the ring carrying Father Time are a rotating annual calendar and a lunar dial with rotating globular moon. Case is shown in Colour Plate 13.

Figure 9/44. Cockey movement with dial removed, showing large 'spider wheel' which rotates in twenty-four hours. Note that motion work is driven from first pinion of train (on right). Main winding arbor on right. Arbor for later auxiliary barrel on left. Large fine toothed wheels rotate once per year and their cams operate sunrise and sunset shutters, see figure 9/45. Cams are shown in position for summer solstice.

Figure 9/44 shows the movement with the dial removed. To avoid the extensive motion work, winding arbors are brought out at the sides. The wheel towards the bottom right is mounted with a friction clutch on the extended arbor of the first pinion of the going train. This wheel drives a pinion on the central arbor and the latter is squared at the front end for the minute hand. A pinion fixed to the wheel and visible in the photograph drives the hour wheel which has a pipe on which is mounted the large 'spider wheel' for the twenty-four hour assembly. Behind the pinion mentioned above is another slightly smaller pinion which drives a wheel behind the hour wheel and which has a pipe to carry the lunar dial. The two pinions are visible in figure 9/46.

The hour wheel carries a pinion which drives a wheel above it. This wheel has a tiny five pin lantern pinion which drives the large fine-toothed wheel on the right (see figure 9/45). This wheel meshes with the similar one on the left. They each have 365 teeth and rotate once per year. They are each provided with a cam and a cam follower to operate the shutters. Note that each follower has a guide screw fitted at the wheel centre to keep it properly positioned on the cam. Note also the counterweights to balance the cams. The followers are connected to two arms pivoted on the hour wheel pipe and with their outer ends connected to the sunrise and sunset shutters. The latter run on grooved guide wheels to reduce friction as much as possible (see figure 9/45).

Figure 9/46 shows the movement from the right hand side, with the drive to the motion work taken off the first pinion. It has a five wheel train, probably of two months' duration. The very tall case permits the use of a large diameter barrel to provide maximum power to the train. Winding is effected by the arbor in the foreground with a contrate wheel engaging with a large wheel fixed to the front of the barrel. The clock has an anchor escapement and a 1¼ seconds pendulum.

The complicated astronomical work imposes a considerable load on the clock and there is little power to spare in any case with a two month movement. There was apparently difficulty with the going of the clock and somebody, possibly Cockey, added a very long, small diameter barrel with a very large contrate wheel driving a pinion on the central arbor carrying the minute hand. The contrate wheel is just visible in figure 9/46 and the winding arbor projects on the left in figure 9/44. It is difficult to see how this auxiliary barrel can have a duration greater than a month or so. Another snag is that it is connected to the minute hand without any form of clutch.

The case (Colour Plate 13) is in the form of a Corinthian half column, ebonised and with gilt columns and other decoration. The height is 10ft. 2ins. The case is of very unusual and striking appearance but the design is somewhat top-heavy.

It is a difficult clock to date, but the design of the half hour marks on the chapter ring and the fact that the movement apparently required modifications to make it go satisfactorily, suggest it was one of Cockey's first productions, probably not later than 1710. In support of this, the clock now at the National Maritime Museum, Greenwhich, and thought to be the one presented to Queen Anne in 1705,[6] appears to be of slightly later date. One peculiar feature of these early astronomical clocks is that setting the annual calendar does not auto-

6. *Ibid.*, pp. 45, 53.

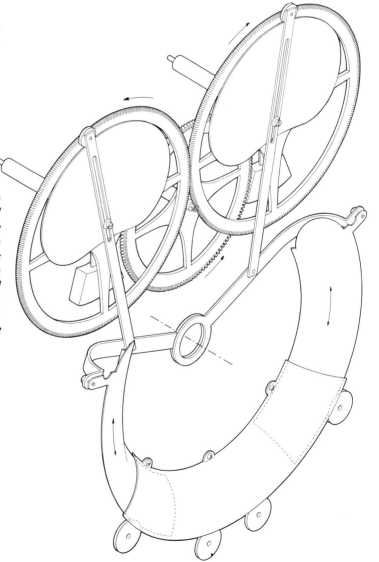

Figure 9/45. Drawing of mechanism to operate sunrise and sunset shutters. Central wheel is driven by pinion on hour wheel pipe and has a five pin open-ended lantern pinion which drives right hand wheel. Latter drives left hand wheel and both carry cams which operate shutters. Note guide screws at wheel centres to keep cam followers in place. Shutter arms pivot on hour wheel pipe. Cams are shown in winter position. Note counterweights to balance cams.

matically set the sunrise and sunset shutters. This could cause problems for an owner whose clock was stopped for some time, but there would be no difficulty where a clockmaker attended regularly for winding and adjusting. This was a common practice in wealthy households and Cockey may have assumed that it would apply with his astronomical clocks.

Figure 9/47 shows the dial of another very similar clock by Cockey which came on the market a few years ago in very dilapidated condition. The later corner pieces fixed with nuts and bolts are furniture mounts showing Adam influence. The minute hand is completely unsuitable and without a figure of Father Time or some other similar device there is nothing to indicate the hour during the time of darkness. The annual calendar and the lunar disc appear to be the same as those already discussd, in which case it is difficult to see how the present pointer can operate correctly. Part of the gearing to drive the rotating moon is visible because a shaped cover is missing. The elaborate fleur-de-lis half hour marks are similar to those on the clock at the National Maritime Museum and indicate a rather later date than that of the dial in figure 9/43.

The movement (figure 9/49 a and b) is very similar to the one in figures 9/44 and 46, but like the Greenwich example, it was designed as a three month movement with a six wheel train. There are apparently difficulties with it and at some stage the duration was reduced

Figure 9/46. Movement from right hand side. Five wheel train probably of two month duration. Winding through a contrate wheel engaging with large wheel fixed to front end of barrel. Auxiliary barrel added later with very large contrate wheel driving pinion on minute hand arbor.

Figure 9/47. Dial of another, slightly later, astronomical clock by Cockey. Basically the same as that in figure 9/43 but very distressed, wrong hands and Adam style furniture mounts as spandrels.

(a)

(b)

Figure 9/48. Two views of movement of the slightly later Cockey clock, similar to that in figures 9/44 and 46. In view (a) note winding on left hand side of movement. It was designed as a three month movement with a six wheel train (b), but its duration was later reduced to obtain more satisfactory running. Cams are balanced by having sections cut out instead of by using counterweights.

to obtain more satisfactory running. It is understood that this clock is at present undergoing thorough restoration.

Figure 9/49 shows a most desirable combination of a very interesting clock in an unusual and beautiful case. The 12ins. dial is signed in a recessed sector above the centre 'John Topping Memory Master.' To accommodate the subsidiary dials the rectangular part of the dial plate is approximately 12ins. × 14ins. high, which almost guarantees that it is in its original case! The corner spandrels are the type with a female head amongst scroll-work (C. & W. No. 21) but those in the arch are an unusual floral type (not in C. & W.) which are also used on the next example (figure 9/50). In figure 9/49 the left hand subsidiary dial is for pendulum regulation and is divided 5, 10, ... 60. The large central dial is for seconds and the right hand one is for strike/silent. The opening below the centre displays a simplified equation table on a large ring which rotates once per year. The top line is engraved 'Sun Slower' or 'Sun Faster' and the next line gives the equation of time to the nearest minute. Below that are shown the months each with their number of days in Roman numerals and the lowest line is divided into days which are numbered 5, 15, 25, for each month. This equation and calendar dial is set by means of the small square adjacent to I on the chapter ring. The hour hand is a later replacement. The month movement is laid out with the winding squares above the centre to provide room for the equation dial ring. Details of a method of providing seconds in the arch are given later in figure 9/108 (Wm. Scafe) and figures 10/4 and 5 (John Ellicott).

The case is veneered with walnut and has a most elegantly shaped trunk door similar to those on some early eighteenth century cabinets. The door has the rare feature of a Vauxhall mirror plate, shaped and bevelled and with a beautifully cut star which matches that in the centre of the seconds dial. The spandrels above the trunk door also have small decorated mirror panels. Note that the lock is on the frame, not on the door, where there is insufficient room. The hood door is hinged independently of the columns, an early use of this method. The base of a caddy is just visible above the cornice. The plinth has a very squat appearance and was probably cut down and eventually restored incorrectly. The present height is 7ft. 5ins. and the date is c.1730.

Figure 9/49. Complicated and elegant clock by John Topping, Memory Master, c.1730. Tall dial to accommodate subsidiary dials, seconds in arch, flanked by pendulum regulation and strike/silent. Signature in recess above centre. Opening below centre for annual calendar with simplified equation table. Calendar set by small square near to I on chapter ring. Incorrect hour hand. Month movement. Walnut veneered case. Hood has detached columns and door hung on ornamental butt hinges, an early example. Base of a caddy just visible. Trunk door with elegantly shaped top and cut and bevelled mirror plate matching star in arch. Spandrels above trunk door with similar mirror panels. Plinth incorrectly restored, now too squat. Present height 7ft. 5ins.

John Topping who normally signed himself 'Memory Master' was a London maker who made other interesting clocks. Another month clock by him has a very similar dial, but the movement has a centre seconds hand. The space occupied by the seconds dial in the above example is used for a rotating globular moon surrounded by a universal tidal dial and a ring giving the age of the moon. The clock is contained in a good quality ebonised case.

Figure 9/50 shows the dial of a clock signed 'Fran Gregg Covent Garden' which is almost identical to the Topping shown in figure 9/49 and is also c.1730. The minor differences are that the corner spandrels are of the turbaned head pattern (C. & W. No. 19) and the top line of the equation dial reads 'Sun too Fast' and 'Sun too Slow' instead of 'Sun Faster' and 'Sun Slower.'

Another contemporary example of Gregg's individuality in style is shown in figure 9/51, where the chapter ring extends right up into the arch and is apparently supported by a figure of Father Time. This idea was quite popular on Dutch clocks but is here flanked by cupids mounted on eagles, which are occasionally found on dials by other makers. The Father Time casting encloses a silvered plaque engraved 'Demi Regla Mi. Valor. Fran. Gregg Covent Garden.' The subsidiary dials are (left) for pendulum regulation and (right) for Strike/Silent. Edwardes[7] shows a timepiece by Gregg with a very similar dial except that the subsidiary dials and cupids are replaced by pierced brass overlays, probably repoussé, to avoid the expense of pattern making for castings.

Clocks by Francis Gregg are often dated wrongly as a result of published evidence that he left Covent Garden in 1714: "Francis Gregg, watchmaker, is removed from the Dial in Russell Street, Covent Garden, to the Dial in St. James Street over against the Palace Gates" (*London Gazette,* October 11-23, 1714).[8] Baillie's entry includes "Great Russell Street in 1711, St. James' 1714-29 bankrupt, York Street 1743 insolvent".[9] This introduces an error: Great Russell Street is by the British Museum, not in Covent Garden. The York Street referred to was in Covent Garden next to Russell Street and now forms that part of Tavistock Street between Wellington Street and Catherine Street. It is evident from his clocks that Gregg must have moved to York Street in 1729 or soon after that date. Wrong interpretation of this information has resulted in clocks of c.1730 or later being dated as "c.1714" because they are inscribed Covent Garden.

At this stage it cannot be stated what relationship, if any, existed between Topping and Francis Gregg, but some association appears probable in view of the close similarity of their work. Both were good makers in their own right, so it is unlikely that they bought in the clocks described above.

The name Pinchbeck usually suggests the gold-like alloy which was so popular for watch cases and jewellery in the eighteenth century, but Christopher Pinchbeck, who invented the alloy, and his son, also Christopher, were both fine clockmakers who deserve fame on that account.

Figure 9/52 shows a most complicated dial of c.1730 and therefore probably the work of Pinchbeck Senior. The chapter ring is about 2ins. smaller than the dial plate to allow room for the five subsidiary dials. The decoration between the dials is of gilt repoussé brass sheet, used because standard spandrel designs were unsuitable and special castings would have involved expensive patterns. The dial in the arch shows the phases of the moon through an opening and its age by a pointer reading across to the outer ring of numbers. It also indicates the times of high tide at thirty seaports, mainly British but also including such places as 'Lisbon', 'Callice' (Calais) and 'Hamburg.' The upper left hand dial has a rotating centre marked with I to XII twice and a sun, and inscribed 'Suns Place in ẏ Ecliptick & Southing of

7. E.L. Edwardes, *The Grandfather Clock,* 3rd edition, 1971, pl. 94.

8. *Britten,* p. 391.

9. Baillie, *Clockmakers,* p. 132.

Figure 9/50. Francis Gregg clock almost identical to Topping example, compare with figure 9/49.

Figure 9/51. Another clock by Gregg, showing his individuality. Chapter ring apparently supported by a figure of Father Time, popular on Dutch clocks. Flanking cupids mounted on eagles. Subsidiary dials for pendulum regulation and strike/silent. Probably c.1730.

Figure 9/52. Very complicated dial of clock by Pinchbeck, probably the father, c.1730. Gilt repoussé mounts between subsidiary dials. Lunar dial in arch shows high tide at thirty seaports. Upper left dial shows position in ecliptic and southing of twenty-four stars. Upper right dial shows position of moon in zodiac. Lower dials show month and day of week respectively.

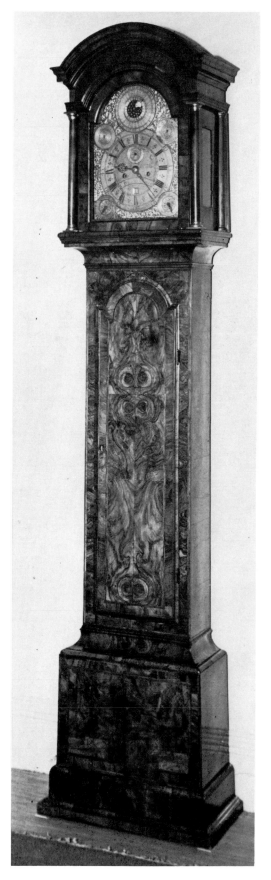

Figure 9/53. Case of Pinchbeck clock with very fine walnut veneers. Hood door hinged independently of columns.

24 Stars.' The outer fixed ring has on its inner edge the twelve signs of the zodiac to which the sun points in turn during its annual path through the heavens. Outside the signs of the zodiac are the names of the stars, such as 'Head of Andromeda', 'Swans Tail' and 'Antares.' The Roman numeral which comes opposite a particular star gives its time of southing, that is crossing the meridian, at that date. The upper right hand dial also has a rotating centre engraved with a crescent moon and inscribed 'This Shews the Sign the Moon is in.' The fixed outer ring has the signs of the zodiac to which the moon points in turn. The lower left hand dial has a hand which points to the month with its zodiacal sign. The lower right hand dial is marked with the days of the week, each with its planetary sign.

The case (figure 9/53) is veneered with very finely figured walnut with the usual herringbone banding and crossbanding. As in the example by John Topping, the hood door is hinged independently of the columns.

This period produced a number of clocks whose makers had apparently vied with one another to produce dials with the greatest possible number of indications and a good example of this is shown in figure 9/54. It is signed 'Daniel Alan London', an apparently unrecorded maker whom Lloyd misread as Daniel Man when he described the clock.[10]

The dial plate has an arch considerably more than a semi-circle to accommodate the large annual calendar. The markings on this dial will next be described, starting from the outside. First are 365 divisions for the days of the year and these are numbered every five starting from the first of each month. The next band of figures gives ordinary sunrise and sunset, sunrise being obtained by taking the hours shown by the inner figure and adding the minutes shown by the middle number. Sunset is obtained by subtracting the number of minutes from the hour shown by the outer figure. For example on 11th December the readings are 8.13.4 which gives sunrise 8.13 and sunset 3.47 for the shortest day. It must be remembered that the Gregorian calendar was not adopted in this country until 1752 when eleven days were omitted. The next band of figures gives the times of nightfall and dawn in accordance with the astronomical definition of night, that is when the sun is a minimum of 18° below the horizon. There is a period of nearly two months in the summer when the sun does not sink so low, hence the inscription 'No Real Night' and the corresponding title of Lloyd's article. The next ring of numbers gives the equation of time to the nearest minute and inside this is inscribed 'Sun Faster' and 'Sun Slower'. Finally, the inner edge gives the months of the year. There is no correction for leap year.

The small dial on the left gives the moon's phases and its age on the outer ring of numerals. The inner ring which is marked I to XII twice is friction tight with a hole near the lower II so that a peg can be inserted to rotate it. It is a universal tidal dial and is set by bringing the time of high tide at the port in question opposite new and full moon, that is 29½ (or 0) and 14¾ days. It is at present set for London, 3 o'clock being opposite those dates.

The clockmaker would no doubt have provided written instructions for setting a complicated clock such as this but unfortunately very few such documents have survived. Universal tidal dials were not very rare and a competent clockmaker would probably have known how to set one for a particular locality, given the times of high tide.

The right hand dial is engraved 'Strike All/Silent Six/Silent All' and provides for silencing only the quarter chimes on six bells (Silent Six), or silencing both quarter chimes and hour strike (Silent All). The urn pattern spandrels (C. & W. No. 26) were in use by Tompion by c.1710 but did not immediately become popular and remained in use into the second half of the century.

The movement is a very early example of a centre seconds mechanism although the hand is not shown in this photograph. It does appear, however, in the illustration to Lloyd's article. Both chiming and striking trains have rack and snail control to permit silencing.

10. H.A. Lloyd, 'No Real Night', *Antiquarian Horology*, Vol. I (December 1953), p. 4.

Figure 9/54. Very complicated clock by Alan, c.1730-35. Dial arch greater than a semi-circle to accommodate large annual calendar dial which indicates times of sunrise and sunset, and the equation of time. Lunar and universal tidal dial on left and dial on right for silencing only quarter chimes or both chimes and strike. Very early example of centre seconds movement although hand is missing.

The handsome case is veneered with finely figured burr walnut and closely resembles the Pinchbeck example in figure 9/53, except that it has a superstructure, and the total height is 9ft. ¾in. The date of the whole clock is c.1730-35.

The dial of an astronomical clock by a 'provincial' maker is shown in figure 9/55, with the signature 'Tho. Budgen Fecit.' Thomas Budgen worked in Croydon and the date is c.1730-35. The twenty-four hour chapter ring is very unusual in having the minute numbers and divisions inside the hour divisions, with noon at the top and midnight at the bottom. The minute hand, which is of conventional design, is rather too long as it points to the quarter hour divisions; the hour hand is gilt with an effigy of the sun at its extremity. The time shown in the photograph is twenty-one minutes past noon. The third hand, with a moon at the end, is discussed below. The left hand aperture in the dial shows the day of the week with its planetary sign, and the right hand aperture has an annual calendar with the signs of the zodiac. The zodiacal and planetary signs[11] are shown in figure 9/56. Below the centre is a subsidiary dial with a simple day of the month indicator read off the long hand.

The two curved scales applied inside the chapter ring are used to find the time of sunrise and sunset. Each is engraved with six zodiacal signs, the left hand one having Cancer (June), to Sagittarius (November) and the right hand one Capricornus (December), to Gemini (May). On both the strips and the annual calendar each zodiacal month is divided into four parts. The curved scales are made non-linear to correspond to the day-to-day changes in sunrise and sunset times, which are rapid at the Equinoxes and very slow at the Solstices. This ingenious layout permits more accurate readings. To find the times of sunrise and sunset for 10th September, the date shown by the annual calendar, the zodiac is read off against a small pointer in the centre of the opening, see figure 9/57. This shows that it is just over half way through the last division of Virgo and a line from the dial centre passing through the corresponding point on the left hand zodiac scale indicates 5.55 a.m., the time of sunrise. To find the time of sunset, a line is taken from the dial centre through the corresponding point on the other zodiac scale, that is in the first division of Aries and gives the time at 6.5 p.m. This is a satisfactory result as it is approaching the Autumn Equinox. A date in late December would indicate Capricornus which is at the top of the right hand zodiac scale and would give a time of around 4 p.m. which would of course be sunset. The corresponding point in Sagittarius at the top of the left hand scale would give sunrise as around 8 a.m. The sun's image on the hour hand also shows the sun's daily passage through the heavens.

In the arch is a globular moon with one half painted with the man in the moon and the other half dark blue, so that the phases of the moon are shown as the globe rotates. The age of the moon in days is shown in an opening in the projection below the moon. The third hand with the moon's image shows its position in the equinoctial and with respect to the sun. At new moon it coincides with the sun and at full moon it is opposite. This is achieved by the moon hand having a period of rotation of approximately 24 hours 50½ minutes. The inner portion of the subsidiary dial below the centre is marked with the signs of the zodiac and the short hand bearing a crescent moon indicates the moon's position in the zodiac. The clock was apparently assembled rather hurriedly for photographing, as some of the indications are not quite correctly set.

The movement (figure 9/58) has, as would be expected, complicated motion work to operate the various astronomical indications. The vertical arbor at the top carries a wheel which meshes with one on the arbor carrying the moon and its number disc. Note the right angle drive by means of ordinary spur gearing. The wheel on the left of the movement carries a pin to operate once per day the seven pointed star wheel for the day of the week. The large wheel on the right carries a six-leaved pinion which meshes with internal teeth on the annual calendar ring. The wheels at the bottom centre are for the day of the month and lunar zodiac

11. Reproduced from L. Dygges, *A Prognostication,* 1555, reprinted 1926.

Figure 9/55. Dial of astronomical clock by Budgen, Croydon, c.1730-35. Unusual twenty-four hour chapter ring with minutes on inside. Hour hand has gilt sun and time shown is twenty-one minutes past noon. Globular moon in arch with its age shown in an opening just below. Left hand aperture in dial centre shows day of week; right hand one has annual calendar with signs of zodiac. The two curved scales marked with signs of the zodiac are used for finding sunrise and sunset. Lower subsidiary dial shows day of month with long hand and moon's position in zodiac with crescent moon hand. Hand with moon disc shows moon's position with respect to the sun.

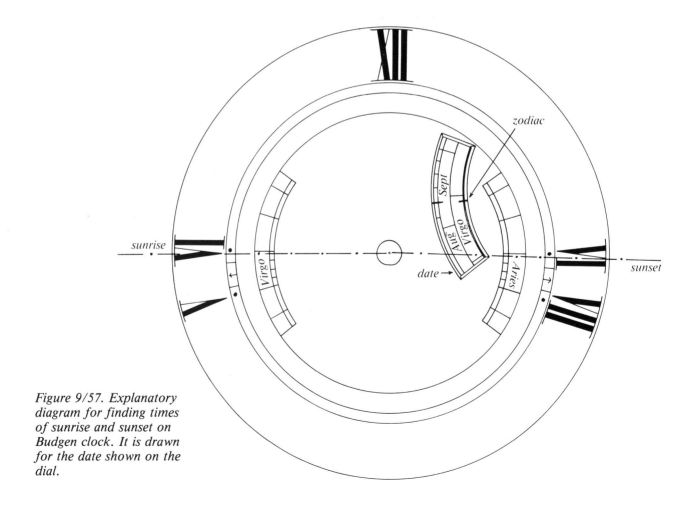

Figure 9/56. Planetary and zodiacal signs reproduced from L. Dygges, A Prognostication, *1555, reprinted 1926.*

Planetes.

♄	♃	♂	☉	♀	☿	☽
Sat-turne	Iupiter	Mars	Sonne	Venus	Mer-curie	Moone

Signes.

♈	♉	♊	♋	♌	♍
Aries	Taurus	Gemini	Cancer	Leo	Virgo

♎	♏	♐	♑	♒	♓
Libra	Scorpius	Sagit-tarius	Capri-cornus	Aquarius	Piſces

Figure 9/57. Explanatory diagram for finding times of sunrise and sunset on Budgen clock. It is drawn for the date shown on the dial.

238

Figure 9/58. Budgen movement showing complicated motion work with simple friction clutches to facilitate setting the astronomical indications. Note right angle drive to moon arbor through ordinary spur gearing. Front of front plate still shows casting and setting out marks.

hands. Simple friction clutches are provided to facilitate setting up the astronomical indications, which is not the easiest of operations. It is worth noting that even on an important movement like this the front of the front plate has been left quite rough and still shows marks from the casting sand. This is often found on more modest clocks.

The clock is housed in a graceful walnut veneered case (figure 9/59) with fine frets and an attractive caddy. Note the attached columns and square topped trunk door. Cescinsky and Webster[12] show an almost identical clock in a similar but shorter case which lacks a caddy and has a squat plinth as well as being shorter in the waist. Although less elegant it appears to be from the same workshop as the case shown here. Cescinsky and Webster state that the moon hand rotates at the same speed as the sun hand and would be used to indicate the time at, for example, the Antipodes! A case of jumping to the wrong conclusion. Lloyd[13] also shows a somewhat similar but later astronomical clock by Budgen.

There are a few clocks which stand completely apart from the mainstream of development, probably because they were designed by amateurs who may have been expert in other disciplines. Figure 9/60 shows a remarkable example which is unsigned but is reliably attributed to Mayne Swete of Modbury, Devon. The magnificent quality burr walnut veneered case is 9ft. 8ins. high, 3ft. 5½ins. wide and 2ft. 2½ins. deep. It has a forward sliding hood, and doors to the front and ends of the middle section and the front of the lower section.

The middle section accommodates the complete movement (figure 9/61), which is weight driven. It provides hour striking, quarter chiming and tune playing at three hourly intervals. It is unique in having a carillon keyboard so that tunes can be played manually, using the same set of hammers as for the mechanical playing.

The going train is on the right and is connected to the dial through leading off rods with universal joints, very much as in a turret clock. As the movement is quite low in the case, the cat-gut lines from the barrels are led up to pulleys fixed in the top of the middle section to provide a satisfactory fall for the weights. These hang at the back of the case and pass behind the mechanism.

A second train in the right hand section provides hour striking on a separate bell and quarter chiming on eight bells of the musical peal. It has a long brass pin barrel hidden from view by the large barrel visible in the photograph.

The musical train is on the left and operates a large wooden pin barrel with seventy-four hammers for thirty-seven bells, to permit rapid repetition of a note when required. It apparently plays every three hours, with a choice of three tunes: Hark! The cock crows; Beau's Delight; Rigadoon.

12. Cescinsky and Webster, p. 183.
13. Lloyd, *Old Clocks*, pl. 40.

Figure 9/59. Graceful Budgen case with well matched walnut veneers, fine frets, attractive caddy, and attached columns. Note square topped trunk door has applied mouldings in place of half round beading.

Figure 9/60. Carillon clock attributed to Mayne Swete, Modbury, Devon, c.1730, probably made by Stumbels or William Clement. Magnificent burr walnut case with sliding hood and opening doors to front and sides. Height 9ft. 8ins., width 3ft. 5½ins., depth 2ft. 2½ins.

Figure 9/61. Movement of Swete clock. Right hand section for going, striking and quarter chiming. Left hand train drives wooden pin barrel for tune playing. Drive to hands through rods with universal joints. Unique in having a carillon keyboard for playing tunes manually as well as by clockwork.

There is reported to be a brass barrel pinned with a psalm tune which can be substituted for the wooden barrel on Sundays. Padded fittings for a spare barrel exist in the lower section but were empty when the clock was inspected. As the clock has not worked for a number of years it has not been possible to verify some of its functions and I am grateful to Bellchambers[14] for some of the information included in this description.

Mayne Swete who made, or more probably designed, this remarkable clock, died in 1735. He took great delight in metal work and in bell ringing which would account for the unique carillon facility. It is in any case very early for a complicated musical clock. It was made as a gift for Mayne Swete's elder brother Adrian who died in 1733 and it remained in the Swete family until acquired by the Victoria and Albert Museum in 1925. A date of 1705 has been ascribed to the clock[15] but c.1730 is much more likely. The dial has a conventional break arch dial unknown in 1705 and the chapter ring and spandrels (C. & W. No. 21) support the later date, as also does the fact that Mayne Swete was apparently abroad from 1705 to c.1730. The most probable explanation is that Swete designed the clock and supervised its making by a professional clockmaker. In this event either William Clement or William Stumbels, both of Totnes, are favoured candidates. Stumbels would appear particularly eligible as he made complicated musical clocks as well as turret clocks and this example shows turret clock practice in the drive to the remote dial and in the hanging of the weights.

SOME COUNTRY CLOCKS

After studying the complex and highly ingenious examples described above it is time, and a relief, to look at the simpler clocks made for people of more modest means.

Figure 9/62 shows an anonymous thirty-hour clock, probably c.1730-40. It was bought nearly fifty years ago in Nottingham, before such objects were sought after, so it was probably made within a few miles of that city. The case is of a plain dark coloured oak with gilt wood capitals and bases and a fruitwood fret made of two halves cut at the same time. It is a blind fret, that is one that is glued on to a wooden backing, so it does not function as a sound outlet. The hood slides forward but has no door. The case is 6ft. 3¾ins. high and has an 11½ins. waist for a 10ins. dial. The trunk door retains its original iron hinges and nails, see figure 9/63. As is usual with thirty-hour clocks, the movement just sits on a seat board nailed to the tops of the trunk sides. The dial (figure 9/64) has the fleur-de-lis pattern half hour marks which came in around 1715 and turban head spandrels (C. & W. No. 19). The hand is a replacement. The movement (figure 9/65) has a plate frame with nicely turned pillars. Practically all Midlands and north country thirty-hour clocks had plate frames from the start, whereas in southern England and East Anglia the birdcage movement was the usual type until almost the end of the eighteenth century. It has been suggested that the rarity of the lantern clock in the north may have caused this different line of development. This movement has several early features, the bell stand mounted on the front plate; the square arbors for hammer, lifting piece and detent; the decorated hammer spring; and the square headed screws. Most clocks of this period had plaited rope for the weight but the sprockets and chain appear to be original, as does the wooden weight pulley. Sprockets and pulleys intended for chain have a groove, or cut-away sections between the pins of sprockets to allow the chain to lie flat. The crutch has been repaired at the lower end. The spare holes adjacent to the spandrels were made by an owner who changed the spandrels because one was missing. He subsequently obtained a replacement for the missing one and replaced the original set.

The clock shown in figure 9/66 is slightly more imposing although the case is made of pine, painted as all pine furniture was originally. There is quite a graceful caddy with gilt

14. J.K. Bellchambers, *Devonshire Clockmakers,* 1962, p. 31, 'Adrian's Clock'.

15. *ibid.*

Figure 9/62. Anonymous thirty-hour clock, probably made in Nottinghamshire, c.1730-40. Plain dark oak, gilt wood capitals and bases and a fruitwood blind fret. Forward sliding hood without door. Height 6ft. 3¾ins. with an 11½ins. waist for a 10ins. dial.

Figure 9/63. Original iron hinge on trunk door of 9/62; note wrought iron nails.

Figure 9/64. 10ins. dial of thirty-hour clock in 9/62. Spandrels extending to edge of dial plate usually means that hood did not have a door. Hand is a replacement.

Figure 9/65. Plate framed thirty-hour movement of clock in 9/62. Note bell stand mounted on front plate; square arbors for hammer, lifting piece and detent; decorated hammer spring; all early features.

wood finials to match the capitals and bases. The hood has a door hinged with intersecting staples. The trunk door has a simple moulding round the edge and is hung on H hinges, with a wooden peg inserted through a hole in the side to secure it. The height to the top of the caddy is 6ft. 10½ins. and it has a 12ins. waist with an 11ins. dial.

The dial (figure 9/67) has an unusual chapter ring with the quarter hour divisions on the outside and each divided into three 5 minute sections. This device enables the time to be read to a minute or so with a single hand and is found on a few other north country thirty-hour clocks. The prominent simple calendar is typical of north country clocks, but is much rarer in the south. It does not require extra motion work as the calendar disc has two teeth per day and is operated by a pin or other projection on the hour wheel. Note the very coarse matting and the ringed decoration which would be produced by a special brace bit similar to that used for ringing winding holes. The engraving is very coarse and heavy, obviously the work of the clockmaker, and the half hour markings are mainly punched work. The spandrels are a well finished variation of the head amidst scrolling foliage type. The original hand is well cut. The maker, Pearson of Dore, is recorded by Loomes as c.1740 and this clock is probably of that date or a little later. Dore is a village in north east Derbyshire, near Sheffield.

Figure 9/66. Thirty-hour clock by Pearson of Dore, c.1740. Painted pine case with gilt wood capitals, bases and finials. Hood door hinged with intersecting staples. H hinges to trunk door and wooden peg to secure it. Height to top of caddy 6ft. 10½ins. 12ins. waist for an 11ins. dial.

Figure 9/67. 11ins. dial of Pearson clock with unusual chapter ring divided into 5 minutes, an idea found on a few other north country clocks. Prominent simple calendar is also typical of the north. Note very coarse matting and ringed decoration. Coarse engraving done by clockmaker and punching for half hour marks. Well finished spandrels and original hand.

Figure 9/68. Pearson movement, heavily built with thick plates and wheels and heavy steel work. Bell stand mounted on back plate, rope drive. Note cut-away sections of dial plate, practice engraving on back of chapter ring and calendar wheel with saw-like teeth.

The movement (figure 9/68) is very heavily built with thick plates, carefully turned pillars and very substantial steel work. Notice also the thickness of the wheels. Although square headed screws are still used, the bell stand is mounted on the back plate and there are no square arbors in the striking mechanism. The second wheel in the striking train has a locking pin instead of a hoop, a somewhat later development. With this type the notches in the count wheel and the end of the detent must both be sloped as the count wheel has to complete the lifting of the detent at the commencement of striking. With the hoop type, this extra lift is obtained by sloping the lower side of the locking piece which rides on the hoop. The going train is as follows:

Great wheel 80
Second wheel 72, pinion 6
Escape wheel 45, pinion 6
Motion work,
    pinion 18, hour wheel 54

This gives a seconds pendulum.

Figure 9/69. Eight-day clock also by Pearson, c.1750, with dial having similar features to thirty-hour example. Oak case also similar but hood has detached columns. Brass finials will have replaced original wooden ones and feet are probably a later addition.

Note the cut-away portions of the dial plate behind the chapter ring, a typical north country feature which is also found in clocks from some other localities such as Cornwall and Berkshire. Some dial plates appear to have been cast with cut-aways, others to have had them chopped out. The general explanation is that they saved brass, but a practical man[16] has pointed out that they would make it easier to flatten a dial plate after matting it. Note the ornamental turning on the dial feet and the practice engraving on the back of the chapter ring. The saw like teeth of the calendar wheel are clearly visible.

The same maker was responsible for the eight-day clock shown in figure 9/69. The oak case bears a marked similarity to the one shown in figure 9/66 and is obviously by the same joiner. The trunk door again has H hinges but is secured by a lock. The hood has detached columns which are too widely spaced for elegance, while the detached columns instead of attached quarter columns at the back are unusual. The brass finials will be replacements for the original wooden ones and the feet are probably a later addition.

The dial is more conventional but has a number of features in common with the previous example. The signature 'Pearson of Dore' is more elegantly written and is on the lower edge of the chapter ring. Although there are no quarter hour divisions, half hour markings identical to those on the thirty-hour dial are provided together with similar half quarter marks. The calendar is also identical but there is a sunken seconds dial. The spandrels are the urn pattern (C. & W. No. 26). The hour hand is closely modelled on the previous single hand. The clock as a whole appears slightly later than the other one and is probably c.1750.

Whilst considerations of space preclude any serious discussion of regional and county variations in the present work, some of the broad differences have already been noted and another specialist group may be of interest. The Quaker clockmakers of north Oxfordshire were a closely-knit community who produced thirty-hour birdcage frame clocks with distinctively decorated brass dials. This unique decoration is applied to the dial centre which is divided into a number of rings filled with radial strips of zigzags. According to Beeson[17] the work was done with a tool which guided the graver and obviated the need for artistic ability, but even so the results varied widely.

16. This suggestion was made by Christopher Elton.
17. C.F.C. Beeson, *Clockmaking in Oxfordshire 1400-1850,* 1962, p. 100.

Figure 9/70. 9½ins. dial of thirty-hour clock by Gilkes, Charlbury, c.1740. Radial decoration with rather amateurish engraving and crude spandrels, typical of Quaker dials.

Figure 9/71. Clock by Gilkes, Adderbury, also c.1740. Better quality dial and hand but generally similar to previous example.

Figure 9/70 shows a 9½ins. dial signed on the chapter ring 'Thos. Gilkes Charlbury.' Note the rather sketchy decoration with flowers in a vase and the amateurish signature. The spandrels, which incorporate a female bust (C. & W. No. 23) are those commonly used and as usual they are cast from a poor mould (possibly from an existing spandrel) and are poorly finished. The movement has an iron loop and spikes like a lantern clock so that it could either be used as a wall clock or, if finances permitted, be housed in a longcase. This was quite a normal design and sometimes one of these clocks will be found hung on a stout hook driven into the back board of its case instead of being fitted on a seat board.

Figure 9/71 shows a clock signed 'Gilkes Adderbury', that is Richard Gilkes. Note the better quality decoration in the centre and more attractive hand, but similar spandrels. Thomas (1704-57) and Richard (1715-87) were brothers who were apprenticed to their father, Thomas Gilkes of Sibford Gower (?1665-1743). Both clocks are probably c.1740.

Figure 9/72 shows a clock signed 'Jno. Seymour Wantage', probably of c.1730. The Seymour family are recorded as clockmakers in Wantage, Berkshire (now Oxon.) from 1525 to 1760 when John died. The case is of pine, now stained, but originally would have been painted. The hood door has half columns applied to the front instead of the customary three quarter ones at the corners. There are quarter columns at the rear and the wooden capitals and bases are gilt. The trunk door has wrought iron hinges. The height is 6ft. 7ins. and the waist measures 12ins. with a 10ins. dial.

The dial (figure 9/73) has a fairly narrow chapter ring with small fleur-de-lis half hour marks and the elaborated cherub spandrels (C. & W. No. 7) favoured by Tompion and other leading makers. The hand is of a type introduced by London makers c.1710. The movement (figure 9/74) is a good quality birdcage, with all brass frame, but without any decoration. The round headed screws appear to be replacements for square headed ones. The weight is suspended on a chain and the sprockets appear to be original. The dismantled movement is

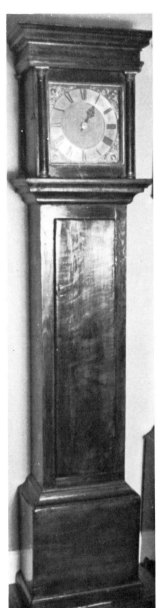

Figure 9/72. Thirty-hour clock by Seymour, Wantage, c.1730. Pine case now stained instead of painted. Unusual half columns applied to front of hood door. Gilt wood capitals and bases. Height 6ft. 7ins., waist 12ins. for a 10ins. dial.

Figure 9/73. 10ins. dial of Seymour clock. Finely matted centre and unusual cherub and flower spandrels.

Figure 9/74. Seymour bird-cage movement. Good quality all brass frame but no decoration. Round headed screws probably replacements. Note nicely pierced hand.

Figure 9/75. Trains of Seymour clock. Note repaired second wheel of going train.

shown in figure 9/75. Note that the second wheel of the going train has been broken and repaired with an applied crossed out disc. The going train is as follows:

Great wheel 84
Second wheel 72, pinion 6
Escape wheel 42, pinion 6
Motion work,
pinion 18, hour wheel 54

This gives 3,528 beats/hour, so the pendulum will have a theoretical length of approximately 40¾ins. compared with 39ins. for a seconds one. This is a reminder of the need to check the train before making a replacement pendulum for a thirty-hour clock as many of them have trains which do not give exact seconds.

Another John Seymour clock examined has a definite family likeness but a number of differences. The 9¾ins. dial is signed 'Seymour Wantage', the chapter ring is slightly broader and has diamond half hour marks, and the spandrels are the later type with a head amidst scrolling foliage (C. & W. No. 21). The hour hand, which is original, is of a slightly earlier type than the one illustrated. The movement is very similar but is unusually shallow for a birdcage and has rectangular iron corner posts. It is chain operated but has a seconds pendulum. The case is in earlier style with a lenticle and small side windows to the hood. It is of black painted pine and is only 6ft. high. This mixture of earlier and later features well illustrates the difficulties encountered in attempting the accurate dating of country clocks.

That Seymour could make other than simple thirty-hour clocks when required is demonstrated by the next two examples. Figure 9/76 shows a most unusual layout with a very large seconds ring intersecting the chapter ring. The seconds ring is in three parts, one engraved on the chapter ring, part above it and the rest below. Whilst it is an interesting lay-

Figure 9/76. Eight-day clock by Seymour with very large seconds ring intersecting chapter ring. A good quality but not very elegant dial. '1752' at centre of arch is presumably its date.

out it is not particularly elegant.[18] The arch has fine scrolled engraving between the seconds ring and the name plate and a leaf border above. The '1752' in the rectangular opening is presumably the date as the clock is c.1740-50. The escapement is in the normal position, but with intermediate gearing to drive the seconds hand. The author has not come across any other dated or numbered clocks by Seymour.

A more conventional eight-day clock is shown in figure 9/77. The dial is signed on an inset plaque in the arch 'John Seymour Wantage' and immediately below this is a square calendar aperture. The rest of the arch is filled with delicate leaf engraving. The chapter ring has no quarter hour divisions but has the fleur-de-lis half hour marks he usually used. An unusual feature is that the minute divisions are in a wavy band, a Dutch device which is occasionally found on provincial English clocks. The spandrels are the urn pattern (C. & W. No. 26) and the hands resemble those in figure 9/76.

The high grade case is veneered with burr walnut with panelled sides, but the most striking feature is the trunk door inset with a panel of bevelled Vauxhall mirror plate. There are also small mirror plates in the spandrels just above the door. Note the cross-grained moulding instead of a half round beading on the trunk door. The hood has a fine sound fret, side windows and detached columns. The hood door is hung on ornamental butt hinges as shown in figure 9/2. The probable date is c.1755.

Figure 9/78 shows an interesting thirty-hour clock by John Inkpen of Horsham, c.1740. The case is of a rich brown oak, the hood has three quarter columns attached to the door and there are side windows (see figure 9/79). The wooden capitals and bases are polished to match the rest of the case and the brass finials are replacements for wooden ones which were presumably gilt. The skirting, which has a bevelled instead of a moulded edge, is a replacement. The height is 7ft. ½in. to the top of the caddy and the waist measures 11⅝ins. for an 11ins. dial.

The 11ins. dial (figure 9/80) is unusually small for one with an arch as they normally measure at least 12ins. For this reason it is almost certain that clock and case were made for one another. The dial is very well engraved and nicely matted. The engraving superimposed on the matted centre is a typical provincial feature. The signature 'Jnͦ Inkpen Horsham' is on a

18. For a description of a similar but probably later example see C.F.C. Beeson, 'A clock by John Hawting Oxford', *Antiquarian Horology,* IV (December 1964), p. 273.

Figure 9/77. Fine eight-day clock by Seymour, probably c.1755. Dial has signature on recessed plaque in arch with calendar aperture just below. Chapter ring has wavy minute band but no quarter hour divisions. Burr walnut case with panelled sides and plinth. Mirror trunk door with mirror inset spandrels above. Hood has detached columns with door hung on ornamental butt hinges and a fine sound fret.

Figure 9/78. Interesting thirty-hour clock by Inkpen, Horsham in brown oak case. Hood has attached columns with polished oak capitals and bases. Brass finials have replaced wooden ones and bevelled skirting is a replacement. Height 7ft. ½in. to top of caddy and 11⅝ins. waist for an 11ins. dial.

Figure 9/79. Hood of clock in 9/78 showing side windows.

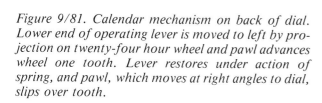

Figure 9/80. The 11ins. dial, unusually small for an arched one. Good quality with typical provincial engraving on matted centre. Calendar in arch is rare on thirty-hour clocks. Good original hands.

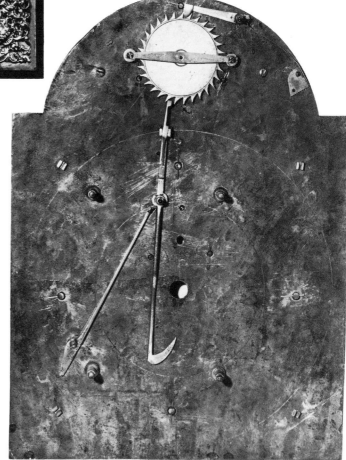

Figure 9/81. Calendar mechanism on back of dial. Lower end of operating lever is moved to left by projection on twenty-four hour wheel and pawl advances wheel one tooth. Lever restores under action of spring, and pawl, which moves at right angles to dial, slips over tooth.

reserve on the plate, not on an applied plaque. The seconds hand necessitates a differently planned movement as will be described below. The seconds ring has the inner edge bevelled so that the hand can be fitted close to the dial to clear the hour hand. The calendar in the arch is an unusual feature which needs a special mechanism. The spandrels are well finished. All the hands are original and are nicely pierced and shaped. Figure 9/81 shows the mechanism of the calendar. The wheel has thirty-one teeth, one per day, and is normally held in position by the spring loaded detent at the top of the dial. The long operating lever is pivoted on a stud just above its centre and has a long restoring spring which presses the lever to the right so that its upper portion moves to the left against a stop pin riveted into the dial plate. The lower end of the lever is moved to the left by a projection on the twenty-four hour wheel of the motion work (see figure 9/83), and the pawl at the top of the lever advances the wheel one tooth. When the operating lever restores under the action of its spring, the spring loaded pawl, which moves at right angles to the dial (see figure 9/82), slips over the tooth.

The clock is designed for hour repeating and figure 9/82 shows the original hardwood pulley on its iron spike which is provided to divert the repeating cord upwards to a bedroom above for telling the time at night. In figure 9/83 note the well made plate frame with nicely finned pillars. It also shows the four wheel going train provided to give a clockwise rotating seconds hand and a shake-free minute hand. Note the long pinion heads on the warning and escape wheel pinions which indicate that these have been renewed. On a movement of this quality it is rather surprising to find a rope drive with its inherent disadvantage of choking the movement with fluff. The front view (figure 9/84) shows how the going train is planted well to the left of centre to allow room for the striking. Rack striking is provided to permit repeating. Note the well cut rack with a deep drop at the end to provide locking on a pin in the pallet wheel. The repeating spring is provided to ensure that the mechanism restores fully after being operated for repeating. It operates by pressing down an extension of the lifting piece. As shown the repeating cord is led down and out through a well worn hole in the side of the trunk. This would probably be used when it was difficult to see the time.

It is interesting to notice that Inkpen also made simple clocks for his less affluent customers. One example inspected has a single hand but the square dial resembles the one just described in having similar ribbon-like engraving on the matting and the signature in a reserve. The movement is a simple birdcage with count wheel striking and no calendar.

Figure 9/85 shows an unusual clock of c.1740 by Thomas Deykin of Worcester in an oak case with the outlines of the trunk door and the raised plinth panel emphasised with a narrow herring-bone banding. The arched dial opening is echoed in the top of the trunk door and the unusual applied panel on the plinth. The hood has unusual corbel brackets supporting the cornice and the attached columns have turned wooden capitals and bases. The bevelled skirting has replaced one with a moulded edge, the caddy top is incomplete and a sound fret in it has been covered over with a plain piece of wood. These alterations have robbed the case of much of its elegance.

The dial is signed on a plaque below the centre and engraving round the calendar aperture extends as far up as the winding holes. In place of a seconds dial there is a plate engraved with a human face with the eyes cut out. A pair of eyes attached to the pallet arbor move in step with the pendulum to give the clock an animated appearance. Similar simple automata operated from the escapement became popular in the second half of the eighteenth century but were usually in the arch, with rocking ships or figures of Father Time as particular favourites. Occasionally much more complicated automata were provided and arranged to operate in conjunction with the striking or musical trains. As with musical clocks, the novelty wears off after a time.

Some country makers were quite ambitious and figure 9/86 shows a simple musical movement. The maker is not known as both the original and a later dial have disappeared. The

Figure 9/82. The movement is designed for hour repeating and cord is shown taken round original hardwood pulley for providing repeating in bedroom above.

Figure 9/84. Front of movement showing going train well to left of centre to allow room for striking train. Well cut striking rack with deep drop at end for locking.

Figure 9/83. The plate framed movement with nicely finned pillars. Four wheeled going train to provide a seconds hand and shake-free minute hand. Long pinion heads on warning and escape wheel pinions indicate renewals.

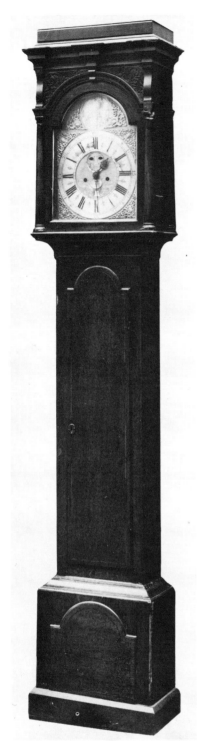

Figure 9/85. Unusual clock by Deykin, Worcester, c.1740. Oak case with narrow herring-bone bandings. Arched dial is echoed in top of trunk door and unusual applied panel on plinth. Note rare brackets supporting cornice. Effect is marred by mutilation of caddy and by incorrect skirting too high on plinth. Dial has human face with moving eyes operated from pallet arbor.

original dial had a calendar operated from a twenty-four hour wheel now missing and a lunar dial operated from a projection of the hour wheel pipe. Although the movement has gut barrels with the usual sixteen turns, the duration is not eight days but only two and a half days.

The striking great wheel has twenty-six pins and the hoop wheel has two cut out sections so it can lock after half a turn. The count wheel (figure 9/87) is driven by a pinion of report on the great wheel arbor, so the barrel has a divided arbor, which is a very late survival of an early practice.

The musical train is warned and let off by pins in the hour count wheel. It is released hourly except at I when there is insufficient movement of the count wheel. The count wheel for the music train is driven by a pinion on the pin barrel arbor and locks the train after one rotation of the pin barrel. There are eight bells (figure 9/88) and the barrel is pinned for two tunes. A tune change lever is mounted on a stud on the front plate and has an operating pin to project through a slot in the dial plate near IX. The lever pumps over the barrel against the pressure of a spring adjacent to the count wheel, see figure 9/87.

The movement is quite well made but is not so well designed. Allowing for sixteen turns of gut on the barrels, the trains have the following durations, going eighty hours, striking and musical each sixty-four hours. This is the reverse of the ideal arrangement as the going train should run out first to avoid the striking getting out of step.

A difficult clock to document, but it could be west country as several makers in that area made simple musical clocks. A rough estimate of the date is c.1740-50.

MORE SOPHISTICATION

This survey of the clocks of the first half of the eighteenth century is rounded off by studying a few good quality ones which illustrate later developments.

Knowledge of the state of the moon was of considerable importance when planning journeys during the hours of darkness, a well known example being that of the Lunar Society of Birmingham, 1766-1813.[19] Members of this small but important scientific society met at each other's houses when the moon was full to light them on their homeward journeys. Lunar dials become very popular in the eighteenth century and continued so into the nineteenth when improvements in street lighting and in public transport made them less necessary.

Two types of lunar indicator have already been described, the rare and expensive rotating globular moon (figure 9/55) and the moon dial with a small circular opening (figures 7/11, 9/11, 9/52, 9/54). The type which became common and which was used into the nineteenth century occupies practically the whole of the break arch and an early example is shown in figure 9/89.

The moon dial caters for two lunations and consists of a large brass disc on which are engraved two moon faces and a scale of days round the edge, marked 1-29½ twice and usually numbered every 5. The ring of markings and the two faces are silvered and the spaces in between

19. R.J. Law, 'The Lunar Society Exhibition at Birmingham', *Antiquarian Horology,* V (December 1966) p. 169.

Figure 9/86. Two-and-a-half day country-made musical movement, maker not known as original and later dials missing. Original dial had calendar operated by a twenty-four hour wheel, and a lunar dial. Probably c.1740-50 and perhaps west country.

Figure 9/87. Back plate showing count wheel with pins for letting off music hourly except at I. Count wheel driven from barrel arbor so latter is divided. Note closely spaced pins on striking great wheel.

Figure 9/88. Musical train showing barrel pinned for two tunes with tune change lever on right. Note conventional eight-day gut barrels and bottom pillars tapped for seat board screws.

painted dark blue with gilt stars. The disc has 118 saw-like teeth, two per day and is usually stepped on by a lever from the hour wheel every twelve hours. The dial arch is cut away as shown, leaving two hemispheres so that a new moon appears on the left and gradually increases in size until it appears complete at 14½-15 days. It then gradually wanes until it disappears behind the right hand hemisphere. A small pointer at the top of the arch points to the age of the moon in days. The two hemispheres and the dial arch are decorated with scrolling foliage. On later dials the hemispheres were engraved as parts of a terrestrial globe and the star spangled sky was replaced by two scenes, a landscape and a seascape, see figure 9/90. By c.1770 the scale of days was often marked on the dial arch instead of on the moon disc with a pointer above each moon face to show the moon's age, see figure 9/91. Another variation with only one moon face is shown in figure 9/92.

The clock in figure 9/89 is signed on a plaque in the dial centre 'Edward Herbert London.' The lunar dial is as described above and the spandrels are the usual type with a head amidst scrolling foliage (C. & W. No. 21). The date is c.1735. The case is veneered with burr walnut picked out with stringing. The hood has a graceful caddy and attached columns but has lost its sound frets. The height is 8ft. 0ins. excluding finials.

Figure 9/89. Clock by Edward Herbert, c.1735, showing early example of type of lunar dial which became common. Burr walnut case with graceful caddy and attached columns but has lost sound frets. Height 8ft. 0ins. excluding finials.

Figure 9/90. Typical lunar dial with a landscape and a seascape, this type followed that in figure 9/89 with a starry sky between moons. Most dials are marked to show 29½ days, not just 29.

Figure 9/91. Later type of lunar dial where the divisions are on the dial arch and each moon has an arrow to point to them. This example comes from a painted dial.

Figure 9/92. North country type of lunar dial used in the upper centre of a square brass dial and making one rotation per lunation. The dial plate would have an aperture to show the phases and a square opening for the moon's age.

A fine walnut cased clock of c.1740 signed 'Robert Cawley Chester' is shown in figure 9/93. It will be the work of the first Robert Cawley who died in 1743. It has retained its elegant original caddy top with gilt wood finials and there are gilt wood capitals and bases to the attached columns. The hood has arched-top side windows. In place of the usual sound frets above the hood door and at the base of the caddy there are glass panels with the rear side decorated with coloured paints backed with gold leaf[20] (see figure 9/94). This is an early form of the decorated panels which became usual on cases made in south west Lancashire. The height is about 8ft. 4ins. excluding the finial. The 12ins. arched dial has a wheat-ear border which is repeated on the name plate in the arch. The spandrels are the usual female head amidst scrolling foliage (C. & W. No. 21). The calendar ring has become displaced.

20. This process is sometimes known as *verre églomisé*.

Figure 9/93. Fine walnut cased clock by Cawley, Chester, c.1740, which still has its original caddy. Height about 8ft. 4ins. excluding finial.

Figure 9/94. Hood of Cawley clock showing elegant caddy. Gilt wood finials, capitals and bases. Early use of decorated glass panels in place of sound frets above hood door and in base of caddy. Panels have rear surface painted in colours and backed with gold leaf. 12ins. dial with wheat-ear border which is repeated on name boss in arch.

Figure 9/95 shows the dial of a fine three train clock signed 'William Lee Leicester.' Note the seconds ring with the divisions outside the numerals, a later style which gradually came into use. As the seconds hand had to reach to the divisions on the outer edge its extra length made a counterpiece desirable and one was normally provided as in this case. The plaque marked 'First/Second', just above the XII is for changing the tune played by the musical movement. The hands are beautifully cut and suit the well engraved dial.

The movement (figure 9/96) is of excellent quality and plays a choice of two tunes on eight bells. To change the tune the pin barrel is pumped across by means of the bevelled end of the lever just visible to the left of the front plate adjacent to the barrel. The other end of this lever projects through the dial above the XII. The barrel is restored to its original position by the flat spring on the back plate. The curved cut away in the top edge of the back plate indicates that either the bells have been repositioned or that larger ones were fitted originally. Chime clocks and early musical clocks had the pin barrel parallel to the other arbors as here but later musical movements had much longer pin barrels to accommodate more hammers and bells and the barrels therefore had to be parallel to the plates. It should be noted that in the seventeenth and eighteenth centuries the term chime was often used to describe a clock playing tunes at intervals of at least an hour (what is now defined as 'musical'). 'Chime' is now used to describe a clock which indicates quarter hours on a number (usually four or more) bells. From what has been said it will be realised that musical clocks give no more accurate audible indication of the time than plain hour strikers. For this reason many of them fell out of use once the novelty had worn off and quite a number had the musical trains stripped out, or were converted to quarter chiming.

Figure 9/95. Dial of fine musical clock by William Lee, Leicester, c.1740. Note seconds ring with divisions on outside and hence longer hand with counterpoise. Tune change lever above XII. Finely engraved dial and beautifully cut hands.

Figure 9/96. Lee movement playing two tunes on eight bells. Cut away in top of back plate indicates that bells have been repositioned or larger ones were fitted originally. Note alternative positions for pendulum suspension on back cock to allow for case leaning back.

The William Lee clock has an elegant walnut case (figure 9/97) very much in the London style of the 1720s. Features suggesting this include the square topped trunk door and the slim proportions. The hood has fine sound frets and quite long side windows but lacks a caddy top. The double skirting to the plinth is quite usual from c.1725. Lee died in 1744 so the clock may be dated c.1740.

Figure 9/98 shows the dial of a chiming clock signed on the chapter ring 'Nicholas Lambert London' and probably c.1740-45. A pair of clocks of c.1715 in arabesque marquetry cases and with dials also signed 'Nicholas Lambert London' on the chapter rings are shown in figure 5/30. All these dials have turban head spandrels (C. & W. No. 19). The only recorded maker of this name is given the dates 1750-70 which makes it unlikely that he was responsible for the clocks illustrated, but there may have been a father or other relative of the same name. In figure 9/98 note the elongated diamond half hour marks and the absence of half quarters. The minute hand is shown broken but has now been repaired. The movement chimes on eight bells and has rack and snail control for both striking and chiming, thus permitting silencing.

The case (figure 9/99) is veneered with burr walnut with chequered stringing. The hood has an elegant break arch surmounted by a caddy and the columns are detached. The brass finials are modern replacements.

Figure 9/100 shows a very similar case to that in figure 9/99, except that it has no caddy to the break arch hood. It is veneered in fine quality burr walnut with narrow herring-bone banding and has a single skirting to the plinth. The escutcheon on the trunk door is an incorrect replacement. The dial (figure 9/101) is signed on a boss in the arch 'Will Avenell Gravesend' and has one or two features which suggest it was not the work of a specialist London dial engraver. The numerals on the seconds ring are too large and are not evenly spaced and the name boss has a rather ineffectual border. The engraving within the seconds ring and the amount of engraving round the calendar aperture also suggest a provincial origin. The minute and seconds hands are incorrect replacements being too late in design. The date of the clock is c.1740.

A very similar dial signed by 'Sam. H. Pape High Street Highgate' is shown in figure 9/102. This conforms more to the London style — less engraving on the dial centre and the seconds ring is much better set out, also the layout of the arch is more satisfactory. The hour hand is too late in style and too long, and the seconds hand is modern and clumsily made.

Some clock cases are so unusual in design, not following the normal progression, that they are very difficult to date. They are usually the work of provincial cabinet makers, not specialist case makers and such an example is shown in figure 9/103. It has a pine carcase veneered with burr and other finely figured walnut which has

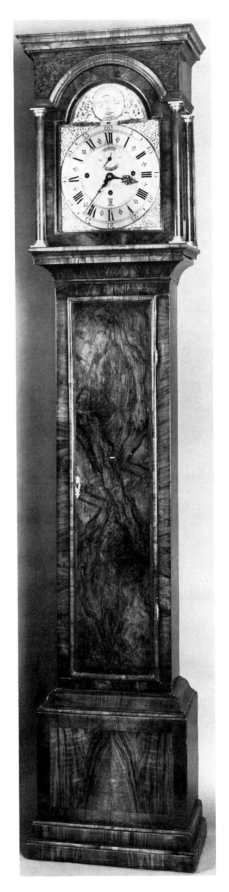

Figure 9/97. Elegant but conservative case of Lee clock, note square topped trunk door, long side windows and slim proportions. Attractive walnut veneers and good sound frets, but lacks a caddy.

Figure 9/98. Dial of chiming clock by Lambert, probably c.1740-45. Strike/silent in arch, hence rack striking and chiming. Broken minute hand has now been repaired.

Figure 9/99. Lambert case with burr walnut veneer and chequered stringing. Elegant break arch hood with caddy and detached columns. Modern brass finials.

Figure 9/101. Dial of Avenell clock. Probably not work of a specialist dial engraver — seconds numbers too large and badly spaced, name boss has weak border. Engraving on matted centre suggests provincial work. Minute and seconds hands incorrect.

Figure 9/100. Clock by Avenell, Gravesend, c.1740, in burr walnut case with narrow herring-bone banding. Break arch hood without caddy and single skirting. Wrong escutcheon on trunk door.

faded to a golden colour. The trunk has Ionic pilasters with enormous capitals and the plinth has flat pilasters to 'support' those above. The hood has strange twisted attached columns with Corinthian capitals in wood. The case is decorated with carved mouldings and carved paterae. A presumably damaged sound fret in the arched hood has been covered with a plain piece of wood. In figure 9/104 note the trunk door hinges which extend the full width of the door.

The dial (figure 9/104) is signed on the chapter ring between 35 and 25 'Geo: Boutcher Broad-clist.' Broadclyst is a village near Exeter in which George Boutcher died in 1745.[21] The clock can therefore be dated c.1740-45. The dial centre is not matted but is covered with scrolling foliage which is repeated on the hemispheres of the lunar dial opening, with simpler engraving above it. The spandrels are the type with a head amidst scrolling foliage (C. & W. No. 21). The lunar dial has the strange feature that in one half there are 10 day divisions from 25 to 5 although ½ is marked midway between them. On the other part of the dial there are only 9 days between 25 and 5 although ½ is shown above two half days. Perhaps this simplified setting out the divisions.

The left hand subsidiary dial is marked 'Chime/Not Chime' and the right hand one lists the six tunes played: 'A March/A Jig/Rummer/Wht: Jack/A. Walpole/113 Psal.' The last tune would be for use on Sundays and a sheet of music, apparently for the 113th Psalm, is

21. Much of this information comes from C.N. Ponsford, *Time in Exeter,* 1978, p. 152.

Figure 9/102. Dial of clock by Pape, High-gate, c.1740. Similar to previous dial but more 'London' style. Seconds ring set out much better and arch layout more satisfactory. Hour and seconds hands incorrect.

Figure 9/104. **Dial and hood of Boutcher clock.** *Dial centre engraved but not matted. Subsidiary dials for chime/silent and tune selector for six tunes. Music for one of them, 113th Psalm, on paper pasted on back board. Note hinge extending right across trunk door.*

stuck on the back of the case. The clock still has its original typical hands (see figure 9/103). A paper stuck on the inside of the trunk door reads:

> To set the clock — Set the hands one hour at a time — that is — let it strike the hour out before you move them again — And the chimes in like manner — It chimes at 3, 6, 9, 12 — The Large Weight must be hung on the right hand side, for the chime part — And observe that it winds up the reverse way. The hand to shift the Tunes, turns the reverse way also — and must not be moved while the tune is playing — Point the hand to Chime or Not Chime, Strike or Silent, according as you wish it — The Moon should be set at New Moon — you can do so by putting your finger to the Plate. N.B. The Works were packed in a Wooden Box — the Pendulum fastened to the back of the case — the weights by themselves.

Figure 9/103. Clock by Boutcher, Broadclyst, in highly individual case of pine veneered with burr and other walnut. Mixture of motifs, pilasters on plinth support Ionic pilasters on trunk and hood has twist columns with Corinthian capitals. Note carved mouldings and paterae. Damaged sound fret covered with plain wood. c.1740-45.

Towards the middle of the eighteenth century dials became much simpler as exemplified by figure 9/105 which shows a clock of c.1745 signed 'Richard Gregg London.' Note there are no quarter hour divisions or half hour markings, just a single line near the edge, and the seconds are numbered only in tens instead of in fives. This simplification, with the absence of any decoration on the matting, produces an elegant dial which is easier to read.

A small number of clocks incorporated a barometer, which had to be the mercury type as the aneroid mechanism was not invented until 1843. A few of these clocks have a wheel type mechanism as fitted in banjo barometers but most of them have a straight tube as in stick barometers. A clock by Finney with a wheel barometer is shown in figure 10/44. Figure 9/106 shows an example with a straight tube barometer, which is signed at the base of the silvered scales 'P. Sullivan London.' This is presumably the Patrick Sullivan who is recorded as working in London 1738-43[22] and the latter date or a little later would be appropriate for the whole clock.

22. N. Goodison, *English Barometers 1680-1860*, 1968, p. 330.

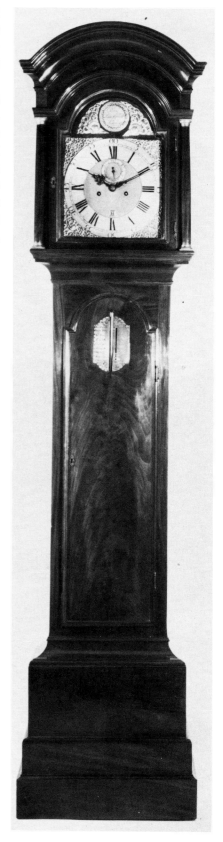

Figure 9/105. Dial of clock by Richard Gregg, c.1745. Early example of simplification which gave greater elegance and improved legibility. Note plain matted centre, absence of quarter hour and half hour markings, seconds numbered only in tens.

Figure 9/106. Clock by Pinchbeck, c.1743. Chapter ring has no quarter or half hour markings and seconds ring has 5, 15 ... etc. replaced by diamonds. Seconds hand has a tail. Straight tube barometer in door with silvered scale signed by P. Sullivan, London. Mahogany case with finely figured veneer on trunk door. Very high double skirting probably due to repairs. Height 7ft. 4ins.

The dial is signed on a boss in the arch 'Christ. Pinchbeck London.' The chapter ring has no superfluous lines, the Roman numerals extending almost to the inner edge. The seconds ring has the 5, 15 .... numbers replaced by small diamonds and the hand has a tail. The spandrels are the popular head amidst scrolling foliage, also known as mask and scroll pattern (C. & W. No. 21).

The mahogany case has a finely figured veneer on the trunk door and is 7ft. 4ins. high. The break arch hood has side windows and detached columns but has apparently had a damaged sound fret covered with plain wood. The plinth has an abnormally high double skirting which may be the result of repairs at some time.

Mahogany was used in this country for furniture making from about 1730 but was rarely used for clock cases until almost the middle of the century. The first mahogany was imported from San Domingo in the West Indies and was very hard and dark in colour, with straight grain and very little figure. Towards 1750 Cuban wood came into use and in this the rich dark colour is accompanied by a fine figure. Later in the century wood was obtained from Honduras. This was lighter in weight, had a more open grain and was of a lighter colour with less conspicuous figuring than Cuban mahogany. The use of mahogany in

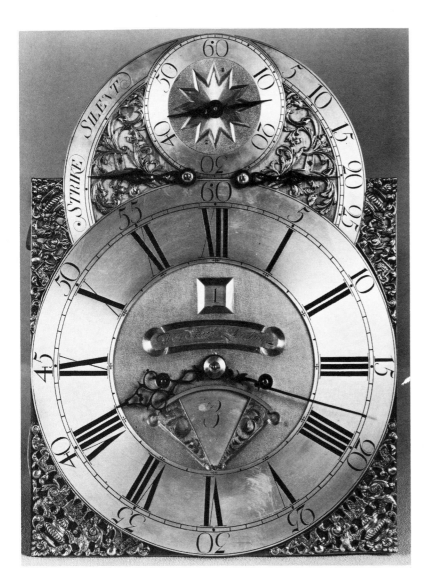

Figure 9/107. Dial of unusual clock by Scafe, c.1745. Chapter ring has half hour divisions but no quarters or half hour markings. Aperture in lower centre for days of week. Large seconds dial in arch, flanked by strike/silent and pendulum regulation dials. Strange feature of no margins of dial plate beyond spandrels and dial rings. Balanced seconds hand but does not reach divisions as other hands do.

Figure 9/108. Scafe movement showing drive to escapement, using two contrate wheels. Note signature on recessed plaque.

provincial casemaking was governed largely by the transport facilities available from the nearest port with trade to the West Indies. Most mahogany cases have a carcase of straight grained mahogany with figured veneer used on the trunk door and perhaps on the plinth.

It should be noted that not all clock cases or other items of furniture which are mahogany coloured are made of that wood. Country joiners used quite a lot of fruit wood, cherry and pear in particular which can closely resemble rather plain mahogany. Another wood which came into use c.1720 is Virginia or black walnut, also known as red walnut, and this can very easily be mistaken for somewhat faded mahogany. It is generally used in the solid and although the grain resembles some solid English and Continental walnut it is not nearly so attractive as much of the European wood. A clock case veneered with Virginia walnut is shown in Colour Plate 15 and is a late use of this wood.

The time lag which occurred in the universal adoption of stylistic changes causes considerable difficulties in the accurate dating of clocks. The dial in figure 9/107 shows the partial adoption of the changes shown in the Richard Gregg dial of figure 9/105. The chapter ring has lost half hour symbols and quarter hour divisions but retains those for half hours. The seconds dial, in the arch, has the divisions on the outer edge and is numbered only every ten. The dial is signed on a recessed plaque just above the centre 'Wm. Scafe London.' The usual type of calendar shows through an aperture just below XII and the opening below the centre shows the days of the week by numbers, 3 as shown will represent Wednesday. The Quakers used numbers instead of names for the days of the week, which could account for this example[22a]. The left side of the dial arch is occupied by a strike/silent device and the right side provides pendulum regulation, by moving the hand to a higher number for faster and to a lower one for slower. Urn spandrels (C. & W. No. 26) are used but the castings in the arch are a special design for this type of clock and are not in C. & W. One strange feature is that the dial plate does not extend beyond the spandrels, chapter ring and arch fittings, which means that the masking frame in the hood cannot overlap the dial plate and therefore may leave gaps. The hour hand is of a pattern which came into use by 1750 and continued until about the end of the century. With a seconds ring over 4½ins. in diameter it is essential to balance the hand, but it would look better if it reached the divisions. The perfect fit of the minute and hour hands should be noted.

Providing a seconds hand in the arch necessitates a considerable rearrangement of the going train. The centre pinion carries a contrate wheel at its rear end (figure 9/108) and this drives a pinion with a long vertical arbor. Another contrate wheel at the upper end of this arbor drives the escape wheel pinion. Contrate wheels can waste a lot of power unless accurately depthed, but the quality of the workmanship is shown by the fact that the clock will run comfortably on 6lb. weights.

The beautifully shaped plates are shown in figure 9/109. Quite often movements which required specially shaped plates had extension pieces screwed on but these must have been special castings. The movement has seven pillars. Note how the escape pinion is carried in a bridge to allow it to mesh with the contrate wheel. The rise and fall mechanism uses a rack engaging with a partly cut wheel. Unlike other types of regulator using a wing nut or micrometer, or an endless screw or worm, this type will run back out of adjustment unless resistance is introduced at some point. This is provided by a stiff bowed spring between the wheel and the back plate. Introducing stiffness into the sliding of the rack would cause jerky movement because of the backlash in the gearing. The top end of the rack has an extension plate fixed to it which is cut away to fit round the pallet arbor cock and carries the pendulum support at the top. Scafe made other clocks with seconds in the arch and this example should be dated c.1745.

The case (figure 9/110) is veneered with burr walnut with herring-bone bandings. The hood has attached columns and good sound frets but no longer has a caddy top.

22a. I am indebted to Francis Wadsworth for this suggestion.

Figure 9/109. Rear view showing rack and pinion type pendulum regulation. Note elegantly shaped plates.

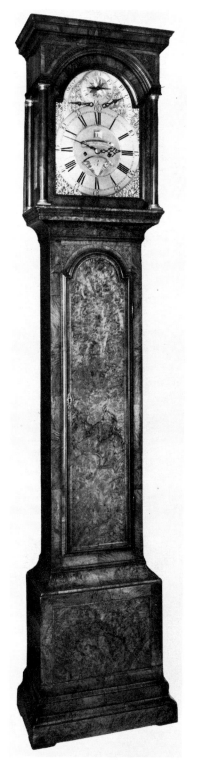

Figure 9/110. Case of Scafe clock with fine burr walnut veneers and herring-bone banding. Hood has attached columns and good sound frets but has lost its caddy.

Figure 9/112. Ellicott movement. Note pinning of chime barrel to ring changes; front plate cut away to facilitate renewing gut. Flat spring on back plate is to shift lifting piece arbor for silencing. Note also large anti-friction wheels for calendar ring.

A very similar case is shown in figure 9/111, differences being the earlier style square topped door, the absence of herring-bone banding and the single skirting to a rather high plinth. The hood has no quarter columns at the rear although these may have existed originally.

The dial is signed on the chapter ring 'John Ellicott London' and has a narrow chapter ring without divisions on the inside, and a large narrow seconds ring although this is still divided on the inner edge and numbered every five. There is a 'Strike/Silent' dial in the arch flanked by dolphins. The spandrels are an early and quite elaborate version of a type (C. & W. No. 36) which came into use about 1750. The hour hand is a cross over loop type which was introduced at about the same time. The whole clock can be dated c.1750.

Figure 9/111. Quarter chiming clock by Ellicott, c.1750. Case similar to previous example except for square topped trunk door and rather high plinth with single skirting. Dial has narrow seconds and chapter rings, and elaborate rococo spandrels. Note cross over loop hour hand.

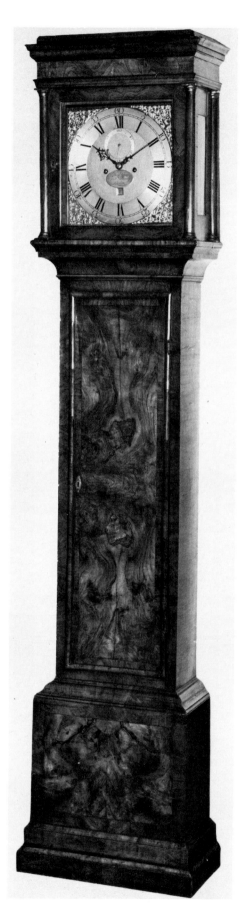

Figure 9/113. Graham no. 778, c.1750. Burr walnut case with raised panel to plinth. Hood has attached columns, fine frets and an elegant caddy. Half round beading to trunk door. Height 7ft. 8ins. 12ins. dial has slim seconds and chapter rings. Slots at III and IX for maintaining power and strike/silent levers.

Figure 9/114. Clock by Gray and Vulliamy, c.1750, in walnut case similar to Graham but without raised panel to plinth. Proportions of hood not very satisfactory, perhaps spoilt by removal of a caddy. Elegant dial with large, very slim seconds ring.

The three train movement (figure 9/112) chimes the quarters on eight bells and unlike most of the early examples it rings changes, not just straight runs down the scale. Such changes normally finish with the lowest pitched bell. The strike/silent hand cuts off both chime and hour strike. The flat spring on the back plate pumps the lifting piece out of the path of the lifting pins. Repeating of hours and quarters can be effected by depressing the lever just to the left of the pin barrel by means of a cord. Note the extra large anti-friction wheels for the calendar ring, also the front plate cut away to facilitate renewing the gut without dismantling. Altogether an excellent quality clock.

A very elegant square dial clock by George Graham of c.1750 is shown in figure 9/113. The burr walnut case has a double skirting and a raised plinth panel as found on some of Delander's clocks but otherwise little used until c.1750. The trunk door has a square top to match the dial and a half round beading. The hood has attached columns, a fine fret and an elegant caddy, which on a bracket clock would be described as inverted bell. The height is 7ft. 8ins. and both case and movement are numbered 778.

The 12ins dial has no divisions on the inside of the chapter ring, a large slim seconds ring divided on the inner edge and numbered every five, and turbaned head spandrels (C. & W. No. 19). The hour hand of the cross over loop pattern is quite narrow, a feature of Graham's hour hands. Slots at III and IX accommodate levers for bolt and shutter maintaining power and strike/silent. The movement has a latched dial and plates and a dead beat escapement.

Another fine square dial clock of approximately the same date as the Graham (c.1750) is shown in figure 9/114. The walnut veneered case has crossbanding to the door and plinth but no raised panel on the latter. There is no sound fret and the proportions of the top of the hood are not very satisfactory, perhaps spoilt by the removal of a caddy.

The 12ins. dial is signed on a plaque below the centre 'Benj:n Gray Just: Vulliamy London.' The large and very slim seconds ring has divisions on the inner edge and is numbered every ten with small diamond marks for the fives. The spandrels have a small head amidst scrolling foliage (C. & W. No. 22). The hour hand is a fully developed version of the cross over loop pattern.

Figure 9/115 shows an interesting dial, signed on the chapter ring 'John Pyke London', which may be dated c.1750 as it does not incorporate the Gregorian calendar adopted in 1752. The corner spandrels include a female bust (C. & W. No. 23) and match those in the arch (C. & W. No. 45). The dial in the arch is for pendulum regulation. The very broad chapter ring has, outside the five minute numbering, a zone on which the creatures of the zodiac are painted. The next three rings show the equation of time: 'Watch Faster/Watch Slower' on the first, then the number of minutes on the second ring and the seconds on the third one. This information is given for the 10th, 20th and last day of each month. For example on December 20th the clock is 3 minutes 38 seconds ahead of solar time. The next ring gives the times of sunrise in hours and minutes for each month on a date between the 15th and the 20th, probably chosen to minimise the error caused by omitting the seconds. The last two rings form an annual calendar. The long hand with the gilt sun makes one rotation per year.

Hindley of York was a very ingenious and individual maker[23] and figure 9/116 shows the full arch dial of a quarter striking clock of c.1750 which is signed on the strike/silent ring 'Henry Hindley York.' Note that the seconds ring is divided on the inside but is numbered every ten seconds. The elaborate arch spandrels which do not appear in C. & W. were also used by Margetts, see figure 11/56.

Figure 9/117 shows the front plate. The maintaining power is all mounted on the front with the bolt projecting through a slot in the plate to engage the teeth of the centre wheel

23. See R.J. Law, 'Henry Hindley of York 1701-1771', *Antiquarian Horology*, VII (June 1971, September 1972) pp. 205, 682.

Figure 9/115. Interesting dial of a clock by Pyke, c.1750. Corner and arch spandrels incorporate female busts. Very broad chapter ring has, outside the minute numbering, the creatures of the zodiac, the equation of time, times of sunrise and an annual calendar. Hand with gilt sun makes one rotation per year. Pendulum regulation dial in arch.

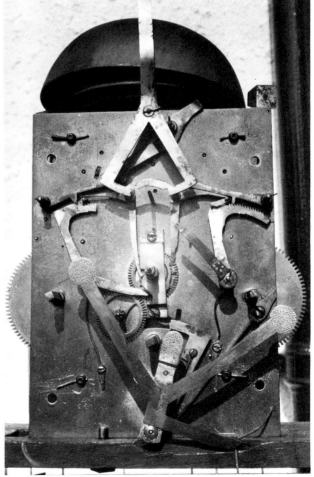

Figure 9/116. Full arch dial of quarter striking clock by Hindley, York, c.1750. Unusual arch spandrels. Dial in arch provides for silencing quarters only or hours and quarters.

Figure 9/117. Front plate, showing maintaining power with bolt projecting through slot to engage centre wheel. Both quarter and hour striking warned and released separately. Diagonal lever behind strike/silent lever intercepts hour fly until quarter rack hook drops at end of striking.

Figure 9/118. Three quarter view showing quarter striking and diagonal lever which intercepts hour fly.

Figure 9/119. Back plate, showing very long crutch and short suspension. Flat springs pressing on discs tension lifting piece arbors against strike/silent lever. Lever passing up through back cock is for repeating and raises both lifting pieces when moved to either side. It is restored by a strong spring. Note L shaped seat board bolt.

which is just behind the front plate (figure 9/121). Rack striking is provided for both trains and the gathering pallets have tails for locking. Both quarter and hour striking trains are warned and released independently by different pins in the cannon pinion which also carries the quarter snail. During quarter striking the hour train is held up by the diagonal lever pivoted just behind the strike/silent lever. The lower end of this lever rests on the quarter rack hook and the upper end has a bent over section which intercepts the fly of the hour train. At the end of quarter striking the rack hook falls into an extra deeply cut tooth on the quarter rack, which allows the diagonal lever to release the fly of the hour striking train, see figure 9/118.

The two lifting pieces are pinned on to arbors which are pressed forward by flat springs on the back plate (see figure 9/119), but with the strike/silent lever in the position shown both lifting pieces are held back so that they are operated by the lifting pins. Moving the hand to 'Quarters Silent' moves the lower portion of the lever to the left, allowing the quarter lifting piece to move forward. Moving the hand to 'Silent' releases both lifting pieces because the left hand part of the lever has a hump on the back which normally holds the quarter lifting piece in the operating position.

The back plate is shown in figure 9/119; note the springs applying pressure to discs fixed to the lifting piece arbors. The lever which passes up inside the back cock is for repeating and is pivoted just below the back cock and has a clearance hole for the pallet arbor. A strong spring holds the repeating lever in its normal position. When the lever is moved to either left or right, the arms at its lower end rotate the two lifting piece arbors via the pins in the discs. The two discs are always turned so as to operate the lifting pieces and warn the striking trains, that is the left one turns clockwise and the right one anti-clockwise. The arrangement permits a cord to be led out at each side of the hood for repeating but causes difficulty in removing and replacing the hood if cords are threaded through holes in its sides. The hood of this clock, like others with the same mechanism, is not drilled for repeating cords. Note the L-shaped fixing bolts which fit holes near the bottom edge of the back and the front plates. An improvement which prevents the fixing screws fouling the pulleys as frequently happens with the usual type which are screwed into the pillars. The very long crutch and short suspension are to give the maximum impulse without jerking the pendulum.

Figure 9/120 shows the quarter striking train. The hammer springs have the tops bent over to form banking springs, a type which is frequently troublesome and a repairer has provided a bent wire stop for the two hammers. Note the double baluster pillars which are typical of Hindley's later clocks.

The movement with front plate removed is shown in figure 9/121. Note the small recoil escape wheel and the small third wheel. The flies have friction springs at the ends instead of the more usual central ones bearing on grooves in their arbors.

The blue japanned case (figure 9/122) is original, the full arch dial (figure 9/123) almost guarantees that. It would have had a caddy top originally. The chinoiserie scenes are of fine quality (figure 9/124), but the case appears to have had some restoration as is usual with japanned cases.

Figure 9/120. Side view, note typical double baluster pillars. Also improvised hammer stop of bent wire.

Figure 9/121. Movement with front plate removed. Note small third and escape wheels. Flies have end friction springs.

Figure 9/122. Blue japanned case of Hindley clock. It would have had a caddy originally.

Figure 9/123. Hood showing full arch door with attached columns.

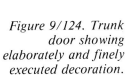

Figure 9/124. Trunk door showing elaborately and finely executed decoration.

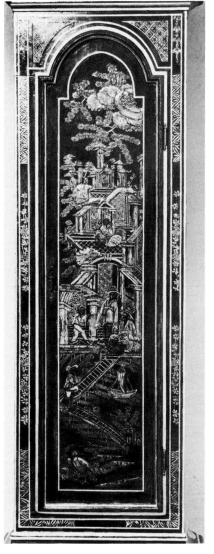

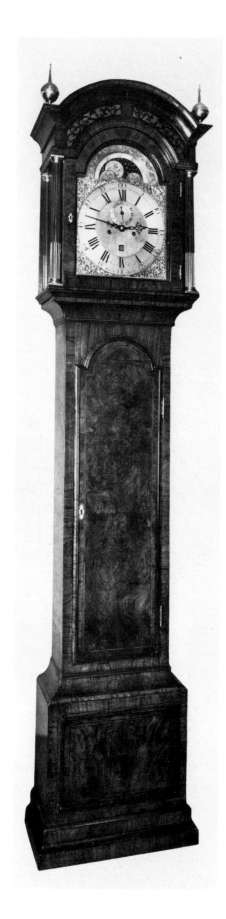

Chapter 10

CAPITAL AND COUNTRY
1750-1800

The main feature of this period is the increasingly important part played by provincial clockmakers, both in terms of a vastly increased output and in the high quality of the clocks produced by the best of these makers. Their work is characterised by a freshness of outlook which resulted in many ingenious pieces of mechanism. It will be appreciated that restrictions on space prevent a comprehensive description and assessment of provincial clockmaking in the present work, but such a survey may be possible at a later date. With the coming of the Industrial Revolution, the Midlands and the north of England became wealthier and more populous so much of the increase in provincial clockmaking took place in these areas rather than in other parts which developed more slowly.

Developments in the field of precision timekeeping are discussed in Chapter 11, but few of these innovations were applied to the ordinary domestic clock. A number of such clocks were made however with dead beat escapements, some of them with wooden pendulum rods, but usually without maintaining power. Rack striking became almost universal except for thirty-hour clocks and there was an increase in the number of three train, including musical, clocks.

There is no doubt that an increasing number of movements and dials were made by specialists who worked mainly or exclusively for 'clockmakers', famous or otherwise. It is difficult to assess the position, but there is evidence that some small town clockmakers were still working independently until at least the end of the century.

The second half of the century saw the gradual adoption of mahogany for the vast majority of cases except for those made in places remote from sea and river ports and for cottage clocks. Where transport costs for mahogany were high, it was often used, particularly in the north, to decorate oak cases, the mahogany being used for crossbanding, columns and other decorative features.

In country districts the fashionable demand for 'mahogany' was often met by the use of fruit woods, particularly cherry and plum, both of which closely resemble solid mahogany. 'Fruit wood' normally means apple, cherry, pear or plum and it is usual to employ this general term.

Figure 10/1. Clock by Behoe, c.1750-54, with moon in arch. Elegant burr walnut case with panelled plinth and herring-bone banding. Detached fluted columns with brass inlay. Replaced finials.

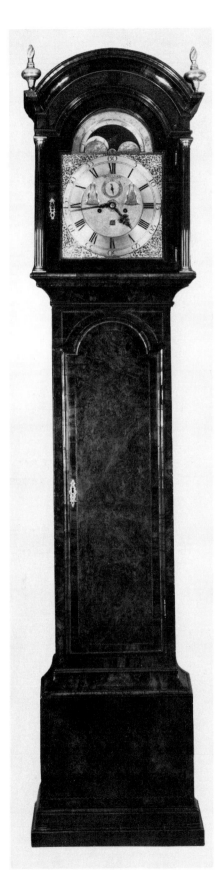

Figure 10/2. Clock by Crolee, c.1750-55. Case similar to previous one but without raised plinth panel and with chequered stringing instead of herring-bone inlay. Good brass flambeau finials.

Figure 10/3. Dial and hood of Crolee clock. Shaped openings for day of week and month with appropriate figures and signs, as well as date. Note alarm setting disc at centre and strike/silent at IX. Possible Dutch influence in type of calendar and in provision of alarm.

Pine continued to be used, particularly in the south and was always painted as was the rule with pine furniture. Some of these cases were very carefully grained to simulate mahogany or rosewood. Japanned cases were still made in the provinces until almost the end of the century. To summarise, away from the main centres of population the choice of woods for cases depended on their availability locally and their cost.

The following extract from an advertisement of 1791[1] raises a few points of interest:

T. and W. Chaplin, Watch, Clockmakers and Silversmiths, ... Bury St. Edmunds.

Best new 8 day clocks in square case, either wainscot or walnut-tree at 5£, the same in arched case at 5£ 5s, new 8 day clocks in mahogany cases at 6£ 6s, the same with moon plates at 6£ 16s 6d; 30-hour clocks with minutes and day of the month, in wainscot or walnut-tree cases at 3£ 13s 6d.....

The fact that walnut cases cost no more than wainscot (oak) ones implies that walnut must have been produced locally and it was presumably used in the solid. This would not have applied in other, more northerly parts of the country.

CONTINUING THE STORY

Walnut veneer continued in popularity for a time and figure 10/1 shows a fine break arch case with panelled plinth and herring-bone banding. The detached hood columns are fluted and inlaid with brass. The finials are later replacements. The dial is signed on the chapter ring 'John Behoe London' and it has urn spandrels (C. & W. No. 26). The moon aperture is bordered with scrolled engraving and the left hand semi-circle is decorated with a moon face and the right hand one with an armillary sphere. The date is c.1750-54.

Figure 10/2 shows another very similar walnut clock. The case does not have a raised

1. Reproduced in A.L. Haggar and L.F. Miller, *Suffolk Clocks & Clockmakers,* 1974, p. 9.

Figure 10/4. Good quality clock by Ellicott with maintaining power and seconds dial in arch, c.1750-55.

plinth panel but has fine chequered stringing and good brass flambeau finials. The dial (figure 10/3) is signed on a plaque 'John Crolee London', an apparently unrecorded maker and the spandrels are C. & W. No. 20. In addition to the date, the day of the week with its deity and planetary sign, and the month with its appropriate figure and zodiacal sign, are shown through openings. The striking may be silenced by a lever at IX with the markings 'S/N' on the chapter ring. There is an alarm with pull-up winding which is set in the normal way by means of the disc behind the hour hand. From this time it is quite normal for seconds hands to have tails although many were still without. The day and month indicators with their shaped openings, and the alarm, which is rare on English longcase clocks, suggest Dutch influence and the name Crolee is not particularly English. Even so there is no reason to doubt its London origin and the probable date is c.1750-55.

Figure 10/4 shows a good quality clock which is signed on the chapter ring 'John Ellicott London.' Apparently watches were signed 'Jno. Ellicott' up to about 1758 when 'Ellicott' only came into use, so if his clocks were signed similarly, it agrees with this example of c.1750-55. The seconds hand is in the arch and maintaining power is provided with a lever at II. The spandrels are C. & W. No. 19. The movement (figure 10/5) has a long vertical arbor and two contrate wheels to take the drive to the dead beat escapement. It has the refinements of a beat setting device on the pallets and banking pins to prevent damage to the escapement if the pendulum receives an excessive swing. The striking train is on the left as usual but with the bell on the right so the hammer strikes it on the inside. The cord near the bell is for hour repeating. The case is of solid red or virginia walnut.

Figure 10/5. Ellicott movement with long vertical arbor to drive escape wheel. Dead beat escapement has beat setting device and banking pins to protect the escapement.

Figure 10/6. Later, more conventional, clock by Ellicott, c.1765, with large seconds ring and strike/silent dial in arch. Fine mahogany case with break arch hood surmounted by early form of pagoda top.

Figure 10/7. Clock by Mayhew, Woodbridge, 1755-60. Lunar dial has tidal markings which appear in opening within seconds ring. Wrong hour hand. Good quality burr walnut case with detached reeded columns but it has lost most of its pagoda top.

A later production signed 'Ellicott London' is shown in figure 10/6. It is more conventional with a large seconds ring within the chapter ring and a strike/silent dial in the arch. It has rococo spandrels, C. & W. No. 40, and C. & W. No. 39 in the arch. The elegant mahogany case has a break arch hood surmounted by an early form of pagoda top. This has a flat top with a small convex moulding round it, whereas the fully developed pagoda top has a convex top and resembles a cross-section of a church bell, so it is also known as a bell top. Note the finely cut sound frets. The probable date is c.1765. A fully developed pagoda topped case is shown in figure 10/18.

A good quality provincial case is shown in figure 10/7, but unfortunately it has lost most of its pagoda top. It has detached reeded columns but without brass inlay. The trunk door is veneered with fine burr walnut. It is signed on an arched name plate 'Willm. Mayhew Woodbridge' who was in business 1751-91.[2] The dial has a matted centre and spandrels with a small head amidst foliage (C. & W. No. 22). The moon dial indicates high tide, no doubt for Woodbridge, which is shown through an opening inside the seconds ring. Such openings within the seconds ring are rare on English clocks but common on Dutch ones, which may have influenced this example. The hour hand is a nineteenth century replacement. The probable date is c.1755-60.

Still looking at East Anglian clocks, figure 10/8 shows a slim, nicely proportioned oak case with typical East Anglian cresting. This type of cresting was developed and used on some American clocks, where it became known as whales' tails cresting. Although the side finials are provided with small plinths, it is strange that they are in the way of parts of the cresting. The hood door has the earlier arrangement of attached columns. The name boss in the arch has a laurel leaf border and is signed 'Thos. Smith Norwich.' The corner spandrels are rococo pattern (C. & W. No. 32) and those in the arch are in matching rococo style (C. & W. No. 39). Quite a lot of dials will be found with rococo corner spandrels, but with dolphins in the arch. The height is 7ft. 10½ins. including the finials, with a 12ins. dial and it dates from c.1760-65.

2. A.L. Haggar and L.F. Miller, *Suffolk Clocks & Clockmakers,* 1974, p. 111.

Colour Plate 16. Fine quality case with trunk section based on right hand design in figure 10/90. Full width hood door without columns, to preserve slim line. Originally had three finials but present one is a replacement. Choice mahogany veneers inlaid with kingwood, tulip wood and ebony. Height 7ft. 7ins. including finial, maximum width of hood 16ins., minimum width of trunk 9⅝ins. Clock with 12ins. dial by Ramsbottom, Hall Green, probably c.1795.

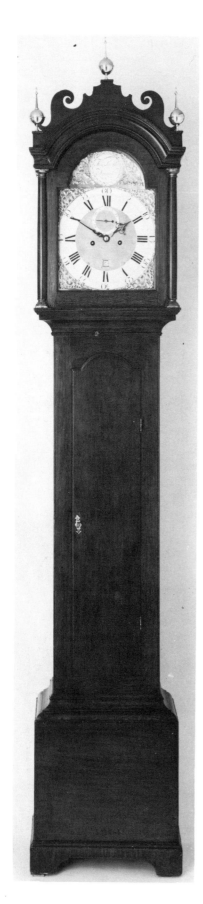

The rococo style had become well established in France by c.1730 but did not become popular in England until about 1750 although some engravers and silversmiths had used it earlier. It is characterised by C-scrolls with flowing, interlaced foliage and is normally asymmetrical but balanced. Clock dials were provided with a variety of rococo spandrels (C. & W. Nos. 30, 32, 36, 37, 39, 40, 41) and some dials, particularly provincial ones, had engraved centres to harmonise with them (see figure 10/119).

Rococo patterns remained fashionable as long as applied spandrels were in use. The rococo style had little effect on clock cases except that some had fine quality key hole escutcheons in this style.

Figure 10/9 shows a very unusual thirty-hour clock which is signed on the engraved dial centre 'Randle Maddock Leek.' The absence of proper minute divisions and numbers indicates that it has been converted from one hand to two and the hour hand is too long. The movement is key wound and the engraving fits neatly round the winding holes which tends to confirm that the dial and movement started life together. The spandrels are C. & W. No. 20.

The motion work is on the back of the movement (figure 10/10) which means that the barrel of the going train must have a divided arbor to permit winding. The hour wheel (next to the back plate) has a long pipe which passes through the movement and carries the hour hand. Inside this pipe is a long arbor with a square at the front end to carry the minute hand and the wheel with the lifting pin fixed to its rear end. If this is a conversion from a one hand clock, the striking would have been let off by a star wheel on the hour wheel, for which an almost vertical lifting piece, as here, would have been suitable. In that case the lifting piece must have been lengthened. Striking is by rack and snail on the front plate (figure 10/11), with locking on a pin in the second wheel of the striking train. Randle Maddock is quoted as c.1760 which is a suitable date for this clock.

There is no doubt that sometimes the name on the dial is that of the purchaser, not that of the maker, which is why some names cannot be traced. A few clocks have both names on the dial, see figure 10/12. The maker's name, 'Barwise Oulton', appears on the chapter ring between 35 and 25 but the owner had a plaque fitted just below XII with the inscription 'Samuel Johnston his Clock 1763' (figure 10/13). It is reasonable to assume that the clock was new when the plaque was fitted and the very large five minute numbers support its date and suggest a north country origin. It is interesting to see the persistence of an early pattern of spandrel (C. & W. No. 8). The hands are replacement brass ones of nineteenth century design. The maker was probably Lott Barwise of Cockermouth, or a relative, as there is a village called Oulton about fifteen miles from Cockermouth.

Figure 10/8. Clock by Smith, Norwich, 1760-65. Slim, nicely proportioned oak case with typical East Anglian cresting, but why do side finials obscure part of it? Hood door has attached columns. Height 7ft. 10½ins. excluding finials, with a 12ins. dial.

Figure 10/9. Key wound thirty-hour clock by Maddock, Leek, c.1760. Converted from one hand to two and hour hand is too long.

Figure 10/10. Back of Maddock movement showing motion work. Lifting piece could have been for a one hand movement.

Figure 10/11. Front plate showing rack striking with locking on a pin in second wheel of striking train.

Figure 10/10

Figure 10/11

Figure 10/12. Thirty-hour clock by Barwise, Oulton, with owner's plaque dated 1763 on dial centre (see figure 10/13). Note late use of crown and cherub spandrels. Wrong hands.

Figure 10/13. Plaque on Barwise dial reading 'Samuel Johnston his Clock 1763'.

Oak furniture was sometimes carved with the initials of the newly married couple for whom the piece was made and figure 10/14 shows the same idea on a clock. Note that the names 'John & Mary Wharton' are on an applied plaque but with a border engraved on the dial plate, whereas the maker's name 'Porthouse Penrith' is engraved direct on the plate. The spandrels are of vaguely rococo design not shown in C. & W. The clock was probably thirty-hour originally but appears to have been fitted with an eight-day movement. The matching steel hands date from about 1800, which could be the date of the clock, but if it is earlier the hands were probably changed at the same time as the movement. The case, of late eighteenth century design, is shown in figure 10/15.

Thomas Mudge is usually associated with precision timekeepers, particularly watches and chronometers, but figure 10/16 shows a musical clock by him which is c.1760-65. A semi-circular plaque in the arch is signed 'Thomas Mudge London' and this is surrounded by a silvered strip listing the six tunes which are played. The upper corners of the dial plate have strike/silent and chime/silent dials and the rococo spandrels are C. & W. No. 32. The mahogany case is of a very elegant design which was used extensively in the second half of the eighteenth century by the leading London makers.

Figure 10/14. Clock by Porthouse, Penrith, probably c.1790. Applied plaque above hands reads 'John & Mary Wharton'. Note vaguely rococo spandrels. Probably thirty-hour originally but now has eight day movement. Hands c.1800.

Figure 10/15. Case of Porthouse clock.

Figure 10/16. Six tune musical clock by Mudge with strike/silent and chime/silent subsidiary dials, c.1760-65. Elegant mahogany case with canted corners to hood.

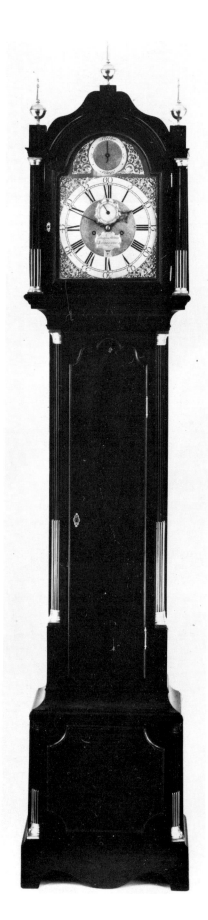

Figure 10/17. Clock by Dawes Northampton, c.1770. Dial has scalloped recesses for name plate and seconds dial. Strike/silent dial in arch. Good provincial mahogany case with quarter columns to plinth, elaborately shaped trunk door and simple cresting.

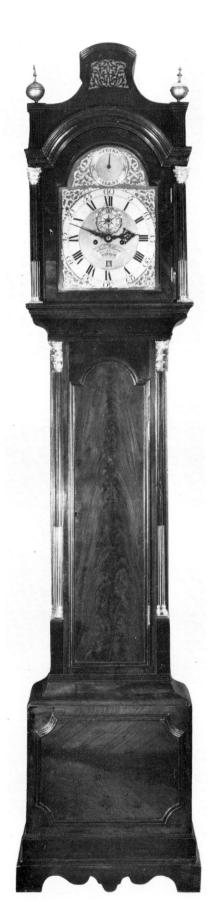

Japanned cases became less popular but were still made, particularly in the provinces, but a good London example of c.1765 is shown in Colour Plate 14. The mainly oak carcase has a deep green ground with well raised gilt decoration and good brass mounts. Note the early type of pagoda top. The height is 7ft. 9ins. The dial is signed on a plaque below the centre 'Wm. Morgan Southwark' and has urn spandrels (C. & W. No. 26) and dolphins (C. & W. No. 38) with a strike/silent dial in the arch.

An excellent quality provincial mahogany case is shown in figure 10/17. Features unlikely to be found on a London case are the quarter columns to the plinth[2a], the elaborately shaped top to the trunk door and the simple cresting to the hood with its suggestion of East Anglian work. The clock is signed on a recessed plaque below the dial centre 'Thomas Dawes Northampton' and this plaque is complemented by an elaborately scalloped opening for a recessed seconds dial. It has urn spandrels and dolphins in the arch. A good quality clock of c.1770.

Figure 10/18 shows a typical London mahogany case of c.1770 with a fully developed pagoda top. After being out of fashion for almost a century, Corinthian capitals were reintroduced and became very popular on the better quality cases. The key hole escutcheons on both doors are the simple flush type which follow the outline of the key hole. Eighteenth century ones are curved at the bottom, as here, whereas modern ones are straight. The dial is signed on an applied plaque in the centre 'John Williams London' and has a sunken seconds dial. The spandrels are rococo (C. & W. No. 32) with C. & W. No. 39 in the arch.

WILLIAM LUDLAM, SCIENTIST AND CLOCK DESIGNER

During the seventeenth and eighteenth centuries a number of clergymen made important contributions to scientific and technical knowledge, including horology. Amongst them was the Rev. William Ludlam, Professor of Mathematics, St. John's College, Cambridge. He was born in Leicester in 1717 and after a distinguished scholastic career in Cambridge he returned to Leicester in 1768 and resided there until his death in 1788. He was one of the six assessors appointed by the Board of Longitude to examine and report on John Harrison's marine timekeepers and was also responsible for the design of at least two domestic clocks. He was known for his skill in practical mechanics.

Figure 10/19 shows what is apparently a very ordinary thirty-hour clock. The 10ins. dial is unsigned and it has neither calendar nor seconds hand. The chapter ring has no half or quarter hour markings

2a. Plinth columns are sometimes found on high quality London cases.

Figure 10/18. Clock by Williams, c.1770. Good mahogany case with fully developed pagoda top. Note reintroduction of Corinthian capitals.

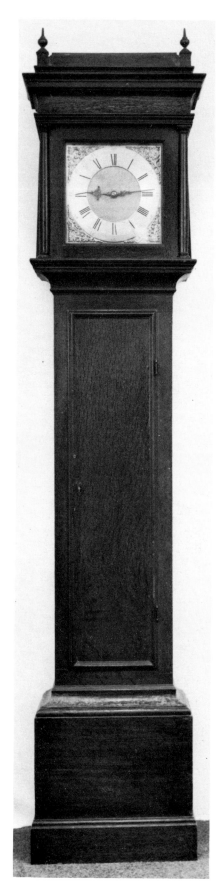

Figure 10/19. Simple, unsigned, 10ins. dial of thirty-hour clock. Plain oak case 6ft. 8½ins. height excluding modern finials and with a 12¼ins. waist.

Figure 10/20. Back plate of thirty-hour clock showing that it was designed by Ludlam and made by Hackings in 1759. Unfortunately the crutch was not removed before the photograph was taken so it obscures the date.

and there are rococo spandrels (not in C. & W.). The hour hand is of the cross over loop pattern. The simple oak case is 6ft. 8½ins. high excluding the modern finials and has a 12¼ins. waist. The hood has long side windows.

The back plate of the movement (figure 10/20) is inscribed 'Made under the Direction of W. Ludlam M.A. by John Hackings: for Mr. James Priest. 1759.' John Hackings was employed by Ludlam as an instrument maker and in 1759 Ludlam wrote of Hackings: "... [he] has worked for me constantly since midsummer, 1753; all my best tools were made by him; whatever has been done by him may be depended on."

The movement is of very good quality with five pillars and is held to the seat board by screws into the bottom pillars. It has a centre pinion to prevent shake in the minute hand and a recoil escapement. The striking mechanism (figure 10/21) incorporates a number of interesting devices, mainly to prevent malfunctioning. Rack striking is provided to permit repeating of the last hour. To ensure accuracy the snail is mounted on a star wheel operated by a pin in the minute wheel at a few minutes to the hour. The spring loaded jumper rapidly completes the movement of the star wheel and holds it in position. The gathering pallet has no tail but, at the end of striking, a pin in the right hand end of the rack raises a lever

Figure 10/21. Front plate of Ludlam/Hackings movement, showing rack striking with snail mounted on a star wheel to ensure accurate repeating of last hour and safety device to allow hands to be turned back safely. It is a centre pinion movement to prevent shake in the minute hand.

squared on to an arbor which carries a locking arm which in turn intercepts a pin in the pallet wheel. There is an unusual device to prevent damage if the minute hand is turned back past the hour. An idea sometimes used is to have a flexible brass lifting piece with a bent out lobe at the end so that if the hand is turned back the lifting pin forces the lifting piece aside. This is not a very good method and on the movement illustrated the lifting piece is quite rigid and is held in its normal position by a pin in a weighted lever pivoted just to the left of the lifting piece. If the hands are turned back, the lifting piece moves to the left and raises the weighted lever until the lifting piece is released by the pin. The slot in the front plate is extended downwards to allow this movement of the warning piece. The repeating lever pivoted near the top of the plate has a spring to ensure that it restores to normal and there are two pins in the plate to limit its movement. The right hand end of the lever has a projection which intercepts the pin in the warning wheel and its tip lifts the rack hook by a pin in the back of the latter.

The substantial pendulum rod (figure 10/22) is $5/16$ in. $\times$ $5/32$ in. steel with a brass scale divided into inches and eighths at its lower end. The octagonal rating nut has its facets numbered in Roman numerals. The highly domed bob is very heavy.

The dial of a very different clock is shown in figure 10/23. It is signed on the silvered centre 'Thos. Lindley Leicester' who is reported as a watchmaker c.1775. The rococo corner spandrels differ from those on the last clock but neither they nor the arch spandrels are shown in C. & W. The clock plays seven tunes which are listed, as follows, on the dial in the arch:

Sunday	Psalm104
Monday	Minuet
Tuesday	Minuet
Wednesday	Song Tune
Thursday	Mint & Rign (minuet and rigadoon)
Friday	Minuet
Saturday	Song Tune

The 'Not Chime' lever to the right of the seconds dial refers to the silencing of the musical part, 'chime' being the common seventeenth and eighteenth century term for that function.

The four train movement (figure 10/24) provides quarter chiming on eight bells (left), hour striking (centre left), going (centre right), tune playing every three hours (except 3 a.m. and 3 p.m.) on fourteen bells (right). The large plates

Figure 10/22. Heavy pendulum of clock in figure 10/19 with inch scale engraved on brass flat and octagonal rating nut with numbered facets.

Figure 10/23. Dial of quarter chiming and musical clock signed by Lindley, Leicester, on plain silvered centre. Selector for seven tunes in arch and 'Not Chime' lever to right of seconds dial for silencing music.

Figure 10/24. Four train movement with chiming on eight bells (left), hour striking (centre left), going (centre right), tune playing three hourly on fourteen bells (right). Eight pillar frame with two central pillars latched. Mechanism at top left is for changing tune and operates from striking train.

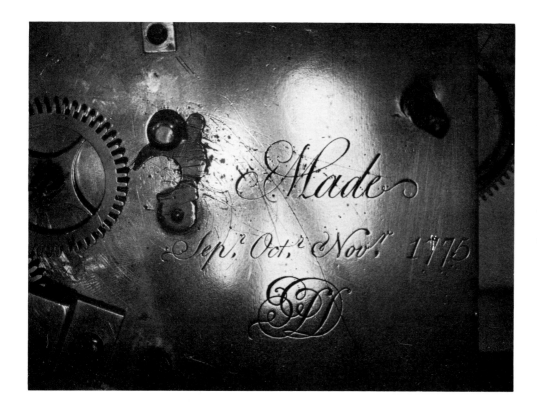

Figure 10/26. Degree scale, with inscription showing that clock was designed by Ludlam.

have eight pillars, of which the two central ones are latched, probably for convenience in assembly. An inscription on the front, between the two right hand winding squares (figure 10/25) makes interesting reading. 'Made Sepr, Octr, Novr, 1775 S D', not only dates the clock and gives some indication of the time spent in its manufacture, but the initials 'S D' indicate that the movement was made by Samuel Deacon of Barton in the Beans, Leicestershire. Deacon, a most ingenious and prolific maker, normally initialled and dated his productions in this manner. He was in business from 1771 until his death in 1816.[3] Figure 10/26 shows the wooden degree plate which is adjustable and is numbered every degree from 0 to 5 to indicate the pendulum arc. Ludlam's part in the design of the clock is proved by the inscription 'Made by the direction of W. LUDLAM for Samuel Darker of Tugby 1776.' This

3. See J. Daniell, *Leicestershire Clockmakers,* 1975.

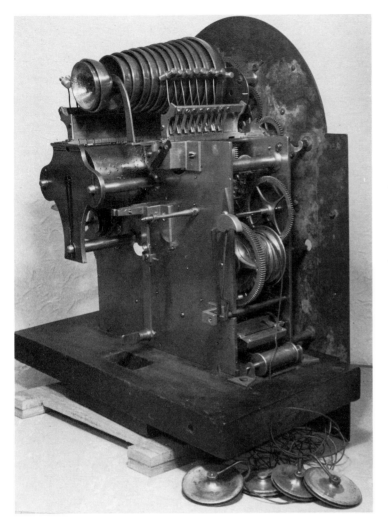

Figure 10/27. Rear view of movement with hour bell removed. Chiming train with count wheel pins in second wheel. Train of wheels behind dial connect tune change mechanism to indicator hand in arch. Fly at bottom right is part of striking train. Note roller mounted on seat board to ensure clearance between weights and beat setting adjustment on crutch.

Figure 10/28. Movement with front plate removed. Pin in second wheel of chiming train warns and releases hour striking train. Pins in striking great wheel operate linked levers to warn and release musical train via combined locking and warning piece which engages pin in third wheel. Endless screw and large three bladed fly provide slow running three wheel musical train. Note roller at bottom right to ensure clearance between weights.

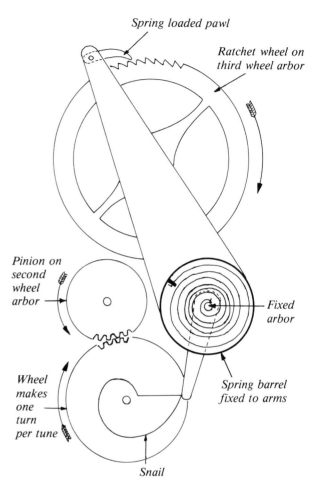

Figure 10/30. Principle of accelerating mechanism. During tune playing snail gradually winds spring and arm carrying pawl moves to left. At start of next run snail releases arm and pawl engages ratchet wheel and so accelerates train.

Figure 10/29. View of musical mechanism. To right of fly is a remontoire-like device to provide rapid acceleration of musical train, see 10/30. Note that each spandrel is fixed to dial with two screws.

bears a great similarity to the wording used on the clock shown in figure 10/20.

Both striking and quarter chiming have count wheel control. This takes the form of pins inserted in the great wheel of the striking train and the second wheel of the chiming train (figure 10/27). This type of count wheel, which was used by Deacon and a number of other makers was apparently introduced in the second half of the eighteenth century. It reverses the action, the count wheel detent *lifts* to lock the train instead of dropping into a notch. Some makers used this idea with count wheels provided with projecting triangular 'teeth'. A pin in the second wheel of the chiming train, on the opposite side from the count wheel pins, warns and releases the hour striking (figure 10/28). In the same way, pins in the striking great wheel warn and release the musical train via the linked levers across the middle of the movement. There is a combined locking and warning piece which operates on a pin in the third wheel of the musical train. The tune change mechanism also operates from the great wheel of the striking train. At the top left hand corner of the front plate (figure 10/24) is a fourteen tooth ratchet wheel which is stepped on every twelve hours by the lever and pawl below and to the right. Mounted on the ratchet is a seven step edge cam so that each alternate step of the ratchet causes the horizontal lever to pump over the large pin barrel against the pressure of a flat spring on the back sub-plate. A train of three wheels (figure 10/27) connects the change mechanism to the hand in the arch.

An endless screw in association with a large three-bladed fly provides a slow running three wheel musical train. The movement incorporates a number of ingenious devices including a spring remontoire-like device to provide a high torque to ensure rapid acceleration of the musical train. The mechanism is mounted on the back plate (figures 10/29 and 30) and is driven by a pinion on the end of the second wheel arbor. This drives clockwise a wheel which rotates once per tune and carries a snail. Just above the snail is a spring barrel with a fixed arbor and an arm attached to the barrel which bears against the snail. Clockwise rotation of the snail winds the spring and at the end of the tune the arm is resting on the highest part of the snail, so the spring is fully wound. The spring barrel also carries a long arm with spring loaded pawl which just clears the teeth of a ratchet wheel on the third (warning) wheel arbor. As soon as the train is released, the snail clears its arm or follower and the pawl engages with the ratchet. The energy stored in the spring is applied to accelerate the train for about one sixth of a turn of the third wheel, by which time it should be running at full speed. After that the ratchet passes freely under the pawl and the snail gradually rewinds the spring ready for the next run.

Other refinements include a shaped cut-out in the back plate to allow the pallets to be withdrawn easily (figure 10/28) and a beat setting adjustment on the crutch (figure 10/27). With four barrels close together, measures must be taken to prevent the weights fouling one another and the two outer barrels have pivoted rollers associated with them to ensure adequate clearance between the weights (figures 10/27 and 28).

The clock is contained in a break arch pine case japanned blue but without any decoration. The trunk door is mounted flush with its frame.

These two clocks prove that William Ludlam was an accomplished horologist. It is interesting to note that in spite of their various refinements they both have recoil escapements. Ludlam's preference for the latter is proved by the following quotation:

> Professor Ludlam, of Cambridge, who had four clocks in his house, three of them with dead-beat escapements and the other with recoil, said, "That none of them kept time, fair or foul, like the last; this kind of escapement gauges the pendulum, the dead-beat leaves it at liberty.[4]

4. P.N. Hasluck, *The Clock Jobber's Handybook,* 10th impression, 1921, p. 33.

Figure 10/31. Complicated clock by Gandy, Cockermouth, 1757. 14ins. dial and very broad chapter ring with wavy minute band surrounded by annual calendar and signs of zodiac. Arch considerably more than a semi-circle to accommodate major part of a twenty-four hour chapter ring which is traversed by sun and has moving shutters to show sunrise and sunset. Outer edge of ring is divided into degrees to indicate sun's amplitude and inner edge has signs of zodiac, Cancer to Saggitarius, on each side. Arch centre has remaining signs of zodiac surrounding a lunar and tidal dial. Case is shown in Colour Plate 15.

SOME NORTH COUNTRY CLOCKS

One surprising fact which emerges from a study of the longcase clock is the number and variety of complicated examples which are signed by makers in small towns remote from London. One explanation that has been advanced on a number of occasions is that these clocks were bought in from makers in London or other large centres of production. Whilst this is undoubtedly true in some cases, a lot of them exhibit such individuality in both design and construction as to rule out this possibility.

Figure 10/31 shows the 14ins. dial of such a clock which is signed in the lower centre 'Gandy Cockermouth' and was made by one of the family engaged in clockmaking through most of the eighteenth century. As will be seen below, an inscription on the dial includes the date 1757, although it appears somewhat later in some of its decoration, such as the engraved and silvered dial centre. Just above the centre is a monogram, possibly that of the original owner. The square part of the dial plate has an engraved border and the very large cherub spandrels are C. & W. No. 13. The very broad chapter ring has quarter hour divisions on the inside and a wavy minute band which is often called Dutch but is found on some provincial English dials also. On the outer edge of the chapter ring is an annual calendar necessary for setting the solar indications in the arch. Just inside the calendar are the signs of the zodiac, each preceded by the word 'Enter'.

The dial arch is considerably more than a semi-circle and has the major portion of a twenty-four hour chapter ring, from 4 a.m. to 8 p.m. This is traversed daily by a gilt sun and there are rising and falling shutters to indicate sunrise and sunset. The outer edge of the chapter ring is marked in degrees to give the sun's amplitude, that is its angular distance north or south of the east point of the horizon at sunrise or the west point at sunset. The inner edge of the ring between 4 and 8 a.m. is marked with the signs of the zodiac, Cancer (June) to Sagittarius (November), and these are repeated between 4 and 8 p.m. Between these groups is inscribed 'The Cause of the Vielssitude (?) of the Seasons'. The remaining signs of the zodiac, Capricorn (December) to Gemini (May), are marked on the corresponding parts of the arch centre, with the following inscription between them, 'The Winter Signs of the Zodiac 1757'. With this layout, Cancer and Gemini coincide, and so on round to Sagittarius and Capricorn, so the appropriate sign must be selected from the annual calendar. This grouping produces some inaccuracy which is greater than with the Julian calendar abandoned in 1752, which is perhaps an argument in favour of dating the clock to 1757 rather than later.

There is a conventional moon dial with Roman numerals to indicate high tide, the latter giving a time of 12 o'clock at new and full moon which would be appropriate for the Cumbrian coast, for example Whitehaven. The Roman numerals are strangely mixed, they run IIII, V, IV (6), VII, VIII, XI (9), X, IX (11), IIX (12). The confusion seems to have arisen because the numbers go from right to left.

The substantial eight-day movement is shown in figure 10/32; note that the barrels are plain, a feature of some Scottish clocks also. The pendulum has a faceted steel rod with heavy bob and there are brass cased weights.

The case (Colour Plate 15) is of Virginia or red walnut with the trunk door and plinth panel veneered and crossbanded. It has ogee feet, canted corners to the plinth and reeded quarter columns to the trunk but plain turned detached columns to the hood. The only brass mounts are the escutcheon on the trunk door and the knob to the hood door. A dignified, well proportioned case, height 7ft. 2¼ins.

A somewhat later clock which seems to have been inspired by the Gandy is shown in figure 10/33. The silvered centre of the dial is signed 'Benson Whitehaven' below the hands and has a coat of arms above. The chapter ring has the later feature of dots instead of a minute

Figure 10/32. Substantial Gandy movement, note ungrooved barrels.

ring and lacks an annual calendar. A simple day of the month ring is engraved on the dial centre. There are bold rococo spandrels of a pattern not in C. & W. but one which is often found on Lancashire and other north western dials. The arch ornaments are pieces cut from corner spandrels. The serpentine minute hand, the chapter ring and the type of calendar suggest a date of c.1780.

In the arch is a smaller and somewhat simpler version of the solar indications on the Gandy clock. There is a gilt effigy of the sun which makes one circuit per day. The outer dial ring lacks the signs of the zodiac but, with the aid of moving shutters, shows sunrise, sunset and the sun's amplitude. The inner ring has Roman numerals on its outer edge to show on

the left daybreak, and on the right the end of twilight. On the inside of the inner ring the left hand side shows the sun's declination and the right hand side the sun's position in the zodiac. These indications are identical with those on the Finney clock in figure 10/41 where they can be seen more easily. The centre of the arch is utilised for a normal lunar disc without markings for the tides. It is not clear how the owner could be expected to be able to set the solar mechanism in the absence of an annual calendar. Benson was a good maker and Lloyd[5] illustrates a fine musical and calendar clock by him.

The case is a restrained example of what is sometimes called the Lancashire Chippendale style. It is veneered with finely figured mahogany with crossbandings and twisted cord inlays. The plinth has a raised panel and chamfered corners with blind frets. The trunk has reeded quarter columns with matching detached reeded columns to the hood. The swan neck pediment has a superstructure behind it which is typical of Lancashire cases. Another Lancashire feature is the panelling of painted glass in the frieze just below the pediment. The fine work on the hood includes a dentil moulding and carved paterae to the pediment.

Figure 10/34 shows the 12ins. dial of another interesting clock signed on the chapter ring 'John Calldwell.' Britten[6] records a Calldwell of Appleton, c.1770, who was probably the maker. The clock is c.1760. There are several villages called Appleton, but this clock was probably made at the one in North Cheshire.[7] The dial plate has a matted centre with ringed winding holes and square apertures for month (left) and day of month (right). There is a very strange engraved lunar dial visible in an opening just above centre. The arch is occupied by a twenty-four hour chapter ring with a rotating disc bearing an effigy of the sun to point to the hours of daylight. A rising and falling plate with a restored painting of a landscape indicates the times of sunrise and sunset. The spandrels are C. & W. No. 20. Like the Benson described above it lacks an annual calendar for setting the solar mechanism.

Figure 10/35 shows the train of wheels to operate the sunrise/sunset plate. The upper wheel has a stud which engages in a slot in the plate in the same way as in the clock by Houlden of Kendal (figures 10/52-54). An additional minute wheel carries a pin which steps a twelve-pointed star wheel which therefore rotates in twelve hours. The star wheel is mounted on a pinion which meshes with the first wheel of the solar train. The three train movement has quarter chiming on six bells with count wheel control and rack striking with inside locking. Figure 10/36 shows the quarter count wheel and the

5. *Old Clocks*, plates 32, 41.

6. 3rd edition, 1911, p. 434.

7. G.H. Stockdale has found evidence of clocks by Calldwell in this village.

Figure 10/33. Clock by Benson, Whitehaven, c.1780, probably inspired by Gandy clock. Dial lacks annual calendar but has simple one inside chapter ring. Twenty-four hour dial in arch with gilt sun and moving shutters for sunrise and sunset. Inner ring in arch shows dawn and nightfall, sun's declination and position in zodiac. Finely detailed case in 'Lancashire Chippendale' style with well chosen mahogany veneers.

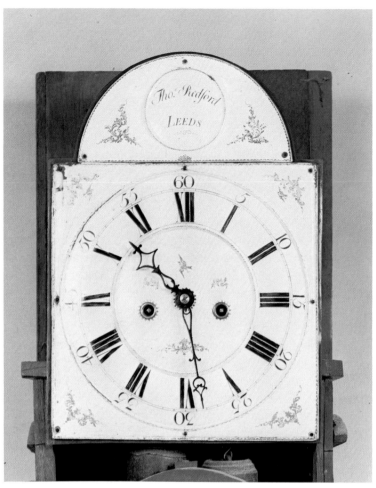

Colour Plate 17. Clock by Radford, Leeds, c.1775. 12ins. dial consisting of two pieces of fired enamel on copper screwed to a brass dial plate. Note very delicate gilt decoration. Wrong hands. See Colour Plate 18 and figure 10/111.

Colour Plate 18. Black japanned case of clock by Radford. Pleasant gilt decoration but without any raised work. Hood has attached columns, but has lost a pagoda top. Good brass finials. Present height 7ft. 2¾ins. excluding finials and 13¾ins. waist for a 12ins. dial. See Colour Plate 17 and figure 10/111.

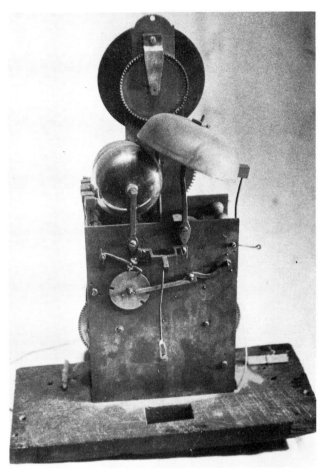

Figure 10/34. 12ins. dial of clock by Calldwell, Appleton, c.1760. Apertures for month, day of month and moon in matted centre. Twenty-four hour dial in arch with gilt sun and rising and falling plate to indicate sunrise and sunset.

Figure 10/36. Rear of movement showing vertical arbor and contrate wheel for disc bearing gilt sun. Note quarter count wheel with pin to warn and let off hour striking. Figures 10/34-36 taken before restoration.

Figure 10/35. Front of movement showing motion work to operate sunrise/sunset plate. Upper wheel carries a stud which engages in a slot in plate mounted on dial. Three train movement with quarter chiming on six bells.

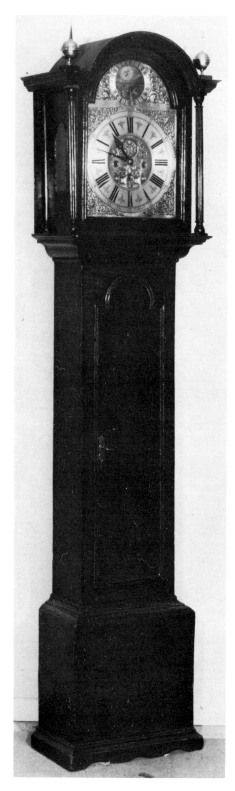

Figure 10/37. Restored Calldwell clock in simple break arch oak case. Height 6ft. 10ins. for a 12ins. dial.

arrangement for letting off the hour striking by a pin in the count wheel and a pivoted lever to warn and release the striking. Note the vertical arbor driving the contrate wheel carrying the solar disc. All these photographs were taken before the clock had been restored. Figure 10/37 shows the restored dial and movement in its simple break arch oak case. The height is 6ft. 10ins.

Figure 10/38 shows the 12ins. dial of an attractive clock which is signed on the chapter ring 'Geo. Booth Manchestr.' and which is c.1760-65. There is attractive acanthus type engraving round the calendar aperture and a laurel leaf border surrounding the moon in the arch. The corner spandrels are C. & W. No. 20, but those in the arch (not in C. & W.) were also used by Hindley, see figure 9/116. The chapter ring has bold fleur-de-lis half hour markings and slender diamonds for the half quarters. In the arch is a rotating globular moon, half silvered and half painted dark blue, with figures to indicate the moon's age engraved round a central band and a fixed pointer.

The break arch hood has detached columns with gilt wooden Corinthian capitals and bases. As with the majority of provincial cases, the hood door is hung on swan neck hinges so as to swing clear of the right hand column. Figure 10/39 shows examples of these hinges, the top two being original and the lower two replacements. London cases and some of the better provincial ones had ornamental butt hinges as shown in figure 9/2 for the hood doors. The case (figure 10/40) is veneered with pollard oak with all the main mouldings made in cross grained wood. The trunk door has the probably unique feature of two concave panels and the plinth has matching concave corners which are carried down through the skirting. A very unusual design executed in a rare wood. The height is 7ft. 9ins.

Figure 10/41 shows the dial of an elaborate astronomical and musical clock which is unsigned but is reliably attributed to Joseph Finney of Liverpool[8] and can be dated c.1765-70. It is known as 'Mr. John Sandforth's Clock', probably after the first owner.

The chapter ring has the spaces between the hour numerals engraved with the names of various places such as 'Verd Isles', 'Agra', so chosen that with the clock set to Liverpool time the hour hand will point to a name when it is 12 o'clock at that place. Round the outer edge of the chapter ring is an annual calendar necessary for setting the solar mechanism, marked with religious festivals and secular anniversaries in abbreviated form. There are such entries as 'K.C.II.R' for 29th May which indicates the restoration of Charles II and for 5th November 'P. Plot', an anniversary which is still celebrated. The calendar hand is in the form of an arm holding a split sword and its two points indicate dates in accordance with both the old and the new style calendars.

In the right upper centre of the dial is a small version of the usual moon dial of the period and just below the centre is an associated tidal dial with rising and falling sea which is flanked by the words 'Flowing' and 'Ebbing.'

8. See Oliver Fairclough, 'Joseph Finney of Liverpool', *Antiquarian Horology,* X (Winter 1976, Summer 1977), pp. 32, 294.

Figure 10/38

Figure 10/38. 12ins. dial of attractive clock by Booth, Manchester, c.1760-65. Note bold half hour markings and unusual arch spandrels. Rotating globular moon, half silvered and half dark blue, with central band of numbers for moon's age. Note gilt wooden Corinthian capitals. Door hung on swan neck hinges.

Figure 10/39. Examples of swan neck hinges. Upper two original, lower two replacements.

Figure 10/40. Pollard oak case of Booth clock. Probably unique feature of two concave panels in trunk door with matching concave corners to plinth and skirting. Height 7ft. 9ins. with a 12ins. dial.

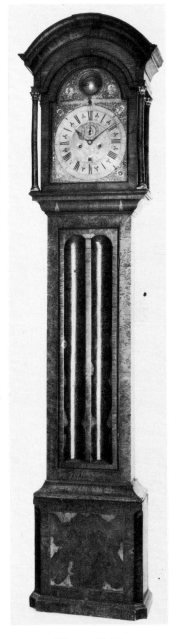

Figure 10/39

Figure 10/40

The arch is used for solar indications. A disc carrying an effigy of the sun rotates clockwise once in twenty-four hours and a pair of rising and falling shutters indicates the length of the day. On the left hand shutter the outer pointer gives sunrise and the sun's amplitude, and the inner pointer shows daybreak and the sun's declination north or south of the equator. On the right hand shutter the outer pointer indicates sunset and the sun's amplitude, and the inner pointer shows the end of twilight and the sun's position in the zodiac. At the bottom of the daybreak and twilight scales are the words 'No night' to indicate the period in the summer when the sun does not sink to 18° below the horizon; compare with the Daniel Alan clock described on page 234 and shown in figure 9/54. The centre of the arch displays an equation table marked for every seventh day.

The dial centre has a decoration resembling quilting which is often found on Lancashire dials but reduces legibility. The large cherub spandrels (C. & W. No. 13) were used extensively on large north country dials. Strike/silent and chime/silent levers are provided and a tune indicator in the left upper centre of the dial lists the tunes played:

> Psalm 104 (for Sunday)
> Lovely Peggy
> Love & Youth
> Nut Brown M(aid)
> A March
> Miller of M(ansfield)
> Merry Toned H

There is a centre seconds hand and the movement has a dead beat escapement with a

Figure 10/41. Dial of elaborate astronomical and musical clock attributed to Finney, Liverpool, c.1765-70. Broad chapter ring has annual calendar with various festivals and anniversaries, with two-pointed hand to indicate old and new style calendars. Lunar dial in upper right dial centre with tidal dial below centre. Tune indicator at upper left of dial centre with chime/silent and strike/silent levers each side of arch. Arch has twenty-four hour dial with sun and moving shutters to indicate sunrise and sunset on outer ring and day break and night fall on inner ring.

Figure 10/42. Movement from striking side, note count wheel with projections, attached to great wheel. Early example of large pin barrel mounted parallel to dial. Note stepped snail for tune changing by bearing on end of pin barrel arbor.

Figure 10/43. Trunk door open showing simple rhomboid pendulum. Back of door removed to show wheel barometer, note calibration scale at base of tube. Illustration also shows hygrometer consisting of long piece of cord round pulleys and used to operate extra hand on dial.

Figure 10/44. Case of Finney clock. Barometer set in trunk door has barometer scale on outside of dial and inner scale for humidity. Ionic columns and pilasters to trunk and Corinthian columns and pilasters to hood. Typical Lancashire brickwork quoins to plinth. Magnificent mahogany case work but rather over-decorated with gilt ornament. Originally surmounted by ornamental armillary sphere, now missing. Height 8ft. 7ins.

simple rhomboid pendulum (figure 10/43) to provide partial compensation. This type of compensated pendulum is discussed in Chapter 11, page 394. The top of the pendulum is visible in figure 10/42. The striking is controlled by a count wheel, with projections instead of slots, which is mounted on the great wheel. The strike/silent mechanism cannot hold up the train as with rack striking, so it is arranged to hold the hammer clear of the bell.

The musical train plays seven tunes on ten bells and is released every three hours and can also be repeated at will. The tunes are changed automatically each night or can be changed by turning the tune indicator hand. The seven-stepped snail which bears on the end of the pin barrel arbor for changing the tune can be seen in figure 10/42. Note that the length of the pin barrel is too great for it to be mounted parallel to the other arbors.

The trunk door accommodates a wheel barometer (figure 10/43) and in addition a hygrometer. The barometer has the usual glass float connected by a cord to a pulley behind the dial and has a counterweight housed in the short glass tube below the dial. Note the paper scale for use when calibrating the barometer. The hygrometer consists of a long piece of cord run round pulleys at the top and bottom of the door and connected to a pulley to operate a hand on the dial. It has a counterweight similar to that for the barometer. The great length of cord is to increase the movement due to changes in humidity. The back of the door has been removed to show the mechanism for the barometer and hygrometer.

The barometer dial set in the trunk door (figure 10/44) is divided into sixty parts for a complete circle with 29ins. marked at 20 and 30ins. marked at 40, so it covers the usual range of 28 to 31ins. The concentric hygrometer dial is inside the barometer markings and has thirty divisions each side of 'Temperate'.

The elaborate case is veneered with finely figured mahogany and is of magnificent quality. It stands 8ft. 7ins. high and was originally surmounted by an ornamental armillary sphere, now missing. Both hood and trunk have fluted pilasters behind the front fluted columns and a mixture of Ionic and Corinthian capitals. The plinth has brickwork quoins, a typical Lancashire feature. The hood is rather over decorated with gilt swag, heads, busts and birds.

Figure 10/45 shows the 13ins. dial of a very interesting month clock signed 'Pannel fecit.' This is apparently the Hugh Pannell of Northallerton who died in 1788 and the probable date is c.1770. Note the very late use of the Latin *fecit*. The dial centre has simple foliate engraving and the spandrels are C. & W. No. 20. The chapter ring has conventional quarter hour divisions but the minutes are marked by two intersecting bands of divisions which may have been inspired by the 'Dutch' type minute band but form a possibly unique variant. The lunar dial in the arch has a disc with two moon faces and a hand which also rotates to indicate the age of the moon on the silvered ring. For some unknown reason the latter is divided into lunations of 29 and 30 days instead of into two of 29½. The seconds hand is a replacement and is rather heavy looking.

Figure 10/46 shows the front of the movement. The unusual train of wheels to operate the lunar dial is a restoration. Note that the simple calendar with its fixed hand is attached to the movement instead of being part of the dial as is usual. This ensures accurate positioning and facilitates adjustment of its operating stud in the hour wheel. There is a four wheel striking train, with closely spaced pins in the pin wheel and a double ended gathering pallet (figure 10/47). Hour repeating was provided by a stout straight spring fixed near the bottom left of the front plate and playing between the two pins in the lifting piece. This arrangement allowed for cords attached to the top of the spring to be led out at both sides of the hood. The rack has the early more reliable rigid tail with a spring supported stud.

This centre seconds movement has the rare, if not unique, feature of having no shake on the minute hand. As the escape wheel has to be planted in the centre, normal centre second movements have an indirect drive to the cannon pinion. Pannell has provided a short hollow centre pinion with the cannon pinion mounted on it as on a non-centre second movement,

Figure 10/45

Figure 10/46

Figure 10/45. 13ins. dial of very interesting month clock by Pannell, Northallerton, c.1770, note late use of 'fecit'. Calendar below centre and lunar dial in arch. Note unusual markings of 30 and 29 days per lunation, rotating hand points to scale. Replaced seconds hand is rather heavy looking.

Figure 10/46. Front of movement. Unusual train of wheels to operate moon. Unusual also to have calendar work mounted on movement instead of on dial.

Figure 10/47. Movement with most of motion work removed. Rare if not unique feature of no shake on minute hand. Hollow centre pinion has normal cannon pinion mounted on it. Note end of seconds pivot visible in end of hollow centre pinion. Four wheel striking train with close spacing on pin wheel and double ended gathering pallet. Note rigid rack tail with spring stud. Hour repeating was provided by spring mounted at bottom left and playing between pins on lifting piece extension.

Figure 10/47

see figure 10/47. The long pivot of the escape wheel pinion can be seen inside the hollow centre pinion.

The layout of the going train, on the left of the movement, is shown in figure 10/48. The centre or third wheel on its hollow pinion is pivoted between the front plate and the stout cock which is secured by two screws. The centre pinion is driven by the second wheel, partly visible below and to the right of the centre wheel which drives the fourth wheel pinion just below the cock foot. The escape wheel pinion is pivoted in the back plate and in the rear end of the hollow centre pinion. This arrangement of long concentric arbors is satisfactory only as long as they are true and the pivots are a good fit in their holes. When it failed some incompetent repairer bodged it and destroyed the centre seconds facility but the present owner has now restored it to a good standard. There is a normal recoil escapement.

Figure 10/49 is a general view of the movement and the back of the dial with its typical north country cut-outs. The elegant shaping of the back cock and the centre wheel cock, and the decoration of the pillars give a strong reminder of the work of Thomas Ogden of

Figure 10/48. Left side of movement showing going train. Hollow centre pinion is pivoted between front plate and large cock. Centre wheel is visible just below cock. Escape wheel pinion is pivoted between back plate and cock and its very long pivot extends inside centre pinion.

Figure 10/49. General view, note finely turned pillars and ornamental cocks, reminder of Ogden of Halifax. Typical north country cut-away dial. Hooks over lower pillars are typical provincial method of fixing. Note apparently original key.

Figure 10/50. Movement from striking side, also shows layout of third and escape wheels. Note punched pivot holes now properly bushed.

Halifax. The bent steel hooks with nuts under the seat board are a typical provincial method of fixing. Note the apparently original key.

The striking train is shown in figure 10/50; note the closely spaced pins in the pin wheel. Many of the pivot holes have at some time been bodged by punching to close them but they have now been bushed.

The case (figure 10/51) is awaiting restoration. It is of oak with mahogany crossbanding and other inlay to the trunk door, and blind frets to the canted corners of the plinth and the top of the trunk. The hood has a dentil moulding below the pagoda top and attached columns with gilt wooden capitals and bases. It probably had gilt wooden finials originally. The plinth lacks a shaped skirting or possibly a moulding and ogee feet. The height will be approximately 7ft. 9ins. when restored.

Figure 10/52 shows the 12ins. dial of an interesting clock signed 'Houlden Kendal.' Loomes[9] quotes of John Houlden of Kendal "No dates known, probably pre-1780", and this example is probably c.1770. The dial plate has an engraved border and a nicely engraved and silvered centre. The spandrels are a variation of C. & W. No. 26. The lunar dial is conventional but should have a long steel pointer fixed by the large-headed screw at the base of the arch. The decoration on the projecting semi-circles is unusual; hour glass, sickle and scythe on the left, and setting sun on the right.

The rare feature of this clock is the miniature solar dial just above the centre. A gilt sun traverses the slot, making one rotation in twenty-four hours and shutters, not visible in the photograph, show sunrise and sunset. Figure 10/53 shows the mechanism on the back of the dial. The wheel just above the centre meshes with the twenty-four hour calendar wheel in the motion work and carries the effigy of the sun. The flat piece of brass partly behind the wheel carries the shutters at its upper end and a slot across the bottom fits a stud in a wheel on the movement which rotates once per year (figure 10/54), thus raising and lowering the shutters. There is no provision for any form of annual calendar to facilitate setting the shutters correctly; compare with the Benson (figure 10/33). At the design stage it would have been quite easy to include a small annual calendar in the space occupied by the simple calendar opening. The solar mechanism was restored at West Dean College and the tutor has stressed that their solution may not be the correct one, but it appears convincing to the author. Figure 10/53 also shows the mechanism for operating the moon. A snail mounted on the hour wheel pipe (figure 10/54) gradually raises the diagonal lever against the pressure of a restoring spring and a spring pawl slips over a tooth of the moon wheel. A spring pawl mounted on the dial plate prevents the wheel slipping back. When the lever is released by the snail it restores and advances the wheel one tooth.

9. B. Loomes, *Westmorland Clocks and Clockmakers*, 1974, p. 106.

Figure 10/51. Pannell case awaiting restoration. Oak with mahogany and other banding. Blind frets to canted corners of plinth and top of trunk. Gilt wooden capitals and bases and probably finials originally. Lacks skirting, or moulding and ogee feet. When restored height will be approximately 7ft. 9ins. with a 13ins. dial.

Figure 10/52. 12ins. dial of interesting clock by Houlden, Kendal, c.1770. Nicely engraved dial plate with unusual subjects on semi-circles of moon aperture. Lunar dial lacks vertical pointer. Twenty-four hour dial just above centre has rotating gilt sun and shutters to indicate sunrise and sunset.

Figure 10/53. Back of dial showing wheel which carries sun and meshes with twenty-four hour calendar wheel. Flat piece of brass partly behind wheel carries shutters and is raised and lowered by stud on a wheel rotating once per year. Long diagonal lever is raised by snail on hour wheel pipe and when spring restores it, lunar disc is stepped on.

The front of the movement is shown in figure 10/54. The wheel at the lower centre rotates once a year and its stud engages in the slot in the plate carrying the sunrise and sunset shutters. It is provided with a clutch spring and the slots in the disc mounted on the wheel are to facilitate setting the shutters with a small screwdriver. The drive to this wheel consists of an endless screw or worm mounted on the twenty-four hour calendar wheel and driving a five leaved pinion. This pinion carries another endless screw which engages with the wheel of seventy-three teeth. The projecting arm on the twenty-four hour wheel is for operating the simple calendar. A number of spare holes in the plates indicate that some changes have taken place over the years. In particular, the pair of holes in the left hand projections, above the rack hook just raise the possibility of a conversion from count wheel striking, and other holes in the front plate may have been to provide a repeating lever and spring. The present striking mechanism is rather unusual. The rack hook is freely mounted on a stud and when it drops deeper at the end of striking a projection near its right hand end intersects a pin, in the warning wheel, not in the wheel on the gathering pallet arbor. This must make the adjustment of the striking very critical. Figure 10/55 shows the skeleton type of plates, very rare on English clocks, but did plates like these inspire the later American makers? A very interesting clock but not of such high quality as others which have been described. Unfortunately the author has not been able to see its case.

Figure 10/54. Front of movement showing snail to operate moon mechanism. On left is twenty-four hour wheel to operate simple calendar and with large endless screw driving a vertical pinion which in turn drives wheel which rotates once per year and carries stud to operate shutters. Unusual striking where deep drop of rack hook causes a projection on it to intersect a pin on warning wheel. Spare holes in plates indicate that changes have been made at some time.

Figure 10/55. Rear of movement showing very rare skeleton plates.

Figure 10/56. Unconventional clock by Walker, Newcastle, c.1770. Calendar above centre and conventional moon below, both operated direct from hour wheel.

Figure 10/57. Eight-day Walker movement with almost triangular plates and three wheel going train. Enormous escape wheel rotating anti-clockwise. Two wheel striking train. Count wheel pins in rim of great wheel and locking pins in rim of second wheel. Hammer lifting pins in enlarged centre of second wheel. Large adjustable fly on arbor of endless screw.

A very unconventional clock of c.1770 is shown in figure 10/56. It is signed on a plaque in the arch 'Jnº Walker Newcastle' and the matted dial centre has very slight ringing to the winding holes. The design of the movement precludes the use of a seconds hand and its space is occupied by the calendar and the usual type of moon disc occupies the lower centre. Both calendar and moon discs are therefore operated direct by a pin in the hour wheel. The corner spandrels are C. & W. No. 40 and those in the arch are C. & W. No. 39.

The eight-day movement (figure 10/57) has almost triangular plates and a three wheel going train. The enormous escape wheel, which rotates anti-clockwise, is just visible in the photograph. The striking great wheel has count wheel pins in its rim and the second wheel has hammer lifting pins in its enlarged centre and locking pins in the rim. A combined locking and warning piece is mounted on the front end of the count wheel detent arbor, outside the front plate. It has two projections, one for locking the train and another diagonally below it to intercept the locking pin when the warning piece is raised. The second wheel drives a large adjustable fly through an endless screw.

It is a very ingeniously designed clock, and Walker advertised in 1766 that his clocks cost less than those with conventional four wheel trains.[10] The clock is contained in an oak case with swan neck pediment and fretwork frieze below.

Both calendar and moon dials were more popular in the north than elsewhere, and figure

10. See B. Loomes, *Country Clocks and their London Origins,* 1976, p. 138.

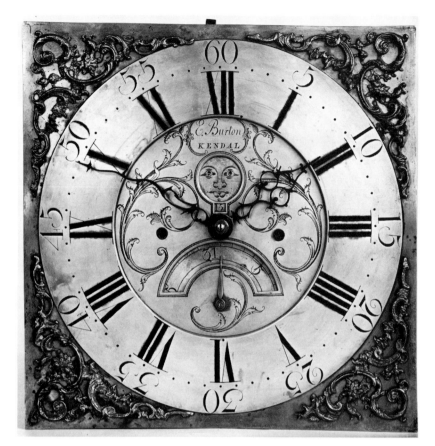

Figure 10/58. Thirty-hour clock by Burton, Kendal, c.1780, with both moon and calendar. Note dummy winding holes with blued steel backing. Lunar disc makes one rotation per lunation.

Figure 10/59. Burton dial shown with moon approaching first quarter. Part of lunar disc is cut away to show star spangled background.

10/58 shows a thirty-hour clock dial with both moon and calendar. It is signed in a cartouche 'E. Burton Kendal'; there were clockmakers of that name through most of the eighteenth century, but this example is c.1780. The dotted minute band is found on both engraved and painted dials of the period and the hands are also typical. The rococo spandrels are a version found on many north country clocks. Note the dummy winding holes with blued steel backing. The moon is shown full in this photograph and approaching the first quarter in figure 10/59.

The so-called 'Lancashire Chippendale' case has a number of distinctive features and figure 10/60 is a good exmple. The clock is signed on the silvered dial centre 'Davison Ecclesham.' Ecclesham has proved very elusive but an R. Davison, Liverpool, is recorded as c.1790, which could be the same man and that date, or a little earlier, would be appropriate for the clock. It has a centre seconds hand and concentric date hand. The spandrels are C. & W. No. 13. Typical case features are the swan neck pediment with built up section behind it and the painted decoration just below, in this case on wood instead of on glass. Other typical features are the brickwork 'quoins' to the plinth and the ogee feet. What is very exceptional is the bulbous or bombé shaping of the plinth which is typical of French or Dutch furniture but not of English. The carved applied fretwork is also very unusual. It probably shows the influence of the left hand design in figure 10/78, from Chippendale's *Director*, see Case Designers and Casemakers (p. 336).

Figure 10/61 shows a most unusual year timepiece with repeating work and an accurate calendar which, in spite of its appearance, probably dates from c.1750. Oval dials are extremely rare, Loomes[11] refers to two, and the author remembers another one on a six-month striking clock. With both the present example and the six-month clock, any makers' names which may have been there originally have disappeared during restoration. Oval dials appear to be a Lancashire feature and this is borne out by the case of the year clock as well as those of the other examples. It is a well designed and beautifully made case veneered with finely figured mahogany with tulip wood crossbanding and boxwood stringing. The case, and the painted dial with its Arabic hour numerals, indicate a date of c.1820. The movement has finely turned pillars which suggest an earlier date and the wheels are mounted on D-shaped collets as used in the late seventeenth and early eighteenth centuries. The concentric calendar hand is a late feature but the mechanism

11. B. Loomes, *The White Dial Clock*, 1974, p. 38.

Figure 10/60. Clock by Davison, Ecclesham, c.1785-90, in a good example of a 'Lancashire Chippendale' case. Exceptional shaping of plinth, probably influenced by design in Chippendale's Director, *see 10/78.*

Figure 10/61. Very unusual year timepiece with accurate calendar and repeating work, outwardly c.1820, but movement probably c.1750. Rare oval painted dial and style of case suggest a Lancashire origin. Maker's name has disappeared.

Figure 10/62. Movement seen from left. Note substantial early part of train and last two wheels between back plate and sub-plate.

Figure 10/63. Top view of movement, showing recoil escapement. Note elegant pillars of sub-frame. Mechanism on left between sub-plate and back plate is for quarter repeating. Train on right between front plate and sub-plate operates calendar and is wound by pulling cord. Note early D-shaped collets.

could equally well have operated a calendar ring showing the date through a small opening. From this evidence it is thought that a mid-eighteenth century clock was provided with a new dial and recased some seventy years after it was made.

The movement has a substantial frame with six main pillars and a sub-plate fixed to five short baluster pillars (figure 10/62). The barrel arbor, first, second and centre pinions are pivoted in the back and front plates, but the remaining pinions are pivoted between the back plate and the sub-plate (figure 10/63). This is the usual arrangement with year clocks to reduce friction and inertia by permitting the use of short light pinions. Figure 10/64 shows the huge rectangular weight and the long handled key necessary for winding such a weight. The photograph also shows the pendulum with its wooden rod and the degree scale fixed to the back of the case.

With a long duration movement it is important to ensure that the calendar does not impose any appreciable load on the movement. The simple concentric 1-31 scale on the dial does not suggest anything more than a simple calendar, but this clock has an annual one which requires correction only for leap year and which is spring driven to avoid overloading the going train. The calendar is powered by a spring in a barrel fixed to the back plate (figure 10/63), and wound by pulling a cord wound round a deeply grooved pulley. Between the front plate and the sub-plate is a train incorporating a hoop wheel and terminating in a fly to regulate its speed. To protect the spring against overwinding, stopwork is fitted. This consists of a pinion on the front end of the barrel arbor engaging with a wheel with a small uncut section (figure 10/65). The calendar train is released once a day and normally locks when the hoop wheel has made one turn. The pallet shown just below the stopwork is mounted on the hoop wheel arbor and therefore advances the thirty-one tooth calendar wheel, mounted behind the dial, by one tooth. One winding should drive the calendar for a year but if it fails the calendar stops without affecting the load on the going train.

Figure 10/66 shows the let off and control mechanism. A twenty-four hour wheel, as used to operate a common calendar, has a pin which raises the lifting piece which is mounted on the arbor of the hoop wheel detent. As the train runs, the hoop wheel raises the detent a little further and this causes a spring-loaded trigger on the lifting piece, which had been deflected, to restore to normal so that it will clear the lifting pin when the lifting piece returns to normal. This type of spring-loaded trigger was used on very early striking systems without warning and is called a 'nag's head'. The short months are catered for by the large count wheel which rotates once per year, being driven from the calendar train by a ten leaved pinion. The count wheel is engraved with the months to facilitate setting the calendar. Each month is allocated thirty-one days so the count wheel has $12 \times 31 = 372$ teeth. The thirty-day months, April, June, September and November, each have one pin inserted in the count wheel and February has three pins inserted. Each rotation of the hoop wheel results in the

Figure 10/64. Huge weight necessary for year movement, with long handled key for winding. Note pendulum with wooden rod and degree scale.

Figure 10/65. Part of calendar mechanism. Stopwork to protect spring, near top of front plate. Pin in twenty-four hour wheel releases calendar train once per day and hoop wheel and pallet shown just below stopwork normally make one turn to advance calendar one day.

328

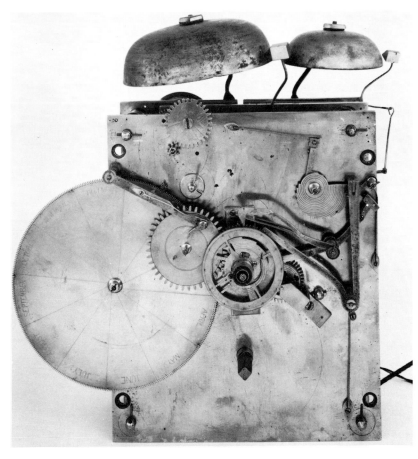

Figure 10/66. Large count wheel driven from calendar train and makes one turn per year. Pins inserted in count wheel for short months prevent calendar train locking and pallet makes extra turns to advance calendar more than one day. Mechanism on right provides for repeating quarters and hours.

Figure 10/67. Rear view showing pull cords and spring barrels for repeating (left) and calendar (right).

Figure 10/68. Right side of movement showing repeating train.

count wheel advancing one tooth. Halfway along the lifting piece is a projection (figure 10/65) which tests for a pin in the count wheel. If it rests on a pin the hoop wheel does not lock so one pin causes the hoop wheel to make two turns and the pallet advances the calendar wheel two teeth. Similarly, at the end of February the three pins cause the hoop wheel and pallet to make four turns, and thus advance the calendar four days.

The repeating mechanism (figure 10/66) is designed like that for a bracket timepiece and repeats quarters followed by hours. It is powered by a coiled spring in a fixed barrel on the back plate, on the left in figure 10/67, and is wound by pulling the cord. The repeating train runs between the sub-plate and the back plate (figure 10/68).

THE WEST COUNTRY AND THE WELSH BORDERS

Bristol was a flourishing port from the fifteenth century and later became an important clockmaking centre which influenced the surrounding counties.

Figure 10/69 shows a typical example of c.1770 in a tall slim mahogany case which does not appear to be veneered. It has reeded canted corners to the plinth and very restrained canted corners to the trunk. The trunk door has a fancy shaped top and a large asymmetrical escutcheon. The hood has attached columns and a rather tall swan necked pediment.

The dial (figure 10/70) is signed on the chapter ring Richd Hardwick Ashwick'. Ashwick is a village about fourteen miles south of Bristol. Even so, the clock has one distinctive Bristol characteristic: the moon dial shows 'High Water at Bristol Key'. This form of wording may have been used because, unlike most ports, shipping came right into the city. This dial has the later type of lunar dial where the scales are fixed to the dial arch and the moon's effigies carry pointers. Note the '29' made into a monogram, which appears on other Bristol dials. The semi-circular projections are engraved with country scenes. The simple type of calendar has an elaborately shaped opening based on a tulip motif. Note the late use of ringed winding holes. The spandrels are a strange rococo design incorporating a human head and are found on a few provincial clocks but do not appear in C. & W.

Figure 10/71 shows a clock of c.1780 by Thomas Williams, Chewstoke with a mahogany case similar to the Hardwick but with a shaped raised panel to the plinth and extensive blind fretwork on the hood. Both these features are typical of Bristol area cases. The dial also is very similar to that of the Hardwick except that the centre is lightly engraved instead of being matted and the seconds dial is engraved on the dial plate. The urn spandrels are C. & W. No. 26 and the serpentine minute hand with its corresponding hour hand is typical of the period.

A fully developed Bristol style case is shown in figure 10/72. It is in fine quality mahogany with beautiful veneers on the elaborately shaped plinth panel and trunk door. The hood door has scalloping round its inner edge. There is blind fretwork on the canted corners of the plinth and trunk and across the hood. The break arch hood has detached reeded columns but lacks the corresponding strips at the back. There is a lunar dial with 'High Water at Bristol Key', a sunken seconds dial and a calendar with a square opening. The rococo spandrels are of a pattern which is not in C. & W. The date is c.1780.

Figure 10/73 shows a very fine clock which has a number of puzzling features. The case is a typical Bristol example with beautifully chosen mahogany veneers and has reeded canted corners to the plinth and trunk with matching reeded columns to the hood. The dial is signed on the chapter ring 'Caleb Pitt Frome Somerset', a maker who is apparently not recorded although a Caleb Pitt was in London from 1790. Including 'Somerset' in the address suggests that the clock was intended for sale outside the county and round the dial arch is a silvered strip engraved 'High Water at London Bridge'. Near the top of the arch is a rotating spherical moon and below it, partly superimposed on the chapter ring, is a dial showing the moon's age with Roman numerals to indicate high tide. The other subsidiary dials are

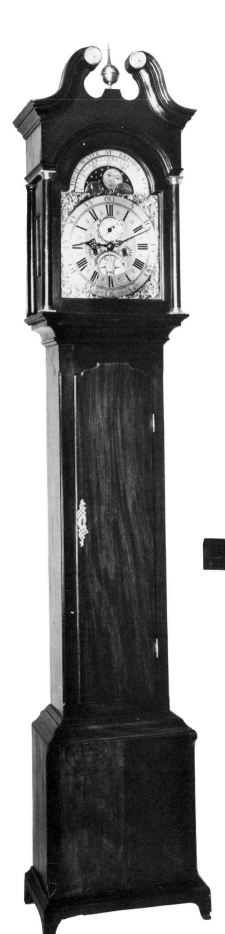

Figure 10/70. Dial of Hardwick clock with characteristic Bristol tidal dial. Lunar dial is later type where scales are on arch. Simple type of calendar with elaborately shaped opening. Note strange rococo spandrels with human heads.

Figure 10/69. Clock by Hardwick, Ashwick, c.1770, in tall solid mahogany case. Reeded canted corners to plinth and small canted corners to trunk. Hood has tall swan necked pediment and attached columns. Note large asymmetrical escutcheon on trunk door.

Figure 10/72. Fully developed Bristol style case, c.1780. Case with fine veneers has elaborately shaped plinth panel, trunk door and inner edges of hood door. Blind frets on canted corners and across hood. Bristol tidal dial.

Figure 10/71. Clock by Williams, Chewstoke, c.1780, with 'Bristol Key' tidal dial and seconds ring engraved on dial plate. Bristol area characteristics of shaped plinth panel and extensive blind fretwork on hood of mahogany case. Note asymmetrical escutcheon.

Figure 10/73. Clock by Pitt, Frome, c.1790, in typical Bristol style case. Dial arch has fine painting of Tower of London framed by a silvered strip 'High Water at London Bridge'. Near top of arch is spherical moon with tidal dial below. Other subsidiary dials are for strike/silent and tune selection. Within chapter ring is a twenty-four hour dial for showing sunrise and sunset.

strike/silent (left) and a tune indicator (right) listing the seven tunes played by the musical train. In the upper part of the dial centre is a twenty-four hour dial with a rotating disc with the sun's effigy and the months and zodiacal signs marked for indicating sunrise and sunset. Horizontal lines at 6 a.m. and 6 p.m. indicate the equinoxes. A simple calendar is engraved round the inner edge of the chapter ring. In the arch is a fine painting of the Tower of London and the lower part of the silvered dial centre has a nicely engraved rural scene. The spandrels have rococo elements but are symmetrical in design and do not appear in C. & W. The date is probably c.1790. Was this clock produced for a London customer about the time that Pitt moved there from Frome? This is assuming that the maker of this clock is the same as the man listed as working in London.

Wales and the border counties was a less prosperous region so it did not produce so many fine clocks. Figure 10/74 shows an anonymous thirty-hour clock. The slim oak case has a shaped sunken panel to the plinth to match the top of the trunk door. The latter is, unununsually, hung on the left. The hood was apparently made without columns and has a rather heavy cornice. The dial (figure 10/75) has the centre decorated with rings and punch marks as a substitute for matting or engraving. The chapter ring has rather uneven engraving and the half hour marks are based on the cross design used by seventeenth century London makers. The rococo spandrels are C. & W. No. 40 with the ends shortened to suit the small dial and they are well finished. From these points it is concluded that the clockmaker bought standard spandrel castings but made the rest of the dial himself. A probable date is c.1770 or it could be later.

A very different example is shown in figure 10/76. The dial has an added arch which was apparently done by the maker, as a silvered strip engraved 'Edward Phillips Monmouth' is fixed over the joint. It appears that he originally intended a square dial as an engraved border goes right round the square portion. The dial plate has a matted centre with heavily ringed winding and seconds apertures. The lower corners have rococo spandrels (C. & W. No. 32) and the upper ones have floral engraving round the subsidiary dials. Dolphins (C. & W. No. 38) are used in the arch. The broad chapter ring has quarter hour divisions on the inside, with elaborate half hour markings and simple half quarter marks on the outside.

There is a full calendar but without correction for the short months. The days of the month are shown in the arch, the months on the top right subsidiary dial and the days of the week just below the centre. The top left subsidiary dial provides a strike/silent facility. The hands are nicely pierced. Certain details of the engraving, for example reversed 'N's, suggest that, in this instance the clockmaker did his own engraving. In fact a most interesting and ambitious clock by an apparently unrecorded maker.

The nicely proportioned case is of pale oak and the hood door has

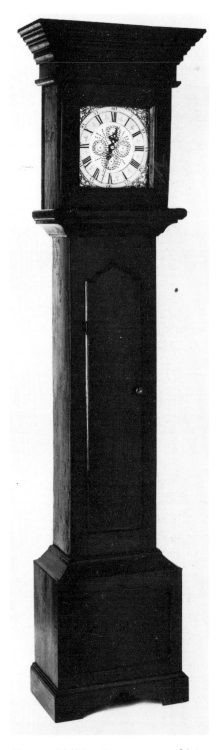

Figure 10/74. Anonymous thirty-hour clock, c.1770 or later, from Welsh borders. Slim oak case, sunken panel to plinth matching trunk door. Hood without columns but with heavy cornice.

attached columns with gilt wood capitals and bases. Below the swan neck pediment is a deep sound fret with a peculiar repetitive pattern. The height is 7ft. 7ins. and the probable date c.1770.

Figure 10/77 shows an elaborate astronomical clock which is signed 'Thos Morgan Leominster' in the arch of the silvered dial. Seconds and minutes are indicated in the arch and hours on the twenty-four hour chapter ring by the black hand which also carries a gilt sun. Inside the chapter ring is a rotating ring marked 1-29½ for the age of the moon and the hand which points to this scale has a small rotating spherical moon to show the phases. Within the lunar date ring is a rotating disc with, on the outside, an annual calendar, then the zodiac with the signs named and each divided into thirty degrees. Within these calibrations are labelled circles representing the Tropics of Capricorn and Cancer, the Equinoctial and the Ecliptic, that is the sun's apparent annual path through the heavens. This is drawn for the northern hemisphere, that is with the north pole at the centre, and the design is based on one by James Ferguson.[12]

It is contained in a fine quality mahogany break arch case with very good sound frets. The provincial origin of the case shows only in a slight heaviness in the design of the hood and in the shaped vertical strips at the back of the hood. The probable date of the clock is c.1790.

12. For a similar example by Philip Lloyd, Lawhaden, see *Antiquarian Horology,* XII (June 1981), p. 597.

Figure 10/75. Dial of anonymous clock decorated with rings and punch marks as substitute for matting or engraving. Note seventeenth century type half hour marks.

Figure 10/76. Very interesting clock by Phillips, Monmouth, c.1770. Dial plate has engraved border and contemporary added arch. Day of month in arch, day of week below centre and month on subsidiary dial top right. Strike/silent at top left. Nicely proportioned oak case with attached columns to hood and deep sound fret. Height 7ft. 7ins.

Figure 10/77. Elaborate astronomical clock by Morgan, Leominster, c.1790. Seconds and minutes in arch, hours read on twenty-four hour chapter ring by spade hand which also carries sun. Hand with rotating spherical moon indicates its age on rotating ring. Inside this is rotating disc with annual calendar, zodiac, ecliptic. Fine mahogany case with good sound frets.

Figure 10/78. Two case designs from 3rd edition of Chippendale's Director, *1762, which also apppeared in the first edition, 1754.*

CASE DESIGNERS AND CASEMAKERS

Little has so far been discovered in the way of published designs for clockcases and those recorded are very exotic and were produced by the authors of well-known books for general furniture. The fantastic nature of both Chippendale's and Sheraton's designs, if interpreted literally, has led some writers, such as Cescinsky and Webster, to condemn them as completely impractical. Even so, a number of cases incorporate features from such designs, but they are usually grafted on rather than formed into a coherent entity. It appears that these 'Chippendale' and 'Sheraton' cases were produced only by provincial cabinetmakers and that the specialist casemakers of London ignored the furniture design books.

Figure 10/78 shows two case designs from the third edition of Thomas Chippendale's *The Gentleman's and Cabinetmaker's Director,* 1762, and figure 10/79 shows a case strongly influenced by these designs. The ogee feet and skirting closely resemble those in the left hand design but the plinth and the trunk are fairly conventional. The hood (figure 10/80) is closely modelled on that of the right hand design and exhibits very fine workmanship particularly in the carving. There are side windows with shaped tops to match the trunk door. The whole

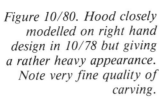

Figure 10/80. Hood closely modelled on right hand design in 10/78 but giving a rather heavy appearance. Note very fine quality of carving.

Figure 10/79. Case strongly influenced by designs in 10/78. Feet and skirting based on left hand drawing. Fine workmanship and well chosen veneers. Height 9ft. ½in. with 15ins. waist and 13ins. dial. By Pridgin, Hull, c.1775-80.

Figure 10/81. Dial with silvered centre and applied brass rims to winding and calendar apertures, a Yorkshire feature. North country type spandrels and chapter ring with dotted minutes. Earlier type of lunar and tidal dial with markings on disc but lacks pointer, probably fixed at base of arch.

Figure 10/82. Pridgin movement striking ting-tang quarters and hours with same train. Arbor carrying disc with pins on both sides is pumped backwards and forwards to operate appropriate hammers.

case is carefully executed in well-chosen mahogany but the heaviness of the hood gives a rather top heavy appearance. The total height is 9ft. ½in. with a 15ins. waist and a 13ins. dial. The probable date is c.1775-80.

The dial (figure 10/81) is signed on a silvered strip in the arch 'William Pridgin Hull'. The silvered centre has engraved seconds dial and scrolled designs. The winding holes and the calendar aperture have applied brass rims, which is a Yorkshire feature. The spandrels are the bold rococo pattern common on north country clocks and the chapter ring has only dots for the minutes and large five minute numbers. The lunar dial is the earlier type with the markings on the rotating portion and includes tidal information, no doubt for Hull. It lacks a pointer which was probably fixed by the collet at the base of the arch.

The movement (figure 10/82) strikes ting-tang quarters and hours from the same train. This is accomplished by having a special pin wheel arbor which is pumped backwards and forwards. It can be identified by the very thick wheel just behind the front plate. A disc on this arbor has pins projecting from both sides so that in the rear position the two quarter hammers are lifted and in the forward position it operates the hour hammer.

Figure 10/83 shows a fine quality case displaying many decorative details taken from Chippendale's *Director,* but the bold cabriole legs with claw and ball feet suggest the baroque designs popular in the first half of the century. The absence of back feet should be noted as they were omitted from a number of provincial cases, no doubt to ensure stability

Figure 10/83. Fine quality case based on designs in Chippendale's Director, *except for bold cabriole legs which suggests pre-1750. Note absence of rear feet, a provincial method of ensuring stability. Height 8ft. 6ins. excluding finial, c.1770.*

Figure 10/84. Hood showing Chinese pagoda top based on right hand design in 10/78. Note fine crisp carving. Musical clock by Walker, Newcastle on Tyne.

by causing the case to lean heavily against the wall. The whole case is embellished with both open and blind fretwork and fine carving in the Chippendale manner. The height is 8ft. 6ins. excluding the finial.

The hood (figure 10/84) has a Chinese pagoda top, similar to that of 10/80 and also based on the right hand design in figure 10/78. The scrolled corner posts flanking the hood door appear to have been copied from a design in the first edition of the *Director* which was omitted from the third edition. This suggests that the cabinetmaker probably worked from the first edition which also included the designs shown in figure 10/78. Note the crisp, high quality carving.

The clock is signed in the dial arch 'Jno. Walker Newcastle' (on Tyne) and has a three train movement playing fourteen tunes. The dial centre is engraved and silvered and the spandrels are C. & W. No. 22. Subsidiary dials in the arch provide for strike/silent and chime/silent. The probable date is c.1770.

The 'Lancashire Chippendale' case of figure 10/60 has a bombe shaped plinth with carved detail which appears to be strongly influenced by the left hand design in figure 10/78. The downward tapering trunk section of the right hand design is used in the elegant case shown in figure 10/85 which also has a matching pilaster applied to the front. Circular dials were introduced in the north c.1785 but were not adopted by the London casemakers until the beginning of the nineteenth century, with the exception of a few regulators. A three quarter view of the case (figure 10/86) shows that the pilaster has been made much more prominent than in Chippendale's design. Figure 10/87 shows the doors open, the trunk door being the full width of the case and providing space for a weight inside. Nothing is known of the

Figure 10/85. Elegant case with downward tapering trunk and matching pilaster based on right hand design in 10/78. Original clock missing but must have been a timepiece, probably a regulator, as there is room for only one weight. Probably c.1800.

Figure 10/86. Three quarter view of case showing prominent pilaster.

Figure 10/87. Case with doors open, showing trunk door full width of case and providing space for a central weight.

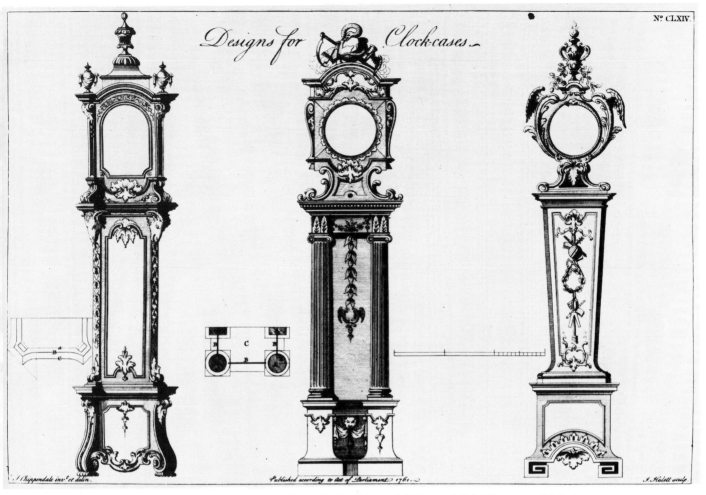

Designs for Clock-cases.

Figure 10/88. Three more case designs from 3rd edition of Chippendale's Director *which show more French influence. Note full arch dial on left, also circular dials. Latter may have influenced design of case in 10/85.*

original clock for this case but it was almost certainly a timepiece, probably a regulator, as there would be inadequate space for more than one weight. A difficult case to date, but probably c.1800.

Figure 10/88 shows three more designs from the same Chippendale publication. These show more French influence than the preceding ones; note the circular dials which were not adopted here until much later as discussed above. Chippendale has been criticised for showing full-arch dials as on the left hand design and on two others in the first edition of the *Director,* but it should be remembered that Hindley of York was using the full arch in the 1750s and Chippendale was also a Yorkshireman!

A case loosely based on the left hand design is shown in figure 10/89. The hood columns are set forward on canted projections and the general outline of the hood cresting and finials is taken from the drawing. The columns are supported by corbel brackets which are a version of those above the rams' heads. The case has well matched mahogany veneers with crossbanding to the trunk door and plinth. The height is 7ft. 4ins. excluding the replaced top finial. The 12ins. dial has a silvered centre engraved with shipping scenes and 'George Penny Wells' engraved round the curved calendar opening. The rococo spandrels are C. & W. No.

37 and the arch has a silvered plaque with an eagle and 'Tempus Fugit', which is flanked by dolphins. Probably c.1780.

Bird[13] shows a case which is based on the second design in figure 10/88. It has two large Corinthian columns which are hollow and accommodate the weights. The rest of the case is fairly conventional and houses a clock by Andrew Veitch of Haddington, c.1775.

Figure 10/90 shows two elaborate designs from Thomas Sheraton's *The Cabinet-maker and Upholsterer's Drawing Book* of 1793. These show the square dial which had been revived by some London makers in the late eighteenth century. The case shown in Colour Plate 16 is obviously inspired by the trunk section of the right hand design. The curved sides of the trunk terminate in scrolls at the top and with oval paterae at the bottom. At the lower end of the trunk the broad band of inlay and the unusual hollow moulding are also taken from the same design. The hood is designed without columns and the door is made the full width, so preserving the slim line. There are arched top side windows. The case is veneered with beautifully figured mahogany, with kingwood, tulip wood and ebony used for inlaying and banding. It originally had three finials but the present one, bearing an effigy of George III, is a replacement. The height is 7ft. 7ins. including finial, the maximum width of the hood 16ins. and the narrowest part of the trunk only 9⅝ins. wide. The dial has an engraved and silvered centre with 'John Ramsbottom Hall Green' inscribed just below the calendar opening. This is apparently the Hall Green near Wakefield and Ramsbottom is recorded at both places. The rococo spandrels are C. & W. No. 40 and the lunar disc is the type with the divisions and numerals round the edge. Note the late use of half hour marks and the very large minute numerals. The hands appear to be too early in style for the clock. The date is probably c.1795.

English casemakers and cabinetmakers, unlike their French counterparts, seldom signed their work and much more research is therefore required into casemakers and their products. At present little is known about the specialist casemakers and our knowledge is restricted almost entirely to the cabinetmakers and joiners who also made clock cases. This is due to the activities of furniture historians in contrast to those of antiquarian horologists which have been concentrated on the clockmakers.

Amongst the few known specialist casemakers mention must be made of possibly the first, Joseph Clifton who was established by 1663, see Chapter 2. An early eighteenth century casemaker was 'John Hall Kace Maker' who thus inscribed the gilt metal mounts of a miniature bracket clock by Claude du Chesne. Mr. Hill 'Clock-case maker of great business' died at his house in Long Lane, near West

13. A. Bird, *English House Clocks: 1600-1850,*1973, pp. 203, 252.

Figure 10/89. Case loosely based on left hand design in 10/88. Hood columns set forward on canted projections and supported on corbel brackets as in drawing. General outline of hood cresting and finials also taken from drawing. Top finial later. Height excluding finial 7ft. 4ins. Clock with 12ins. dial by Penny, Wells, probably c.1780.

Smithfield in 1743.[14] Haggar and Miller quote 'George Goodwin (from London), Clock Case Maker, Woodbridge', 1812.[15]

From what evidence has so far been brought to light it appears that the vast majority of provincial cases were made by men or firms who also did more general work. In 1968 Goodison[16] drew attention to the relevant material in the archives of the Lancaster cabinet-making firm of Gillows and produced much useful information. Loomes,[17] one of the very few other writers to have studied casemaking, has devoted a chapter to the subject, in which, apart from treating the Gillow information in more detail, he supplies very interesting particulars of the supplying of cases by a country joiner in the mid-eighteenth century. Towards the end of the eighteenth century and in the nineteenth some makers pasted labels in their cases, for example:

Summerscales

Cabinet and Clockcase Maker

Lincoln

No. 423

which is in the mahogany case of a clock by James Wilson of Stamford (1786-99).

14. M. Harris, *Old English Furniture,* 3rd edition, 1946, p. 21, source unknown.

15. *Suffolk Clocks and Clockmakers,* pp. 87, 185.

16. N. Goodison, 'Gillows' Clock Cases', *Antiquarian Horology,* V (March 1968), p. 348.

17. B. Loomes, *Complete British Clocks,* 1978, p. 172.

Figure 10/90. Elaborate case designs from Sheraton's Drawing Book, 1793. Note square dials as revived by some London makers in the late eighteenth century.

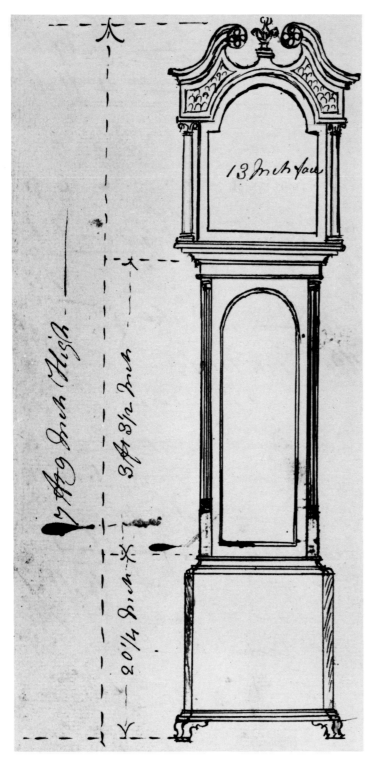

Figure 10/91. Gillow drawing of 1787 for a mahogany case 7ft. 9ins. high excluding finial, with a 13ins. dial; compare it with 10/92.

Figure 10/92. Mahogany case with many features in common with the design in 10/91. Hood door has moulded front, a Lancashire feature, and apparently a carved and gilt frame within it.

Within case drawing annotations: 13 Inch face; 7 ft 9 Inch High; 3 ft 8½ Inch; 20¼ Inch

The Gillow records referred to above give details of a number of cases from 1784 onwards although the firm was making them as early as 1743. Their products included: solid mahogany cases decorated with exotic veneers, pine cases veneered with mahogany, oak cases with mahogany trimmings and painted deal cases. The firm started stamping its name on some productions in the late eighteenth century and this became normal practice after 1820, but no stamped clock cases have yet been recorded.

Figure 10/91 shows a drawing for a mahogany case. 9ins. high, the estimate for which is dated 1787. It should be compared with figure 10/92 which shows a very similar case housing a clock of similar date with the dial signed 'John Lawrence Lancaster' round the arch. Note the carved paterae and finial ('a shield and 2 roses gilt' in the estimate) and the scale like frieze fret. The hood door has an ogee moulded front which is a typical Lancashire feature and within this is what appears to be a gilt gesso frame ('gilding the glass frame in moulding'). Other estimates have entries for gilding glass frames, a finish which follows the tradition with looking glass frames. In the absence of documentary evidence, a definite attribution cannot be made, but this case is probably by Gillow.

Figure 10/93 shows a drawing for a fine case, possibly showing Chippendale influence in the pagoda-like top, Gillows had subscribed to the *Director*. In figure 10/94 is shown a good quality mahogany case with the circular dial which became popular in the north. These give some idea of the range of designs produced and used by the firm.

The magnificent case in figure 10/95 is of an original design incorporating a variety of motifs. Basically it consists of an Ionic column surmounted by a spheroid containing the

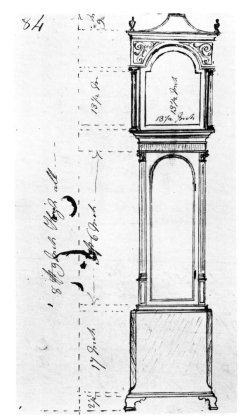

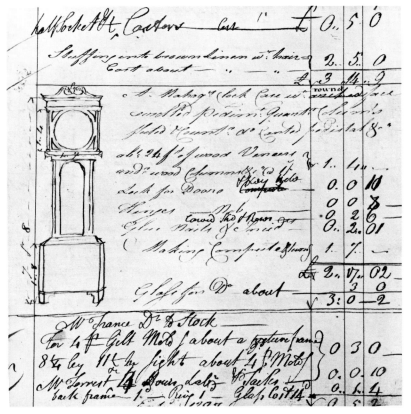

Figure 10/93. Gillow drawing, also of 1787 for a fine case with a pagoda-like top possibly showing Chippendale influence. Height 8ft. 9ins. with 13½ins. dial opening.

Figure 10/94. Gillow drawing of 1786 showing case for a round dial, height 7ft. 8ins. excluding pediment.

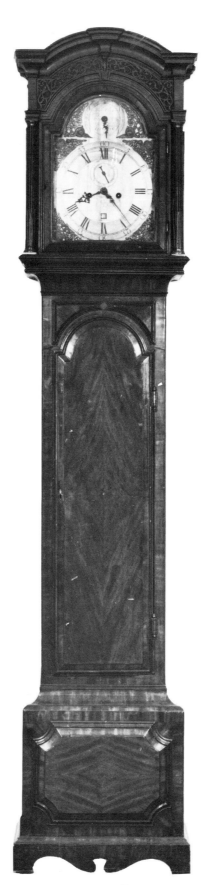

Figure 10/95

Figure 10/96

Figure 10/97

movement. Neo-classical influence is shown in the rams' heads, and the rope swags and tassels which decorate both the column and the spheroid are inspired by the naval victories of Nelson. The lotus petals which unite the column to the top section and also form the finial reflect a taste for Egyptian ornament following Napoleon's conquest of Egypt. From this evidence it may be dated to the first few years of the nineteenth century. The design and the quality of execution suggest a possible attribution to Thomas Chippendale the younger. The dial is signed by Thomas Lister of Halifax but is something of a puzzle as it has an applied chapter ring which does not resemble his usual style but is more in the manner of c.1700.

DIAL DEVELOPMENTS

Starting about 1770 there were a number of changes in dial design and construction which greatly changed the appearance and had the effect of considerably improving legibility, particularly with the poor lighting of the time.

Plain silvered brass dials had been introduced for regulators by about 1750 (see Chapter 11) and from about the same date Ellicott used plain square silvered dials on bracket clocks with circular dial openings. In spite of these developments flat silvered dials were not introduced on ordinary longcase clocks until c.1775.

The first stage was the abandonment of the matted dial centre whilst still retaining the applied chapter ring and spandrels. The usual arrangement was to engrave the seconds ring and the maker's name on the dial plate, the central part of which was then silvered. Figure 10/96 shows a dial signed on the dial plate, in the arch, 'Sam! Cox Long Acre London'. Surrounding the signature is engraved a strike/silent dial, and the dial centre has an engraved seconds ring and a square calendar aperture. There are the usual applied chapter ring and spandrels but the latter are the crown and crossed sceptre design (C. & W. No. 10) which are too early for this clock so must be replacements. The slim, elegant mahogany case is 8ft. 0ins. high and has chamfered panels to the trunk door and the plinth. The date is c.1775.

An alternative design, less commonly used, had a chapter disc engraved with the seconds dial and maker's name or other information and silvered all over. For a strike/silent mechanism there would often be a matching disc in the arch. Figure 10/97 shows a clock with a dial of this type which is signed at the centre 'Thos Mudge Willm Dutton London'. The corner and arch spandrels are of an unusual foliate design which is not in C. & W. The beautifully designed mahogany veneered case is of a type normally used by Mudge and Dutton as well as by several other makers of high quality clocks in the second half of the eighteenth century. The probable date is c.1770.

The final development, the one piece silvered dial, is shown in figure 10/98. This example is signed just below the centre 'Chas Newman Lynn' and probably dates from c.1780. There is a strike/silent dial in the arch and a square calendar aperture just above VI. Being a provincial dial it has decorative engraving, in this case simple but effective scrolling foliage with a touch of rococo. The chapter ring is indicated by engraved lines just inside the hour numerals and outside the minute numbers. At a later date there was a tendency to omit these

Figure 10/95. Magnificent mahogany case basically consisting of an Ionic column surmounted by a spheroid containing the movement decorated with rams' heads, rope swags and tassels, and lotus petals, which suggest c.1800-10. Clock by Lister, Halifax, but dial has some strange features.

Figure 10/96. Clock by Cox, Long Acre, c.1775, showing silvered dial centre engraved with seconds ring and signature engraved on arch within strike/silent markings. Crown and sceptre spandrels are replacements. Slim elegant mahogany case with chamfered panels to plinth and trunk door. Height 8ft. 0ins.

Figure 10/97. Clock by Mudge and Dutton, c.1770, with rather unusual silvered chapter and strike/silent discs. Rare foliate spandrels. Elegant mahogany case of type normally used by these and other leading makers of the period.

Figure 10/98. Clock by Newman, King's Lynn, c.1780, with one-piece silvered dial which, being provincial, has decorative engraving. Note chapter ring indicated by engraved lines which were omitted on later dials. Fine quality mahogany case with brass inlay and good sound frets.

Figure 10/99. Clock by Thwaites, c.1785, showing typical one-piece London dial devoid of decoration. Note reintroduction of square dial. Mahogany case has square topped trunk door to match dial but truncated pagoda top is unusual with latter.

circles. The serpentine minute hand was introduced c.1780. The fine quality mahogany veneered case has brass inlay to the trunk and hood columns and fine sound frets.

In contrast to provincial dials, London ones were usually quite plain and figure 10/99 shows a good example of c.1785 which is signed just below the centre 'Aynsth Thwaites' with 'London' just above the VI. Note the complete absence of decoration. The chapter ring is still indicated by engraved circles as in figure 10/98, but the minute ring consists of a single circle with lines across it. There was a revival of the square dial on London clocks late in the eighteenth century, perhaps part of a search for simplicity. The good quality mahogany case is unusual in combining a square dial opening with a truncated pagoda top. Note the square topped trunk door to match the dial.

Flat silvered dials were quite popular in the southern half of the country but were used very little, if at all, in the north. Northern makers, if they continued to use the brass dial, preferred the traditional applied chapter ring and spandrels.

A few provincial makers adopted the applied chapter disc as in the Mudge and Dutton clock of figure 10/97, and figure 10/100 shows a late example (c.1795), signed just above the VI 'Thos Templer Portsmouth Common'. Portsmouth Common was where Portsea now stands but there is apparently no record of this maker. Note that the minutes are now marked only with a circle of dots and that there are no engraved circles. The seconds ring is located on a cloud and the calendar opening is flanked by engravings of a fort and a warship, both probably of local significance. Note the dial fixing steel screws with polished heads, which were often used from about the end of the eighteenth century. The rococo spandrels are a variation not shown in C. & W. The hands are of the matching type introduced shortly before 1800 but they differ slightly so one must be a replacement.

The changes which have been discussed so far relate only to changes in the design of brass dials, but in 1772 an advertisement in the *Birmingham Gazette* announced a much more fundamental development, the production of dials in sheet iron painted white.[18] These became extremely popular, particularly in the north, as they offered superior legibility and were much cheaper to make. Even so, some makers quoted the advantages of legibility and permanence *at the same price as brass dials!* John Benson of Whitehaven was one who advertised thus in 1782.[19] The importance attached to the improved legibility can be gauged from the fact that some existing clocks had their brass dials painted over or replaced with painted iron ones. Also, some good quality clocks are found with original painted dials of brass instead of iron, so economy was not always the motive.

The new dials have been variously described as white, painted or japanned and Goodison quotes a contemporary reference to a 'china' dial.[20] They are also incorrectly described as enamelled. The white or tinted paint which forms the ground was hardened by heat treatment but this is quite different from true enamelling which requires a high temperature to fuse the glass-like coating. Decoration in the spandrels, in the arch and possibly in the dial centre was painted on after the ground coating had been baked. The decoration was then varnished to protect it. The painting of the numerals, divisions and maker's or seller's 'signature' seems to have been the last stage and not to have been protected by varnish. As a result, the black markings have often suffered from domestic cleaning operations and are in a much worse state than the rest of the dial. The signature is a frequent casualty but can often be deciphered by faint discoloration of the ground, which is most easily detected by applying a strong light at an angle. It is a great mistake to repaint the ground if this can be avoided.

One consequence of the introduction of the painted dial was that the average clockmaker purchased a complete dial with the dial feet riveted in before painting, whereas he probably

18. See B. Loomes, *The White Dial Clock,* 1974, particularly pp. 27-28. This is the only book devoted to the subject.

19. See J. Penfold, *The Clockmakers of Cumberland,* 1977, p. 142.

20. N. Goodison, 'Gillows' Clock Cases', *Antiquarian Horology,* V (March 1968), p. 358.

Figure 10/100. Clock by Templer, Portsmouth Common, c.1795, showing provincial use of chapter disc with engraved scenes and dotted minutes. Note steel screws for fixing dial feet. Matching type hands introduced about this time but these differ slightly so one is a replacement.

made up a brass dial even though he had it engraved by a specialist. This change in procedure gave rise to two possible difficulties:

1. Without a degree of standardisation between dial makers and clockmakers, the winding squares and the seconds hand might not coincide with their holes. This would apply only to eight-day clocks, except for a very few thirty-hour clocks with seconds hands.

2. The dial feet might coincide with the movement pillars or some of the striking parts, which again is less likely to occur with the simpler thirty-hour clock.

The more independent smaller maker probably made his movements to suit the dials he had purchased, but movements were certainly available from specialist suppliers so there must have been some agreed standards to prevent the difficulties discussed in 1 above. There is some evidence for this and Harlow, in 1813, states of his *Guide,*[21] "I feel confident, that if Dial and Movement Makers observe the rules here laid down, the movements and dial will fit with the utmost exactness – ." He continued: "S. HARLOW respectfully informs the Trade, that he manufactures ... also Caliper Plates correct for Dial Makers". These must have been templates to enable dial makers to drill the winding and seconds holes to suit movements made according to Harlow's drawings. Research is necessary to establish, from surviving clocks of the period, the extent to which this proposed standardisation was followed in practice.

The second difficulty, that of the dial feet being in the wrong place was overcome by using what Harlow called "...the back plate, commonly used by the Birmingham Dial Makers", but what is now usually called a false plate. This consists of an iron plate with the centre cut out, which is attached to the dial by four short feet, about ⅜in. long. This plate is almost invariably of cast iron[21a], often with the dial maker's name and the dial feet holes cast in. It was drilled at convenient points and provided with feet to suit the movement. False plates were provided for most but not all eight-day movements but were not provided for thirty-hour ones. In the nineteenth century false plates gradually ceased to be used, probably because the same entrepreneur was supplying dials and movements already fitted together, so that by mid-century it was usual for the dial to have long feet fitted direct to the movement.

Figure 10/101 shows a false plate marked 'Wilson' attached to its 12ins. dial. James Wilson was in business as a dial maker in Birmingham 1778-1809.[22] The dial (figure 10/102) is signed 'Jnº Fordham Brainteee', probably the man who is recorded at Coggeshall, a few miles away, 1784-93,[23] and the date of the clock is c.1785-90. The dial has raised gilt decoration resembling the applied spandrels of a brass dial and which is found on a number of early white dials. The painting in the arch is well executed but the effect is spoilt by the protective coat of varnish having become discoloured and crazed. Note the typical dotted minute and seconds rings, but the seconds numbers have been rather badly repainted. The clock is a little early to have matching hands so they may be replacements. The movement (figure 10/103) is well made, the minute wheel has a steel pinion pivoted in a cock and the snail is fixed by a screw to facilitate removal for cleaning. These refinements suggest that Fordham was in fact the maker, not just a retailer. The striking mechanism has had one or two rather clumsy repairs.

Figure 10/104 shows a dial with a simple raised gilt decoration and with a calendar dial with a pointer, which was introduced about 1780 and very gradually superseded the rotating calendar disc. The hour and minute hands are nineteenth century style matching brass ones and the minute hand has been shortened to fit. As so often happens, the maker's name has disappeared but the date is c.1780. The mahogany case is beautifully proportioned and has

21. S. Harlow, *The Clock Makers' Guide to Practical Clockwork...with instructions for the Dial Makers,* 1813, republished 1978.

21a. Some false plates were made of sheet iron.

22. Loomes, *White Dial,* p. 47.

23. C.A. Osborne, *Essex Clock & Watchmakers,* 1979.

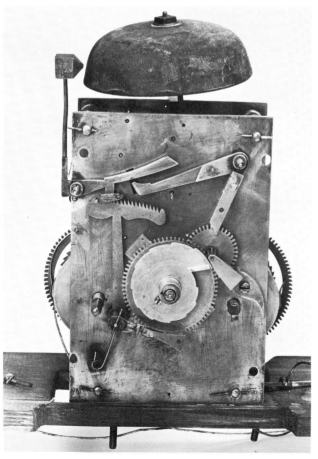

Figure 10/101. False plate marked 'Wilson' attached to its 12ins. dial.

Figure 10/102. Wilson dial signed by Fordham, Braintree, c.1785-90. Note raised gilt spandrel-like decoration and attractive painting in arch marred by aged varnish. Typical dotted minute and seconds rings but seconds numbers rather clumsily repainted. Note brass collets to winding holes. Hands probably replacements.

Figure 10/103. Fordham movement with refinements suggesting it was probably a local product, note minute wheel pinion pivoted in cock. Rather clumsy repairs to striking mechanism.

Figure 10/104. Dial, c.1780, with simple raised gilt decoration and calendar dial with pointer which gradually superseded rotating disc. Signature now missing. Hour and minute hands are replacements. Good quality mahogany case with fine veneers and brass inlaid columns.

Figure 10/105. Dial by Scholfield, Rochdale, c.1785, with simple fruit and flower decoration. Traditional calendar and lunar dial with markings on dial arch. Usual paintings of earth's hemispheres below moon now worn away. Original hour hand, minute hand later.

finely figured veneers and delicate sound frets. The trunk and hood columns are reeded and have brass inlay as well as brass capitals and bases. This is very much a London style case with no provincial characteristics which probably indicates a home counties origin for the clock. This example shows that fine quality cases were made for painted dial clocks, but many of these cases have now been used to rehouse earlier brass dial clocks whose cases had become dilapidated or had been destroyed.

Figure 10/105 shows a dial of c.1785 which has simple fruit and floral decoration in the spandrels and dial centre. It has the traditional calendar disc showing through a curved aperture and the usual type of moon in the arch. Note the scale for the moon's age is now on the dial plate, not on the lunar disc. The semi-circular areas just below the lunar dial had the usual representations of the earth's hemispheres but this has become worn away and, unlike the other markings, has not been restored. The dial is signed, as usual just below the centre, 'Edm. Scholfield Rochdale'. Note the brass collets

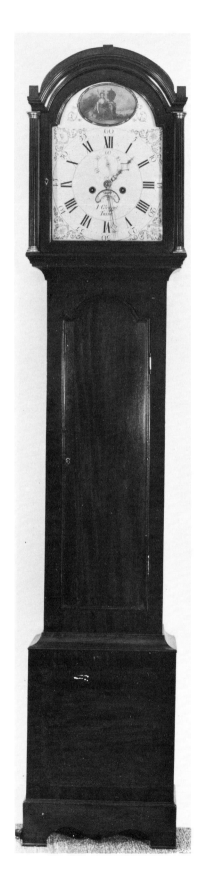

Figure 10/106. Dial very similar to that in 10/102 and possibly also made by Wilson. Clock by Clement, Tring, c.1785-90. Brass replacement hands. Neat mahogany case but lacks finials.

Figure 10/107. Clock by Iles, Stroud, c.1810, with minutes numbered only every fifteen and concentric circles for minute and seconds divisions. Probably original matching steel hands.

which were always fitted to prevent damage to the paint by careless use of the winding key. The hour hand is original but the later pattern minute hand has replaced the probably serpentine original.

Figure 10/106 shows a dial very similar to that in figure 10/102 and possibly also made by Wilson. It is signed 'I. Clement Tring', an apparently unrecorded maker but the date is c.1785-90. The matching brass hands are a replacement. Matching hands, but in steel, were introduced in the 1790s. It is contained in a neat mahogany case with crossbanding to the plinth panel and reeded hood columns with brass mounts. The simple break arch hood has plinths for three finials.

Early painted dials had simple restrained decoration with a large area of the white ground exposed whereas later dials had more complex and colourful decoration which gradually spread to fill all the available space outside the minute ring. The development of dial decoration is covered in detail by Loomes (see above) and by Hudson.[24]

After about 1800 the minutes were numbered only every fifteen and the divisions were generally between two concentric circles as on brass dials. An example of this type of c.1810 by 'Wm. Iles Stroud' is shown in figure 10/107. It has matching steel hands which are probably original.

During the first quarter of the nineteenth century there was a fashion for using Arabic hour numerals instead of Roman ones. Usually they were upright as in figure 10/108 which shows a clock with a 12ins. painted dial signed 'J. Balling Shepton Mallet'. It has the early scroll type of decoration so is probably c.1800. In spite of the seconds hand and the (dummy) winding squares this is a thirty-hour clock. A number of these imitation eight-day clocks were made as status symbols for those unable to afford the real thing. The oak case has the swan neck pediment used on many provincial clocks and is 7ft. 6ins. high. Occasionally the Arabic numerals were made radial, with the lower ones facing outwards as in figure 10/109. This dial is signed 'G. Mawman Beverly' and is probably c.1810. It is in a very good quality case veneered with finely figured mahogany and inlaid with box, satin-wood and probably kingwood. The fluted hood columns have brass Corinthian capitals. Note the Hepplewhite style feet at the front and the absence of rear feet to ensure that the case stands firmly against the wall. This idea is found on some Yorkshire and other provincial cases. The probable date is c.1810 for the case also.

The final stage in dial development was the complete abandoning of minute numbering, which was introduced about 1815-20. Figure 10/110 shows a typical plain London dial of this type c.1815 signed 'Barwise London' with a strike/silent dial in the arch. The good quality mahogany veneered case is almost devoid of ornament and should be compared with the provincial version of the same design in figure 10/109.

The ordinary painted dial is often incorrectly described as being enamelled, but there are a few longcase clocks with dials which merit this description. Colour Plate 17 shows a 12ins. dial made up of two pieces of fired enamel on copper. These dials are very rare because of the brittleness of the enamel and the risk of distortion during the firing. To help overcome these difficulties, the arch section was made separately and both the name boss and the chapter ring were made slightly convex to give added rigidity. Both sections are fixed with small screws to a rigid brass dial plate, which is however skeletonised in true north country fashion (figure 10/111). The gilt decoration on the dial (Colour Plate 17) bears a relationship to that found on some of the earliest painted dials but is more delicately executed. The dial is signed 'Tho.ˢ Redford Leeds' which is obviously intended for Thomas Radford, a known Leeds maker. Apparently, his order to the enameller was not very clearly written and once

24. F. Hudson, 'Scottish Painted Dials', *Antiquarian Horology*, X (Winter 1976-Summer 1977), pp. 55, 173, 317. Reprint, with other material, entitled *Scottish Longcase Clocks 1780-1870*, available from the Antiquarian Horological Society.

Figure 10/108. Thirty-hour clock by Balling, Shepton Mallet, c.1800. Dial has upright Arabic hour numerals and minutes numbered every fifteen. Seconds hand and dummy winding squares to simulate an eight-day clock. Oak case with swan neck pediment, 7ft. 6ins. high.

Figure 10/110. Clock by Barwise, London, c.1815. Dial completely without minute numbering or decoration. Typical matching steel hands. Good quality mahogany case almost devoid of ornament. Compare with provincial equivalent in 10/109.

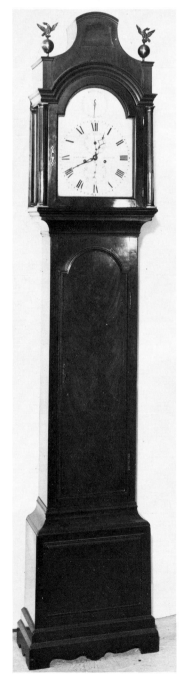

Figure 10/109. Clock by Mawman, Beverley, c.1810. The Arabic hour numerals are radial with the lower ones facing outwards and the minutes are numbered similarly every five. Fine quality inlaid mahogany case with Hepplewhite style feet at front and none at back.

Colour Plate 19. Clock by Wright and Woolley, Tenterden, c.1790, with well painted dial. Slim, nicely proportioned mahogany case with square topped trunk door and caddy to hood. Gilt wood capitals, bases and finials. Height 7ft. 4½ins.

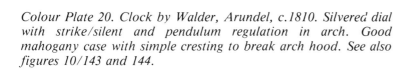

Colour Plate 20. Clock by Walder, Arundel, c.1810. Silvered dial with strike/silent and pendulum regulation in arch. Good mahogany case with simple cresting to break arch hood. See also figures 10/143 and 144.

Figure 10/111. Rear of Radford dial showing thick dial plate but with north country cut-out sections, also domed name boss and chapter ring for rigidity. Note nineteenth century replacement movement and dial foot moved to fit. See Colour Plates 17 and 18.

fired the lettering could not be amended. It was probably made at Bilston in south Staffordshire.

The hands do not match and both are too late in date for the clock. The present movement (figure 10/111) is a nineteenth century replacement, note the rather mean looking pillars. It was presumably new when fitted to the dial as there are no surplus holes in the front plate, but one dial foot had to be moved to avoid a pillar.

The black japanned case (Colour Plate 18) has lost its pagoda top but retains three fine brass finials. The columns are attached to the hood door, and there are rectangular side windows. The gilt decoration is the simple type without any raised work. The present height is 7ft. 2¾ins. excluding finials, while the waist is 13¾ins. The probable date for the whole clock is c.1775.

THE LATER CLOCKS

Some clocks will now be described which continue the story to the end of the eighteenth century, and in a few cases, just into the nineteenth.

Figure 10/112 shows a very unusual clock which is signed in the dial arch 'George Borrett Stowmarket'. The centre of the 12ins. dial plate and the chapter ring are silvered and the spandrels are C. & W. No. 21. An opening in the arch has a picture of death in the form of a skeleton which alternates every few minutes with a picture of a man drinking. Was this an early advocacy of temperance? The movement is a centre seconds timepiece of month duration with dead beat escapement.

The fruitwood case (figure 10/113) has a curious cresting where the typical East Anglian design is modified to suggest a swan neck pediment. The hood has detached columns and side windows with Gothic shaping. The probable date is c.1770-75.

Another East Anglian clock, of superb quality, is shown in figure 10/114. The 13ins. dial is signed across the engraved and silvered centre 'Moore Ipswich' and it dates from c.1775.

Pieces of rococo spandrel are fitted round the four subsidiary dials which serve the following purposes. Top left: strike/silent. Top right: tune selector for the musical train, inscribed:

104 Psalm
Tamo Tanta
Happy Clown
Foots Minuet
Brittons strike home
Collin & Phebe
Miller of Mansfield

The lower left hand dial indicates the days of the week and the lower right hand one the months. The day of the month is shown through the usual square opening. The minute hand is a ninetenth century replacement. The arch has a painted scene with automata consisting of a lady and a gentleman at dinner with servants and musicians. Eight figures are animated, being operated by a pin wheel driven by the musical train. A lever in a slot near III is for changing the date, an unusual but very useful refinement. Other levers just above are for releasing and stopping the musical train.

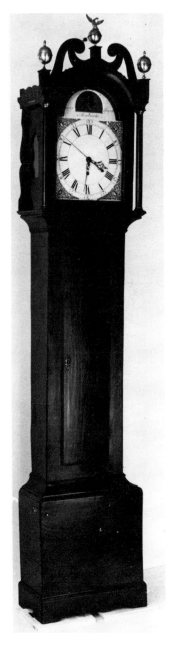

Figure 10/112. Clock by Borrett, Stowmarket, c.1770-75. 12ins. dial has silvered centre and opening in arch where figure of death alternates with that of a man drinking. Month centre seconds time-piece movement with dead beat escapement.

Figure 10/113. Fruitwood case of Borrett clock with curious cresting suggesting a swan neck pediment. Hood side windows with Gothic shaping.

The movement (figure 10/115) has three trains, the right hand one playing the selected tune twice each hour, on ten bells with seventeen hammers. The left hand train provides quarter chiming on six of the ten bells and hour striking on a larger bell. This is accomplished by having pins in the end of the chime barrel to operate the hour hammer when the barrel is pumped over. This method is used on a clock by Cobham shown in figure 7/13. The going train has an anchor escapement and the pendulum has a wooden rod and heavy brass faced bob.

The elegant case (figure 10/116) is veneered with finely figured mahogany, with reeded

Figure 10/114. 13ins. dial of a very fine musical clock by Moore, Ipswich, c.1775. Upper subsidiary dials for strike/silent and tune selection, lower ones for day of week and month. Day of month in usual square opening. Painted scene in arch with automata operated by musical train. Wrong minute hand.

Figure 10/115. Moore movement showing musical train with large pin barrel. Left hand train provides quarter chiming and hour striking. Note wooden pendulum rod.

Figure 10/116. Elegant case of Moore clock with finely figured veneers and good gilt brass mounts. Height 8ft. 10ins. including flambeau finial.

Figure 10/116

quarter columns to plinth and trunk, and reeded columns to hood, all with brass inlay. The hood has cast brass frets to the side windows and sound frets, and brass flambeau finials, all the brass mounts being gilt. The height including the central finial is 8ft. 10ins.

Provincial makers in general used more decorative engraving on dials than the London makers and figure 10/117 shows an attractive unsigned example of c.1775-80. The centre is engraved with two groups of buildings, some of which have a vaguely Oriental air and a small vessel sails between them. In the upper centre a parrot enjoys cherries and the sky is filled with small birds. The chapter ring is rather unusual in having separate rings of quarter hour and half hour divisions. The 11ins. dial plate has cut-away sections behind the chapter ring, which together with its plate framed movement indicates a north country origin. The dial plate has been resilvered all over as traces behind the chapter ring proved that this was done originally. Despite the quite good quality engraving the dial had the chapter ring and the spandrels riveted in position, a strange economy. The hand, although an old one, is not original and is rather early for the dial. The case has disappeared.

An unusual dial of c.1780 with possible Dutch influence is shown in figure 10/118. It is signed on a curved plate near VI, 'Willm Bull Stratford Essex', the county name being a rare addition to a 'signature'. The dial centre is matted and the heavy rococo spandrels are a

Figure 10/117. Anonymous 11ins. dial, c.1775-80, of north country origin. Dial plate silvered all over and with attractive scene in centre. Unusually set out chapter ring and spandrels both riveted in position. Hand rather too early.

pattern found on many north country clocks but not recorded in C. & W. The chapter ring has the arcaded minute band typical of Dutch clocks and which is also found on a number of provincial English examples. There are very decorative half hour marks, a late use of such devices. The sunken seconds dial has a scalloped edge to the dial opening. There is a full calendar but without correction for the short months, all provided in typically Dutch fashion. The day of the month appears in a square opening in the seconds dial, a position very rarely used on English clocks. The month is shown in the left hand key hole shaped opening together with the appropriate figure and sign of the zodiac. The day of the week with its deity and planetary sign appears in the right hand opening. The lunar dial in the arch is the earlier type where the scale of days is engraved on the disc. The left hand subsidiary dial is for 'Strike & Chime/Silent' and the right hand one for indicating the seven tunes played by the movement. The mahogany case has fine quality veneers and brass mounts.

Figure 10/119 shows the dial of a 'London' clock which has the very decorative engraving on the silvered centre more usually associated with provincial work. The dial is signed on a sunken plaque in the arch 'John Farley Southwark' and the engraved centre harmonises with

Figure 10/118. Unusual dial of musical clock by Bull, Stratford, Essex, c.1780, showing provincial and possibly Dutch influence. Chapter ring with arcaded minute band and elaborate half hour markings. Day of week and month in openings in dial centre and day of month in aperture in seconds dial. Subsidiary dials for strike/silent and tune selection. Note early type lunar disc with scale marked on it.

Figure 10/119. Musical clock by Farley, Southwark, c.1785. Dial centre has decorative rococo engraving, despite being a 'London' clock. Note Victorian style lettering on tune selection dial, indicating modernisation last century.

the late rococo spandrels (C. & W. No. 30). Note that the seconds ring is engraved on the dial plate. The left hand subsidiary dial is for strike/silent and the right hand one is a tune selector for the four tunes played:

Home Sweet Home
Chimes
Annie Laurie
Auld Lang Syne

The Victorian style lettering, as well as the choice of tunes, indicates that the pin barrel was renewed or repinned in the nineteenth century.

The movement (figure 10/120) has ten bells with only ten hammers so the music is relatively simple, and automatic change of tune is not provided. The movement is of excellent quality; note the large anti-friction wheels supporting the calendar ring.

The case (figure 10/121) is veneered with finely figured

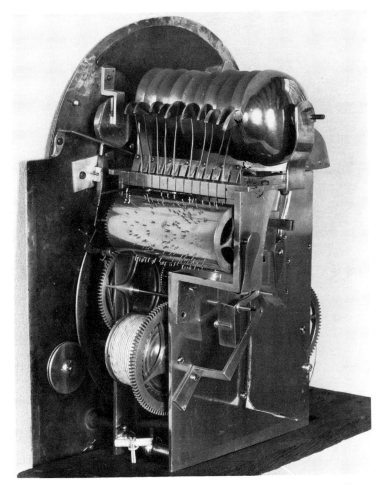

Figure 10/120. Movement of Farley clock. Excellent quality but relatively simple musical mechanism. Note large anti-friction wheels for calendar ring.

Figure 10/121. Case of Farley clock. Fine proportions and carefully chosen veneers. Quarter columns of plinth and ogee skirting are unusual on a London case.

mahogany and is beautifully proportioned. The quarter columns to the plinth and the ogee skirting are rather unusual on a London case. The whole dates from c.1785.

After discussing two clocks made in what is now London, it is instructive to examine one of typically London appearance from a small town in West Sussex. Figure 10/122 shows the 12ins. dial which is signed 'John Taylor Petworth' on the silvered centre and which is completely free from the decorative engraving usually found on provincial work. The rococo spandrels (C. & W. No. 30 as on the Farley dial) are partnered by matching arch spandrels, not in C. & W. and not often used.

The movement is of good quality with five pillars and there is a rigid rack tail with spring stud. The spandrels are fixed with square headed screws. These two survivals of earlier practice suggest that Taylor was an independent maker, not one buying in from a trade supplier such as Thwaites, see Makers and Retailers (p. 373). Figure 10/123 shows the brass cased weights and the large pendulum bob supported on a graduated rating nut.

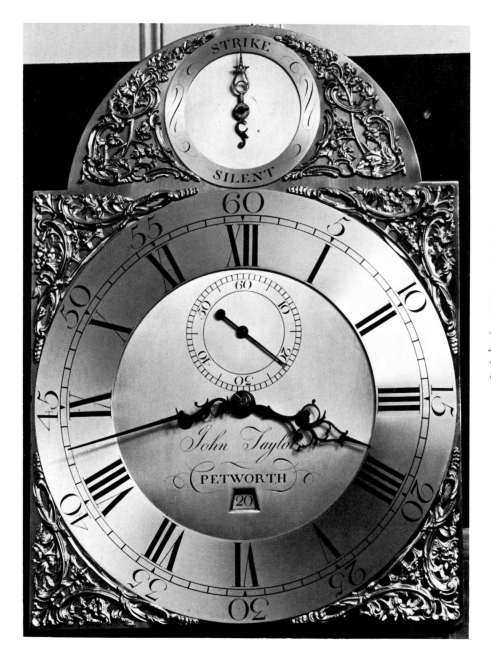

Figure 10/122. 12ins. dial of London style clock by Taylor, Petworth, 1774. Note unusual arch spandrels matching late rococo corner spandrels. Dial has no provincial features but movement suggests an independent maker.

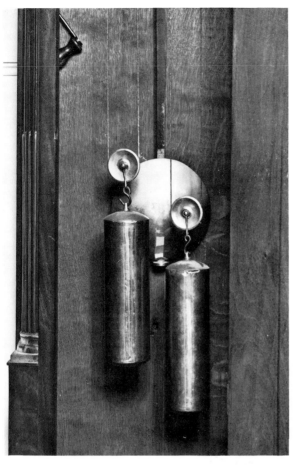

Figure 10/123. Original brass cased weights and heavy pendulum bob with graduated rating nut.

Figure 10/124. Pagoda topped case of Taylor clock, showing typical London design with well chosen veneers. The flambeau finials are of gilt wood, a provincial touch. The height is 7ft. 11½ins. excluding finials and it has a 14¼ins. waist for a 12ins. dial.

Figure 10/125. Fine sound fret in hood of Taylor clock.

Figure 10/126. Elegant dial of a musical clock by Gatton, London, c.1785. Note slimness of chapter and seconds rings and fine matted centres of main and subsidiary dials. Signature on dial plate in arch between strike/silent and chime/silent dials.

The pagoda topped case (figure 10/124) is of mahogany with well chosen veneers and is of typical London design. It is not known whether it was made locally or was supplied from London. It has the usual brass inlay to the trunk and hood columns but the flambeau finials are of gilt wood. There are very fine sound frets in the front and the sides of the hood (figure 10/125). The height is 7ft.11½ins. excluding the finials and it has a 14¼ins. waist for a 12ins. dial. The back plate of the movement is dated 1774.

Figure 10/126 shows the elegant dial of a musical clock of c.1785, signed direct on the dial plate in the arch 'Edwd Gatton London'. The elegance results from the slimness of the chapter and seconds rings, and the very restrained decoration. There are matching strike/silent and chime/silent rings in the arch and the dial plate within all the rings is finely matted. The late rococo spandrels are C. & W. No. 30. The seven tunes played are engraved on a curved strip on the arch:

> Easter Hymn
> Waterman
> March
> Hornpipe
> Air
> Lango Lee
> Minuet

The movement (figure 10/127) has the pin barrel arranged parallel to the dial because of its length. There are twelve bells with twenty -three hammers to permit rapid repetition of

Figure 10/127. Gatton movement with long pin barrel parallel to dial and twenty-three hammers for twelve bells, and therefore capable of playing quite complicated music. Note large adjustable fly.

notes when required. The larger number of bells and hammers and the consequent layout of the pin barrel as here are characteristic of the later musical clocks.

Figure 10/128 shows a rather humbler clock of c.1785 which is signed round the arch 'John Draper Chelmsford'. The silvered dial plate is lightly engraved with floral designs and the calendar shows through a curved slot. The arch has three painted country scenes and in front of the central one an automated figure marches in sympathy with the pendulum. This works on the same principle as the more common figure of Father Time with a scythe.

A painted dial clock of 1780-90 is shown in figure 10/129. As often happens, the maker's name and address have worn away with cleaning but the case suggests an East Anglian or possibly Lincolnshire origin. There is a particularly fine pierced cresting to the hood and the case is nicely proportioned except for the very high cut-away skirting. The material is mainly oak, with a little crossbanding and other decoration, probably in mahogany.

Figure 10/130 shows a London case of c.1790 of traditional pagoda top design but with the addition of fan type inlays of boxwood and crossbanding, probably satinwood. Such cases are often loosely described as 'Sheraton' because of the inlaying but they bear very little relation to Sheraton's published designs. The height is approximately 7ft. 10ins. The 12ins. dial has the usual silvered centre and is signed on a plaque in the arch 'John Philp St. John's St. London'. The subsidiary dials are chime/not chime (left) and tune selector for four tunes. The tunes are played hourly on ten bells.

A fine quality case of c.1790-1800 is shown in figure 10/131. It has fan inlays and crossbanding like the previous example, but the trunk door has a central inlay of musical instruments and the plinth panel has a decorative shell. Just below the trunk quarter columns are panels of blind fretwork and these, together with the plinth quarter columns, suggest a provincial origin. The present clock, by David Hubert, London, is earlier, c.1740.

Colour Plate 19 shows a nicely proportioned mahogany case of c.1790 with a painted dial inscribed 'Wright & Woolley Tenterden'. The case has slim lines resulting from small-section mouldings and attached columns. The trunk door is square topped and the hood has a caddy top and sound frets. The capitals, bases and finials are of gilt wood. A conservatively designed case but very pleasing. The height is 7ft. 4½ins. The dial is well painted and the false plate is stamped 'Wilson'. It has the usual type of lunar dial and a calendar through a curved opening.

A cottage clock in a simple oak case is shown in figure 10/132. The plinth is rather high and the hood has a simple rectangular superstructure which probably should have finials.

Figure 10/128. Clock by Draper, Chelmsford, c.1785, with one-piece silvered dial. Three painted country scenes in arch and marching figure operated from pallet arbor.

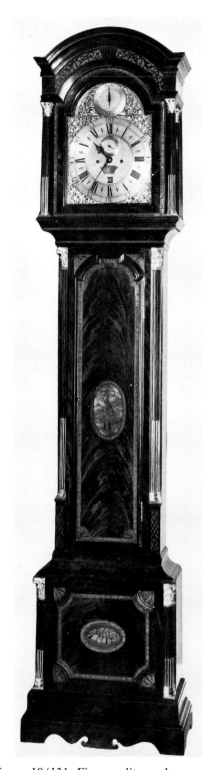

Figure 10/130. Musical clock by Philp, c.1790, with 12ins. dial. Traditional pagoda topped mahogany case with fan inlays and crossbanding, probably in satinwood. Height 7ft. 10ins.

Figure 10/129. Painted dial clock of c.1780-90, maker's name now missing. Case mainly oak with crossbanding and other decoration, probably in mahogany. Fine pierced cresting suggests East Anglian or possibly Lincolnshire origin. Case nicely proportioned except for very high cut-away skirting.

Figure 10/131. Fine quality mahogany case, c.1790-1800, with large oval inlays on trunk door and plinth panel as well as fan inlays and crossbanding. Quarter columns to plinth and blind frets below trunk columns suggest provincial work. Present clock is earlier, c.1740.

The plinth and trunk door have mahogany crossbanding and the fluted columns and a fluted strip in the frieze are probably also of mahogany. The dial (figure 10/133) has had the numerals repainted but unfortunately the signature was not replaced. The hands are odd and too late in date. The date is probably c.1795-1800. Apart from cheapness, square dialled clocks required less headroom so were popular for the humbler homes.

From late in the eighteenth century Vulliamy and a few other good London makers housed their clocks in architectural style cases, no doubt inspired by the neo-classical movement. Figure 10/134 shows a good example although later than some, c.1810. Note the square topped trunk door, square dial opening and triangular pediment. It has reeded quarter columns to the trunk and matching detached columns to the hood. It is a simple but very elegant design and is carried out in the choicest mahogany veneers. The silvered dial is

Figure 10/132. Cottage clock, c.1795-1800, in oak case with mahogany crossbanding and other decoration. Rather high plinth and rectangular superstructure which should probably have finials.

Figure 10/133. Dial of cottage clock. Numerals repainted but unfortunately signature not replaced.

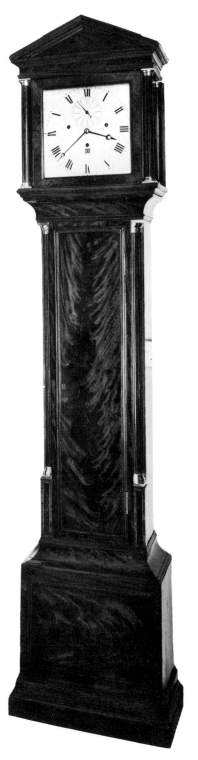

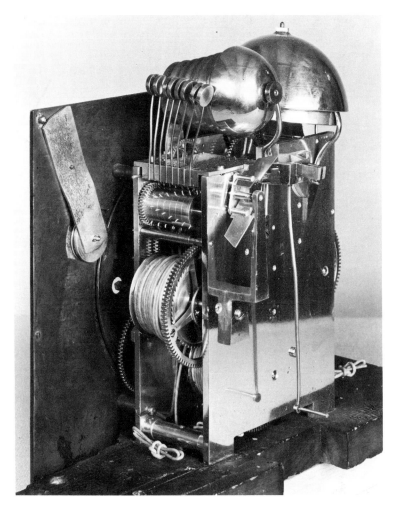

Figure 10/135. Anonymous quarter chiming movement of superb quality, resembling work of Benjamin Vulliamy. Note very long crutch.

Figure 10/134. Anonymous three train clock, c.1810. Silvered dial has observatory markings for seconds but no minute numbering. Fine quality architectural style case with triangular pediment and square topped trunk door. Choice mahogany veneers.

unsigned, note the absence of minute numbering, a nineteenth century development. The seconds dial has the radial marks known as 'observatory markings' to facilitate reading seconds from a distance.

The movement (figure 10/135) provides quarter chiming on eight bells and is built to a very high standard with a dead beat escapement with very long crutch and many other refinements. It closely resembles the work of Benjamin Vulliamy.

MAKERS AND RETAILERS

Although the name on the dial of a clock is usually referred to as that of the 'maker', it is well known that there were trade suppliers who furnished retailers with movements and dials. The difficulty is in knowing how widespread this practice was and the extent to which a particular maker was dependent on other manufacturers.

Lee[25] has produced stylistic evidence that even in the seventeenth century Joseph Knibb, for example, sometimes supplied other makers with movements. Joseph Williamson's part in supplying equation mechanism to the trade has already been discussed (Chapter 8). Similarly, John Shelton has been credited with supplying regulators to Mudge and others who were journeymen with him in the Graham workshop.

No doubt many of the trade suppliers were well known and did not need to advertise. That some thought it worthwhile is proved by the following advertisement which appeared in the *Ipswich Journal* of 30th June 1750:[26]

> All sorts of Clock and Mathematical work also Brass plates for coffins, &c., by Mandeville Somersall, Clock-engraver and Varnisher in Fore-Street, near Moorgate London, where Country Chapmen may be furnished with all sorts of Clock Dial Plates, completely fitted up; as also all sorts of Tools or Materials for Clock and Watchmaking at the lowest prices.

Samuel Harlow's *Guide* of 1813, which has already been discussed in connection with painted dials, was directed at dial makers and movement makers, so obviously these makers to the trade were playing a prominent part by the early nineteenth century.

Some country or small town makers were independent of such suppliers, an example being Samuel Deacon of Barton in the Beans, Leicestershire, who made the four train clock to Ludlam's design which is described earlier in this chapter. Deacon's workshop, now re-erected in Leicester, was equipped for both the casting of brass parts and the forging of steel ones.

Another example of a complete clockmaker is furnished by William Lasseter of Arundel in Sussex, who was apparently established by c.1750. His workshop also had facilities for forging and brass founding. The business survived into the 1950s and their lathe and wheel cutting engine are in a private collection. In 1788 Thomas Walder joined Lasseter to learn the trade, although he was twenty-two years old, which is somewhat elderly for an apprentice! He kept a detailed notebook (see figures 10/136-138) which has fortunately survived. The entries are in random subject order, obviously the order in which he received the instruction. One entry proves that Lasseter cast his own bells:

> For Clock Bells.
>
> Take one pound of copper to one Quarter of a pound of Block Tinn. Melt the copper first before you put in the Tinn, cast in a little Salt peter to clear it.

One contemporary thirty-hour Lasseter clock perhaps shows evidence of apprentice work in the form of casting holes in the front plate and the bell.

An early page of the notebook is reproduced in figure 10/137 and the upper part reads as follows:

> Observations in Makeing an Eight day Clock
>
> Pillars two Inches and half long
>
> Barrel laps one Inch, one Qu. and one Eight broad
>
> Barrel Heads are Qu. of an Inch from the fore plate
>
> Take the end chace (shake?) off the Back plate
>
> Lay your Barrels the same distance from the center and both upon a line,
>
> Lay the centre wheel half an Inch above the barrels
>
> Lay the Swing (escape) Wheel one Inch and ¾ above the center for a 12 Inch Plate.
>
> Lay your warning Wheel a little into the frame to make roome for a lon (long) Pallett tail.

After three miscellaneous recipes, the page concludes:

> Proper Divisions for the Hours and Mts. of a 13 Inch Dial plate
>
> Take two thirds for the Hours and one third for the Mts.

25. *Knibb.*

26. Reproduced in A.L. Haggar and L.F. Miller, *Suffolk Clocks & Clockmakers,* 1974, p. 8.

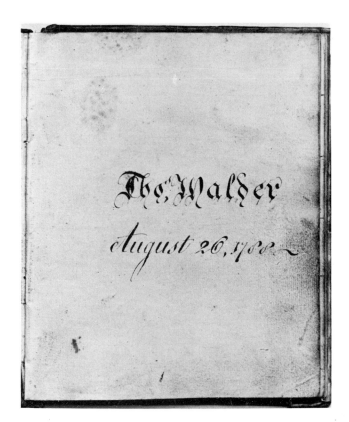

Figure 10/136. Title page of apprentice notebook started by Thomas Walder in Arundel in 1788.

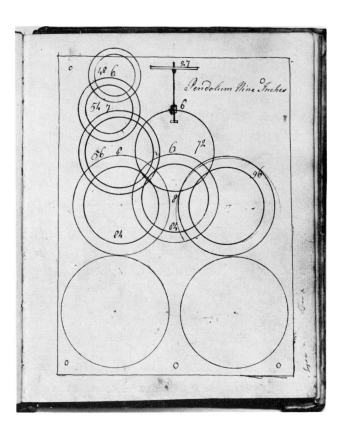

Figure 10/137. An early page of Walder notebook with observations on making an eight-day clock and miscellaneous recipes.

Figure 10/138. Another page of Walder notebook with details of a bracket clock movement.

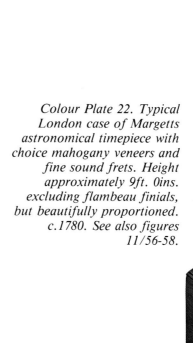

*Colour Plate 21. Regulator
with conventional dial by
Henry Frodsham, Liverpool,
c.1830-35. Very decorative
pulley and stirrup for
mercury jar. Note small
weight which indicates a good
quality movement. Fine
quality late Regency case in
form of an obelisk. Rect-
angular plinth has tapered
chamfers which lead into
tapered trunk and applied
beading continues this line on
the hood. Egyptian influence
combined with classical
ornament. Gadrooning as on
the hood is a common
feature of late Regency
furniture. Choice mahogany
veneers combined with ebony
inlay which is another early
nineteenth century feature.*

*Colour Plate 22. Typical
London case of Margetts
astronomical timepiece with
choice mahogany veneers and
fine sound frets. Height
approximately 9ft. 0ins.
excluding flambeau finials,
but beautifully proportioned.
c.1780. See also figures
11/56-58.*

A later page (figure 10/138) shows that Walder was interested in the design of spring clocks even though he may not have made them. At a later date it is intended to analyse thoroughly this important notebook.

Having looked at the written evidence, it is now appropriate to look at some of the clocks.

Figure 10/139 shows the 10ins. dial of a thirty-hour clock, signed 'Willm Lasseter Arundell', and c.1775-80. The silvered centre has scrolled engraving to complement the rococo spandrels (C. & W. No. 33) and the original hands fit the chapter ring. The movement (figure 10/140) is well made and has a four wheel going train with a brass centre pinion. Striking is by count wheel with hoop wheel locking. The slim pine case has most of its original Georgian green paint but is at present too dilapidated to be photographed.

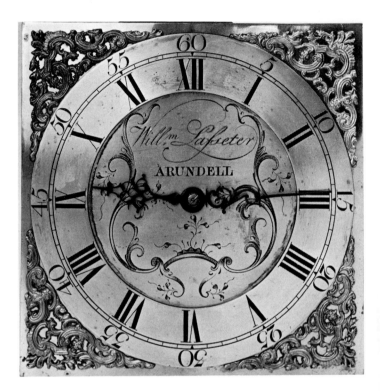

Figure 10/139. 10ins. dial of thirty-hour clock by Lasseter, Arundel, c.1775-80. Engraved centre in keeping with spandrels.

Figure 10/140. Lasseter movement, showing centre pinion. Note casting faults in front plate.

Figure 10/141. 12ins. silvered dial of thirty-hour clock by Lasseter junior, c.1785-90. Well engraved dial with seconds hand, thus showing that movement has a centre pinion.

The next illustration, figure 10/141, shows the 12ins. silvered brass dial of a thirty-hour clock signed 'Wm. Lasseter Junᵣ Arundel'. The probable date is c.1785-90 and indicates that he was then working independently of his father, the first William, who at this time signed some clocks 'Wm. Lasseter Senᵣ' The dial is well engraved, note the seconds ring and the typical serpentine minute hand. The presence of the seconds hand indicates that the movement has a centre pinion which was almost invariably used on thirty-hour. clocks by Arundel makers. The oak case (figure 10/142) is 7ft. 4½ins. high and is nicely proportioned. Note that at this late date the hood still has attached columns.

Figure 10/143 shows the 12ins. silvered dial of an eight-day clock by the Thomas Walder who wrote the notebook. Although this is later (c.1810), note points of similarity with the Lasseter Junior dial already discussed. The main difference is in the type of lettering used for the signatures. The arch is used for strike/silent and pendulum regulation dials. The matching hour and minute hands are of early nineteenth century design in steel and the subsidiary dials all have simple matching hands. The movement (figure 10/144) is well made, with the up and down regulator consisting of a bell crank riding on a snail behind the dial. The strike/silent mechanism has a bell crank which engages with a long pin in the rack when in the silent position.

The case (Colour Plate 20) is well designed and is veneered with finely figured mahogany. The break arch hood has a very simple cresting and the detached columns are reeded and have brass inlay. Altogether a good quality and very pleasing clock by a small town maker, proving that he could make other than cottage clocks when opportunity offered.

Apart from documentary evidence, the unorthodox designs used by some makers are sufficient to indicate that they worked independently rather than buying movements from trade suppliers. Figure 10/145 shows a most unusual thirty-hour movement by Robert Apps of Battle. The striking train has only two wheels and an endless screw or worm on the vertical fly arbor. The hammer is lifted by a pin in the second or locking wheel and a combined locking and warning piece with two projections intercepts a pin in the rim of this wheel. The count wheel has pins instead of slots and ratchet teeth so that it is stepped on by a gathering pallet squared on to the locking wheel arbor. The going train has a centre pinion to avoid shake on the minute hand. The clock has a square painted dial and the date is c.1790. Apps made a number of movements on this plan.

Some clocks show evidence of changes of plan on the part of the maker; perhaps they were apprentice efforts? Figure 10/146 shows such a movement; note the multiple scribing for the going great wheel. It is quite a good quality with centre pinion and long pivot for a seconds hand. With the motion work removed (figure 10/147) the efforts at planting the great wheel are even more obvious. The same

Figure 10/142. Oak case of Lasseter junior clock. Nicely proportioned, note late use of attached columns. Height 7ft. 4½ins.

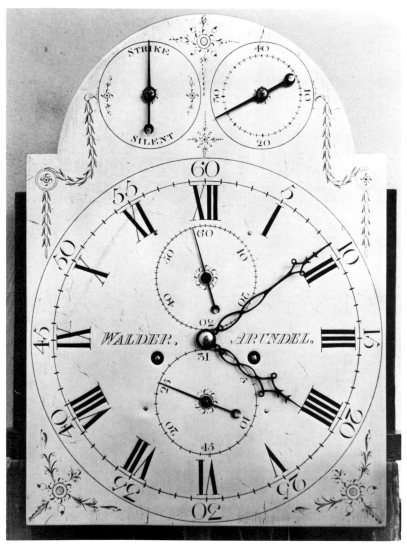

Figure 10/143. 12ins. silvered dial of eight-day clock by Walder, Arundel, c.1810. Note similarity to Lasseter dial in 10/141. Typical matching steel hour and minute hands. Strike/silent and pendulum regulation in arch. Case shown in Colour Plate 20.

Figure 10/144. Walder movement. Note snail for pendulum regulation and strike/silent which operates by holding up rack by means of a bell crank.

Figure 10/145. Highly original design of thirty-hour movement by Apps, Battle, c.1790. Two wheel striking train with endless screw carrying large vertical fly. Pin type count wheel with ratchet teeth stepped on by gathering pallet. Four wheel going train with centre pinion.

problem seems to have arisen in locating the holes for the dial feet also. Unfortunately the dial has disappeared so nothing is known of the maker of this movement.

Having looked at some independent country makers, it is now necessary to consider the activities of a firm which supplied many London clockmakers. Aynsworth and John Thwaites (father and son) carried on an extensive business throughout the second half of the eighteenth century with the firm becoming Thwaites and Reed in 1805 and continuing until after the Second World War. Buggins[27] has produced evidence that they supplied many clocks to the Ellicotts as well as to numerous other makers, including such famous ones as John Arnold, Francis Perigal, James Tregent and the Vulliamys.

A note book with the title page inscribed 'Jno. Thwaites April 17th. 1771'[28] has a number of interesting entries. The following indicates that even a large concern like Thwaites bought in some parts:

Thos. Hampson New Street Prescot; Lancashire
Price of Spring Pinions according to sizes given to be filed up
Hardened; Polished; & the front Centre Pivot finished

No 1 Centre Pinion		8	Leaves	12^s	pr. Dozen
2	....	6	....	7	do
3	....	6	....	8	do
4	Pin Wheel........	8	....	10	do
5	....	8	....	8	do

and so on.

27. G. Buggins, 'John Ellicott — Clockmaker or Clock Designer?', *Antiquarian Horology,* IV (December 1964), p. 275.
28. Now in the library of the Antiquarian Horological Society.

Figure 10/146. Movement where maker apparently had difficulty in planting going great wheel. Quite good quality with centre pinion and long seconds pivot.

Figure 10/147. The same movement with motion work removed, showing scribing more clearly. Same difficulty apparently experienced in locating dial feet.

Although this refers to pinions for bracket clocks they probably bought longcase pinions also. On another page:

Observations on Mr. Ellicotts Regulators

First that they are month ones
Second that all the Wheels take off the
Pinions the Numbers are

Great Wheel	96/12
Second Do	96/12
Centre Do	96/12
third Do	90/12

The Pillers rivet into the frames.

Figure 10/148 shows a drawing entitled: 'Mr. Vulliamys Length for the bars of a Gridiron Pendulum, Each bar measuring from the Centre of the Pin to Do.' This is another interesting indication of the type of work undertaken by Thwaites.

Much more research is necessary before any sound assessment can be made of how the trade was conducted and how dependent makers were on the products of specialist suppliers.

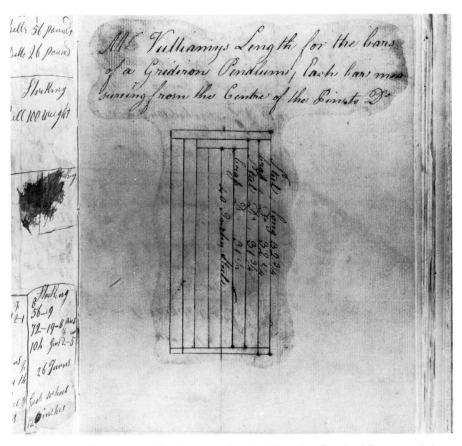

Figure 10/148. Page in Thwaites notebook giving details of gridiron pendulum for Vulliamy.

Chapter 11

ACCURACY ACHIEVED

In Chapter 8 an account was given of the main developments which led to more accurate timekeeping in the period up to c.1750 and directly resulted in the production of the extremely accurate astronomical clocks or regulators of the second half of the eighteenth and the whole of the nineteenth centuries. This is not to say that research and innovation then ceased, many very able horologists applied themselves to the search for even greater accuracy, particularly in temperature compensation and escapements, but few of their inventions offered any real challenge to the simple and reliable devices of Graham and Harrison. A general work such as this is not the place for a detailed examination of the regulator, but the broad development will be considered on the same lines as in the earlier chapter.

MAINTAINING POWER

The main development in the application of maintaining power was the adoption of Harrison's going ratchet to the eventual exclusion of the bolt and shutter by about 1800. The latter has the disadvantage that extra power is applied to the train at the end of winding until the bolt is clear of the wheel, which has a slight effect on the timekeeping. The defect is not present with the going ratchet.

A refinement fitted on some of the best regulators is stopwork which prevents further winding once the barrel is filled with cat gut. It operates on the same principle as the stopwork fitted to fusee clocks and watches, and avoids the risk of straining the gut by overwinding. It also operates and prevents a tangle if the line spreads across the barrel instead of feeding on evenly. A movement fitted with stopwork is shown in figure 11/25.

ESCAPEMENTS

Graham's dead beat escapement was used in nearly all the precision clocks made and as time went on a greater proportion of the high grade examples had jewel inserts to the pallets. This improved their performance by reducing friction and wear. Pivot holes were also jewelled in step with the increased jewelling used in high grade watches.

As only the tips of the escape wheel teeth come into contact with the pallets of a Graham dead beat escapement, it is possible to use pins projecting from the side of the wheel instead of conventional teeth. A regulator with such a dead beat escapement, made by James Prince of Peover in 1815, is shown in figure 11/1. The pins must have adequate strength to prevent flexing and at the same time they must be kept as fine as possible to prevent excessive drop. Even so, the drop is likely to be greater than with a conventional escape wheel.

In figure 11/1 note the sturdy plates with the baluster pillars secured by screws and washers. The pendulum is hung between the plates, near the front and has loops in the rod to clear the various arbors. The crutch also has a loop to clear the escape wheel arbor. The train (figure 11/2) has very light six armed wheels with high numbered wheels and pinions. The very large great wheel is necessitated by the use of a centre pinion of sixteen leaves. The front plate is cut away in a Gothic design and thus requires a bridge for the centre pinion. Harrison maintaining power is provided, but the pendulum is not compensated.

Figure 11/1. Regulator by James Prince of Peover with pin wheel dead beat escapement. Note the sturdy plates and the baluster pillars secured by screws and washers. The crutch and pendulum are in between the plates, towards the front with loops to clear various arbors. Date 1815.

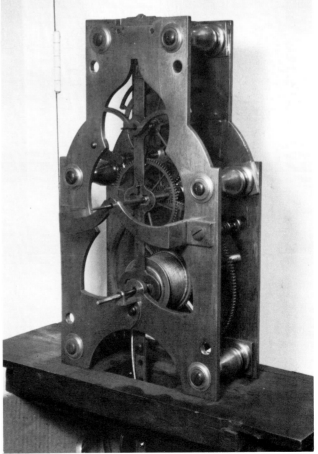

Figure 11/2. Gothic design of cut-away front plate with bridge supporting centre pinion. Very light six armed wheels with high numbered train. Harrison maintaining power but plain iron pendulum rod.

The circular dial (figure 11/3) is signed 'Hemingway, Manchester.' and is partly skeletonised. The rotating hour dial is crossed out into six arms which tend to be confused with the fixed vertical pointer. The centre of the seconds ring is pierced and engraved to form an elaborate Prince of Wales' Feathers design, perhaps in honour of the Prince Regent. Its practical effect is to obscure the hand! The clock is contained in a lancet top case[1] with a glazed lower door. It was made for a Mr. Thornley, saddler and watchmaker, Altrincham.

The grasshopper escapement was given limited revival in a modified form by Benjamin Vulliamy in the late eighteenth century, but never became popular.

A number of inventors produced escapements which gave a constant impulse independent of variations in driving power due to roughness in the train or varying viscosity of the oil. The usual method was to have independently mounted pallets which were raised by the action of the train and in falling under the influence of gravity gave impulse to the pendulum. Thomas Mudge, Edward Massey and others produced escapements of this type[1a] but they had only limited use and were treated with some mistrust as liable to trip. It was only with the perfection of Edward Beckett Denison's gravity escapement, 1852-59,[2] for the Palace of Westminster clock (usually known as 'Big Ben'), that such escapements became completely acceptable.

1. That is, shaped like a pointed arch.

1a. See *Rees*, pp. 187-218 (Escapement).

2. See Vaudrey Mercer, *Edward John Dent and his Successors,* 1977, p. 389; also W.J. Gazeley, *Clock and Watch Escapements,* 1956, p. 93.

Figure 11/3. Dial of Prince regulator, signed 'Hemingway, Manchester'. Rotating twenty-four hour dial driven from cannon pinion. Decoratively pierced dial which tends to obscure seconds hand and hour dial.

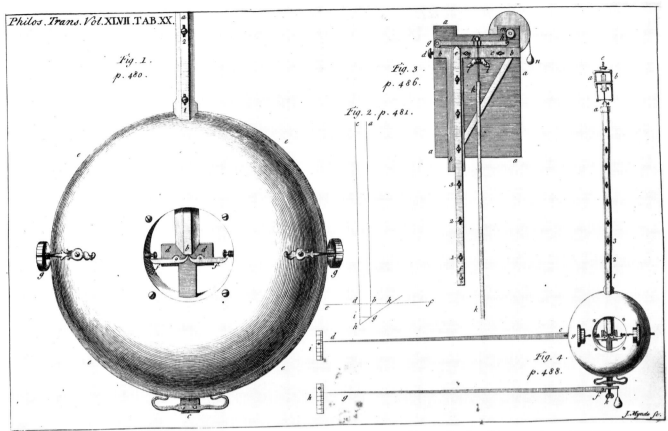

Figure 11/4. Drawing used by John Ellicott when describing his methods of temperature compensation to the Royal Society in 1752. Figs. 1 and 4 show his first method where a bimetallic pendulum rod maintains the bob at a constant height. Fig. 4 also shows his apparatus for adjusting this compensation. Fig. 3 shows his second method where a bimetallic strip operates a rise and fall mechanism to maintain the pendulum at a constant length.

Some regulators were made with variations of this gravity escapement but as they belong to the second half of the nineteenth century they are beyond the scope of the present volume.

In 1820 William Hardy invented an escapement which had four spring mounted pallets[3] and which gave a constant impulse. It was capable of very great accuracy but was liable to failure through metal fatigue of the pallet springs and therefore fell out of use. Modern metallurgical knowledge would have overcome the fatigue problem.

TEMPERATURE COMPENSATION

The compensated pendulums of Graham and Harrison fulfilled all requirements but several interesting alternatives were developed as well as minor changes to the existing designs. With a more general knowledge of the relative rates of expansion of different metals the more expensive but less suitable brass rod was almost abandoned for longcase clocks but continued in spring clocks. Wooden rods were quite often used on better quality house clocks and the middle grade of regulators, and gave good results.

The work of Ellicott

In June 1752 John Ellicott read a paper to the Royal Society, entitled *A Description of Two Methods by which the Irregularities in the Motion of a Clock, arising from the Influence of Heat and Cold upon the Rod of the Pendulum, may be prevented.* The illustration used in Ellicott's publication is reproduced in figure 11/4.

3. See Christopher Wood, 'What's Wrong with Hardy's Escapement?', *Antiquarian Horology*, IX (September 1976), p. 882.

Figure 11/5. Transportable regulator by Ellicott with detachable levelling stand and clamping facilities for pendulum, c.1760. It has Ellicott's first type of compensation, that is an iron rod fixed to the suspension and on which the bob slides. A brass rod is fixed to the top end of the iron rod and held parallel to it by screws in slots. With a rise in temperature the lower end of the brass rod descends and raises the bob with respect to the iron rod to maintain a constant length, see figure 11/6.

Figure 11/6. Mechanism in the bob. The lower end of the brass rod depresses the levers which are pivoted in the iron rod and their outer ends raise the bob. Compensation is varied by screwing the rods in or out by the knurled nuts. The bowed spring takes part of the weight of the bob to obtain a smoother action.

The first method he described is shown in figs. 1 and 4 of that illustration and a clock made with this type of compensation is shown in our figure 11/5. The pendulum rod consists of an iron bar which carries the suspension at its upper end and upon which the bob slides. A brass bar is rigidly fixed at its upper end to the bar and held parallel to the latter by screws passing through slots in the brass and fixed in the iron. With a rise in temperature the greater expansion of the brass causes its lower end to descend with respect to the iron. Two levers are pivoted on the iron rod (see figure 11/6) so this motion of the brass rod depresses the inner ends of the levers and raises the outer ones. The outer ends of the levers bear against two rods in the pendulum bob, so a rise in temperature causes the bob to rise with respect to the iron rod. By suitably proportioning the arms of the levers, the upward movement of the bob can be made to equal exactly the downward movement of the iron rod. This is obtained as accurately as possible by calculation but can be adjusted by varying the effective length of the outer arms of the levers. For this purpose the two rods can be screwed in or out by the knurled nuts and they have projections at their ends so that the levers always bear on those points. The bowed spring below the pendulum bob is adjusted to take part of the weight to secure a smoother action of the compensation levers.

The month movement (figure 11/7) is of high quality with six substantial latched pillars and the dial is also latched. It has a Graham dead beat escapement with steel pallets but the escape wheel is apparently a replacement, the crossing out suggesting a nineteenth century origin. Bolt and shutter maintaining power is fitted (the operating cord is visible in figure 11/5). The temperature compensation mechanism precludes the use of a rating nut under the pendulum bob so a micrometer type of regulator is fitted to the suspension. This has an endless screw or worm and wheel operated from a hand in the dial arch through a wheel and pinion so' that moving the hand to a higher number will increase the rate.

The earlier precision clocks were often quite complicated and had dials similar to ordinary domestic clocks. By about 1750, however, it was realised that for the best possible performance a movement should have no unnecessary mechanism which could cause variations in the power reaching the escapement and therefore affect its rate. This movement is an early example of this simplification. It is a plain timepiece, no calendar or equation work and the distinctive dial layout (figure 11/5) serves the same purpose. The hours are engraved on a toothed disc which engages direct with the cannon pinion, thus eliminating unnecessary friction. Although the shape of the dial plate is highly individual, the layout and the plain silvered finish became the standard. It first appeared on regulators by Graham in the late 1740s.

The mahogany case (figure 11/5) has a detachable folding stand with adjustable feet for levelling and has fittings inside the trunk on the right for clamping the pendulum after it has been removed from the movement. These two features prove that the clock was intended to be transportable, presumably for use in connection with some form of astronomical observations. There were great preparations for the transits of Venus in 1761 and 1769 and, as Howse indicates, the Royal Society bought a timepiece for this purpose from Ellicott for £35 8s.[4] From this evidence it is very likely that the regulator just described, or the next one to be considered, is the one bought by the Royal Society.

Ellicott's communication to the Royal Society describes and shows two methods of temperature compensation (figure 11/4), and the clock shown in figure 11/8 is provided with the second type. It is very similar to the clock already described and the mahogany case has similar arrangements for clamping the pendulum. There is no sign of it having had an adjustable stand and the plinth shown in the photograph is modern. It was, no doubt, screwed to a stout post when set up (see screwholes in back board), this being the method which Howse quotes from a contemporary account. Both cases are slightly tapered, probably to improve stability.

4. D. Howse, 'The Admiral's Clock', *Antiquarian Horology,* X (Spring 1977), p. 164.

Figure 11/7. Month movement of Ellicott regulator. Six latched pillars and latched dial feet. Bolt and shutter maintaining power. Dead beat escapement with replaced escape wheel. Micrometer adjustment to suspension with endless screw operated from hand in dial arch via wheel and pinion. Note typical regulator dial layout with hours engraved on wheel which engages with cannon pinion.

The movement (figure 11/9) is similar to the previous one but is pinned instead of being latched, probably to reduce cost. The escape wheel appears to be original and the bolt and shutter mechanism is well shown in the photograph. The dials of both clocks are similarly signed 'Ellicott London', which would accord with a date of c.1760.

A general view of the compensation system is shown in figure 11/10 and a close up view in figure 11/11. It depends on a bimetallic strip as used on Ellicott's compensation pendulum. A flat iron bar is rigidly attached to the horizontal bar across the top of the movement. A flat brass bar is firmly attached to the bottom of the iron bar and held parallel to it by screws through slots in the brass in the same manner as in the compensating pendulum. The upper end of the brass bar supports a lever which is pivoted at its left hand end and which supports the pendulum suspension. The suspension passes through a slot in the back cock in the usual way so that only the portion of the suspension below the cock is effective.

With a rise in temperature the iron pendulum rod expands at the same rate as the iron bar of the compensation. The brass bar expands more than the iron one so the top end of the brass bar rises and lifts the lever, thus shortening the pendulum suspension slightly. If the mechanism is correctly adjusted the pendulum will remain a constant length. This adjustment is obtained by varying the point at which the brass bar operates on the lever and thus varying the amount of movement of the suspension spring for a given temperature change. The horizontal bar supporting the compensation bars is held by two screws in slots and can be moved by means of the knurled headed screw on the left.

To prevent any tendency for the compensation bars to buckle or to move in jerks, most of the weight of the pendulum is taken by a small counterweight. This is shown in figure 11/12 which is an explanatory drawing produced by the National Maritime Museum. The right hand end of the lever is attached to a small chain which is coiled round a small diameter pulley. A larger pulley on the same arbor has a cord attached which carries the counterweight. Unfortunately the cord is shown coiled the wrong way round its pulley in figures 11/10 and 11, so that it would increase the pressure on the brass bar. The counterweight is on the left and the pull cord for the maintaining power is on the right in figure 11/8.

Ellicott, in his communication to the Royal Society, expressed a preference for the first method, that is the compensation on the pendulum. This was apparently because he had designed a contrivance to enable him to correct the compensation directly (figure 11/4), whereas the second type could be corrected only by trial and error. His inventions were criticised at the time, and have been since, as liable to move in jerks, which is apparently the case.

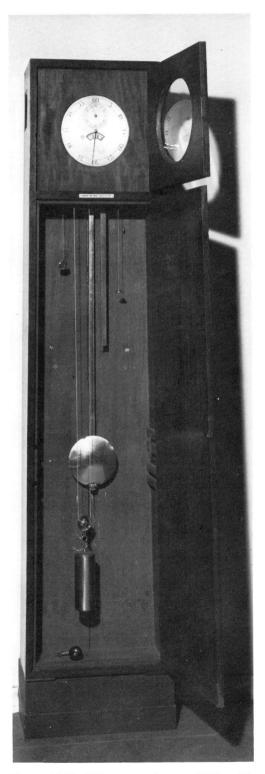

Figure 11/8. Ellicott regulator c.1760, with his second type of compensation. Note pendulum clamps, similar to those on previous clock. No sign of it having had an adjustable stand, and screw holes in back indicate that it was screwed to a post. Present plinth is modern.

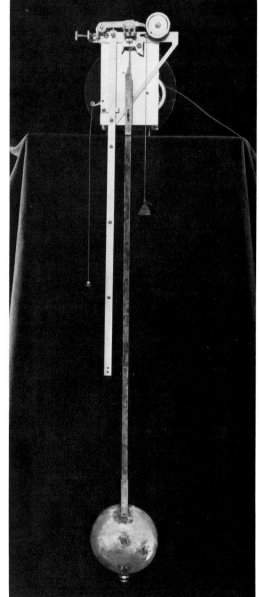

Figure 11/9. Movement of second regulator, similar to that in 11/7 except pinned not latched. Escape wheel apparently original. Note bolt and shutter.

Figure 11/10. Temperature compensation. Bimetallic strip to left of pendulum has brass rod fixed at bottom but free to move vertically at top. With rise in temperature brass rod rises and raises pivoted lever carrying suspension.

Figure 11/11. Details of compensation system. The brass strip is in front of the iron one and held parallel to it by screws in slots. The upper end of the brass rod bears against the lever which is pivoted on the left and carries the suspension. With a rise in temperature the suspension is raised and its length below the back cock reduced to compensate for the expansion of the iron pendulum rod. The amount of compensation is varied by means of the knurled screw on the left which moves the horizontal bar carrying the compensation bars, thus changing the point at which the brass bar operates on the lever. To ensure smooth operation, a small weight hung from the pulley on the right is arranged to take most of the weight of the pendulum. This is shown in 11/12. Unfortunately in this photograph, and in 11/10, the cord is coiled the wrong way round the pulley, so it would increase the pressure.

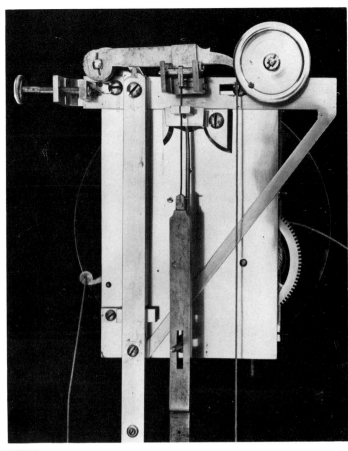

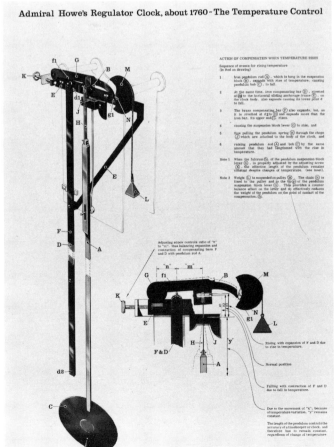

Admiral Howe's Regulator Clock, about 1760 - The Temperature Control

Figure 11/12. Explanatory drawing of the operation of the compensation system, produced by the National Maritime Museum. Compare with 11/10 and 11, noting particularly the action of the counterweight.

Figure 11/13. Principle of the rhomboid pendulum. The unshaded rods are of iron or steel and the shaded one of brass. With a rise in temperature the greater expansion of the brass diagonal causes the rhombus to become broader and so reduces the lengthening of the pendulum. As drawn it provides only partial compensation.

Figure 11/14. Multiple rhomboid pendulum providing correct compensation without excessive breadth. As in 11/13 the diagonals are of brass.

The rhomboid pendulum

Robert Hooke (died 1703) is credited with the invention of the rhomboid pendulum,[5] the principle of which is shown in figure 11/13. The greater coefficient of expansion of the brass than that of the steel causes the rhombus to become broader, whilst its vertical measurement remains constant. Unfortunately to obtain perfect compensation the pendulum needs to be broader than it is long, which precludes its use in a domestic clock! However, by proportioning the pendulum as in figure 11/13 a partial compensation is achieved and it can be accommodated in a really broad longcase. Joseph Finney of Liverpool made several of this pattern and one of c.1765-70 is illustrated in figure 10/43. Williamson of Ulverston in north west Lancashire is credited with the invention around 1750 of a pendulum with five rhombi (figure 11/14) which made it of more manageable proportions and Edward Troughton, apparently independently, designed a pendulum with seven rhombi some fifty years later.[5] A few Lancashire makers, other than those mentioned, also used the rhomboid pendulum.

Partial compensation

Apart from using properly compensated pendulums, some makers were content to apply partial compensation to their good quality domestic clocks. This was probably perfectly adequate for all except the most fastidious owners. The Finney clocks with their simple rhombic pendulums were an example of this approach and an entirely different idea will now be described.

Figure 11/15 shows the lower part of the pendulum of a complicated clock of the third quarter of the eighteenth century. The dial is signed on the chapter ring 'Joshua Squire', an

5. See *Rees,* p. 240.

apparently unrecorded maker of northern, probably Yorkshire, origin. The pendulum rod is a flat iron strip and the smaller, lower, pendulum bob is fitted to this strip and is regulated by a rating nut in the usual way. The light coloured strip between the two bobs is of brass and is fixed to the iron strip at its lower end. The upper end of the brass strip is free to move and has the large bob attached to it. With a rise in temperature the greater expansion of the brass causes the upper, heavier, pendulum bob to rise with respect to the rod, so effecting partial compensation.

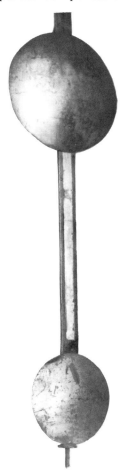

The 12ins. arched dial (figure 10/16) has complicated calendar indications; in the arch is a gilt sun which should rise on the left and, after traversing the blue sky, sink on the right. There is a shutter on the left to vary the time of sunrise according to the time of the year. The ringings to the winding holes are applied turnings (figure 11/19), as were used by Thomas Ogden of Halifax, and are one of the features suggesting a Yorkshire origin. The dial has urn pattern spandrels (C. & W. No. 26) and the movement is designed for a centre seconds hand which is missing.

Figure 11/15. Partially compensated pendulum of north country clock by Joshua Squire, c.1770. Flat steel rod which supports smaller lower bob via rating nut. Central brass strip is fixed at lower end, but upper end is free to move and supports large bob. With a rise in temperature, greater expansion of brass causes upper bob to rise with respect to the rod, so giving partial compensation.

Figure 11/16. Complicated dial of Squire clock. Domed blue sky in arch and gilt sun which should rise on left and set on right. Other indications are shown in 11/17-22. There should be a centre seconds hand.

In the upper part of the dial centre is a lunar dial (figure 11/17) which is a variation of the 'Halifax' type. The top left opening shows the age of the moon, 14½ days, which is almost full moon and the top right opening shows high tide. High tide at 6 o'clock at new moon and full moon is approximately correct for the port of Bridlington so the clock was probably made in and for that area. Figure 11/18 shows the shaded or obscured moon used to indicate new moon, the dial is actually shown on day 27. In the lower part of the dial centre (figure 11/19) is a day of the week indicator (note 'Tuseday'), the appropriate deity and planetary sign being shown in the upper opening.

Openings near III, VI and IX show different zones of a large annular calendar dial with internal teeth which should rotate once per year; this has unfortunately been fixed and the operating mechanism removed. It is actually fixed about ⅛in. to the right of its proper position so some of the indications are a little out of place.

Figure 11/20 shows the day of the month opening at III with the days numbered every five. Due to the incorrect positioning of the calendar dial the divisions appear outside the edge of the dial plate. The outer inverted numerals are for the times of sunrise and appear in the aperture at IX. Portions of the calendar ring projecting beyond the dial plate are normally hidden by the masking frame in the hood of the case. The opening below VI (figure 11/21) gives the months with their numbers of days and above this the position of the sun in the zodiac, that is in its passage through the heavens, with the appropriate zodiacal signs, that for Cancer appearing just above, and to the right of, June. The time of sunrise, 3.35, is shown in the opening to the left of IX (figure 11/22). The sunrise time is approximately ten minutes earlier than for the same date (12th June) at London and thus confirms the suggested area of origin.

Figure 11/23 shows the movement which, as can be seen by the low position of the escapement, is designed for centre seconds. Note the very large calendar ring with internal teeth and the domed section behind the arch to give a realistic sky.

The case (figure 11/24) is of high quality and is veneered with very finely figured mahogany. The plinth has a raised panel, chamfered corners and ogee feet. The trunk has reeded quarter columns and applied fretwork above the door. The hood has a swan neck or

Figure 11/17. Lunar dial based on the 'Halifax' type. It is showing almost full moon, with its age, 14½ days on the left and high tide at 6 o'clock on the right. The tidal times are suitable for the port of Bridlington which suggests an area of origin for the clock.

Figure 11/18. The lunar dial shown at day 27. Note the obscured moon. The central pivot for the seconds hand is visible just above the pin holding the minute hand.

Figure 11/19. Day of week indicator, note spelling of 'Tuseday'. The upper opening shows the deity and planetary sign for the day. Note the applied turnings to the winding holes, which were used by Ogden of Halifax and therefore suggest a Yorkshire origin for the clock.

Figure 11/20. Day of month markings on large annual calendar ring which has been fixed about ⅛in. to the right of its correct position. The sunrise times to the right of the dial plate are normally covered by the dial masking.

Figure 11/21. Opening showing month with its number of days and above it the zodiac with each sign divided into thirty degrees. The sign for Cancer is above and just to the right of June.

Figure 11/22. The indicator for sunrise reading 3.35 for 12th June. This is approximately ten minutes earlier than for London and is about right for the latitude of the suggested area of origin.

Figure 11/23. Movement of the Squire clock showing low position of escapement for centre seconds. Note very large annual calendar ring and domed section behind arch to give realistic sky.

curly horn pediment with carved paterae and open fretwork below. The finial, probably of mahogany, is missing. The hood door has a moulded frame and the detached reeded columns have turned wooden capitals and bases. A fine quality case with many northern features and containing an equally fine clock. This is yet another example of the interesting and important clocks by almost unknown makers which exist in some numbers and which often do not receive the attention they deserve.

THE CONVENTIONAL REGULATOR

Apart from the complicated precision clocks described in Chapter 8, Graham, towards the end of his career, made simpler precision clocks which closely resembled the conventional regulator. Even so he had apparently not fully realised the importance of avoiding any non-essential mechanism which could cause extra friction, as he included a common calendar and conventional motion work even though the hours were indicated by a rotating disc behind an opening in the dial plate.[6] After Graham's death in 1751 several of his journeymen, including John Shelton and Thomas Mudge, produced similar regulators and a somewhat altered example by Mudge is shown in figure 11/25.

The 10ins. dial is the normal regulator type except for the provision of a calendar. The radial markings inside the seconds ring are to facilitate reading seconds at a distance and are known as observatory marks. Note that the dial is fixed to the dial feet by small steel screws with polished heads. This became the normal method for regulators and was also used for silvered dials on good quality domestic clocks from about 1800. The substantial movement had six latched pillars but the bottom two are now pinned to allow the repositioning of the front movement fixing brackets to suit a cast iron bracket which has replaced the original seat board. The present nine rod gridiron pendulum hangs from the iron bracket but the pendulum was originally supported on the back cock. Other changes include the provision of Harrison type maintaining power although the shutter mechanism of the original bolt and shutter has been left in position. The vertical arbor visible on the left of the movement is part of the stopwork and carries an arm which is pushed across by the last turn of gut to go on to the barrel. A detent on the arbor intersects the barrel to prevent further winding. The month movement has end plates to the pivots to reduce friction and a dead beat escapement. The signature 'Tho. Mudge London' appears on the back plate as well as on the dial.

The case (figure 11/26) has an oak carcase which was probably exposed originally but is now veneered with walnut. The glazed trunk door and the shaped skirting are other probably nineteenth century, 'improvements' and an additional section appears to have been added immediately below the hood door. The height is 5ft. 10½ins. and the date c.1751-55.

The next stage in the development of the regulator was the elimination of practically all the motion work. This was accomplished

Figure 11/24. Case of Squire clock veneered with fine mahogany. Plinth has raised panel, canted corners and ogee feet. Reeded columns to trunk and hood with turned wooden capitals and bases. Blind frets above trunk door and open frets in frieze. Moulded hood door frame. Carved paterae to swan neck pediment and probably had carved or turned wooden finial.

6. One of these early regulators is shown in *Antiquarian Horology*, VI, pp. 394-395 and shows a close resemblance to the Mudge in figures 11/25, 26.

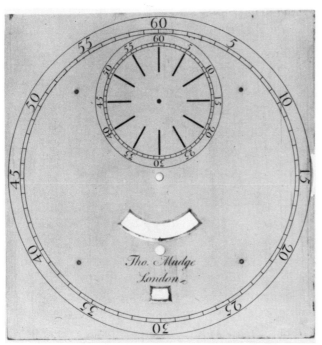

Figure 11/25. Regulator by Thomas Mudge, c.1751-55. At top the 10ins. dial, normal regulator type except for calendar. Radial lines every five seconds, known as observatory marks, are to facilitate reading at a distance. Dial fixed to dial feet by steel screws. Lower illustration shows substantial month movement originally with six latched pillars. Lowest ones now pinned to allow for repositioning of movement fixing brackets. Vertical arbor of stopwork is visible on left.

Figure 11/26. Case of Mudge regulator. Oak carcase now veneered with walnut. Glazed trunk door, shaped skirting and additional section below hood door are other, probably nineteenth century, improvements. Height 5ft. 10½ins.

either by providing the hour disc with teeth which engaged with a pinion on the centre arbor or by providing a pair of extra wheels between the plates, one attached to the great wheel and the other on an arbor carrying the hour disc or hand. This absence of conventional motion work is evident in the dial layout as the hour slot or hour hand will not be concentric with the minute hand.

The classic break arch case used by Mudge, Dutton, Holmes and others was occasionally used for examples with the standard type of 'regulator' dial (figure 11/27). The effect is likely to be unbalanced unless the arch is used for a pendulum regulation dial or a flamboyant signature. The example shown has been unbalanced by the loss of a name plate which was secured by the two holes near the base of the arch.

Regulators became an important part of the furnishings of retail 'watchmaker and jeweller' shops in the nineteenth and early twentieth centuries and were usually inscribed with the names of the proprietors. These changed from time to time so the name on the dial was changed to suit and may therefore bear no relationship to that of the maker or the date of manufacture. This could account for the removal of the name plate from the example in figure 11/27.

This is a rather difficult clock to date. The breadth of the mahogany case, the cut-away lower skirting and the brass inlay to the reeded corners of the hood suggest a possibly provincial, rather late version of this style. The five minute numerals from 20 to 40 face outwards and are probably a provincial feature of c.1790. The elaborately shaped seconds and hour hands also support a date of around 1800, so the probable date for the whole is c.1790-1800.

Figure 11/28 shows the 12ins. dial of a fine regulator which is signed 'Arnold London No. 34'. The dial is fixed by four steel screws with polished heads which fit into stout dial feet pinned to the front plate (figure 11/29). The heavy radial lines at five second intervals (figure 11/28) are to facilitate reading seconds from a distance under observatory conditions and are probably an addition. Note the extremely slender seconds and minute hands, designed to have the minimum effect on the movement. A small arrow above the winding square indicates the anti-clockwise winding for the month movement.

The movement (figure 11/29) is very heavily built with six pinned pillars and is secured to the seat board with substantial angle brackets. Harrison maintaining power is fitted, and the pallets and the pivot holes for the escape pinion and pallet arbor are jewelled.

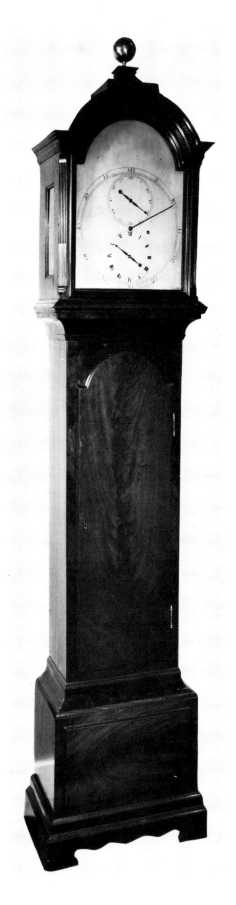

Figure 11/27. Regulator with dial now unbalanced by loss of name plate from arch. Position of hour hand shows that it has minimal motion work, with hour wheel engaging direct with cannon pinion. Note that minute numerals from 20 to 40 face outwards. Elaborately shaped hour and seconds hands. Good quality mahogany case based on classic break arch type used by leading makers. Probably provincial and c.1790-1800.

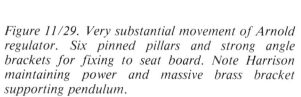

Figure 11/28. 12ins. dial of fine month regulator by Arnold, No. 34. Note extremely fine hands and usual rotating hour disc, also arrow to indicate anti-clockwise winding.

Figure 11/29. Very substantial movement of Arnold regulator. Six pinned pillars and strong angle brackets for fixing to seat board. Note Harrison maintaining power and massive brass bracket supporting pendulum.

The pendulum is supported by a massive brass bracket screwed to the back board of the case, which is the normal method of hanging a really heavy pendulum so that there will be no tendency to rock the support. The gridiron pendulum (figure 11/30) has three steel and two zinc rods, an early use of zinc in a compensation pendulum.[7] As the coefficient of expansion of zinc is a little over twice that of iron, this arrangement provides complete compensation. The rating nut is graduated and there is a scale fixed to the back board for levelling and indicating the arc of vibration in degrees. Note the large finely spoked pulley to reduce friction and variations in driving power and the small weight for a month movement, a sign of quality.

The case (figure 11/31) is solidly constructed of mahogany and is of a simple dignified design which became standard for regulators. The height is 6ft. 4ins. and the waist measures 14⅛ins. To obtain good results from a regulator it should be rigidly fixed to a wall, otherwise the heavy pendulum will cause rocking of the case and probably swinging of the weight when it is at the right height to form a seconds pendulum.

7. Smeaton had recommended and Hindley had used zinc for compensation by c.1755. See R.J. Law, 'Henry Hindley of York', *Antiquarian Horology,* VII (September 1972), p. 682.

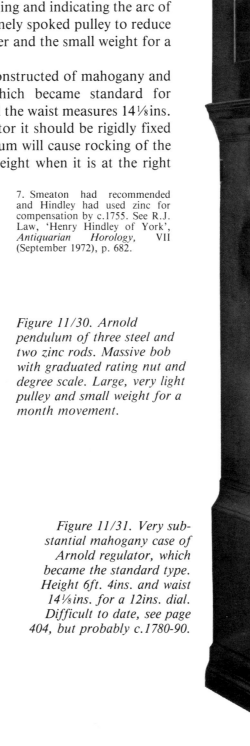

Figure 11/30. Arnold pendulum of three steel and two zinc rods. Massive bob with graduated rating nut and degree scale. Large, very light pulley and small weight for a month movement.

Figure 11/31. Very substantial mahogany case of Arnold regulator, which became the standard type. Height 6ft. 4ins. and waist 14⅛ins. for a 12ins. dial. Difficult to date, see page 404, but probably c.1780-90.

As the author was in some doubt about the date of this regulator he consulted Vaudrey Mercer, author of the standard work on the Arnolds.[8] He suggested that the signature 'Arnold' could mean that it was made by John Arnold and Son (1787-99) as this signature was used on some of their watch dials. Arnold supported the pendulum bobs of his earlier regulators at their centres so that temperature changes affected only the rods. No. 34 does not have this feature, which suggests a later date, unless the pendulum has been modified. On the other hand the low number could mean a date c.1780 and No. 34 does closely resemble No. 101 which is presumably pre-1787 as it is signed 'John Arnold'.

Regulators were used by three distinct groups, astronomers, watch and chronometer

makers who needed to be able to check their work, and well-to-do householders who used them to set their watches and domestic clocks. No doubt many of these latter gentlemen were satisfied with the normal type, such as in figure 11/31, but there are some regulators enclosed in elegant cases which were obviously specially designed to harmonise with the rich furnishings of a wealthy home. Such a clock is shown in figure 11/32. The case is veneered with beautifully grained mahogany with a shell inlay above the dial and the design was probably influenced by one in Thomas Sheraton's *Cabinet Maker and Upholsterer's Drawing Book,* published in 1793, see figure 10/90. The conventional regulator dial is inscribed 'Cragg Southampton', probably the John Cragg whom Baillie records as c.1790, and the whole clock is probably c.1795-1800.

Figure 11/33 shows the 10ins. dial of another regulator which was presumably intended for domestic use as it has concentric hour, minute and seconds hands. The maker, Penton, London, is probably the Charles Penton recorded as 1760-78 (Britten and Baillie), but the date of this example is probably nearer to 1800. The month movement has six pillars and Harrison maintaining power. The pendulum (figure 11/34) is a variation of the gridiron, being essentially a five rod type as in figure 11/30, but the two zinc rods are replaced by a tube. Several makers were experimenting with concentric tube pendulums around 1800-10 and the present example is probably an early development of that idea.

The mahogany case (figure 11/35) is veneered with finely figured wood and its elegance results from the shaping of the hood cornice and the top of the trunk door to match the serpentine or ogee shaped dial arch. It is unusually small, 5ft. 11½ins. high and with an 11½ins. waist.

8. R.V. Mercer, *John Arnold & Son Chronometer Makers 1762-1843,* 1972.

Figure 11/32. Conventional regulator by Cragg, Southampton in very elegant mahogany veneered case probably based on a Sheraton design. Obviously designed to harmonise with the furnishings of a wealthy home. Probably c.1795-1800.

Figure 11/33. 10ins. dial of regulator, by Penton. Concentric hands indicate that it was probably for domestic use. Month movement with six pillars and Harrison maintaining power.

Figure 11/34. Penton pendulum, based on gridiron of 11/30 but with the zinc rods replaced by a tube. An early example of a concentric tube pendulum. Note channel in door to accommodate weight.

Figure 11/35. Small, elegant case of Penton regulator. Finely figured veneers and ogee shaping of dial reflected in cornice and in top of hood and trunk doors. Height 5ft. 11½ins. and 11½ins. waist for 10ins. dial.

Figure 11/36 shows a domestic regulator which is also of small proportions. The silvered dial is signed 'Robert Green Edinburgh' and shows twice I-XII hours, and twice sixty minutes numbered every five, with the seconds numbered every ten. The movement has Harrison maintaining power, a dead beat escapement and a wood rod pendulum. Green was a good maker and this example should be dated c.1810.

A conventional regulator but with a case fit to grace any mansion is shown in Colour Plate 21. The dial is signed 'Henry Frodsham Liverpool', a maker who was apprenticed in 1823 and, judging by the case, this example dates from 1830-35. The dial has the usual regulator layout but the hours are now shown on a sub-dial instead of having a rotating disc or ring behind an opening as on earlier regulators. Another nineteenth century development was the use of a glazed panel in the trunk door to display the compensated pendulum and, incidentally, the beautifully finished pulley and weight. An elegantly shaped stirrup supports the mercury jar of the pendulum. The case is an excellent specimen of Regency design and cabinet work and is conceived in the form of an obelisk. The plinth is rectangular but has tapering chamfers which lead in to the tapered trunk section. The trunk has a half round beading and this continues the taper effect in the hood section which is rectangular. This Egyptian influence is combined with classical ornament, the antefixes (corner ornaments) being a popular feature of Sheraton designs.[9] Gadrooning became common in the later Regency period. The case is veneered with very choice mahogany, including the now important back board. The use of ebony inlay is another characteristic of early nineteenth century furniture.

It is interesting to compare this Frodsham regulator with an almost identical one shown in Smith's *Dictionary*[10] which has the dial signed 'Jones Gray & Co. Liverpool' and the movement signed 'James Condliff Liverpool'. This has a little box inlay instead of ebony and has a third skirting which could be an addition. It also has a small wooden knob finial in place of the brass ball finial of Colour Plate 21. In both cases the dial glass is held in a hinged brass bezel as used on bracket and wall clocks of the period. It is obvious that both cases came from the same workshop. It may well be that both movements also came from the same clockmaker, James Condliff, but the author has not been able to check this.

There is no difficulty in dating the domestic regulator shown in figure 11/37, where the 12½ins. diameter dial is engraved 'J.R. Arnold. A.D. MDCCCXXXIV'. Arnold was in partnership with Dent 1830-1840, so with this signature the clock must have been made for personal or family use, not for sale. Vaudrey Mercer has made the very reasonable

9. Thomas Sheraton, *Cabinet-maker, Upholsterer and General Artists' Encyclopaedia,* 1804-6.
10. Alan Smith (ed.), *The Country Life International Dictionary of Clocks,* 1979, p. 119.

Figure 11/36. Small domestic regulator with silvered dial by Robert Green, Edinburgh. Shows twice I-XII hours, and twice sixty minutes numbered every five. Harrison maintaining power, dead beat escapement and wood rod pendulum. Probably c.1810.

Figure 11/37. 12½ins. dial of domestic regulator by J.R. Arnold, 1834. As he was in partnership with Dent at this time, the clock must have been made for personal or family use, not for sale. The dial, without minute numbering, is typical of its date and the very unusual hands appear to be original.

Figure 11/38. Sturdy eight-day movement of Arnold regulator. Harrison maintaining power, jewelled dead beat pallets and beat setting adjustment at top of crutch. Mercury compensated pendulum hung from back cock.

Figure 11/39. Typical late Regency mahogany case of Arnold regulator with break arch hood following shape of dial and reeded canted corners with brass inlay to both hood and trunk. Central brass finial is missing. Height 6ft. 9½ins. and waist 13½ins. for 12½ins. dial.

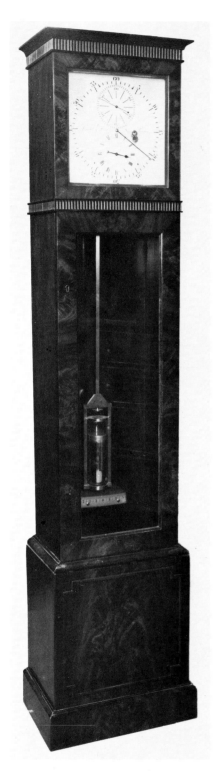

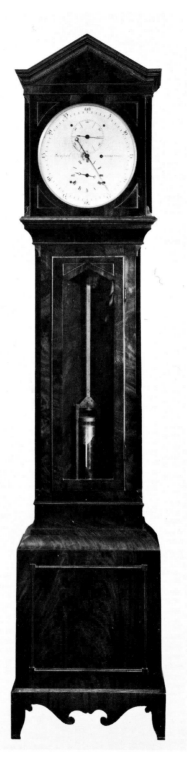

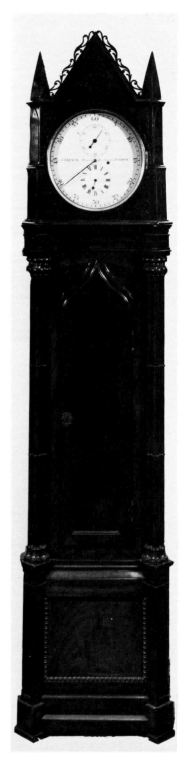

Figure 11/40. Fine quality regulator by Arnold and Dent, 1830-40. Winding hole in glass with brass shutter to permit winding without opening hood door. Severely designed mahogany case relieved by applied beading on plinth and fluting on hood.

Figure 11/41. Elegant mahogany cased 'gentleman's regulator' by Benford, c.1835. Note balanced minute hand. Broken architectural pediment to case is reflected in shape of trunk door opening.

Figure 11/42. Regulator by French in late Regency Gothic case, c.1835. Fine quality mahogany case with canted pilasters to plinth surmounted by cluster columns on trunk. Trunk door with ogee shaped top. Applied Gothic tracery to hood section.

suggestion that it could have been made to commemorate Arnold's silver wedding. The dial, without minute numbering, is typical of the date and the very unusual hands appear to be original. The sturdy eight-day movement (figure 11/38) has Harrison maintaining power, jewelled dead beat pallets and beat setting adjustment at the top of the crutch. It has a mercury compensated pendulum hung from the back cock.

The mahogany case (figure 11/39) is a typical late Regency design with break arch hood following the shape of the dial and reeded canted corners with brass inlay to both trunk and hood. The central brass finial is missing from its plinth. The height without finial is 6ft. 9½ins. and the waist measures 13½ins.

A fine regulator with the dial signed 'Arnold & Dent Strand London' is shown in figure 11/40 and must date from 1830-40. Considerable importance was attached to the exclusion of dust from regulators and this one is designed to be wound without opening the door. A hole in the glass is provided with a brass cover which may be turned aside for the insertion of the cranked key. The severely designed case is relieved by the applied beading on the plinth panel and the fluted decoration of the hood section.

Figure 11/41 shows a regulator of c.1835 with the silvered dial signed 'Benford Clerkenwell', presumably the John Benford who is recorded 1832-38.[11] Note the balanced minute hand; some were balanced by means of a weighted arm attached to the minute hand pipe behind the dial. The case has a broken architectural pediment which is reflected in the shape of the trunk door opening. The whole case is elegantly designed and well finished and was probably made as a 'gentleman's regulator'. The lightly decorated hands also probably indicate a domestic setting.

A late Regency Gothic case of c.1835 is shown in figure 11/42. The dial of this regulator is signed 'J. French Royal Exchange London', which will be the Santiago James Moore French recorded as being in Sweetings or Swithins Alley 1808-38 and at 18 Cornhill 1839-42. French's products are usually signed 'Royal Exchange' and Sweetings Alley was on the east side of the Exchange which is situated in Cornhill, hence the address used on the dial. The fine quality mahogany case has canted pilasters to the plinth with cluster columns to the trunk and the glazed trunk door has an ogee shaped top. The upper part of the case has applied Gothic tracery. The height is 7ft. 2ins.

Figure 11/43 shows the final form of the regulator case where there is no separate hood section and the long glazed door gives access to both the dial and the pendulum. The mahogany carcase, including the back board, is veneered with finely figured mahogany and there is typical Victorian carving just below the dial. The quality of the movement is shown by the mercury com-

11. Britten, *Old Clocks*, 3rd edition.

Figure 11/43. Final form of regulator case, c.1860-70, without separate hood section and with one door giving access to both dial and pendulum. Well figured mahogany veneers and typical Victorian carving. Quality of movement shown by mercury compensated pendulum with finely divided degree scale and by smallness of weight. Dial inscribed 'Wm. Gibson Aspatria', but he probably bought it as his shop clock.

pensated pendulum with its finely divided degree scale and the smallness of the weight. The silvered dial is signed 'Wm. Gibson. Aspatria' (Cumberland). Loomes' *Clockmakers* lists Gibson as being in business in 1873 and the probable date of this example is c.1860-70. Little clockmaking was being done by small town makers at such a late date so Gibson probably bought the regulator as his shop clock.

COMPLICATED PRECISION CLOCKS

A group of precision equation timepieces by Graham was described in detail in Chapter 8 and a few similar clocks, apparently owing their inspiration to Graham's work, were made later in the eighteenth century.

Figure 11/44 shows the 10¼ins. dial of a fine month equation timepiece signed 'Wm. Dutton London' of c.1775 which is in the Fitzwilliam Museum. This clock should be compared with the Graham shown in figures 8/37-44. The annual calendar ring has been simplified by the omission of the equation of time and the sun's declination, but the times of sunrise are still shown. Note the pictorial representation of the signs of the zodiac. There is a separate inner ring which indicates the age of the moon in days and quarters of days and the phases are shown by a rotating globe, half silvered and half painted dark blue. In this photo-

Figure 11/44. 10¼ins. dial of a fine month equation timepiece by Wm. Dutton, c.1775, which should be compared with the Graham clock in 8/37-44. Annual calendar ring simplified by omission of equation of time and sun's declination, but times of sunrise still shown. Note pictorial signs of zodiac. Separate inner ring indicates age of moon and phases are shown by rotating globe, half silvered and half dark blue. In this photograph phase and age of moon do not agree. Gilt hand with sun indicates solar time direct. Chapter disc, calendar and age of moon rings are of high grade fired enamel and dial plate is gilt. Repoussé or stamped silver spandrels, compare lower pair with those in 8/37.

graph the phases do not agree with the age of the moon as shown on the rotating ring. The gilt hand with the sun indicates solar time direct as with the Graham examples.

The chapter disc, calendar and age of moon rings are of high grade fired enamel and the dial plate is gilt. The spandrels are of repoussé or stamped silver fixed with small screws at the front. The lower pair should be compared with those on the Graham dial (figure 8/37). These spandrels have now been removed to show the attractive original engraving (figure 11/45). They were probably a nineteenth century 'improvement'.

The month movement (figure 11/46) has four latched pillars, but the dial feet are pinned. The inverted train has a dead beat escapement (figure 11/47) but with Harrison maintaining power and the barrel on the right (figure 11/46). End plates are fitted to the pivot holes of the train and motion work but not to the equation work. The drive to the lunar work consists of an endless screw or worm on the hour wheel pipe which drives a vertical arbor mounted on the back of the dial. A pinion on the upper end of the arbor drives the moon arbor through a wheel and friction spring and the moon arbor carries a bevel wheel which meshes with a similar one at the centre of the age of the moon ring. This gearing is just visible in figures 11/46 and 49.

The drive to the calendar consists of a wheel between the plates driven by the first pinion

Figure 11/45. Dutton dial with spandrels removed to show attractive original engraving. Silver spandrels were probably a nineteenth century 'improvement'.

Figure 11/46. Month movement with four latched pillars but with pinned dial feet. Inverted train with barrel on right and Harrison maintaining power. End plates to pivots of train and motion work but not to equation work.

Figure 11/48. Drive to calendar consists of large wheel between plates driven by first pinion of train. This wheel is mounted with a friction spring on a long arbor squared at front end for setting calendar. Pinion squared on to this arbor drives large calendar wheel through an idler pinion to reverse direction of rotation. Equation cam is mounted on rear end of calendar arbor.

Figure 11/47. Movement seen from below. Note inverted dead beat escapement. Endless screw on hour wheel pipe drives a vertical arbor for lunar mechanism.

of the train (figure 11/48). This wheel is mounted with a friction clutch on the arbor which is squared at its front end for setting the calendar with a key. A pinion squared on to this arbor drives the large calendar wheel through an idler pinion to reverse the direction of rotation. The equation cam is mounted on the rear end of the calendar arbor (figure 11/49). In contrast to Graham's practice of using a light wheel, the bell crank has a fixed stud riding on the periphery of the equation cam and the parts are more solidly made.

Figure 11/50 shows the principle of the differential gearing used to drive the solar time hand and should be studied together with figures 11/47 and 48. The internally cut rack at the lower end of the bell crank (figure 11/49) drives a pinion with a bevel wheel (a) fixed at its front end. The arbor carrying the minute wheel (b) is pivoted in the front end of this arbor and carries round with it a similar bevel wheel (c) which projects between the arms of the minute wheel to turn a third bevel wheel (d). The latter is free to rotate on the minute wheel arbor and has a wheel (e) fixed to it which drives the cannon pinion carrying the solar time hand. This differential assembly works in just the same way as the epicyclic gearing used by Graham. As long as the first bevel wheel (a) remains stationary, the solar hand rotates at the same speed as the mean time hand and maintains a constant distance from it. Any movement of the bell crank causes rotation of the first bevel wheel (a) and the solar hand is advanced or retarded with respect to the mean time hand.

The pendulum (figure 11/51) is a nine rod gridiron with the rating nut divided into thirty and provided with an index. The pendulum is suspended from a bracket in the seat board and the pin type crutch hangs below the seat board (figure 11/49).

The case (figure 11/52) has a mahogany carcase with figured mahogany veneer. The break arch hood with reeded chamfered corners instead of columns produced a most elegant case which was used by Mudge, Dutton, Holmes and other good makers of the second half of the

Figure 11/49. Rear view showing balanced equation cam and bell crank with fixed stud riding on cam. Internal rack at lower end of bell crank drives pinion on an arbor with a bevel wheel at front end, see 11/48. Note crutch hanging below movement.

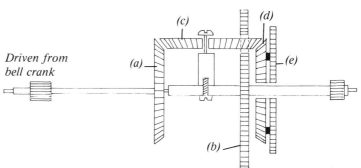

Figure 11/50. Principle of differential gearing used to operate solar time hand. Arbor of pinion driven by rack on bell crank has bevel wheel (a) at front end. As long as this remains stationary, solar hand rotates at same speed as mean time hand, but any movement of bell crank causes rotation of (a) and solar hand is advanced or retarded with respect to mean time hand.

eighteenth century. It is a small clock, only 6ft. 5½ins. high excluding the finial and its plinth, and the waist measures 11½ins. for the 10¼ins. dial. Probably because of the slimness of the case, the sides were hollowed out to accommodate the swing of the enormous pendulum bob. In the circumstances this does not necessarily indicate that anything is not original.

A perpetual calendar equation timepiece signed on the dial, just above the centre, 'Eardley Norton London', is shown in figure 11/53. The mahogany case is to the same general design as the Dutton in figure 11/52 but is quite a lot broader and the whole clock is probably c.1780. It has a silvered one piece dial and the seconds ring appears to have

Figure 11/51. Nine rod gridiron pendulum with rating nut divided into thirty and with an index. Note sides of case hollowed out to allow for swing of enormous bob. As case is very slim this does not necessarily indicate that anything is not original.

Figure 11/52. Elegant Dutton case, mahogany carcase and figured mahogany veneer. Reeded chamfered corners to hood. Finial not original. Height only 6ft. 5½ins. excluding finial and plinth, with 11½ins. waist for a 10¼ins. dial.

had observatory markings added. The annual calendar in the arch caters for leap year and a vertical pointer moves up or down to indicate the appropriate date. Just below the calendar dial is a small dial marked 'Leap Year/First after/Second after/Third after' with a hand to point to the correct year.

The calendar dial (figure 11/54) has dates for four years spiralled round it, starting on the outside at 'Leap Year' which shows February with twenty-nine days. The four years are so spaced that they occupy exactly four turns of the disc. At the centre is a pinion which meshes with a wheel on the arbor of the year hand and this arbor carries a snail to raise or lower the date pointer as required. The remaining rings on the calendar disc show the signs of the zodiac, the sun's declination and the times of sunrise.

Figure 11/53. Perpetual calendar equation timepiece by Eardley Norton, c.1780. Mahogany case similar to the Dutton but broader. Inverted movement has one piece silvered dial with observatory markings on seconds ring. Sub-dial at centre of arch is marked with leap year and three following, and pointer above it rises and falls to point to appropriate part of calendar.

Figure 11/54. High grade Norton movement with six latched pillars and similar to Dutton in 11/46. Calendar dial has dates for four years spiralled round it, starting on outside at 'Leap Year' showing February with twenty-nine days. Four years occupy exactly four turns of the disc. At the centre is a pinion which operates mechanism for the year hand and the vertical pointer. Remaining rings on calendar disc show zodiac, sun's declination and times of sunrise. Drive to calendar consists of six pointed star wheel stepped on by twenty-four hour wheel and carrying contrate wheel which drives pinion having endless screw engaging with calendar disc of 487 teeth. Equation work is all on front plate and has epicyclic gear train similar to Graham in figures 8/37-44.

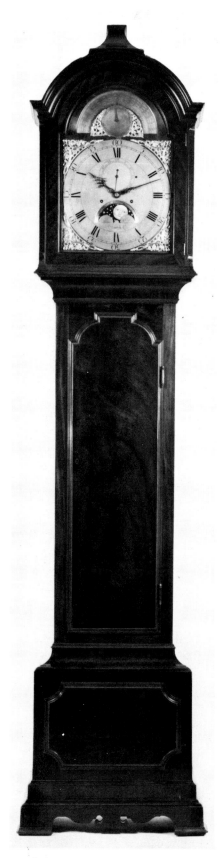

To drive the calendar disc, a twenty-four hour wheel, driven from a wheel on the hour wheel pipe, has a pin which moves a six pointed star wheel once per day. The star wheel is mounted on a contrate wheel driving a pinion with an endless screw engaging with the calendar wheel. There are 1,461 days in a four year period and the factors of that number are 3 and 487 so the calendar disc is cut with 487 teeth and the contrate wheel and pinion are arranged to rotate the endless screw $1\frac{1}{3}$ times per day so the disc advances $1\frac{1}{3}$ teeth per day.

The equation cam is mounted just behind the calendar disc and a bell crank follows the periphery of the cam, and the rack at its lower end applies the necessary movement to an epicyclic gear train which operates on the same principles as the one in the Graham equation clock in figures 8/37-44. The usual gilt hand with the sun's effigy shows solar time on the dial.

Figure 11/55 shows a perpetual calendar striking clock signed on the silvered chapter disc just above VI 'Edmund Prideaux London' and probably of slightly earlier date (c.1775) than the Eardley Norton. This is not an equation clock so the calendar disc does not give any solar information but its calendar layout is identical with that of the Eardley Norton and the drive to the calendar wheel is also identical. It is probable that both mechanisms came from the same specialist maker as few workshops would have been equipped to cut these high-numbered calendar wheels. Below the dial centre is the usual type of moon dial stepped on twice a day by the hour wheel. The dial has rococo spandrels (C. & W. No. 30).

The movement is of similar high quality to the Eardley Norton with six latched pillars and end plates to the pivots. The going train has Harrison maintaining power, a dead beat escapement and a wood rod pendulum. There is rack striking with a strike/silent lever at III. The calendar is set by the squared end of the star wheel arbor, just to the right of the seconds ring.

The mahogany case is similar to that of the Eardley Norton but has finer shaping to the trunk door and plinth panel, and sound frets in the sides of the hood.

Figure 11/56 shows the 14ins. dial of a month astronomical time-piece which is signed on the chapter ring 'George Margetts London'. The rococo corner spandrels are C. & W. No. 36, but the very detailed arch spandrels with female busts are not recorded in C. & W. The serpentine minute hand and its matching hour hand

Figure 11/55. Perpetual calendar striking clock by Prideaux, c.1775. Dial has silvered chapter disc and rococo spandrels (C. & W. No. 30) and conventional lunar dial below centre. It is not an equation clock so calendar disc does not give any solar information, but layout of disc and its drive are identical to those of the Eardley Norton in 11/54. Calendar is set by square to right of seconds dial. Mahogany case similar to but slightly finer than that in 11/53.

Figure 11/56. 14ins. dial of month astronomical timepiece by Margetts, c.1780. Lunar and tidal dial in arch. Hands on age of moon ring point to times of high tides. Large disc within chapter ring rotates clockwise in one sidereal day and carries ecliptic ring. Hand carrying sun (pointing to 4.30) rotates clockwise in twenty-four hours and indicates date and sun's position in zodiac. At noon it shows sun's declination on vertical scale and can be used to find approximately daybreak, sunrise, sunset and nightfall. Hand carrying moon (pointing to IIII) rotates in 24 hours 50 minutes, shows moon's position relative to sun and at 12 noon gives time of moon's southing. Case is shown in Colour Plate 22.

Figure 11/57. Month movement of Margetts. Twin great wheels engage with a common pinion. Astronomical gearing between dial and front plate, note continuous drive to lunar work in arch.

Figure 11/58. Well made mahogany inner case of Margetts timepiece to exclude dust from movement.

came into use c.1780 although the hour hand was also used with the earlier style 'straight' minute hand. The centre seconds hand matches the others. In the arch is a lunar dial with a rotating disc carrying a spherical moon to show the phases and a pointer to indicate its age on the fixed outer ring. On the latter are two engraved hands which point to the time of high tide on the band of Roman numerals. This dial shows high tide at 12 o'clock at new and full moon, and was probably made for Portsmouth or some port in the south east.

Within the chapter ring is a large disc which rotates clockwise in one sidereal day and is engraved with the 'Tropic of Capricorn', the 'Equator' and the 'Tropic of Cancer', as well as various stars. Fixed to this disc is an eccentric ring representing the ecliptic, with the inner edge divided into the twelve signs of the zodiac, each divided into thirty degrees, and the outer edge marked with an annual calendar. A hand bearing an effigy of the sun (pointing to 4.30 and just visible in figure 11/56) rotates clockwise in one mean solar day. As the ecliptic ring makes 366 turns per year to the solar hand's 365, the ecliptic ring will advance $^1/_{365}$ of a turn per day with respect to the hand, that is one day on the calendar markings. The vertical scale extending downwards from XII is marked to show the sun's declination north or south of the equator and is divided to show up to 30° although the maximum declination is 23° 27′ north in summer and south in winter. At noon when the solar hand coincides with the vertical scale, the sun's declination is read by noting where the central line on the ecliptic ring cuts the vertical scale.

The solar hand can also be used to find the approximate times of sunrise and sunset. First it is necessary to imagine a 2×12 hour dial with 12 noon at the top. The point where the solar hand on the central line of the ecliptic ring cuts the outer edge of the horseshoe shaped dial indicates sunrise on the left and sunset on the right. Similarly, where the solar hand and ecliptic ring cut the inner edge of the horseshoe gives the times of daybreak and darkness, these being marked 'Twilight Begins' and 'Twilight Ends' respectively. Correctly, there is a period of nearly two months in the summer when the ecliptic ring does not cut the inner edge of the horseshoe, thus indicating 'no real night', see the clock by Daniel Alan, figure 9/54.

The hand with the effigy of the moon (pointing to IIII in figure 11/56) rotates once in 24 hours 50 minutes and shows the moon's position relative to the sun. At 12 noon, the lunar hand points to the time of the moon's southing for that day.

Figure 11/57 shows the movement. It is of month duration with two barrels and two weights, but both great wheels engage with a common pinion. The layout was adopted to reduce the pressure on the pivots and also provides maintaining power. The gearing to operate the astronomical mechanism is just visible between the dial and the front plate. Note the continuous drive to the lunar work in the arch.

The movement is enclosed in an accurately fitting mahogany box to exclude dust, the sides and top being hinged for access, see figure 11/58. The case (Colour Plate 22) is a good quality but typical London example with choice mahogany veneers. It has fine sound frets in spite of there being no striking train, which may indicate that the case was not ordered specially for the clock. The height is approximately 9ft. 0ins. excluding the flambeau finials, and it is beautifully proportioned. The date is c.1780.

SIDEREAL TIME CLOCKS

Sidereal time is used by astronomers as it can more easily be measured accurately than can solar time. There are 366 sidereal days in a year, so the sidereal day is slightly shorter than the mean solar day, its duration being 23 hours 56 minutes 4.1 seconds of mean solar time. A clock can therefore easily be converted to keep sidereal time by slightly shortening the pendulum. However, to indicate both sidereal time and mean solar time with the same mechanism requires very complicated gearing.

Figure 11/59 shows the twin dials of a regulator which keeps sidereal time and shows it on

Figure 11/59. Twin dials of sidereal and mean solar time regulator designed by Vines in 1836 and made by Walsh. On sidereal dial normal hands indicate hours, minutes and seconds with minute hand rotating once per hour. Hand with gilt sun indicates mean solar time. Hand with moon has shutter to show phases and also indicates position of moon relative to sun. Mean solar dial is straightforward except that inner part of seconds dial rotates anti-clockwise to show sidereal seconds.

the right hand dial. Mean time is obtained through a train of wheels and used to control the mean time hands on the left hand dial. The mean solar dial is inscribed 'J. Vines, Inv^{r}', that is Joseph Vines who designed the clock in 1836. The sidereal dial is engraved 'Walsh, Newbury, Maker', presumably the Henry Walsh who is recorded in 1830.

The sidereal dial has a twenty-four hour chapter ring, note that IX to XVI on the lower part of the dial point outwards. The normal hands indicate hours, minutes and seconds, the minute hand rotating once per hour. The hand with the effigy of the sun indicates mean solar hours and should agree with the time shown on the left hand dial. The hand showing the moon makes one rotation less per lunar month than the mean solar hand and therefore shows the position of the moon with respect to the sun. A black shutter, operated by a cam, moves in front of the white disc to indicate the phases of the moon. The mean solar dial is straightforward, except that the inner portion of the seconds dial rotates anti-clockwise at such a rate that the hand shows mean seconds on the outer dial and sidereal seconds on the inner one. This provides for easy comparison of sidereal and mean solar seconds.

The sidereal movement terminates in a special type of gravity escapement which bears some relationship to the Delander duplex described in Chapter 8. It has two thirty-toothed escape wheels, the larger one for locking and the smaller one for impulsing. There is a weighted crutch which engages only with the left hand side of the pendulum. At the end of a swing to the right the escapement is unlocked and lifts the crutch to the left. When the pendulum has swung to the left the crutch is released and its weight gives a constant impulse to the pendulum. This is a single beat escapement so the hands move every two seconds and the sidereal seconds dials are marked accordingly. The seconds pendulum is of the gridiron type with five steel and four brass rods.

The mean solar movement has its own driving weight and wheel train, but instead of being controlled by an escapement and pendulum, there is a small train of wheels connecting its seconds hand arbor to the corresponding arbor in the sidereal movement. Figure 11/60 shows the arrangement of this wheel train. A thirty-two toothed wheel mounted on the sidereal seconds arbor engages with a wheel of 247 teeth. Mounted on the arbor of this wheel is a 331 toothed wheel which meshes with one of forty-three teeth mounted on the arbor of the mean solar seconds hand. This arrangement is accurate to within about 0.0005 seconds per day, or less than a quarter of a second per year.

The clock is housed in a handsome case (figure 11/61) in nineteenth century Gothic style which is veneered with mahogany that has faded to a delightful golden colour.

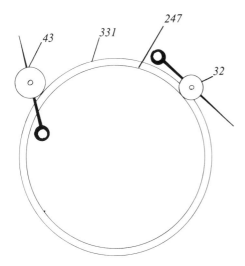

Figure 11/60. Principle of gearing used to interconnect sidereal seconds and mean solar seconds arbors. The wheels of 247 and 331 teeth are mounted on the same arbor.

Figure 11/61. Handsome nineteenth century Gothic case veneered with mahogany now faded to a lovely golden colour.

Chapter 12

REPAIR, RESTORATION AND FAKING

Repair, restoration and faking are all different aspects of one vast subject where there are few laws and much is a matter of personal opinion. Most owners or purchasers want their clocks to look as beautiful as possible and to show little or no evidence of the ravages of time in spite of being anything up to three hundred years old. During most of their existence clocks were, of course, just useful objects with a furnishing value, so from time to time they needed repair and were modernised, visually to make them fit in with later furnishings and mechanically to improve their functioning. The quality of this work varied from craftsmanship at least equal to the original down to pure bodging, often being governed by the amount the owner was prepared to spend. Quite a lot of clocks which required considerable attention or which had come to be regarded as misfits from the furnishing point of view were stored away and probably forgotten. With the increase in interest over the last twenty years, many of these clocks have been brought out of storage and refurbished.

The objects of restoration are to put a clock, or other object, as far as possible, into the state in which it was when new. This involves the replacement of poor or incorrect repairs, the removal of later improvements and possibly of incorrect previous restoration, and the provision of missing items. All this must be done with great care as over-restoration can result in an 'as new' effect which many people find distasteful. Some changes, especially those made early in a clock's life, have become a part of its history and should be retained.

It is impossible to define exactly what constitutes faking although some examples are very obvious. To provide any decorative or mechanical feature without definite evidence of its previous existence on the clock or on other truly comparable examples constitutes faking. This applies particularly to any 'improvements' carried out for financial gain.

Purchasers and owners generally like restoration work to be matched to the original so that it is inconspicuous or even virtually undetectable, which is fair enough providing that the clock is not eventually offered for sale as being all original. Turret clocks are not subject to the same financial pressures as are domestic clocks and a recommended practice is to paint replaced parts a distinctive colour. To the purist this is an attractive scheme but a restorer who followed it would have only a very limited clientele, although some sympathy with this idea was expressed in the correspondence columns of *Antiquarian Horology* during 1977. The organisers of some antiques fairs specify a maximum percentage of restoration as being acceptable, which is a good idea but must be very difficult to implement. It is worth commenting, that earlier this century when good clocks were plentiful and antiquarian horological studies were in their infancy, the faker's job was much easier but the rewards were correspondingly less than obtain today.

DIALS AND MOVEMENTS

Repairs

Before longcase clocks were valued as antiques many of them were repaired very crudely. Worn pivot holes were reduced by punching, either by making a number of dents with a centre punch or by using a special punch which produced a circular indentation round the pivot hole (see figures 9/17, 10/50). Both methods result in badly cut pivots which may have to be replaced. Escapements were adjusted by bending the crutch arbor, deforming the back cock, or by sticking pieces of metal on to the pallets with soft solder. Calendar or lunar work, suspected of stopping the clock, was rendered inoperative, not by removing the operating pin or stud, but by throwing away the twenty-four hour wheel or even by breaking off a group of teeth from the calendar disc. Sometimes whole trains were discarded. Broken hands were mended with soft solder or were replaced with any pattern which happened to be readily available.

In contrast to the horror stories above, much repair work was very competently and conscientiously executed. Worn pinions were replaced or the appropriate wheels shifted to mesh with unworn sections; or in some cases complete trains were renewed. Worn escapements had both escape wheel and pallets replaced with an up-to-date assembly with its larger pendulum arc. The difficulties this caused are discussed in Chapter 3, p. 46. Much of this work is nineteenth century and is easily detected as no attempt was made to match the existing work. The pinions have long heads with thick parallel arbors and the wheels are mounted on heavy cheese headed collets.

With modern repair work it is usual to make new parts to match the rest of the movement in style, colour and finish, which is satisfying artistically but makes it difficult to detect new work, particularly if the whole movement is subsequently given a high polish. A well polished movement has a very satisfying look and resists corrosion but the use of high speed polishing buffs in careless hands can easily cause excessive removal of metal, particularly from corners, edges and wheel teeth. Any fine engraving will also be adversely affected.

There is considerable controversy over the methods used in preparing chapter rings and similar items for silvering. The commonest way is to spin the component in a lathe or similar device and apply emery cloth or other abrasive, using a block to prevent rounding of edges and cutting in to the engraving. Using a course abrasive results in concentric grooves, a result disparagingly described as resembling a gramophone record. The alternative method is to apply the abrasive by hand, again using a block, and working in all directions. Here again the coarse abrasive may cause marks which can have a very unpleasant effect. Whatever method is adopted, coarse abrasives should be avoided because of the wear caused to the engraving, apart from the unsatisfactory final result. In the author's opinion, there is no objection to spinning chapter rings providing the speed is kept low and only a fine abrasive is used.

Improvements

Over the years many clocks were modified to improve their performance or to provide additional facilities.

Some verge escapement longcase clocks were converted to anchor to improve their timekeeping and there seems little objection to restoring them to verge except in the case of very early conversions such as that of the Fromanteel in figure 2/1. In assessing the ethics of such a reconversion the points to be considered are the date of the change and the relative rarity of the two types of mechanism.

With the demand for more accurate indication of the time, many one hand thirty hour clocks were provided with two hands. This was done either by modifying the motion work or, probably the more usual method in fairly recent times, by fitting a spare movement. Figure 12/1 shows an early clock converted to two hands, note the absence of minute divisions and numbers. The chapter ring is inscribed 'Giles Thorner Fecit', an apparently unrecorded maker. On many of these conversions the chapter ring was provided with simple minute divisions in the form of shallow drillings round the outer edge.

The winding of thirty-hour clocks came to be regarded as a serious drawback, so many

Figure 12/1. Early eighteenth century thirty-hour clock by Giles Thorner, originally only one hand but now converted to two hands. Note absence of minute divisions and numbers.

Figure 12/2. Thirty-hour clock by Henry Gamble, Bramley, c.1775, now provided with an eight day movement. Note how the winding holes cut through the engraving.

were converted to eight day, usually by using the movement from a spare painted dial, sometimes complete with false plate. Figure 12/2 shows a thirty-hour dial by Henry Gamble, Bramley, c.1775, and now with an eight day movement. Note how the winding holes cut through the engraving, which always shows a later alteration. Most of these changes of movement are easily spotted, but if in doubt it is worth examining both the front plate and the dial plate for spare holes which may perhaps have been plugged. Other points to check are whether the movement has a long seconds pivot without a corresponding seconds dial and whether dial or movement has provision for calendar work lacking on the other partner. A few plate framed thirty-hour movements were converted by being provided with an extra pinion and wheel with barrel for each train accommodated in extensions to the plates. Britten[1] describes a conversion requiring only one wheel and pinion plus the two barrels but the author does not recollect seeing a clock so modified.

A simple improvement applied to many thirty-hour clocks was to provide chains instead of ropes. To be successful this needs new sprockets in the movement and preferably a new weight pulley. For many years 'conversion sets' have been available and these are easily recognised by the striking sprocket having a pivoted click instead of the usual spring click.

Some eight day clocks with count wheel striking were converted to rack and snail in order to provide hour repeating, an example being the Gould clock in figures 4/47 and 48. The introduction of wire gongs in the nineteenth century resulted in some clocks having them fitted in place of bells. Chimes were often added, indeed Walder's notebook, referred to in Chapter 10, has a section headed 'A proper Quarter part to be added to a Common Eight Day Clock'. This was usually done by extending the plates on the right, resulting in a third winding hole somewhere near III, see figure 12/3, which shows such a clock by Foster, Carlisle, c.1800. Asymmetrically placed winding holes, as in this case, always indicate an alteration. Sometimes a new three train movement was provided and the dial centre renewed, which is usually fairly easy to detect from the style of movement and the decoration of the dial centre.

The introduction of the painted dial with its excellent legibility led to the painting of some brass dials after removing all applied parts.

Faking

By definition, faking presupposes an intention to describe an object as genuine when it is not. If an enthusiastic collector acquires the remains of an interesting clock and has all the missing parts made so that it looks as it would have done originally, there

Figure 12/3. Eight day striking clock by Foster, Carlisle, c.1800, later provided with a quarter chiming train. Note asymmetrical winding hole at III.

1. F.W. Britten, *Horological Hints and Helps,* 4th edition, 1947, p. 254.

Figure 12/4. Provincial style lantern clock made from a thirty-hour birdcage movement. Nicely proportioned and well engraved.

is no question of faking unless he, or someone who subsequently becomes the owner, attempts to pass it off as being completely genuine. This point has been discussed because some honest and knowledgeable collectors derive great satisfaction from this sort of salvage operation, particularly if they are capable of doing the greater part of the work themselves. Many of the improvements described in the previous section come under the heading of faking if efforts are made to remove all traces of the alterations.

Traditionally, brass dial clocks are more valuable than painted ones although the latter are now appreciated much more than they used to be. This preference has led to the fitting of old brass dials, usually thirty-hour ones, in place of painted dials. This is easy for clocks in cases with square dial openings, but the majority of the better quality cases with painted dials to be replaced are arched and most of the spare brass dials square. Many of these replacement dials therefore have arches added, often very crudely attached with strips soldered on at the back and with 'Tempus Fugit' on a boss in the arch. An attached arch is always a suspicious sign particularly when the dial is complete with signature, calendar and so on without an arch. Some square dials were modified soon after the arch came into fashion but these were well done and the new work matched to the old, including provision of matching engraved borders if present on the old dial. New brass dials, as well as chapter rings, spandrels and other parts have been readily available during most of this century, but the poor engraving without any fine lines, the generally weak design, and the fixing of chapter rings with screws, usually render detection easy. This does not apply to 'tailor made' dials carefully designed and made by craftsmen to suit particular movements. The main clue will probably be the condition of the back of the various components. Restorers normally leave the backs of dial plates in a tarnished state.

Dials have also been 'improved' by changing spandrels for those of an earlier design, although this has probably become less prevalent. One-piece silvered dials are occasionally found with spandrels added, and one such dial was seen fitted with seventeenth century style cherub spandrels! A suitable name can add considerably to the value of a clock so signatures have been changed in some cases. A good engraver can make a satisfactory copy of a particular maker's 'signature' but to erase the old signature it is necessary to hammer up the metal from the back. This leaves a slightly thinner section of the dial plate or chapter ring, which can be seen or felt at the back. The job is of course much easier in the case of unsigned dials such as that in figure 3/9, so the number of such anonymous clocks decreases.

Movements have received less attention from fakers than have dials and cases, because until recently fewer purchasers were interested in mechanisms than were interested in other aspects. Dials and movements which have lost their original partners are married together and this is difficult to detect if they are suitable and of similar age — and the work is done by a good craftsman. It is almost certain that the dial feet will not have fitted the holes in the front plate, so there should be some signs of plugged holes in either dial plate or front plate.

A few movements have been made up from a mixture of old and new parts to suit particular dials. Fairly recently there was in circulation a month Roman striking clock, where the movement had been so made to suit a very good early dial with IV on the chapter ring, thus indicating it should have Roman striking. The faker had taken the precaution of using period hands.

Collectors who are interested in fragments may have been surprised by the relatively high prices for birdcage thirty-hour movements without dials and may even have been told that they were used for making lantern clocks! Figure 12/4 shows an interesting eighteenth century style lantern clock with a nicely engraved dial and a sensible provincial signature not likely to lead to such careful examination as would a well known name. Figure 12/5 shows a side view and the only unusual feature is the excessive distance between the dial and the front train bar. Figure 12/6 provides the answer to the problem. A thin line on both top and

Figure 12/5. Movement of made up lantern clock, note excessive distance between dial and front train bar.

Figure 12/6. Bottom plate of made up lantern clock showing strip of brass fitted at front to make square plate essential for a lantern clock. Top plate treated similarly.

bottom plates shows how they were extended to convert them from the rectangular shape of the longcase movement to the square necessary with a lantern clock. An example of fine craftsmanship, what a pity it was not used for honest restoration.

CASES

Repairs

In many ways cases are more vulnerable to damage and inexpert repair than are the clocks they contain. By modern standards houses were damp until quite recent times and the liberal washing of tiled or stone paved floors made matters worse. These conditions encouraged rot and woodworm attack, the feet or skirting and plinth, and sometimes the back board, being most affected. Even today good clocks are sometimes seen with the skirting or feet bleached as a result of careless floor washing.

Cases were mutilated when removal to premises with lower ceilings caused difficulty and those which suffered most were the taller, better quality clocks which had started life in fine houses with lofty ceilings. Finials, caddies and pediments were removed and if this action proved insufficient, the plinths were cut down as necessary. See figure 12/7 which shows a case shortened at both ends. Note also the imitation fan inlays in place of the sound frets, which suggest that the case was modified about the end of the eighteenth century. The clock and case date from c.1740. An alternative idea very occasionally adopted was to remove a section of floor and sink the case into the ground, when damp would soon cause deterioration of the plinth.

Before the introduction of modern chemical solutions, woodworm infestation was regarded with dread and frequently badly infested articles were burnt or, if the attack were localised, the affected parts ruthlessly cut out.

Repairs necessary because of woodworm attack or accident were frequently entrusted to a joiner or estate carpenter who in many cases used oak, pine or whatever wood was readily available and made no attempt at matching the mouldings. The author remembers visiting a country house with much fine furniture where clock cases and other items exhibited such repairs in oak from the estate. He also recollects seeing a fine floral marquetry case with the plinth rebuilt in thick slabs of pine stained brown! Bun feet were often replaced with a skirting, which may have been an improvement made to increase the stability of the case (see the discussion on bun feet in Chapter 4).

As the plinth is the main part to suffer incorrect restoration a few such examples will now be examined. Figure 12/8 shows a marquetry case of c.1710-15 which may perhaps have had a square dial opening originally. The marquetry in the spandrels above the hood door is later in style than that on the rest of the case and replaces sound frets. The dial has an added arch which looks later, so it may not be the original dial. When the plinth needed repair it was provided with a strange arched top skirting decorated with

Figure 12/7. Walnut case of c.1740 which has been reduced in height to suit a low ceiling. Caddy removed and plinth cut down, then provided with incorrect skirting. Note imitation fan inlays in place of sound frets.

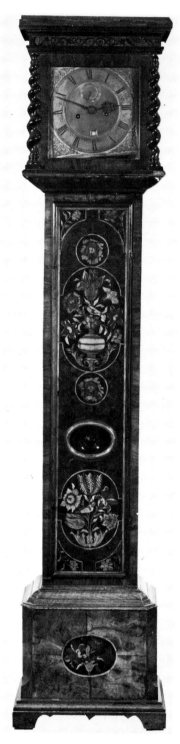

Figure 12/8. Marquetry case, c.1710-15, with plinth incorrectly restored with arched skirting decorated with later marquetry. Straight-grained replacement moulding at bottom of trunk. Dial opening possibly square originally, note very late marquetry in spandrels above hood door. Clock by Samuel Stevens, dial has added arch.

Figure 12/9. Marquetry case, c.1680, completely rebuilt from bottom of trunk downwards. Moulding not cross-grained, canted corners, incorrect skirting. Plinth panel veneered with non-matching wood but has one original marquetry panel. Clock by Daniel Quare.

Figure 12/10. Marquetry case, c.1695-1700, with cut down plinth which has been tidied up with matching border and crossbanding. Apparent skirting is flush with plinth. Trunk door also shortened, note extra banding just below it. Clock by Richard Baker.

marquetry in an attempt at matching it to the existing work. The moulding between the plinth and the trunk is not cross-grained so must be a replacement.

In figure 12/9 a fine floral marquetry and olive oyster case of c.1680 has been completely rebuilt from the bottom of the trunk downwards. It has a modern moulding with longitudinal grain, canted corners which did not come in until c.1725, and a cut-away skirting of even later design. It looks as though one panel of marquetry was salvaged from the original plinth and reused. The clock is signed at the base of the dial 'Daniel Quare, London'.

Figure 12/10 shows a marquetry case of c.1695-1700 where the plinth had been severely cut down and subsequently tidied up by running a matching border and crossbanding across the bottom of the marquetry panel. The bottom of the door has been shortened too, note the banding just below it. What appears to be a skirting is in fact flush with the panel. Good workmanship but quite unsatisfactory proportions. The clock is by Richard Baker.

Figure 12/11 shows a highly imaginative reconstruction of the plinth of a fine arabesque marquetry case of c.1700. The moulding at the top of the plinth is completely wrong in design and the plinth front consists of a good panel of floral marquetry from the trunk door of a late seventeenth century case which is flanked by strips of high grade, probably Victorian, carving. The whole is topped, or rather bottomed, by a carved skirting!

The seaweed marquetry case in figure 12/12 apparently required new twist columns, probably because the original ones were worm eaten, but unfortunately they were made detached in late eighteenth century style. The clock is by Samuel Jenkins, London.

In figure 12/13 a late seventeenth century marquetry case has been rebuilt, only the trunk section with its door being original. The plinth is both too high and too wide and the marquetry, although superficially similar to the original, is much more open in design. The hood is also a complete replacement, the fancy turned columns suggesting that the work was done in the nineteenth century. The clock is by Essaye Fleureau.

Marquetry case restoration is discussed in Chapter 5 but even so it was thought worthwhile to include these examples of how it should not be done.

In more recent times much good restoration work has been done with proper regard to the original appearance of the case, but it is noticeable that until about the middle of this century it was the custom to provide a skirting rather than bun feet on seventeenth century examples. In this connection it is interesting to note the extreme scarcity of bun feet on early clocks shown in the older horological books and to compare them with possibly the same clocks in more recent publications. It is worth pointing out that so many cases have restored plinths that this is not regarded as a serious drawback if the work is well done. The correct restoration of caddy tops is also well worthwhile if space permits as the proportions of cases are greatly improved by this operation.

The original polished surface should be retained if this is possible and very often the dirt can be removed by repeated careful washing or by the use of a combined cleaner/polish. Only as a last resort should a case have the polish stripped off, nor should it be rubbed down with sandpaper to produce an even surface. Marquetry and other early veneered surfaces often have what appears to be glue which stands slightly proud of the joints and this should not be removed. French polish is an inappropriate finish and unsuitable because it tends to emphasise any blemishes. Japanned work deteriorates with age and is easily damaged by atmospheric changes and by rough treatment, so most japanned cases need, or have already received, restoration, varying from a light touching up to a complete rejapanning.

Improvements

Many early clock cases were modified to give them added stature to suit higher ceilings when these came into fashion or to make them harmonise with later furnishings. Figure

Figure 12/11. Fine arabesque marquetry case, c.1700, entirely rebuilt below the trunk. Completely wrong moulding, and plinth panel consists of earlier marquetry panel from a trunk door between strips of, probably, Victorian carving. Note carved skirting.

Figure 12/12. Seaweed marquetry case with replaced twist columns detached in late eighteenth century style.

Figure 12/13. Late seventeenth century marquetry case where only trunk section has not been rebuilt and this has been shortened. Plinth too wide and too high with looser design of marquetry and incorrect skirting. Hood completely renewed. Probably done early in nineteenth century.

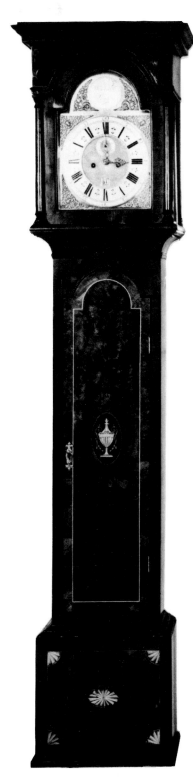

Figure 12/14. Panelled ebony case, 1670-75, made more imposing by addition of high double skirting instead of bun feet. Hood modified by insertion of extra section above frieze and provision of a larger triangular pediment. Compare with figure 12/19.

Figure 12/15. Marquetry case, c.1695, with plinth panel cut down then later provided with double skirting. Hood frieze and cornice replaced by truncated pagoda top with late eighteenth century inlay.

Figure 12/16. Walnut case c.1725 with caddy and most of skirting removed, but with added banding and late eighteenth century inlays. Clock is by Windmills.

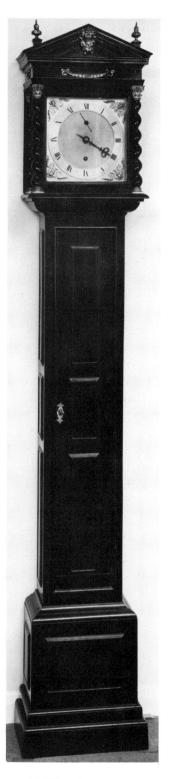

Figure 12/17. Oak case, probably c.1770-80, heavily embellished and carved in Victorian times. Note triple skirting with paw feet. Plinth and trunk panelled by applying carved mouldings. Good quality carving. Clock by Richard Reed, Chelmsford.

Figure 12/18. Hanging alarm time-piece by Joseph Carswell, Hastings, c.1760, in almost contemporary oak 'grandmother' case. Note Chippendale style fret and attached columns. Height 5ft. 10ins.

Figure 12/19. Accurate copy of 1670-75 case made c.1930 by Van Winsum. Carcase of old oak with ebony veneer and mouldings. Good quality gilt mounts and old iron hinges on trunk door. Height 6ft. 4ins. for a 9ins. dial. Ignore incorrect dial.

12/14 shows a panelled ebony case of 1670-75 which was made more imposing by the addition of a high skirting plus a cut-away late eighteenth century skirting. This was balanced by adding an extra section just above the frieze of the hood and then replacing the triangular pediment with a larger one. Compare this mutilated specimen with the original ones in Chapter 2 or the correct reproduction in figure 12/19.

The case in figure 12/15, having lost part of its plinth panel, now has a double skirting and the top section of the hood has been replaced by a truncated pagoda top with inlay suggesting a late eighteenth century date for the 'improvements'.

Another case which was probably modified around the same date is shown in figure 12/16. It has lost its caddy and most of the skirting but has been enlivened by the addition of light coloured banding, and fan and urn inlays. The clock is by Windmills and the date c.1725.

Quite a number of square topped hoods had swan neck pediments provided, some of them probably in place of caddy tops which had been removed. Another method of giving a case added stature was by converting it to take an arched dial and then either modifying the dial or making a new one, or in some cases fitting a new dial and movement complete.

There was a considerable vogue for carved oak furniture in 'Elizabethan' taste during the Victorian period and many pieces were made to nineteenth century designs incorporating both period and modern carving. Wood carving also became a fashionable hobby for amateurs. During this time many period oak cases were carved and some of them were considerably altered structurally, no doubt to accord with the Victorian idea of Elizabethan furnishings. Figure 12/17 shows a case probably of c.1770-80 which has been much modified. It now has three skirtings, the lowest one having widespreading paw feet. The plinth and the trunk have been panelled by applying carved mouldings and the hood has acquired a very fine carved cresting. The trunk door and the front of the plinth are decorated with good quality carving in high relief and most of the mouldings and the columns have also been carved. It is just possible to visualise the original appearance of the case.

An improvement of a different nature is shown in figure 12/18, where a wall mounted alarm timepiece of c.1760 was provided with a long case within a few years of it being made. The oak case has a Chippendale style fret and attached columns to the hood and the height is 5ft. 10ins. so it qualifies as a 'grandmother'. The clock is by Joseph Carswell of Hastings and it has a 5-5½ins. dial.

Faking

Most of the work described in this section is concerned with altering cases to improve their saleability. Early this century clocks in ebony veneered or ebonised cases were very difficult to sell as most collectors preferred more decorative cases veneered with such woods as walnut or kingwood. It must be realised that in those days really serious collectors were interested mainly in seventeenth century examples and many of them took no interest whatever in clocks with arched dials.

This preference for the more decorative cases led to the stripping of black cases which were then reveneered with the 'show' woods, perhaps with the inclusion of marquetry panels. For a satisfactory job the mouldings had to be remade with cross-grain wood, which involved a lot of work. Due to the more perishable nature of cases, there has always been a surplus of movements, so some fine quality reproduction cases were made. Generally they had a carcase of old oak with carefully chosen veneers and after fifty or sixty years' wear they can be very difficult to detect if the design is correct.

Figure 12/19 shows a case made c.1930 by Van Winsum, a noted casemaker of the time. It is an accurate copy of a case of 1670-75, note the double skirting as found on very many cases when this one was made. A later reproduction would have been provided with bun feet. The carcase is all of old oak with ebony veneer and ebony mouldings. The hood slides up and is provided with the correct type of hook, and the trunk door has old wrought iron hinges. The hood has good quality gilt mounts. After fifty years of use the case has cracked veneers across the top and bottom of the door and has acquired the usual minor damage. Consequently it needs careful examination to establish its true age. The dial shown in the photograph is incorrect and should be ignored. The height is 6ft. 4ins. for a 9ins. dial.

In more recent times humble painted pine cases have not been immune from the craze for stripped pine furniture, which is quite fair providing the purchaser realises that originally all such cases were painted.

It is a more dubious procedure when such pine cases are japanned or veneered with fine woods. As mentioned above, remaking the mouldings is a big job so the old ones may have been disguised with stain. Another point to check is that modern veneer is normally very thin, unlike the saw-cut veneer used in the seventeenth and eighteenth centuries. It is always more difficult to disguise the unpolished areas, so if a case is stained or painted with flat paint on the inside, it is as well to examine it really thoroughly.

MARRIAGES

The term marriage[2] normally implies a more or less permanent union, but when used horologically it is more akin to the swopping of partners, a practice which has had a certain vogue in recent times. Specifically it means putting together a clock and a case which did not start life together. The general idea is to ensure that a fine clock has a fine case and vice versa. The low demand for black cased clocks has already been mentioned and this led to fine or valuable clocks being rehoused in good walnut, marquetry or similar cases at the expense of the original less valuable inmates. Walnut was not always as valued as it is today and some of the arch dial clocks in walnut cases were put into mahogany ones. See, for example, McIver Percival, *The Walnut Collector* (1927), p.142, "I know one old clock-repairer who some ten years ago told me that in the fifty years in which he had specialised in repairing long-case clocks, he had put more than a hundred clocks which had come to him in walnut cases into what he described as 'good solid mahogany'"!

When a clock is in an unsuitable case it is quite acceptable to put it in a more appropriate one if this can be done without disturbing another clock which is thought to be in its original case. It is very difficult to detect a marriage when the clock and case fit one another perfectly, are of similar quality and are of the same period. In fact there are not many examples where one can be certain that clock and case have always been together, so a successful marriage is not a serious disadvantage. The clocks most likely to be in their original cases are the humble ones where their low value makes it unlikely that a change would be worthwhile, and clocks with unusual shaped or sized dials, such as rectangular instead of square and those with non-standard arches.

Whilst proof of a case being original is hard to find Tompion, for example, numbered both case and movement, but even that could be faked. There are many points which can be checked for ascertaining whether a case has been changed. The most obvious check is whether the dial fits the opening, bearing in mind that the masking frame may have been changed, so look for new work, or even for plywood here. Some perfectly original country cases were made with, for example, a hood door suitable for an 11ins. dial and a masking frame for a 10ins.one, possibly so that it could be opened out if required. A dial which is too large for the opening never looks right, see figure 12/20 which shows a fine marquetry case of c.1690-95 intended for an 11ins. dial and now equipped with a 12ins. one.

Other things to check are whether with the dial in the right place the weights are so far

2. Often now described as 'associated'.

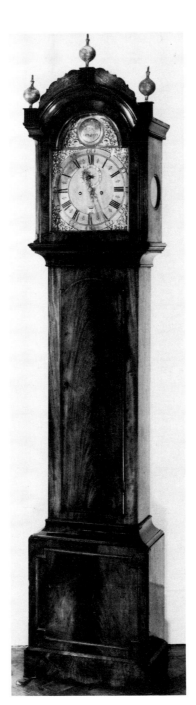

Figure 12/20. Fine marquetry case of c.1690-95, made for an 11ins. dial and now provided with a 12ins. one, note how chapter ring is partly obscured. Clock by Joseph Foster is c.1700. Case height 7ft. 5ins.

Figure 12/21. Clock by William Clark, London, c.1760, in provincial mahogany case probably c.1775. Note hood has reeded canted corners with break arch cornice bearing heavy plinths for finials. Circular side windows and shaped cresting are also provincial features.

Figure 12/22. Case veneered with satinwood and inlaid in late eighteenth century style but with much earlier style banding and twist columns. Thirty-hour single hand cottage clock by Richard Pettit, New Sampford, converted to two hand eight day. Very much a made up case and clock.

forward that they rub on the front of the case, or the pendulum is too close to the back board. The pendulum should also agree with any rubbing marks on the back board and come opposite the lenticle if the case has one. Pieces cut out of the sides to allow for an increased swing indicate either marriage or the fitting of a later escapement at some time. Another indication of a marriage is when a month or other clock having heavy weights is found in a lightly built case intended for a thirty-hour clock.

Movements vary in height with some of them having a lot of spare room below the barrels whilst others are more squat. Month movements are normally taller than eight day ones because of the extra wheels required. Therefore the height of the seat board with respect to the dial opening varies considerably and freshly cut tops to the sides of the case where the seat board fits, or fresh packing pieces under the seat board, are worth investigating. When the seat board is well above the bottoms of the hood windows it suggests either a marriage or that the side openings originally had frets backed with material, rather than glass. To avoid having packing pieces under a seat board, restorers sometimes cut back the case sides to below the level of the moulding under the hood and provide fresh upper parts to the sides with the joints out of sight.

In figure 12/21 the dial fits the masking frame and the only misfits are stylistic ones. The clock is a London example by William Clark, c.1760, but the case is later and of provincial design. Note the combination of a break arch hood with the reeded canted corners and shaped cresting with heavy plinths for the gilt wooden finials. The circular side windows are another provincial feature.

Figure 12/22 shows a most interesting specimen. The case is veneered with finely figured satinwood with inlay in a copy of late eighteenth century style but the banding used round both doors and to edge the trunk and plinth is the type found on marquetry cases at the beginning of the eighteenth century. Note also how the inlay on the lower trunk moulding stops about 2ins. from the back. The twist columns are a rather slim version of those used on late seventeenth century cases. It has a thirty-hour one hand dial from a cottage clock now provided with a two hand eight day movement. Altogether a clock to be avoided.

GRANDMOTHER CLOCKS

Whilst 'grandfather' clocks have the well known descriptive title 'longcase' as well as earlier names, it is perhaps significant that there is no such equivalent for 'grandmother'. With very few exceptions those now in existence were produced in the last hundred years. There is always a demand for extra small pieces of antique furniture and these therefore command high prices. To meet this demand, bureaux, chests of drawers and similar items were, and are, carefully reduced in size to make them more valuable. The demand led to the making up of grandmother cases, sometimes from full-sized ones and sometimes by using old wood from badly damaged or large, relatively valueless pieces of old furniture. A lot of japanned furniture was made between the Wars and this output included a number of red japanned grandmother cases.

The usual definition of a grandmother clock is one which has a height of less than six feet, which restricts the fall for the weights so much that a normal eight day movement will have difficulty in running its full time. Sometimes a bracket clock dial and movement was used, either remaining spring powered or being provided with small barrels to take cat gut. It is relatively easy to provide a longer pendulum on a movement with an anchor escapement by changing the escape wheel and pallets. Difficulty caused by the pendulum striking the sides of the narrow trunk was overcome by fitting a cylindrical pendulum bob. The movements used in tavern clocks and the later weight driven wall clocks were suitable also, but had to be fitted with new dials.

To be nicely proportioned, a case less than 6ft. high needs a dial 8ins. or at the most 9ins.

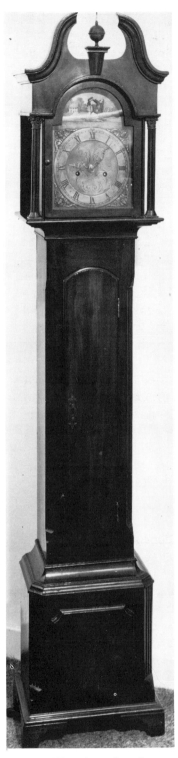

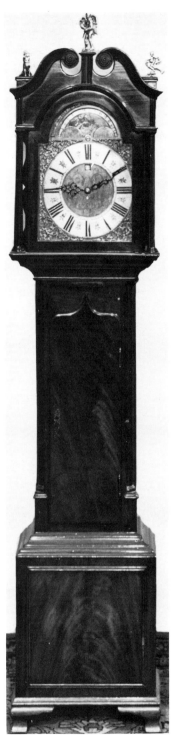

Figure 12/23. Grandmother case which is a beautifully scaled down version of a late eighteenth century longcase. Modern dial with early cherub spandrels and painted scene in arch with dancing Scotsman! Height 5ft. 7ins. with an 8ins. dial. Probably made early this century.

Figure 12/24. Very fine mahogany grandmother case showing 'Lancashire Chippendale' influence. Unsuitable figure finials. Single hand dial, now with two hands, a little large for opening. Height only 5ft. 2ins. without finials, and 9ins. dial. Again, probably made early this century.

Figure 12/25. More sensibly proportioned grandmother case which allows for a normal longcase dial with adequate room for the pendulum, probably c.1790-1800. Thirty-hour single hand dial by Mark Metcalf, Askrigg, now converted to two hand eight day. Height not known but presumably under 6ft.

across, which restricts the choice very considerably. For this reason many grandmother clocks have specially made dials and an example is shown in figure 12/23. It has an 8ins. dial with modern, poor quality, engraving and the minutes are number 10, 20, etc. The spandrels are the early cherub pattern (C. & W. No. 3), nearly a century too early in style for this clock. The arch has a painted scene with the added bonus of a Scotsman dancing in time to the pendulum! The mahogany case is a beautifully scaled down version of a late eighteenth century provincial case with swan neck pediment and the height is 5ft. 7ins. Note the reeded canted corners to plinth and trunk and the reeded columns with Corinthian capitals.

An even finer mahogany case showing 'Lancashire Chippendale' influence is shown in figure 12/24. The hood is surmounted by three rather improbable brass figures and the height is only 5ft. 2ins. without figures. The 9ins. dial is a little large for the opening and has a single hand chapter ring but is now equipped with two hands. There is a lunar dial in the arch and a calender aperture just below XII. It is not known whether it still has a thirty-hour movement.

The example shown in figure 12/25 is rather more convincing. Instead of being a scaled down version of a normal longcase it was designed to take a normal longcase dial and movement and has a trunk broad enough for the pendulum to swing freely. It is described as a grandmother although the height is not stated. The ogee feet suggest a north country origin and it probably dates from about the end of the eighteenth century. The dial, by Mark Metcalf of Askrigg who died in 1776, is for a one hand thirty-hour clock but has now been provided with an eight day two hand movement.

Eighteenth century hooded wall clocks were relatively uncommon but usually had dials 6ins. to 9ins. across so were suitable candidates for making into grandmother clocks. Most of them were thirty-hour timepieces, usually with alarm, but they were generally 'improved' by being equipped with eight day movements when used for grandmothers.

Chapter 13

SOME LATER DISCOVERIES

As mentioned in the original Introduction to this work, finality is never reached and interesting items continue to surface and in some cases further research necessitates a revision of existing theories and opinions. This short chapter includes a few of the more interesting of these developments.

BALANCE LONGCASE CLOCKS

The first serious book on the history and collecting of clocks, *Former Clocks and Watchmakers and their Work* by F.J. Britten, appeared in 1894 and the section on longcase clocks has in its introduction the statement: 'The escapements were either of the ancient balance or bob pendulum description' and goes on to say 'As the conversion [to pendulum] was a simple process, it is now very difficult to meet with an example having the original escapement'. Britten's book became *Old Clocks and Watches and Their Makers*, which passed through many editions and retained the statements quoted above until just after the First World War, when the wholesale destruction of thirty hour clocks must have made balance-controlled longcase clocks very rare. Most of the survivors which had been converted to anchor escapement probably went unrecognised, with the result that there are no references to balance longcase clocks in modern horological literature.

The example shown in figure 13/1 came to light recently having been converted to anchor escapement and long pendulum and with its duration increased from fifteen to thirty hours. Balance clocks always had separate weights for each train so that the timekeeping could be regulated by adding or subtracting small pieces of lead or shot in a space at the top of the going weight, see page 22. This clock had been converted to Huygens' single weight and continuous rope system, which involved reversing the direction of one train as the two great wheels originally turned in opposite directions and must both turn the same way when a pulley with single weight is provided.

The following changes were made to the going train, the direction of rotation was reversed and the duration increased by replacing the forty-eight tooth hour wheel driven by a four pin pinion formed on the great wheel arbor by a pinion of sixteen leaves driving an hour wheel of forty-eight via an idler pinion. The escapement conversion involved replacing the crown wheel with a third wheel and pinion and providing a small escape wheel and anchor pallets.

The duration of the striking train was doubled by increasing the number of pins in the great wheel from eight to sixteen, cutting an extra slot in the hoop wheel and changing the pinion of report from the four pin pinion to one of eight leaves. It was also necessary to slow down the striking by providing a warning wheel with twice the number of teeth and remaking the fly pinion.

The clock is laid out like a lantern clock of the 1660s, but with plates six inches square it is larger than the normal lantern. The frame was made without turned columns, feet or finials and with no provision for side doors or frets, which rules out any possibility of it having been made for a lantern clock.

The maker was obviously accustomed to making lantern clocks and the tapered arbors with

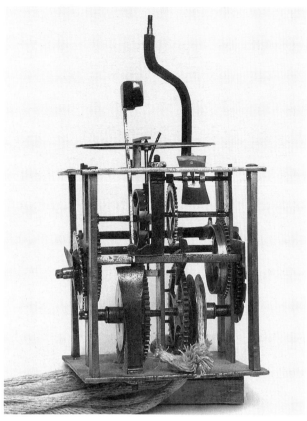

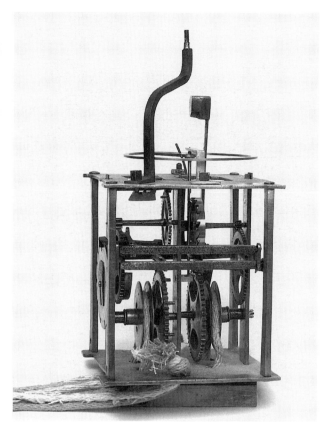

Figure 13/1. Restored movement of balance clock seen from the right, replaced verge escapement and balance, and new warning wheel. The balance is planted high on the verge to avoid the fly which projects well above the top plate.

Figure 13/2. Left hand view of balance movement.

the wheels riveted on without collets are a reflection of early practice. It is of interest to note that the original train numbers are identical with those of the lantern clock in Chapter 1. All 'improvements' have now been removed and the clock completely restored to balance control with its original short duration (figures 13/1 to 13/3). However the bottom plate had been drilled to permit the use of pulleys to double the duration, before the conversion to pendulum, and this facility has been utilised to simplify winding. The trains are now as follows:

Going	Great wheel	56	Pinion of report 4, Hour wheel 48
	Second wheel pinion	7	
	Second wheel	54	
	Crown wheel pinion	6	
	Crown wheel	19	
Striking	Great wheel	56	8 pins, pinion of report 4, count
Hoop wheel pinion		7	wheel gear 39
Hoop wheel		54	
Warning wheel pinion		6	
Warning wheel		48	
Fly pinion		6	

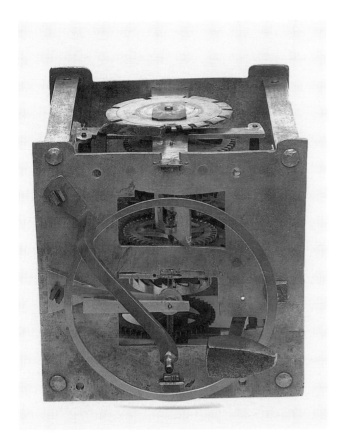

Figure 13/3. Top view of movement showing replaced balance and cock, and new bell stand.

Figure 13/4. Anonymous 10ins. dial of balance clock.

Unfortunately the clock is not signed, see figure 13/4, so the maker cannot be traced, but he was probably working in the provinces. The ten inch dial, which is obviously original to the clock, cannot be earlier than about 1680, so the clock is a survivor made in an earlier style, rather than a precursor of the pendulum clock.

The case is contemporary and is of ebonised pine, with a forward sliding hood without a door. It is interesting to note that the exceptionally wide side windows coincide with and give a complete view of the very deep movement (figure 13/6), suggesting that the case was made to house a similar type of movement originally. It is of provincial construction and the height is 6ft. 10ins.

Figure 13/6. Hood of balance clock case showing exceptionally wide side windows which line up with and display the whole of movement. Note that wood strips behind rear columns extend to top of hood, an early feature.

Figure 13/5. Case housing balance clock. Ebonised pine with forward sliding hood but without a door. Height 6ft. 10ins.

TOMPION EQUATION CLOCK CASES

Some years ago, when the author was engaged in cataloguing clocks in the Fitzwilliam Museum, Cambridge, he came to the conclusion that the upper portion of the hood of the Drayton House Tompion clock (figure 13/7) had been modified, probably soon after it was made. Similar superstructures, incorporating concave mouldings, are found on a number of clock cases dating from the early years of the eighteenth century, see figure 13/8, which shows the hood of a fine clock by Edward Speakman dating from c.1710. It was then decided to examine the slightly earlier but closely related clock in the Royal Collection (figure 13/9), originally supplied to William III and now in Kensington Palace.

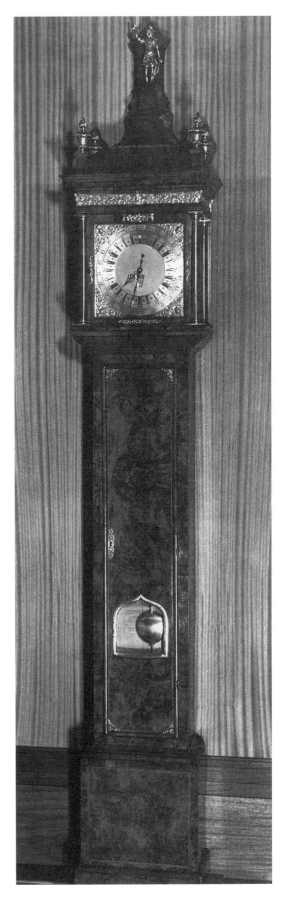

Figure 13/8. Hood of a fine longcase clock by Edward Speakman, c.1710. Compare the superstructure of the hood with that of the Tompion case in figure 13/7.

Figure 13/7. The Drayton House Tompion of c.1695 in its present position in the Fitzwilliam Museum.

Figure 13/10. The dial of the Drayton House clock. The chapter ring and spandrels are contained within an 11 ⁄4ins. square, which is the only part visible with the door closed.

Figure 13/9. The Kensington Palace Tompion supplied to William III, c.1690.

THE DRAYTON HOUSE CLOCK

According to Symonds[1] this clock was supplied by Tompion to Drayton House, the home of Lady Mary Mordaunt, Duchess of Norfolk. She separated from the Duke and lived at Drayton House with Sir John Germain from around 1692. The clock probably dates from c.1695.

The case has the normal oak carcase which is veneered with burr walnut. The caddy part of the hood also has an oak carcase but the wood differs from that in the rest of the case. Some of the walnut on the caddy differs from that on the main part of the case and the piece of solid walnut behind the figure of a warrior, which forms an integral part of the caddy, seems rather strange as other cases with pedestal figures lack this backboard, the figures being silhouetted against the wall, see figure 13/8.

The hood slides up and was constructed without a door, as was normal with early cases. Traces remain of the spoon lock for securing the hood when the trunk door was closed and of the catch for holding the hood in the raised position. Bearing in mind the very high position of the winding square, at the upper XII, it may even have been necessary to remove the hood for the annual winding. The hood was subsequently cut to provide a door so that the clock could be wound and corrected without having to raise the unwieldy hood. There is no masking frame to the dial.

The dial plate (figure 13/10) has an 11¼ins. square engraved on it which contains the chapter ring, the spandrels and the decorative engraving between them. This is the only part of the dial plate visible when the hood door is closed, the subsidiary dials being completely covered, as they were before the door was provided. Opening the door gives access to the maintaining power lever on the right and the lower of the two subsidiary dials in the arch, the annual calendar. The upper dial, indicating the zodiac, remains covered unless the hood is raised, which provides additional evidence that the door was a later modification. The annual calendar was provided to enable the clock winder to set the equation of time mechanism correctly, it being directly associated with the calendar. The latter was not intended for daily use, being difficult to read except at close quarters. A similar, but later, equation clock by Tompion and Banger (figure 13/21) has a separate day of the month indicator at the base of the dial for normal use. The movement of the Drayton clock is described on pages 178, 179.

It is suggested that this case was modified at the customer's

1. *Symonds*, p.269.

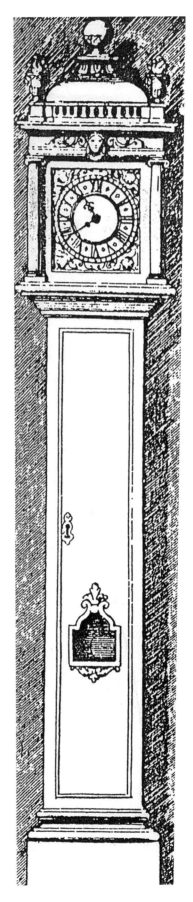

Figure 13/11. Drawing for a clock case by Daniel Marot, a Huguenot architect who worked for William III. Note the shaping of the pendulum window.

Figure 13/12. The trunk of the Royal case. Note the brass replacement hinges, also the cut-away section above and behind the pendulum to accommodate a wide-swinging pendulum in the normal position. The rebated oak strip on the right, level with the pendulum bob, is one of two used to fix a silvered degree plate.

Figure 13/13. Illustration of the Royal clock in the Pictorial Inventory of c.1827, showing the clock very much in its present form except for the bun feet.

request, soon after it was delivered, to make it more imposing to suit a lofty room. The design of both caddy and mounts is similar to that of other important but somewhat later clocks by both Tompion and Quare. Increasing the weight and instability of the hood would have made a door essential.

THE ROYAL CLOCK

According to Symonds[2] this clock was made for William III and is slightly earlier in date than the Drayton House clock as indicated by the foliated cherub spandrels (figure 13/14). It probably dates from c.1690.

The case is very similar to the Drayton one up to the top of the trunk section, the corresponding dimensions of the two cases being identical or within a small fraction of an inch of one another. It also has an oak carcase veneered with burr walnut. Both trunk doors have the same gothic shaped pendulum window frames, possibly inspired by a design of Daniel Marot (figure 13/11). They also have small spandrel pieces in the corners and, exceptionally, three hinges per door, although the original iron ones have been replaced by later brass examples on the Royal case (figure 13/12). Both cases now have skirtings but the one on this case is of

---

2. *Symonds*, p.268.

Figure 13/14. Dial of the Royal clock as seen through the hood door. Note the absence of decoration round the subsidiary dials.

Figure 13/15. Movement of the Royal clock showing how the calendar disc was modified.

Figure 13/16. Hood of the Royal clock case showing replacement door.

450

Figure 13/17. Inside of hood of the Royal clock case showing alterations carried out with pine carcase wood.

Figure 13/18. Rear view of top hood of the Royal clock case showing how the arched section stops short of the back.

Figure 13/19. Clock No.231 by Thomas Tompion, c.1695, showing typical domed hood of the period.

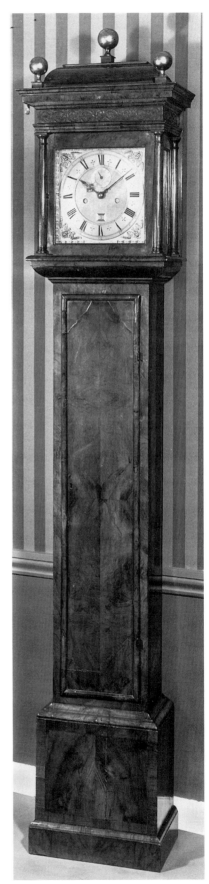

eighteenth century design and as it covers the crossbanding on the plinth it cannot be original. The drawing in the Pictorial Inventory[3] of c.1827 (figure 13/13) shows a skirting which does not obscure the crossbanding, with bun feet below. The skirting on the Drayton House case is certainly of seventeenth century design but it may also have replaced bun feet.

The dial (figure 13/14) is very similar to the Drayton House dial (figure 13/10), with the chapter ring and spandrels enclosed within an 11¼ins. square and curved slots for the annual calendar and zodiac above. It will be noticed that there is no decoration around the slots, the scrolled engraving between the spandrels being confined within the square. The original square dial opening did not expose either of these subsidiary dials, but the present opening has a small break arch to display the calendar and zodiac slots, an arrangement which is very unsatisfactory aesthetically. Tompion designed his dials with great care and would not have produced an unfinished effect on such an important clock.

When the Gregorian calendar was adopted in England in 1752 the loss of eleven days necessitated corrections to solar indications on clocks and on this example the change was apparently made by cutting off the outer, calendar, ring and refixing it in the correct position (figure 13/15).

The hood slides up and was originally without a door. The present door (figure 13/16) is of later construction, the oak being quite different from that of the rest of the carcase. The arched section of the hood is built up in pine (figure 13/17) in contrast to the original oak sides and strip across the top. A strange feature is that the arch stops about 1½ins. short of the back (figure 13/18), probably done to avoid weakening the hood when it was altered. The finial and its pedestal with supporting brackets appear to be original, but the supporting plinth is almost certainly later. The hood probably started life very similar to the one in figure 13/19 which shows Tompion No.231 of slightly later date.

Tompion enjoyed the lavish patronage of William III which resulted in the production of a number of very fine and expensive clocks. Queen Anne also patronised Tompion but on a much more modest scale. With the

3. Royal Collection, Pictorial Inventory taken for George IV, c.1827.

Figure 13/20. Year equation clock by Tompion and Banger, supplied to Prince George of Denmark, c.1703. The hood is designed to display the subsidiary dials.

advent of George I there was little royal interest in the fine and applied arts, a state of affairs which continued until the time of George III, who was keenly interested in the arts and sciences.

There is conclusive evidence that this case housed a more conventional clock at some period in its history. These year clocks each have their pendulum hung low down on the front plate, so that the pendulum hangs immediately behind the trunk door. Figure 13/12 shows a cut-away section in the side of the trunk to accommodate a wide-swinging pendulum suspended from the back of a movement in the normal higher position. A similar cut-away exists in the left hand side of the trunk. The only reason for thus modifying the case would be to fit another movement and dial.

The Drayton House clock has a silvered brass plate embodying a degree scale fixed immediately behind the pendulum and in front of the weight. This plate would have had to be removed when a conventional movement was fitted in the Royal case as it would have interfered with the fall of the weights. The rebated oak strip fixed to the right hand side of the trunk (figure 13/12) is one of the fixings for the silvered plate and together with its partner proves that the present case is the one originally provided for the clock.

Year-going clocks normally require skilled maintenance if they are to give a reliable performance and it is suggested that some time after Tompion's death in 1713 the clock became unreliable and a

Figure 13/21. Dial of clock in figure 13/20, showing how the engraved border to the dial is upswept to include the subsidiary dials.

shorter-duration clock was fitted in its place, thus necessitating the alterations described above. It is also suggested that at the time of the substitution the dial opening in the hood was still square without the arch, as a special dial would otherwise have been necessary and would probably have made the change not worthwhile.

George III had a deep and continuing interest in horology, examples of this include some notes he made on how to dismantle and re-assemble a watch[4] and the steps he took to ensure that John Harrison received the proper reward for his work on marine timekeepers. It would have been appropriate for George III to have arranged for the restoration of this clock and for the modification of its case to show the annual calendar and the signs of the zodiac, bearing in mind his interest in astronomy also. These alterations had certainly been carried out before the preparation of the drawing in the Pictorial Inventory of c.1827 (figure 13/13).

A third year equation clock, also in the Royal Collection (figure 13/20), was made by Tompion and Banger for Prince George of Denmark c.1703[5] and in this case the subsidiary dials for the calendar and zodiac are accommodated in an upswept section of the original hood door. A proof that the subsidiary dials were intended to be permanently on view is provided by the engraved border to the dial plate which sweeps upwards to include them (figure 13/21). This layout is much more satisfying aesthetically than the small break-arched opening now on the earlier clock and is probably the first clock by Tompion to have other

4. C.B. Drover, 'George IIIrd's Directions for Mounting and Unmounting a Watch', Antiquarian Horology, 9 (March 1975), 169.
5. Symonds, p.269.

than a rectangular dial opening.

The Kensington Palace year clock has long been claimed as the earliest English clock to have a break-arch dial, but there was always the unexplained gap until c.1709 when the next examples appeared on the clock presented to the Pump Room, Bath, in 1709[6] and on the similar Iscoyd Park clock[7]. It now appears that the introduction of the break-arch dial must be attributed to the latter date, from when it was quickly adopted by many makers.

THE FIRST SIDEREAL TIMEPIECE?

Sidereal time is briefly discussed and defined on page 168. Because it can be determined more accurately than solar time it became increasingly important to astronomers, but its changing indication with respect to solar time made it unsuitable for domestic purposes. Any normal clock can be converted to indicate sidereal time merely by slightly shortening the pendulum to make it gain approximately four minutes per mean solar day, so there is nothing to show that an ordinary clock has been so used.

Clocks which indicate both mean solar time and sidereal time are rare and the example by Thomas Tompion shown in figure 13/22 is probably the earliest to have survived. The 12ins. dial plate is signed on a reserve in the matting 'Thos:Tompion Edw: Banger London' and this is covered by a silvered oval plaque engraved 'Thos. Tompion London'. This probably means that the clock was made in 1708-09 about the time of Banger's dismissal when George Graham was working for Tompion but had not yet been made a partner. The clock may well have been made by Graham as it shows similar work to that on a sidereal clock, no.634 which he made some fifteen years later. The outer chapter ring is divided into minutes on its inner

6. *Symonds*, p.74.
7. E.L. Edwardes, *The Grandfather Clock,* 3rd edn. (Altrincham, 1971), pl.90, p.165.

Figure 13/22. 12ins. dial of sidereal timepiece by Tompion, no. 483. The inner chapter ring is mounted on the matted centre which is separate from the rest of the dial plate. The gilt minute hand rotates with the steel one and can be pre-set to show local time.

Figure 13/23. Dial with centre section removed. Clockwise-rotating outer chapter ring is supported on anti-friction wheels and driven from the normal motion work via the minute wheel arbor which extends to rear of movement.

edge and makes two complete rotations in a clockwise direction in 366¼ days. The gilt brass minute hand rotates with the steel one and can be pre-set up to approximately fifteen minutes ahead or behind it; it was probably used to give a direct reading of local time.

The month-going timepiece movement (figure 13/23) has bolt and shutter maintaining power and, exceptionally for a 'special' clock is numbered, 483. The clock now has a dead-beat escapement, presumably a later modification by Graham. Like Tompion's equation clocks described earlier, the central part of the dial plate is separate and is supported on its own dial feet.

The rotating chapter ring is supported on four anti-friction wheels and the drive for it is taken from the normal motion work. The large diameter wheels with teeth of fine pitch are to produce regular motion and reduce shake. The minute wheel is mounted on an arbor which passes through the movement and is supported by cocks at each end. The rear end of this arbor (figure 13/24) carries a wheel of 288 teeth which meshes with a wheel of 144 teeth. The latter has an endless screw or worm on is front end which drives a pinion of fifteen leaves on a vertical arbor. The upper end of this arbor has an endless screw which engages with the 586-tooth ring gear fixed to the rear of the chapter ring. This gear train gives the required rotation in 183⅛ days.

The whole clock is of very fine quality and is latched throughout. It is numbered 483 on the back plate.

The ebonised case, shown in figure 13/25, has gilt metal finials and other mounts and stands 7ft. 5ins. high.

There is considerable controversy as to exactly how the clock was intended to be used. In its present state there is no obvious index point against which the rotating ring can be read. If a fixed point had been used one would expect there to be a fixed hand or an engraved pointer on the normal chapter ring, but there is no trace of any such device. In addition this method does not give a direct answer but requires an arithmetical operation.

It seems far more likely that originally the clock had an hour hand with an extended tip which reached the minute divisions on the rotating chapter ring. Such an hour hand would have been very vulnerable and if a later owner of the clock were not interested in astronomical matters he may well have had the hand replaced by one of a more conventional design. With such an extended hour hand there are two possible answers, the choice between them depends on the priority on the use of the clock.

If it is regarded as a mean-solar time clock which also indicates sidereal time, the pendulum is regulated to show mean time on the main dial. Sidereal time is then obtained by reading the time shown against the tip of the hand on the outer chapter ring and subtracting this from twelve hours.

However, if the clock is regarded as a sidereal time clock which also indicates mean solar time, the pendulum is adjusted to show sidereal time on the main dial. Mean solar time is then shown directly on the

Figure 13/25. Ebonised case of Tompion no. 483 with gilt metal mounts. It stands 7ft. 5ins. high. Probably 1708-09.

Figure 13/24. Three quarter rear view of movement showing drive to rotating chapter ring. Note high-numbered wheels to give smooth drive with minimum shake.

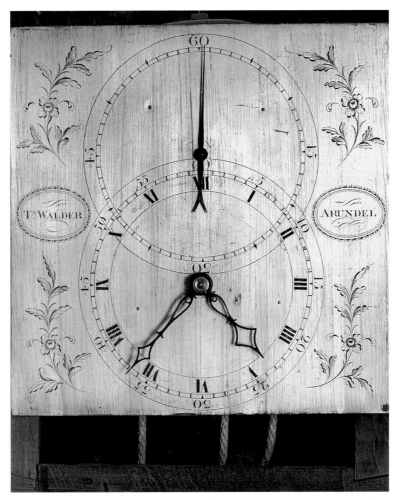

Figure 13/26. 11ins. dial signed T. *Walder Arundel, with very prominent seconds ring, possibly for doctor's use.*

rotating chapter ring.

If further research could establish the occupation or primary interests of the original owner this would help to decide how the clock was used originally. If he were a practising astronomer, professional or amateur, this would suggest the clock was adjusted to keep sidereal time.

SOME PROVINCIAL CLOCKS

The dial shown in figure 13/26 is by Thomas Walder of Arundel, a maker discussed at some length on pages 374 to 379. Another clock by him with the same dial layout has survived[8] and it is suggested that this arrangement with prominent seconds indications may have been designed for a doctor's use when taking a patient's pulse, as watches with seconds hands were not in common use until later in the century. This clock probably dates from c.1800-05, as his later clocks had a single circle for the minute divisions and 'Thomas' is abbreviated to 'T' or is omitted altogether.

8. See *Antiquarian Horology,* Vol. VII p.78.

Figure 13/27 shows the movement which is laid out the same as an ordinary centre-pinion movement, but with an additional centre pinion mounted low in the frame with normal two-hand motion work. There is a recoil escapement so the large seconds hand puts up a lively performance.

The original oak case (figure 13/28) is of a typical Sussex design with a rather insignificant cornice to the hood.

The individual design of this clock proves that Walder was no mere retailer and further proof of his ability as a maker exists in the form of a clock very similar to the one on page 380 with the front plate inscribed 'Thos. Walder made this clock for W. Dendy Augt, 1801'.

Figure 13/27. Thirty-hour clock by Walder showing striking train on right. Note additional centre-pinion planted low down in plates.

Figure 13/28. Original oak case of Walder clock, a typical Sussex design with rather insignificant cornice to hood.

William Dendy of Arundel was a corn merchant who died in February 1842, so the clock may well have been made for him when he got married.

Although many provincial makers were buying-in movements from trade suppliers by the end of the eighteenth century, some of them continued to make their own movements in the nineteenth century, although they may have bought-in rough wheels and pinions. Some of these clocks displayed great originality in design, an outstanding example being the year-going striking clock in figure 13/29. It is by Hardeman & Son of Bridge near Canterbury. Samuel Hardeman was in partnership with William Nash at Bridge until 1794 when he set up business on his own; it is not known when he was joined by his son William. Samuel is last recorded in a trade directory of 1838 and the clock was probably made c.1810.

The silvered brass dial (figure 13/30) measures 16ins. by 22½ins., note the absence of minute numbering. Below the dial centre is a simple thirty-one day calendar and in the arch is a month dial with the hand operated from the motion work by a long vertical arbor with an endless screw or worm at its upper end.

The massive movement (figure 13/31) has seven pillars and the plates are approximately 9¼ins. wide and 11ins. high.

The going train is as follows:

Great wheel	108
Second wheel pinion	12
Second wheel	72
Third wheel pinion	9
Third wheel	64
Centre pinion	8
Centre wheel	60
Fifth wheel pinion	8
Fifth wheel	56
Escape wheel pinion	7
Escape wheel	30

So the clock has a seconds pendulum and the barrel rotates once in twenty-four days, so sixteen turns give a duration of 384 days. The striking train consists of five wheels (see figure 13/32):

Figure 13/29. Year-going striking clock by Hardeman & Son, Bridge. Case with substantial mahogany carcase and fine veneers. Separate double skirting which supports plinth. Height 9ft. 2ins. including finial.

Great wheel	120
Second wheel pinion	10
Second wheel	96
Pin wheel pinion	8
Pin wheel	78 26 pins
Locking wheel pinion	6
Locking wheel	72 2 locking pins
Warning wheel pinion	6
Warning wheel	54
Fly pinion	7

With this train the striking barrel also turns once in twenty-four days, so the weights should descend equally. The weights are each of 96lbs. and are suspended on specially strong catgut with large wooden pulleys.

This clock represents a magnificent achievement by a little known provincial maker, year-going striking clocks being particularly rare because of the difficulty of obtaining a reliable performance from the striking train.

The very substantial mahogany case (figure 13/30) with well-chosen veneers, stands freely in the double skirting which supports the lower end of the plinth. The total height, including finial, is 9ft. 2ins.

Figure 13/30. 16ins. dial of year clock, note counter-balanced minute hand. Hand of month dial in arch is stepped on daily from motion work.

Figure 13/31. Left hand side of year movement showing striking train. Note long vertical arbor with endless screw at upper end operating month hand.

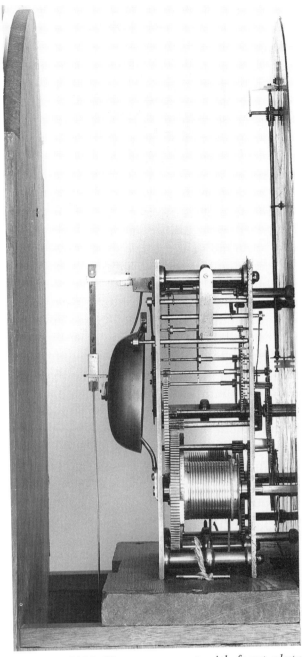

Figure 13/32. Year movement with front plate removed. High-numbered wheels in striking train to obtain required duration from five wheels. Also skeletonised fly for lightness.

461

Glossary

ACANTHUS. Herbaceous plant with coarsely serrated leaves used in Greek architectural ornament. Found on Corinthian capitals and in floral marquetry.

ADAM, Robert (1728-92). Architect and furniture designer who led the classical revival in England. His furniture was ornamented with fine marquetry and painted panels. He did not publish his designs.

ANEROID. A type of barometer which measures the effect of varying air pressure on a partially exhausted metal box. It was invented in 1843.

ANTEFIX. An ornamental corner piece above a classical cornice.

ARABESQUE. Form of decorative design including interlacing scrolls, leaves and strap-work in a symmetrical layout. Used in late marquetry work which often also includes grotesque figures and animals.

ARBOR. An axle or spindle on which is mounted a wheel, pinion or other rotating part.

ASTROLABE. An instrument for measuring the altitude of heavenly bodies and thus used for determining time and latitude.

BASE. Bottom, ornamented portion of a column, sometimes used for the plinth of a long-case.

BERAIN, Jean (1637-1711). Designer to Louis XIV who published many drawings which incorporated grotesque and other figures, draperies, arabesques and trailing foliage. His designs influenced arabesque marquetry in this country.

BIRDCAGE. Type of thirty-hour longcase movement with top and bottom plates joined by vertical posts and trains carried in narrow bars, usually one behind the other.

BOLT AND SHUTTER. A type of maintaining power used mainly on early clocks to keep them going during winding.

BOULLE, André Charles (1642-1732). French furniture designer and cabinetmaker who developed marquetry designs which incorporated metals, tortoiseshell and other exotic materials. This is often known as 'Boulle' work. It is only rarely found on English clock cases.

BRACKET CLOCK. Popular name for a spring driven clock normally placed on a mantelpiece, a piece of furniture, or occasionally on a wall bracket. Other names are spring clock and table clock, but the latter can lead to confusion with the pre-pendulum clocks in metal cases.

BRIDGE. A bracket with a foot at each end, used to support an arbor or other device. A common example is the hour wheel bridge.

CAM FOLLOWER. An arm which follows the contours of a cam.

CANNON WHEEL OR PINION. The cannon wheel or pinion has a pipe which carries the minute hand at the front end.

CANTED CORNER. One which is bevelled or chamfered, see figure G/1.

Figure G/1. Canted corner on trunk of an early nineteenth century case. This example is fluted.

CAPITAL. Top ornamented portion of a column. The different types are described under the appropriate headings Doric, Ionic and Corinthian.

CARTOUCHE. Engraved scroll with rolled-up ends used to contain the maker's name on a clock dial.

CASE PARTS. Figure G/2 shows the main parts of a longcase.

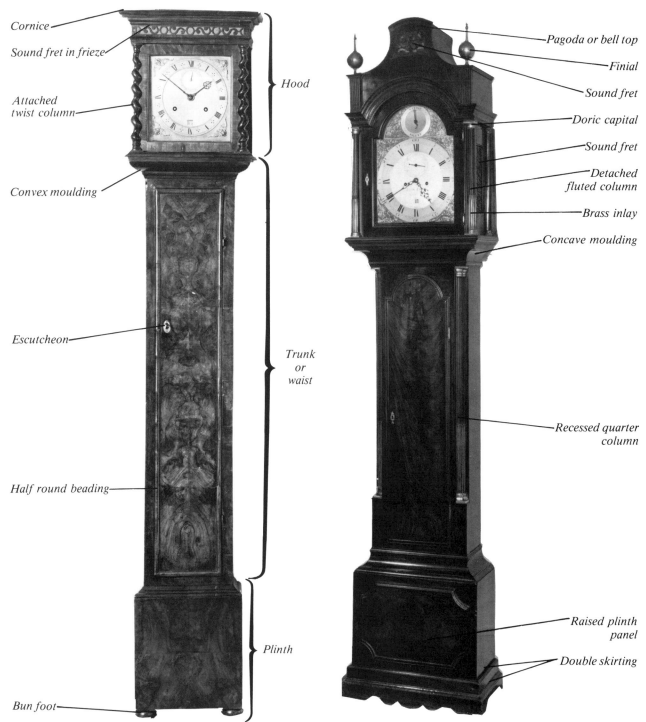

Figure G/2. Parts of a clock case. The left hand example is in walnut, 6ft. 6ins. high and houses a month clock by Joseph Knibb, c.1675-80. Right hand one is in mahogany, approximately 8ft. high and houses a clock by John Ewe, London, c.1775-80.

CAVETTO. A hollow or concave moulding.

CHAPTER RING. The ring carrying the hour numbers or chapters, also known as the hour circle, see figure G/5.

CHINOISERIE. Imitation Chinese motifs, often with some European features. Used on japanned clock cases and on some late eighteenth century dials.

CHIPPENDALE, Thomas (1718-79). Prominent furniture designer and manufacturer who published well known books of designs (the *Director*). His clock case designs were rather fanciful, see Chapter 10, but cases showing traces of his influence are loosely described as 'Chippendale'.

CIRCULAR ERROR. The error introduced by a pendulum following a circular rather than a cycloidal path. The result is that large arcs take longer than small ones. This is also known as a lack of isochronism.

CLOCK. Apart from the general meaning, a time measuring instrument, 'clock' was formerly used to refer to the striking train. See also: 'Watch'.

COCK. A bracket, normally with only one foot, which supports an arbor or other device. A bracket with a foot at each end is called a bridge. An exception is the pendulum cock or back cock which is really a bridge but may have got its name from some of the early pendulum cocks having only one foot.

COCUS WOOD. A rich dark brown wood with a rather pronounced grain, occasionally used as a veneer in the seventeenth century. It comes from a West Indian tree, granadilla (*brya ebenus*) and is also known as green, Jamaican or American ebony.

COLLET. A collar which holds a part in place on an arbor. Used to describe the domed washer which retains the minute hand and for the collar which holds a great wheel in place, but the most usual application is for the mounting of a wheel on an arbor. See figure G/3 which shows how collet design changed over the years.

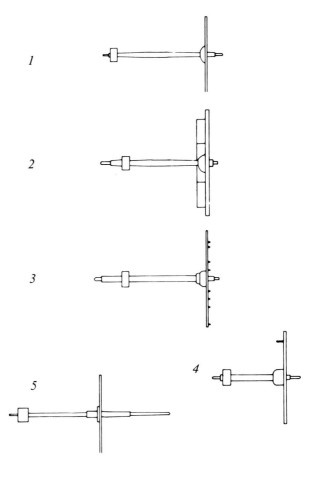

Figure G/3. The development of wheel collets. 1. Third wheel; note very short domed collet and tapered pinion with short head, late seventeenth century. 2. Thirty-hour hoop wheel, rather heavier domed collet, pinion still tapered, early eighteenth century. 3. Pin wheel, ornamented collet on straight pinion with short head, early eighteenth century. 4. Thirty-hour warning wheel, with heavy cylindrical collet, mid-eighteenth century. 5. Escape wheel with cheese headed collet, introduced about mid-eighteenth century and continued up to date.

COLUMN. A vertical shaft of circular cross-section, usually with capital and base. Columns used on clock cases are attached to the corners of the hoods of earlier cases but are detached on later examples.

CONTRATE WHEEL. A wheel with teeth parallel to its arbor, used to drive a pinion at right angles to the wheel.

CORBEL. A bracket used to support an overhanging member. Corbel brackets are fitted under the hoods of some cases.

CORINTHIAN COLUMN. Most ornate of the three Greek orders of architecture. The capital has horizontal rows of acanthus leaves. Corinthian capitals were used on some seventeenth century and some late eighteenth century cases.

CORNICE. Top horizontal moulding on a clock case.

CORNUCOPIA. A horn of plenty, overflowing with flowers, fruit and corn. Some finials incorporate this device.

CRESTING. Carved decoration above the cornice of some seventeenth century clocks, see figure G/4.

CROSSBANDING. Decoration consisting of a strip of veneer with the grain at right angles to its length.

CROSS-CUT or cross-grained. A moulding which is made with the grain at right angles to its length. It is built up on a base with the grain parallel to its length.

CROWN WHEEL. The escape wheel of a verge escapement. It has teeth parallel to its axis.

CRUTCH. A rod attached to the pallet arbor which connects it to the pendulum.

CUSHION MOULDING. A bold convex moulding, found immediately under the cornice of some seventeenth century cases. Also known as a pulvinated frieze.

DECLINATION. The angular distance of the sun north or south of the celestial equator. The maximum declination is 23° 27′ north in June and south in December.

DETENT. Catch or lever which acts as a stop piece to lock a wheel.

DIAL PARTS. Figure G/5 shows the main parts of a dial.

DOLPHIN. A conventional representation of this marine animal was commonly used on lantern clock frets and for the arch spandrels of long-case dials. The latter ornaments are often loosely referred to as 'dolphins'. The motif was also employed on furniture. Probably used because the dolphin was formerly a symbol of friendliness.

DORIC COLUMN. Simplest of the three Greek orders of architecture. Doric capitals were used on many clock cases, see figure G/2.

DUPLEX ESCAPEMENT. An escapement with two escape wheels invented by Daniel Delander. The principle is the same as in the duplex watch escapement which was introduced later.

Figure G/4. Early type of cresting on a walnut case, clock by Joseph Knibb, c.1680.

466

Dial plate

Matting

Floral engraving

Ringed winding hole

Calendar aperture

Foliated cherub spandrel

Chapter ring or hour circle

Seconds ring

Minute divisions

Quarter hour divisions

Half hour mark

Half quarter mark

Figure G/5. The parts of a dial. This example is by Robert Morey, London, and is c.1710.

DUTCH MINUTE BAND. A type of minute marking which is arched between the five minute numbers. It is common on Dutch clocks and is occasionally used on English ones.

DUTCH STRIKING. A system where either the last or the next hour is struck at the half hour, using a higher toned bell.

ECLIPTIC. Apparent path of the sun amongst the stars during the year, as viewed from the earth.

ENDLESS CORD. A descriptive title for Huygens' maintaining power where the weight is hung on an endless cord.

EPICYCLIC GEARS. A system where a wheel or pinion travels round the circumference of a stationary wheel. Also known as sun and planet gearing. Used in equation and astronomical clocks.

EQUATION OF TIME. The difference between apparent solar time, as shown by a sundial, and mean solar time.

EQUINOX. The dates on which day and night are of equal length, that is when the sun crosses the equator or its declination is zero. The spring equinox is on 20th or 21st March and the autumn equinox on 22nd or 23rd September.

ESCUTCHEON. Applied surround to a key hole, usually of brass.

FEATHER BANDING. Decoration consisting of two strips of veneer with the grain running diagonally in opposite directions. Often known as herring-bone banding.

FINIALS. Decorative terminal ornaments, used on top of the hoods of clock cases.

FLAMBEAU FINIAL. A type where the upper part resembles a flaming torch.

FLEUR-DE-LIS or fleur-de-lys. Heraldic lily flower, former royal arms of France. Used for half hour marks on many eighteenth century dials.

FLUTING. Vertical hollows separated by sharp ridges, usually in a column or pilaster.

FRET. An area of pierced wood, or occasionally metal, on a clock case to allow the sound of striking to be heard more clearly, see figure G/2. Blind frets, that is fretwork backed with solid wood, were introduced as a decorative feature by Chippendale. Some country clock cases have blind frets in imitation of sound outlets.

FRIEZE. Horizontal section below a cornice, see figure G/2.

GADROONING. A border ornament of convex ridges, the opposite of fluting.

GOING RATCHET. Another name for Harrison maintaining power, which comes into operation automatically.

GRANDE SONNERIE. A striking system where the quarters and the last hour are sounded at each quarter.

GRANDMOTHER. A small longcase clock, under 6ft. high. A modern term for what is usually a modern clock.

GRASSHOPPER ESCAPEMENT. Accurate but delicate escapement invented by John or James Harrison.

GRAVITY ESCAPEMENT. One which gives a constant impulse provided by the force of gravity.

GREAT WHEEL. The first wheel of a train where the power is applied.

GREGORIAN CALENDAR. More accurate calendar introduced by Pope Gregory XIII in 1582 but not adopted in England until 1752. The correction was then made by omitting eleven days.

GRIDIRON PENDULUM. Compensation pendulum consisting of alternate bars of two dissimilar metals, invented by the Harrisons.

HARRISON MAINTAINING POWER. Method of providing maintaining power by means of an extra ratchet wheel. Invented by John Harrison and sometimes known as the going ratchet.

HERRING-BONE BANDING. Decoration consisting of two strips of veneer with the grain running diagonally in opposite directions. Also known as feather banding.

HOOP WHEEL. A wheel with a hoop attached to the side of it. A cut-away portion provides for locking a striking train.

HOUR CIRCLE. A ring bearing the hour numerals, also known as a chapter ring, see figure G/5.

HOUR WHEEL. A wheel which usually rotates in twelve hours and carries the hour hand.

HUYGENS MAINTAINING POWER. An endless rope maintaining power system invented by Huygens and used on thirty-hour clocks.

HYGROMETER. An instrument for measuring the humidity of the air.

IONIC COLUMN. One of the three Greek orders of architecture. The Ionic capital has two lateral spirals. It is rarely used on clock cases.

ISOCHRONOUS. The property of a pendulum (or balance) of swinging through large or small arcs in equal times.

JAPANNING. An opaque varnished finish, usually with gilt decoration, in imitation of Chinese lacquer work. Painted dials are sometimes described as japanned.

LACQUER. True lacquer work is an Oriental product, but the term is often applied to japanning. Lacquer is also the name of the special varnish used to prevent metal tarnishing.

LAMBREQUIN. Engraved drapery panel sometimes used on an early dial to take the maker's signature.

LANTERN PINION. A pinion consisting of thin steel rods, occasionally made from the solid end of an arbor, but usually consisting of rods between two discs.

LENTICLE. A glazed aperture, usually round or oval, to show the pendulum bob. Although often used, something of a misnomer as it implies a lens-shaped glass whereas it should be flat.

MAINTAINING POWER. A device to keep a clock going during winding.

MINUTE WHEEL. A wheel in the motion work which meshes with the cannon wheel or pinion and which has a pinion to drive the hour wheel.

MOTION WORK. Collective name for the gearing, normally behind the dial, which drives the hands and calendar work.

OGEE MOULDING. Moulding of double curvature, concave below, convex above.

OYSTER. Slice of veneer cut across a sapling or a small branch so that the grain exhibits oyster-like markings. Olive is the wood most commonly used.

PALLET. Acting part of an escapement or other device which acts upon teeth of a wheel or rack.

PARQUETRY. A geometrical pattern formed of pieces of veneer.

PASSING STRIKE. A striking mechanism where the hammer is operated direct from the motion work.

PATERA. Round or oval decoration, usually applied, carved or inlaid, much used in the late eighteenth and early nineteenth century.

PEDIMENT. Triangular or curved section above the cornice of a case.

PILASTER. Pillar of rectangular cross-section attached to a vertical surface. Rarely used on longcases.

PINCHBECK. Alloy of four parts copper to three parts zinc used as a cheap substitute for gold. It was named after the inventor, Christopher Pinchbeck Sr.

PINION. A small wheel, usually of not more than twenty teeth, or 'leaves' as they are known. Unless stated otherwise it refers to a pinion with solid radiating leaves, as opposed to a lantern pinion. The complete arbor is often referred to as a pinion.

PIPE. The horological name for a tube used to act as a bearing.

PIVOT. The turned down end of an arbor which runs in a bearing known as a pivot hole.

PLINTH. The section of a clock case below the trunk, see figure G/2.

PORTICO TOP. Alternative name for pediment of architectural style case.

PRINCE'S WOOD. Seventeenth century name for kingwood.

PULVINATED FRIEZE. Frieze with a convex or cushion moulding.

PUMP ACTION. A device for sliding an arbor lengthwise to modify a striking or other operation.

RECOIL ESCAPEMENT. One where the supplementary swing of a pendulum or balance after a tooth has escaped causes the escape wheel to be pushed back. Common examples are the verge and the anchor, the latter often being referred to as the recoil escapement.

REEDING. Moulding consisting of small parallel rounded elements resembling reeds.

REPEATER. A clock or watch which strikes the last hour and perhaps the last quarter on demand. Also used in the seventeenth century to describe grande sonnerie striking.

REPOUSSÉ. Ornamental metal work hammered into relief from the reverse side.

RESERVE. Space on an engraved or matted surface left plain to accommodate an inscription.

RHOMBOID PENDULUM. One using one or more rhombi to provide temperature compensation.

ROCOCO. A style of decoration based on C-scrolls with flowing foliage, rocks and shells. It is normally asymmetrical but balanced.

ROMAN STRIKING. A system invented by Joseph Knibb which uses two bells, a small one to represent the Roman I and a larger bell for the Roman V. Four is marked on the dial IV.

SEAWEED MARQUETRY. A late type of marquetry with fine scrolling foliage but without strapwork or figures.

SHAKE MINUTES. A term applied to the more common type of thirty-hour movement which does not have a centre pinion but has an indirect drive to the minute hand.

SHERATON, Thomas (1751-1806). Well known furniture designer who published books of designs. His clock case designs were fanciful, see Chapter 10, but many inlaid mahogany cases are very loosely described as 'Sheraton'.

SIDEREAL TIME. A system based on the actual rotation of the earth compared with a fixed point, instead of its apparent rotation compared with the sun. A sidereal day is 23 hours 56 minutes 4.1 seconds of mean solar time.

SKIRTING. Board fixed round bottom of clock case, see figure G/2.

SOLAR TIME. Time based on the earth's rotation with respect to the sun, as indicated on a sundial. When averaged over a year it becomes mean solar time, the system in common use.

SOLSTICE. Dates on which sun is at greatest distance from equator, that is around 21st June (summer solstice) and 22nd December (winter solstice).

SPANDREL. Space between an arch and its surrounding rectangle. On a clock dial, the spaces between the chapter ring and the corners of the dial plate, or the decorative castings fitted in these spaces, are called spandrels. The term is also used loosely to describe the similar decorative fittings on a dial arch. Cescinsky and Webster's *English Domestic Clocks* has a comprehensive set of illustrations showing the development of spandrels. These are reproduced in figures G/6-12. For convenience these are identified in the text as 'C. & W. No. --'.

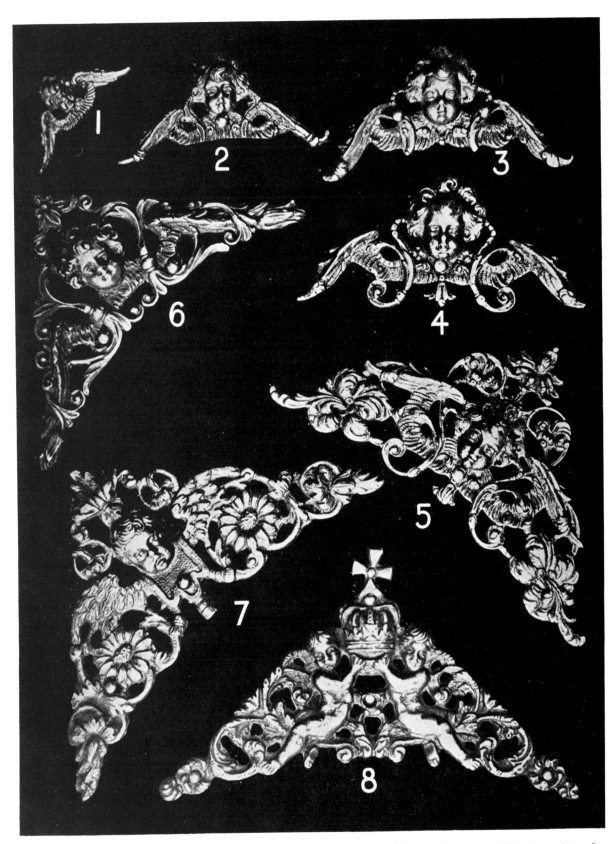

Figure G/6. Early spandrels. 3 is found on the earliest longcase dials and 4 came into use c.1670. 5 was introduced by Tompion c.1675 but was rare until c.1685. 7 was used mainly by Tompion and his associates from c.1700. 8 also came into use c.1700. The very small spandrels in figures G/6-10 are not from longcase dials.

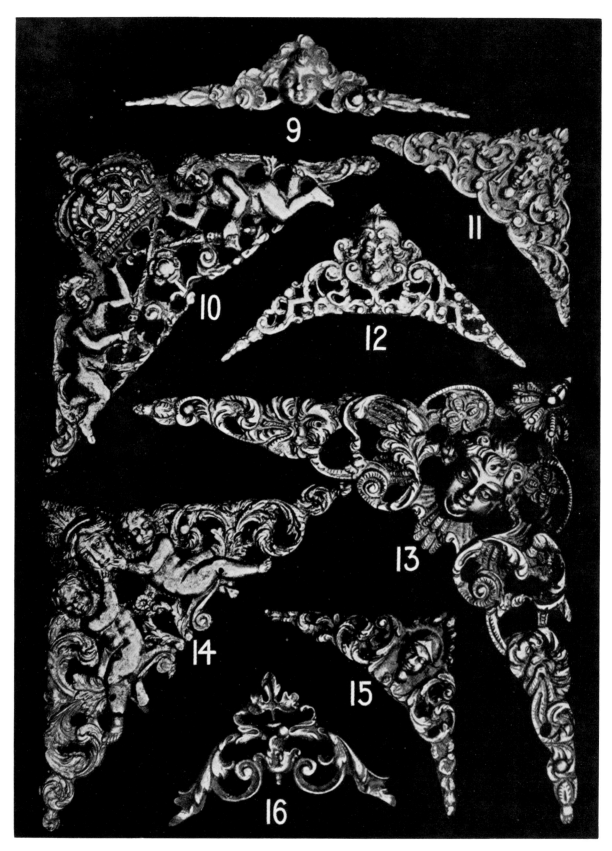

Figure G/7. 10 was introduced c.1710 and 14 a little later but it did not become popular. 13 is often found on 13 or 14ins. north country dials of the second half of the eighteenth century.

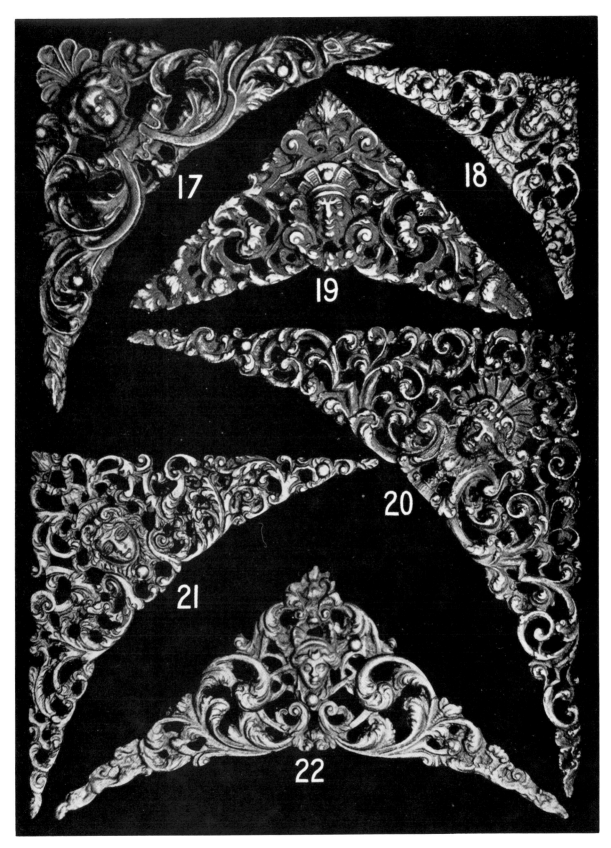

Figure G/8. 19 was introduced by Tompion around 1700, 21 came into use c.1720 and had great popularity. 20 and 22 are variations of 21 which were introduced later.

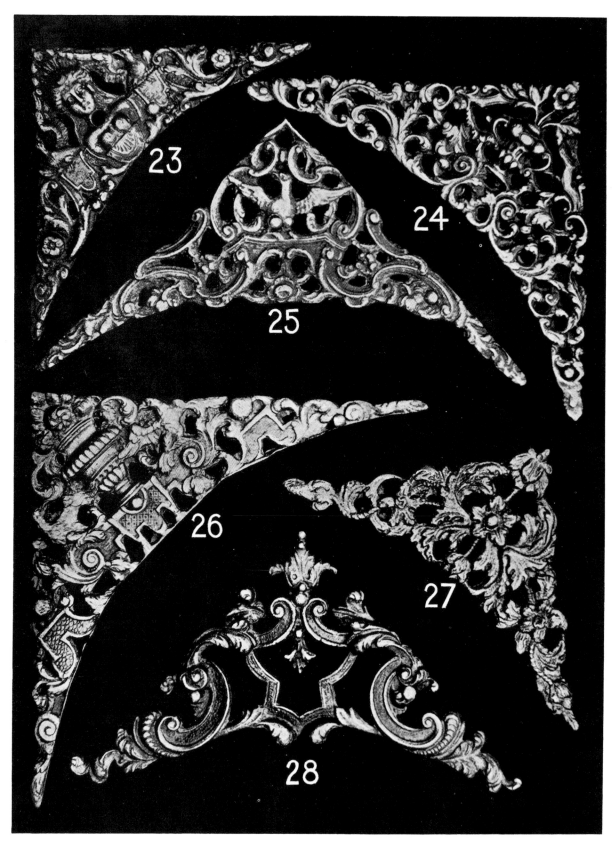

Figure G/9. 26 was introduced c.1710 and lasted a long time. 28 was occasionally used on good quality clocks around mid-eighteenth century. 23, 24 and 25 are found mainly on provincial eighteenth century clocks.

Figure G/10. 32 and 33 mark the introduction of the rococo style, c.1760. 30 is later, c.1780.

Figure G/11. 38, the dolphin, was introduced c.1715 and was used with all types of corner spandrels through most of the century. 36 and 40 date from c.1760 and 39 is a corresponding arch spandrel. 37 is found on small provincial dials of the second half of the eighteenth century.

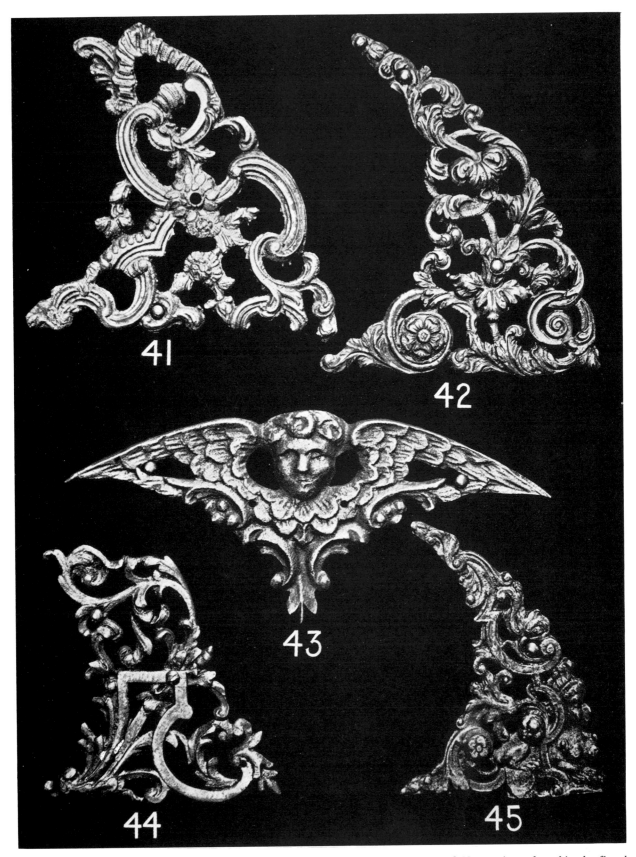

Figure G/12. 41 is another rococo arch spandrel, but the others are earlier. 42 and 45 were introduced in the first half of the eighteenth century but are not very common. 44 matches 28 (figure G/9).

Figures G/13 a and b. Spoon lock on a seventeeenth century marquetry case. View (a) shows it from the outside with the hood removed. Closing the trunk door presses on the rounded lower end and the bent-over top of the lever enters a mortice in the frame of the hood. View (b) shows the lever pivoted at the bottom of the mounting plate and with a restoring spring to ensure release of the hood.

SPOON LOCK. A safety device fitted to a longcase with a rising hood to lock the latter until the trunk door is opened. It consists of an iron bar pivoted just below the hood and with its lower end shaped like a spoon handle. Closing the trunk door pushes the lower end backwards and the bent-over upper end enters a mortice in the bottom rail of the dial frame, see figures G/13 a and b.

SPROCKET. A pulley with a ring of spikes on a great wheel arbor in a thirty-hour movement. Sprockets for rope have a smooth bottom to the groove, but chain sprockets have a central groove, or cut-away portions, to accommodate alternate links.

(a)   *(b)*

STRINGING. Very narrow band of inlay.

TIMEPIECE. A clock which does not strike.

TRUNK. The middle section of a longcase, see figure G/2.

VERGE. The pallet arbor of the verge or crown wheel escapement. Verge is occasionally used to describe other types of pallet arbor also.

WAIST. Another name for the trunk of a longcase, see figure G/2.

WATCH. An old name for the going part of a clock. See also: Clock.

WHEEL BAROMETER. Type where the atmospheric pressure is indicated on a dial, also known as a banjo barometer from the shape of the case.

ZODIAC. A broad band in the heavens, centred on the ecliptic, which encloses the paths of the sun, moon and major planets. The zodiac was divided by early astronomers into twelve parts, each of 30° and named after an appropriate constellation as follows: Aries (Ram), Taurus (Bull), Gemini (Twins), Cancer (Crab), Leo (Lion), Virgo (Virgin), Libra (Scales), Scorpio (Scorpion), Sagittarius (Archer), Capricornus (Goat), Aquarius (Water Carrier), Pisces (Fishes). The signs are illustrated and named in figure G/14. As each sign lasted for approximately thirty days they were often used on the annual calendars of complicated clocks.

Figure G/14. The signs of the zodiac and those for the planets, from L. Dygges, A Prognostication, *1555, reprinted 1926, p. 13*

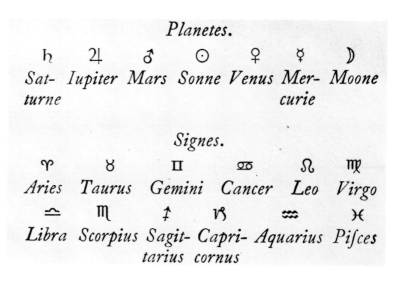

Planetes.

♄	♃	♂	☉	♀	☿	☽
Sat-turne	Iupiter	Mars	Sonne	Venus	Mer-curie	Moone

Signes.

♈	♉	♊	♋	♌	♍
Aries	Taurus	Gemini	Cancer	Leo	Virgo
♎	♏	♐	♑	♒	♓
Libra	Scorpius	Sagit-tarius	Capri-cornus	Aquarius	Pifces

478

Conversion Table: Imperial to Metric Measurements

FEET	INCHES	MILLIMETRES	FEET	INCHES	MILLIMETRES
	8	203	7	0 } 84	2133
	9	229			
	10	254	7	3 } 87	2209
	11	279			
	12	305	7	6 } 90	2285
	13	330			
	14	356	7	9 } 93	2361
6	0 } 72	1828	8	0 } 96	2438
6	3 } 75	1904	8	3 } 99	2514
6	6 } 78	1980	8	6 } 102	2590
6	9 } 81	2057			

Bibliography

This list has been restricted almost entirely to books published in the last thirty years, or to earlier works which have been reprinted during that period. In every case the date quoted refers to the first publication of that edition, reprints generally being ignored as they do not incorporate later ideas or discoveries. Books dealing only with relatively small areas such as counties have been omitted in spite of the best of these publications containing much useful information for collectors interested in these areas.

The price and availability of horological books can change rapidly and possible purchasers are advised to consult an up-to-date catalogue from a reliable horological bookseller.

Asprey & Co., *The Clockwork of the Heavens,* 1973. Catalogue of an exhibition of astronomical clocks, watches and allied scientific instruments. Contains useful information on astronomical clocks.

G.H. Baillie, *Clocks and Watches: An Historical Bibliography,* 1951. Extensive survey of horological literature up to 1800, with useful comments and illustrations.

G.H. Baillie, *Watchmakers and Clockmakers of the World,* 3rd edition, 1951. An essential tool, it contains about 35,000 names of makers up to 1825. Now entitled 'Volume I', see Volume 2 of same title by B. Loomes.

G.H. Baillie, C. Clutton and C.A. Ilbert, *Britten's Old Clocks and Watches and their Makers,* 7th edition, 1956. Completely re-written and excellent general survey which includes a list of nearly 14,000 makers, with more detail than in *Watchmakers and Clockmakers of the World.* An 8th edition has been prepared by C. Clutton (q.v.).

A. Bird, *English House Clocks: 1600-1850,* 1973. Good general survey full of practical information on cases and movements.

F.J. Britten, *Old English Clocks: The Wetherfield Collection,* 1907, recent reprint. Valuable record of an early but important collection long since dispersed.

F.J. Britten, *Old Clocks and Watches & their Makers,* 6th edition, 1932. The 3rd (1911) and 6th editions have been reprinted, the former with additional illustrations. A very good general survey which grew with each fresh edition so that by the 6th the layout had become very confused. Britten's contained the first extensive list of makers. For the 7th edition see Baillie and for the 8th see Clutton.

E. Bruton, *The Longcase Clock,* 2nd edition, 1976. Useful book which includes information on thirty-hour and other clocks for the 'small' collector.

H. Cescinsky, *The Old English Master Clockmakers and their Clocks 1670-1820,* 1938. Good illustrations of the earlier clocks by well known makers, but little on mechanism.

H. Cescinsky and M.R. Webster, *English Domestic Clocks,* 2nd edition, 1914, recent reprint. Valuable for its large number of photographs, mainly of fine clocks, but much of the information is now out of date.

C. Clutton, G.H. Baillie and C.A. Ilbert, *Britten's Old Clocks and Watches and their Makers,* 8th edition, 1973. An enlarged and revised version of the 7th edition, see under Baillie, Clutton and Ilbert.

C. Clutton and G. Daniels, *Clocks and Watches, The collection of the Worshipful Company of Clockmakers,* 1975. Gives details of only a dozen or so longcase clocks, but these include the three important Harrison examples owned by the Company.

P.G. Dawson, *The Design of English Domestic Clocks 1660-1700,* 1956. A small book but full of important information.

P.G. Dawson, C.B. Drover and D.W. Parkes, *Early English Clocks, A discussion of domestic clocks up to the beginning of the eighteenth century,* 1982. Very important and detailed study of both clocks and cases of this vital, formative period.

D. de Carle, *Watch and Clock Encyclopaedia,* 2nd edition, 1959. Very comprehensive illustrated dictionary which includes an antique clock section.

D. de Carle, *Clocks and their Value,* 4th edition, 1979. Covers a wide field but is most useful for its list of Tompion numbers.

W. Derham, *The Artificial Clock-maker. A Treatise of Watch, and Clock-work,* 1st edition, 1696, to 4th edition corrected, 1759. 1st edition reprinted 1962. Very important early textbook full of interesting information.

J. Drummond Robertson, *The Evolution of Clockwork,* 1931, recent reprint. Important for the history of the pendulum and of the anchor escapement.

E.L. Edwardes, *The Grandfather Clock,* 4th edition, 1980. Comprehensive well illustrated survey showing many provincial examples.

E.L. Edwardes, *The Story of the Pendulum Clock,* 1977. Contains the complete text of Huygens' *Horologium* in both Latin and English and a translation of the Coster/Fromanteel contract. Includes details of a number of early longcase clocks.

W.J. Gazeley, *Clock and Watch Escapements,* 1956. Theoretical and practical details of a wide range of escapements, an invaluable work.

G.F.C. Gordon, *Clockmaking Past and Present,* 1925. Contains much interesting historical and practical information not available elsewhere.

H.C. King and J.R. Millburn, *Geared to the Stars,* 1978. The sub-title *The Evolution of Planetariums, Orreries and Astronomical Clocks* indicates that much of the information is not directly applicable to the longcase clock but there is an important section on astronomical clocks.

W. Laycock, *The Lost Science of John 'Longitude' Harrison,* 1976. Important scientific study of Harrison's improvements in pendulum clocks.

R.A. Lee, *The First Twelve Years of the English Pendulum Clock,* 1969. Catalogue of an exhibition of Fromanteel and other clocks, 1658-70. Important source of information for this vital period.

R.A. Lee, *The Knibb Family, Clockmakers,* 1964. Apart from its importance as an investigation and record of the work of the Knibbs, this book provides much interesting information applicable to clocks made by their contemporaries.

H.A. Lloyd, *Some Outstanding Clocks over Seven Hundred Years 1250-1950,* 1958, recent reprint. This survey of unusual and complicated clocks gives details of many important developments.

H.A. Lloyd, *The Collector's Dictionary of Clocks,* 1964. Very comprehensive reference book, full of interest.

H.A. Lloyd, *Old Clocks,* 3rd edition, 1964. Excellent general introduction to antiquarian horology.

B. Loomes, *The White Dial Clock, 1974.* Pioneer study of the white or painted dial longcase clock with useful details of the dial makers.

B. Loomes, *Country Clocks and their London Origins*, 1976. Contains much useful information on the Fromanteels and Loomes as well as interesting details of clock-making in the provinces.

B. Loomes, *Watchmakers and Clockmakers of the World,* Volume 2, 1976. Companion volume to Baillie's of the same title, it augments and extends the list to c.1875 and includes a further 35,000 entries. It is equally essential.

B. Loomes, *Complete British Clocks,* 1978. A good general survey with some emphasis on provincial makers and information on case making.

H. Quill, *John Harrison, the Man who found Longitude,* 1966. Although most of the book is devoted to Harrison's development of marine timekeepers, there is an interesting section on his precision pendulum clocks.

A. Rees, *Rees's Clocks Watches and Chronometers (1819-20),* 1970. An invaluable selection from *The Cyclopaedia; or Universal Dictionary of Arts, Sciences and Literature.* The horological sections were written by Dr. W. Pearson, the astronomer.

A. Smith (editor), *The Country Life International Dictionary of Clocks,* 1979. Extremely comprehensive work written by a team of specialists. It is notable for its illustrations.

J. Smith, *Horological Dialogues,* 1675, reprinted 1962. Written mainly for the clock owner but full of interest. There is an appendix on designing clock trains.

J. Smith, *Horological Disquisitions Concerning the Nature of Time,* 1694, reprinted 1962. This book has an explanation of the equation of time together with a table, also tables of lengths of pendulums and instructions for setting up long pendulum clocks.

J. Stalker and G. Parker, *A Treatise of Japaning and Varnishing,* 1688, reprinted 1971. Complete textbook on japanning or lacquering with a large selection of chinoiserie designs.

R.W. Symonds, *A History of English Clocks,* 1st edition, 1947, 2nd edition 1950. A small book which gives a good introduction to the subject.

R.W. Symonds, *Thomas Tompion, his Life and Work,* 1951. Important study of this most famous maker with many detailed illustrations of his work.

Indices

Makers' Index

Illustrations are listed after text references and are identified by chapter/figure number

Subject Index

This is a selective index. An exhaustive one would have produced a daunting document with a book of this size. Main entries are in bold type, and other entries have been restricted to those which make a useful contribution. Illustrations are listed after text references and are identified by chapter/figure number.

The Antique Collectors' Club

The Antique Collectors' Club was formed in 1966 and quickly grew to a five figure membership spread throughout the world. It publishes the only independently run monthly antiques magazine, *Antique Collecting*, which caters for those collectors who are interested in widening their knowledge of antiques, both by greater awareness of quality and by discussion of the factors which influence the price that is likely to be asked. The Antique Collectors' Club pioneered the provision of information on prices for collectors and the magazine still leads in the provision of detailed articles on a variety of subjects.

It was in response to the enormous demand for information on 'what to pay' that the price guide series was introduced in 1968 with the first edition of *The Price Guide to Antique Furniture* (completely revised 1978 and 1989), a book which broke new ground by illustrating the more common types of antique furniture, the sort that collectors could buy in shops and at auctions rather than the rare museum pieces which had previously been used (and still to a large extent are used) to make up the limited amount of illustrations in books published by commercial publishers. Many other price guides have followed, all copiously illustrated, and greatly appreciated by collectors for the valuable information they contain, quite apart from prices. The Price Guide Series heralded the publication of many standard works of reference on art and antiques. *The Dictionary of British Art* (now in six volumes), *The Pictorial Dictionary of British 19th Century Furniture Design, Oak Furniture* and *Early English Clocks* were followed by many deeply researched reference works such as *The Directory of Gold and Silversmiths,* providing new information. Many of these books are now accepted as the standard work of reference on their subject.

The Antique Collectors' Club has widened its list to include books on gardens and architecture. All the Club's publications are available through bookshops world wide and a full catalogue of all these titles is available free of charge from the addresses below.

Club membership, open to all collectors, costs little. Members receive free of charge *Antique Collecting*, the Club's magazine (published ten times a year), which contains well-illustrated articles dealing with the practical aspects of collecting not normally dealt with by magazines. Prices, features of value, investment potential, fakes and forgeries are all given prominence in the magazine.

Among other facilities available to members are private buying and selling facilities, the longest list of 'For Sales' of any antiques magazine, an annual ceramics conference and the opportunity to meet other collectors at their local antique collectors' clubs. There are over eighty in Britain and more than a dozen overseas. Members may also buy the Club's publications at special pre-publication prices.

As its motto implies, the Club is an organisation designed to help collectors get the most out of their hobby: it is informal and friendly and gives enormous enjoyment to all concerned.

For Collectors —By Collectors —About Collecting

ANTIQUE COLLECTORS' CLUB
5 Church Street, Woodbridge Suffolk IP12 1DS, UK
Tel: 01394 385501 Fax: 01394 384434
—— or ——
Market Street Industrial Park, Wappingers' Falls, NY 12590, USA
Tel: 914 297 0003 Fax: 914 297 0068

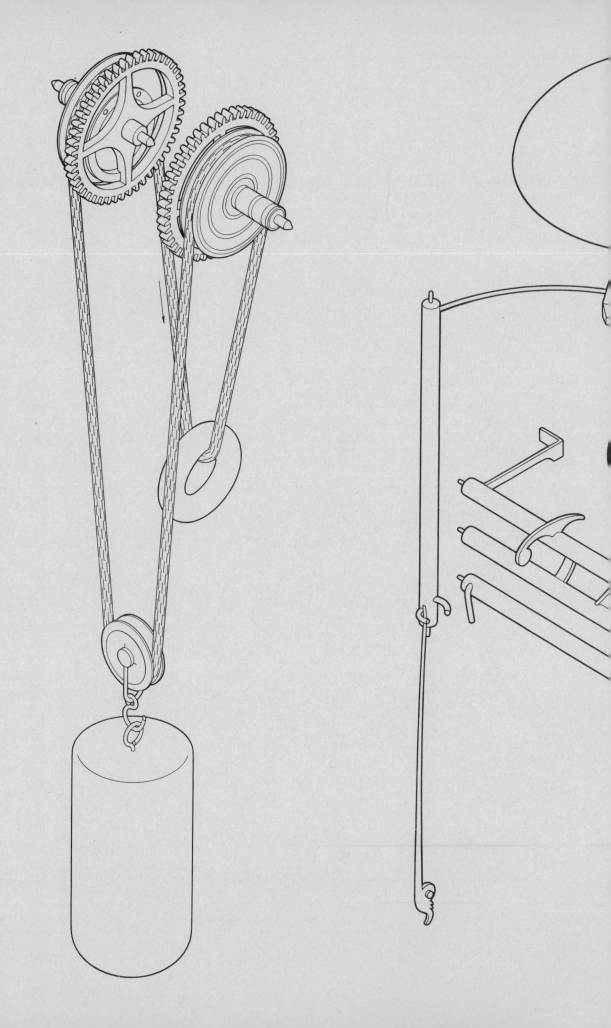